Studies in the History of Art
Published by the National Gallery of Art,
Washington

This series includes: Studies in the History of
Art, collected papers on objects in the Gallery's
collections and other art historical studies
(formerly *Report and Studies in the History of
Art*); Monograph Series I, a catalogue of stained
glass in the United States; Monograph Series II,
on conservation topics; and Symposium Papers
(formerly Symposium Series), the proceedings
of symposia sponsored by the Center for
Advanced Study in the Visual Arts at the
National Gallery of Art.

*Forthcoming

The Architectural Historian in America

CAVE IVDICES
A D·XFIDES·B
M·CMVI

HIAN·ORDER

STUDIES IN THE HISTORY OF ART · 35 ·

Center for Advanced Study in the Visual Arts

Symposium Papers XIX

The Architectural Historian in America

A Symposium in Celebration of the Fiftieth Anniversary
of the Founding of the Society of Architectural Historians

Edited by Elisabeth Blair MacDougall

National Gallery of Art, Washington

Distributed by the University Press of New England

Hanover and London 1990

Editorial Board
DAVID A. BROWN, *Chairman*
DAVID BULL
NICOLAI CIKOVSKY, JR.
HENRY A. MILLON
CHARLES S. MOFFETT

Editor
CAROL ERON

Copy Editor
ELLEN COCHRAN HIRZY

Designer
CYNTHIA HOTVEDT

Editorial Assistants
ULRIKE MILLS, ABIGAIL WALKER

This publication was produced by the Editors Office, National Gallery of Art, Washington
Editor-in-chief, Frances P. Smyth
Printed by Schneidereith & Sons, Baltimore, Maryland
The text paper is 80 pound LOE Dull text with matching cover
The type is Trump Medieval, set by BG Composition, Baltimore, Maryland

Distributed by the University Press of New England, 17½ Lebanon Street, Hanover, New Hampshire 03755

Abstracted by RILA (International Repertory of the Literature of Art), Williamstown, Massachusetts 01267

Proceedings of the symposium "The Architectural Historian in America," sponsored by the Center for Advanced Study in the Visual Arts, National Gallery of Art, and the Society of Architectural Historians, 8–10 December 1988

The symposium program was planned by a committee composed of David B. Brownlee (chairman), William Jordy, Spiro Kostof, Elisabeth Blair MacDougall, Henry A. Millon, and James O'Gorman

"Sigfried Giedion at Harvard University" © 1990 Trustees of the National Gallery of Art, Washington, and Eduard F. Sekler

ISSN 0091-7338
ISBN 089468-139-7

Cover: Architectural details from the Temple of Hera, Paestum. From William Robert Ware, *Greek Ornament* (Boston, 1878), pl. 12. By permission of the Trustees of the Boston Public Library

Frontispiece: H. M. Seabury, *A Frontispiece.* From *Year-Book of the Columbia University School of Architecture,* 1905–1906, 67. By permission of Avery Architectural and Fine Arts Library, Columbia University

The motif that appears throughout this volume is a detail of the cover illustration

Contents

Preface

In December 1988 the Society of Architectural Historians and the Center for Advanced Study in the Visual Arts jointly sponsored a symposium on "The Architectural Historian in America," held at the National Gallery of Art in celebration of the then-forthcoming fiftieth anniversary of the society. This volume of *Studies in the History of Art* contains nineteen of the papers presented at that gathering; its appearance coincides with the semicentennial of the founding of the Society of Architectural Historians in 1940.

The idea of commemorating this golden anniversary with the kind of scholarship that the Society of Architectural Historians has promoted for fifty years was first proposed by Victoria Newhouse, president of the Architectural History Foundation. The ultimate decision to hold a symposium on the historiography of architectural history in the United States, and the formulation of the symposium program eventually involved a number of officers and members of the society, whose contributions are acknowledged with gratitude here: Richard Betts, David Brownlee, William Jordy, Spiro Kostof, Elisabeth Blair MacDougall, James O'Gorman, and Osmund Overby. The Society of Architectural Historians is also grateful to the Architectural History Foundation for support during the planning process. The Center for Advanced Study was pleased to be able to hold the meeting, and is pleased now to thank David A. Bahlman, executive director of the society, for his scrupulous attentions in preparation for the meeting. Both the Society of Architectural Historians and the Center for Advanced Study would like to express their appreciation to the Samuel H. Kress Foundation and the Samuel I. Newhouse Foundation for making this joint gathering possible. Greatest thanks of all go to Elisabeth Blair MacDougall for her willingness to undertake the demanding task of editing the symposium papers for publication.

The volume was prepared for publication by the Editors Office of the National Gallery. Unfortunately, it was not possible for several papers to be included: Homer Thompson's "Greece and Rome"; Renata Holod's "From Olana to Nerangestan: Americans and the Architectures of the Islamic World"; and Richard Pommer's "History in the Service of Architecture: Postmodernism and the Reappraisal of the Past." The Center for Advanced Study and the Society of Architectural Historians are pleased that the publication could appear in time for the 1990 annual meeting of the Society of Architectural Historians in Boston–Cambridge, where the society was founded fifty years ago.

The symposium series of *Studies in the History of Art* is designed to document scholarly meetings held under the auspices of the Center for Advanced Study in the Visual Arts and to stimulate further research. Future volumes in the series will chronicle additional symposia, including those jointly sponsored by the Center for Advanced Study and sister institutions.

HENRY A. MILLON
Dean, Center for Advanced Study in the Visual Arts

Introduction

From the outset, the symposium on "The Architectural Historian in America" was intended to cut a wide swath across the practice of architectural history in the United States. The resulting papers, gathered in this special volume of *Studies in the History of Art*, comprise a fascinating, albeit selected, intellectual and cultural history of the field. The emphasis here is on the period between about 1880, when the professionalization of architecture began to demand increased attention to architectural history, and the 1950s, when many of the senior members of the profession in the 1980s began their careers.

A number of poignant and important themes recur in these papers. Perhaps the largest common theme is the relationship between the study of architectural history and the practice of architecture. As will be seen, the rise of architectural history in America corresponded closely to the professionalization of architecture, the creation of our first architectural schools, and the birth of the first architectural magazines. For architectural historians, these new circumstances provided both a social niche and a serious purpose, and architects gained, too, by tying their calling to a branch of humane letters. This somewhat opportunistic connection between architecture and architectural history persisted, sometimes even in the face of almost unanimous antihistorical philosophy. In-

deed, the association of architects and architectural historians often seems to be a matter of culture rather than ideology, although, of course, there almost always have been earnest historicists who saw the relationship more seriously.

Largely cultural, too, is the story of the growth of the profession of architectural history. Always a relatively tiny band, architectural historians were long sheltered by their architect (and sometimes art historian) colleagues. They were rarely assembled in any one place by academic life, and, unlike scholars in such cognate fields as archaeology and art history, they waited until almost the middle of the century before founding their own national professional organization. This means that an account of the early years of architectural history in America is largely a story of powerful individuals and of the emergence of schools of thought, not usually tied to a single institution, in certain areas of specialization.

The life of ideas that has woven these individuals and schools together (or kept them apart) is as broad and varied as the world of architecture that it has sought to understand. It has always been reaching outward, preoccupied with the borders of the field. Sometimes it has been concerned with interchange with other disciplines—anthropology, literary history, general history, politics, or architectural design—and sometimes with the relationship between American architecture and architecture elsewhere or with the relationship between American and foreign scholarship. In these ways, American architectural historians have been horizon gazers, even more than their persistent study of distant architecture would suggest.

Readers of this volume will find that these themes are joined by others, and I hope that they will be emboldened to write about what they discover and to push the inquiries begun here further and in new directions. Ours is still a young discipline with much to understand about our subject and ourselves. As we celebrate what we have been and what we are, I hope that we continue to look outward.

DAVID B. BROWNLEE
University of Pennsylvania

The Architectural Historian in America

ELISABETH BLAIR MACDOUGALL

Harvard University (emerita)

Before 1870:

Founding Fathers and Amateur Historians

The beginning of professional architectural history in America is usually dated in the 1880s, when courses were first introduced in the early schools of architecture and in some college art history curricula. These courses, however, served the specific function of educating and training students to be professional architects or of supplementing their cultural background in a humanistic educational system. This does not mean that there was no interest in or knowledge of architectural history in the first hundred years of the Republic. To the contrary, the architecture and hence its history played an important role from the earliest years in discussions about the creation of the new nation. As we shall see, there were also publications devoted solely to architecture, and architecture was included in books and articles on all the arts.

It is my belief that the discussions and published writings were an expression of generally held ideas about the role of architecture as a symbolic expression of a culture's ideals and achievements and as an instrument for intellectual and moral improvement, "enabling [the common citizen] . . . [to] feel a community of interest with his wealthier neighbor."[1] Furthermore, public architecture served to give the citizen "his due share alike of the burden and glory [of the nation]."[2] The most obvious example of this thinking occurs in the discussion of and the designs for the capital in Washington.

The decision was made to found a new city instead of selecting one of the old colonial capitals, such as New York or Philadelphia, to serve as the seat of the national government. This clearly set the stage for an architecture that would represent the ideas already discussed and also brought into focus the beliefs expressed by the founders of the nation that a new style of architecture was needed. As the City Commissioners of Washington wrote in 1793,

our ambition [is] to express in some Degree in the Stile of our Architecture, the sublime sentiments of Liberty which are common . . . to Americans . . . to exhibit a grandeur of conception, a Republican simplicity, and that true Elegance of proportion which corresponds to a tempered freedom excluding Frivolity, the food of little minds.[3]

The commissioners' statement reflects several beliefs about architecture that were widely held at that time. First, as Benson Lossing was to write nearly fifty years later, "Architecture . . . presents an index by which to determine [a people's] social advancement and the progress of knowledge among them."[4] R. Cary Long, to whom I shall return, put it more succinctly. "Architecture," he said, "is the Geology of humanity."[5] Social advancement was usually equated at this time with a nation's or a culture's form of government. However, architecture could be more than a passive symptom of a state of affairs, as these writers seem to imply was true of architecture of the past; they believed it could also be used in a conscious way to create a symbolic image of the aims and ideals of the new nation. But, since they could not conceive of an architecture created *ex novo*, they recommended seeking historical precedents from democracies and republics of the past. Naturally these were judged to have produced the highest forms of architecture.

By "tempered freedom," surely a phrase that reflected their beliefs in a limited franchise as well as an approach to design, and "Elegance of proportion," the commissioners were stating their belief in an architecture controlled by rules—of proportion, of decorum in the sense of appropriateness of form to function, of styles of ornament. "Republican simplicity" and the exclusion of "Frivolity" were a rejection of the extravagance and of the eccentricity of the architecture of the *anciens régimes*. A comparison of designs for the Capitol in Washington with the almost contemporaneous Moorish fantasy, the British Prince Regent's Brighton Pavilion, will make their ideas clear.[6]

One more belief common in the early years of the Republic, but not explicit in the commissioners' letter, was the uplifting character of architecture. Arthur Gilman, in 1844, states that architecture is "among those causes which affect the character of the age, and exert a prominent influence on the *moral* [emphasis mine] and intellectual habits of a people."[7] This belief in the moral value of intellectual and, in this case, aesthetic experience was frequently expressed in the planning stages of the capital and was extended to other projects, such as the plans for a national botanic garden on the Mall at the foot of the hill below the Capitol.

There is no need to discuss the actual buildings of these first years of the Republic. We all know how these beliefs and ideas were given form—not, as one might expect from the emphasis accorded to historical precedent, in exact imitation of earlier buildings. There are of course a few

exceptions, such as Jefferson's design for the Virginia State House in Richmond. Nor is this the place to discuss whether the new buildings expressed, as the commissioners desired, "the sublime sentiments of Liberty" or "a grandeur of conception." It is important to recognize that these concepts not only determined the forms and placement of our earliest national architecture, but they also formed the underlying ideology of the literature of architectural history for many decades.

A brief review of architectural books published between the 1790s and the 1870s shows they may be divided into several categories.[8] In the first are the books that give instructions for the use and correct construction of the orders and other types of ornament. Examples include Owen Biddle's *Young Carpenter's Assistant or A System of Architecture adapted to the Style of Building in the United States . . .* of 1805 or William Brown's *The Carpenter's Assistant; Containing a Succinct Account of Egyptian, Grecian, and Roman Architecture . . .* , first appearing in 1848.[9] Although their titles suggest some component of historical text, in fact they are no more than pattern books of the type popularized in England in the preceding century, written by and for architects and builders.

A second category consists of books on the history of art that include sections on architecture; important examples are William Dunlap's *A History of the Rise and Progress of the Arts of Design in the United States*, the first published history of American art (it came out in 1834), Benson Lossing's *Outline History of the Fine Arts Embracing a View of the Rise, Progress, and Influence of the Arts among Different Nations, Ancient and Modern . . .* of 1842, and Miss Ludlow's *A General View of the Fine Arts*, 1851.[10] In a class by itself is Louisa Caroline (Huggins) Tuthill's *History of Architecture from the Earliest Times; Its Present Condition in Europe and the United States*, published in Philadelphia in 1848.

A third category includes books originally published in Great Britain or Europe but reprinted in the United States. The first general history of art published here was John Memes' *History of Sculpture, Painting, and Architecture* of 1831, a reprint of the 1829 Edinburgh edition.[11] German and French authors were also published in translation, but oddly enough, standard European and British texts such as James Elmes' *Lectures on Architecture* or James Fergusson's *History of the Modern Styles of Architecture*,[12] although they are referred to by American writers, had no American editions. Of course, importation of books printed in England and on the continent was common in the period, so only inventories of library or private owners' holdings at that time would give a true picture of the literature of architectural history available in the United States.

Finally, many important articles were published in periodicals, such as the *North American Review, Proceedings of the New-York Historical Society,* and *Papers of the New-England Historic Genealogical Society.* These constitute some of the most interesting and revealing writings of the period.

Most of the authors seem to have had no professional connection with the arts. Of the authors I have enumerated, only Dunlap was a professional; an artist who had studied with Benjamin West in London, he gave painting lessons, and on the title page of his book he is called vice-president of the National Academy of Design. Except for the pattern books, or those specifically intended for builders, the publications were not addressed to a professional audience or intended for professional use. Instead the books seem to have addressed a general cultivated audience or, in the case of the periodical articles, the intellectuals and amateur scholars who made up the readership or membership of the society. Implicit in most of the writing is a belief that a knowledge of the arts elevates the intellect and acts as a positive force to improve morals. Benson Lossing is more explicit:

The cultivation of the Fine Arts, and a general dissemination of a taste for such liberal pursuits, are of the highest importance in a national point of view, for they have a powerful tendency to elevate the standard of intellect, and consequently morals, and form one of those mighty levers which raise nations as well as individuals to the highest point in the scale of civilization. . . . Cultivation of the Fine Arts has invariably attended . . . a corresponding improvement in the social, moral and intellectual character of the people.[13]

Implicitly or explictly all the writers view the architecture of the past as a reflection of a period's culture and achievements. Even Louisa Tuthill, whose text is the most factual and least interpretive of those I have named so far, says, "The study of ancient architecture is the study of history. It reveals the religion, government, social institutions, science and art of the mighty past."[14]

Also common to all is the concept of development and progress, the latter used in titles by many authors, for example, Dunlap and Lossing. The idea of development is usually tied to the advance from primitive forms and cultures to the higher state of more evolved civilizations. Depending on the author's point of view, prehistorical times or Egyptian and Assyrian architecture are the starting points. The development of the orders is constantly discussed, of course, and one author, R. Cary Long, postulates a development of building shapes. The concept of progress is more nebulous, but seems to contain the idea of improvement—like Coué, every day, in every way, getting better and better. Sometimes it is related to recent history, as in "The Progress of the Arts in the United States." Concepts of cyclical patterns, such as the biological analogy of birth, maturity, and decay familiar from Renaissance writing, seem not to exist at all.

In the general histories, architecture is recognized as one of the fine arts—the others are usually painting, sculpture, engraving, and sometimes poetry and music—but its functional or technical side is also acknowledged. Dunlap says, "Of the four arts . . . architecture alone is the offspring of necessity." For Mrs. Tuthill architecture is both an essential and an ornamental art, a "mechanic art" when "strength and convenience are alone regarded . . . when it adds to these, beauty of design, or a regard for effect, it becomes an ornamental or fine art."[15] Lossing, in recognizing the double character of architecture, says it is superior to the other arts because it "administers to our physical comforts and enjoyments, as well as elevates and refines the intellectual powers, while its sister arts only excite our admiration and love by imitations of the sublime and beautiful of the world around us"; elsewhere he implies that architecture's superiority derives from the fact that it is "the creation of man's invention," unlike the other arts, which are "a process of imitation."[16] All agree that it was the desire for beauty or luxury, plus the creation of rules of design, that elevated the craft of construction to the art or science of architecture.

Their typology and periodization need little comment. Most writers differentiate military and civil architecture and include within civil "monumental," chiefly tombs, ecclesiastical, public, and domestic. Discussion of buildings is almost entirely confined to the first three categories of civil architecture, with the heaviest emphasis on funeral and church architecture. Dunlap says, "Public architecture [he is including monumental, ecclesiastical, and civic] seems principally connected with our subject, but the effect of domestic architecture upon the moral feeling and character of mankind, renders it a subject not to be disregarded by us."[17]

Histories start with the pyramids of Egypt, include Assyria, sometimes considered a predecessor of Egypt, "Hindoo," and Persia, both of which are usually considered outgrowths of Egyptian design, and usually include a section on China, but rarely Japan. Greece follows chronologically, always as an improvement on Egyptian design. Dunlap says "contemplation of the natural perfection" of forms in nature "led to the improvement of Egyptian architecture by the Greek colonists of Asia Minor."[18] For Lossing, "the pure architecture of Greece is undoubtedly superior to that of every other nation."[19] Roman architecture is seen as unoriginal, "distinguished rather by new applications than by fresh invention."[20] Romans are criticized for failing to adhere to the rules developed by the Greeks.

Discussion of the architecture of the Middle Ages often begins with some reference to Early Christian and Byzantine monuments (St. Peter's and Hagia Sophia), although no style or period name is given them. The rest of the medieval period is usually divided into two successive styles, Romanesque, or round arch, and Gothic, or pointed arch. Despite the emphasis throughout these writings on classical rules of proportion and of the orders and ornaments, the Middle Ages are not seen as a period of corruption or barbarism, nor is Renaissance architecture hailed as the return to true architecture.

There is little discussion in the general histories about the causes of change or the origins of a given style. Greek temples originated as wooden structures; medieval churches, especially the Gothic, were inspired by groves of trees. Lossing alone suggests that medieval church architecture developed from "the necessities of religious rites."[21]

The writers are critical of contemporary architecture. Memes refers to the "inferiority of modern architecture," and Lossing says the United States Capitol is our only worthwhile monument. Defects are blamed on the influence of Roman architecture, often condemned despite the high regard in which Roman law and other institutions were held. A typical statement is that of Memes, who criticizes the Romans for treating the Greek orders as "so many conventional ornaments which might be changed or superseded. . . . This it is important to mark, for the same [desire for novelty and restless spirit of innovation] have been the sources, and are still the operating causes, of inferiority in modern architecture."[22]

Unlike contemporary writing in England and Europe, the American publications frequently devoted space to pre-Columbian and pre-Revolutionary architecture.[23] The interest seems to have been inspired by nationalist sentiment. An example is R. Cary Long's article, "The Ancient Architecture of America: The Historical Value and Parallelism of Development with the Architecture of the Old World," published in the *New-York Historical Society Proceedings* in 1849. Long states, "the great historic problem of the present day [is to investigate] when and by what kind of people was ancient America inhabited; what is their place in the past?"[24] Even more indicative are passages in which the servile dependence of artists in England on aristocratic patronage is contrasted to the equality and independence of American artists (Dunlap) or the individuality and independence of settlers; a resulting individuality in church architecture is contrasted to feudal dependence in the Old World.[25]

After the first decades, history writing became less theoretical and philosophical. Publications of the 1840s and later were usually factual and biographical, such as Miss Ludlow's and Louisa Tuthill's histories, or anecdotal, such as Shearjashub Spooner's *Anecdotes . . .* or Celine Fallet's *The Princes of Art*.[26] Although a few essays appeared on Gothic architecture, American writers were not involved in the controversies that divided the critics and architects in England over the validity of the Gothic revival and historicism in general.[27] However, the number of American editions of Ruskin and Viollet-le-Duc suggests that Americans were no strangers to the debates.[28]

A new audience for architectural history began to appear by the 1840s. Women writers such as Miss Ludlow and Louisa Tuthill were addressing a female audience. As Mrs. Tuthill's dedication of her book, "To the Ladies of the United States of America, the Acknowledged Arbiters of Taste," makes clear, women had begun to exert an influence as patrons of the arts. A literature developed to inform and educate this hitherto neglected group.

Finally, one should mention the existence of an antihistorical and profunctionalism trend. This can be exemplified by remarks of Horatio Greenough, the sculptor. In an article published in the *North American Review* in 1843, he urges the creation of an original United States architecture, saying that it is wrong to adopt forms created for different purposes. "In our eagerness to appropriate," he says, "we have neglected to adapt, to distinguish,—nay to understand. . . . Like the captive king, stripped alike of arms and purple, and drudging amid the Helots of a capital, the Greek Temple, as seen among us, claims pity for its degraded majesty."[29]

NOTES

1. Anonymous, "Remarks on the Progress and Present State of the Fine Arts in the United States," *Analectic Magazine* 6 (1815), 375.

2. *Views in Philadelphia and Its Environment from Original Drawings taken in 1827–1830* (Philadelphia, 1830), unpaginated. I would like to express my gratitude here to Bates Lowry, whose *Building for a National Image: Architectural Drawings for the American Democracy, 1789–1912* (Washington, D.C., 1985) was the source of these quotations and whose text substantiated the hypotheses with which I embarked on this study.

3. Commissioners of Washington, D.C., to Commissioners of the municipality of Bordeaux, 4 January 1793, quoted in Lowry 1985, 24.

4. Benson J. Lossing, *Outline History of the Fine Arts Embracing a View of the Rise, Progress, and Influence of the Arts among the Different Nations, Ancient and Modern* (New York, 1842), 12.

5. R. Cary Long, "The Ancient Architecture of America: The Historical Value and Parallelism of Development with the Architecture of the Old World," *New-York Historical Society Proceedings* 7 (1849), 119.

6. The various designs submitted for the Capitol are published by Glenn Brown, *History of the United States Capitol*, 2 vols. (Washington, D.C. 1899–1904). For the Pavilion at Brighton, see John Morley, *The Making of the Royal Pavilion, Brighton* (London, 1984).

7. Arthur Gilman, review of *Rural Architecture*, by Edward Shaw, *North American Review* 58 (1844), 436.

8. I have based my analysis on the lists in Henry-Russell Hitchcock, *American Architectural Books*, 2d ed. (New York, 1976). No list of the architecture books published in these years is appended here, because they may be found easily in William H. Jordy's "Chronological Short-title List of Henry-Russell Hitchcock's American Architectural Books," appended to the second edition.

9. Owen Biddle, *Young Carpenter's Assistant or A System of Architecture adapted to the Style of Building in the United States* . . . (Philadelphia, 1805; later editions to 1858); William Brown, *The Carpenter's Assistant; Containing a Succinct Account of Egyptian, Grecian, and Roman Architecture* . . . (Worcester, Boston, New York, 1848; ss. to 1856).

10. William Dunlap, *A History of the Rise and Progress of the Arts of Design in the United States* (New York, 1834); Lossing 1842; Miss Ludlow, *A General View of the Fine Arts* (New York, 1851). I have not been able to find any information, not even a first name, for "Miss" Ludlow.

11. J. S. Memes, *History of Sculpture, Painting, and Architecture* (Boston, 1831).

12. James Elmes, *Lectures on Architecture* (London, 1831); James Fergusson, *History of the Modern Styles of Architecture* (London, 1862).

13. Lossing 1842, iii, f.

14. Tuthill 1848, viii.

15. Dunlap 1834, 11; Tuthill 1848, 17.

16. Lossing 1842, 12–13.

17. Dunlap 1834, 325.

18. Dunlap 1834, 10.

19. Lossing 1842, 69.

20. Memes 1831, 270.

21. Lossing 1842, 82–83.

22. Memes 1831, 272.

23. An exception to European neglect of pre-Discovery architecture in the Americas is Franz Theodore Kugler's 1841 *World History of Art and Architecture*. See George Kubler, "Architectural Historians before the Fact," in this volume.

24. Long 1849, 120.

25. Nathan Henry Chamberlain, *A Paper on New-England Architecture, Read before the New-England Historic Genealogical Society, September 4, 1858* . . . (Boston, 1858), 10.

26. Shearjashub Spooner, *Anecdotes of painters, sculptors and architects, and curiosities of art* . . . 3 vols. (New York, 1850 and later editions). Celine Fallett, *The Princes of Art: architects, painters, sculptors and engravers*, trans. Mrs. S. R. Urbino (New York, 1870). The first French edition appeared in Rouen, 1855. French editions were published in Boston and New York in 1870.

27. See, for example, John Henry Hopkins, *Essay on Gothic Architecture* . . . (Burlington, Vt., 1836), chiefly a manual for church designers.

28. Hitchcock lists over one hundred editions, issues, or printings of Ruskin titles and six of Viollet-le-Duc in *American Architectural Books* (nos. 1023–1129, 1310–1315, respectively).

29. Horatio Greenough, "American Architecture," *North American Review* 10 (1843), republished in Henry T. Tuckerman, ed., *A Memorial of Horatio Greenough* (New York, 1853), 117–130.

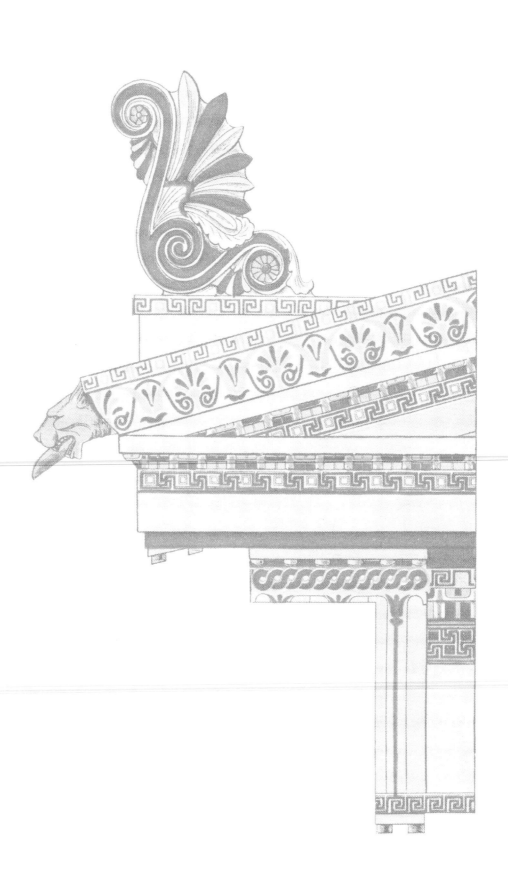

WILLIAM B. RHOADS
State University College at New Paltz

The Discovery of America's Architectural Past, 1874–1914

The discovery and celebration of America's architectural past began well before 1874. True, Thomas Jefferson in 1781 and Louisa Tuthill in 1848 had uncomplimentary things to say about the country's old buildings, and from London in 1873 came James Fergusson's widely read opinion that before 1814 "there was hardly one single building erected in North America . . . worthy of being mentioned as an example of Architectural Art."[1] Yet as early as the 1790s the Reverend William Bentley, an antiquarian cited by Abbott Lowell Cummings as "New England's first architectural historian," described seventeenth-century buildings in diary entries.[2] Washington Irving wrote amusingly about the quaint architecture of the Hudson Valley Dutch, but took it seriously enough to rebuild one of their old stone houses for his own use in 1835.[3] Architects Benjamin Latrobe, William Strickland, and John Hubbard Sturgis recorded the appearance of vanishing landmarks,[4] while Arthur Gilman, Thomas Tefft, and Richard Upjohn in the mid-nineteenth century wrote admiringly of designs from a century earlier.[5]

The 1870s were marked by celebrations of the centennial of independence and a new zeal for recording old buildings, especially as sources for the rising colonial revival. In 1874 students of Professor William Robert Ware at the Massachusetts Institute of Technology measured and drew late Georgian church towers in Boston. Two were published in the *Architectural Sketch Book* (1875; fig. 1). By 1874 William Edward Barry, a draftsman in the Boston office of Peabody and Stearns, had published *Pen Sketches of Old Houses* (fig. 2).[6] Also in 1874 a photo of Bishop Berkeley's house (1728) near Newport, Rhode Island, appeared in the *New-York Sketch Book*, edited by Charles McKim. It showed the picturesque rear roof of the Berkeley house, but McKim's taste was broad enough so that he later published the Georgian entrance of the Ford house (Washington's headquarters; fig. 3) in Morristown, New Jersey, drawn by Bassett Jones, and the formal classicism of New York City Hall, "the most admirable public building in the city." McKim argued for the "architectural merit" of these buildings in the face of those who considered them "ugly." McKim himself was then a colonial revivalist (e.g., in his Blake house of 1875), but he did not believe it was enough to gather graphic documentation of colonial buildings. He insisted it was time that architects "write about them as Architecture," in contrast to popular magazines such as *Harper's* where colonial buildings were illustrated simply as a quaint background for "some story or other."[7]

In 1876 architects and architectural students were invited to submit "careful drawings" for publication in a new journal,

the *American Architect and Building News*. These drawings, including plans and details, would surpass in value the "picturesque views published in books and magazines." It was observed that "the architecture of the Colonies" stemmed from England and the "narrow formalities of the Georgian period." The writer on the one hand condemned this colonial work as "feeble, lifeless, monotonous," while on the other proposing that its "ancestry was good. . . . the precepts of Vignola and Palladio had been translated, illustrated, and codified, by Wren and Chambers" and applied by "skilful mechanics" to American buildings.[8]

Boston architect Robert S. Peabody was impressed by the English revival of the "Queen Anne" on an 1876 visit[9] and soon came to advocate that Americans revive the colonial, which he thought equivalent to the Queen Anne, as "our legitimate field for imitation" and "our only native source of . . . inspiration." His taste ran to the "picturesque pile" of the Fairbanks house in Dedham, but more to "Georgian houses" like the Vassall-Longfellow house in Cambridge, which provided "the richest and finest models." He thought classical details had been "the common language of every carpenter, and treated freely . . . with no superstitious reverence for Palladio or Scamozzi, those bugbears of later years." Peabody's sketches of "old houses at Lenox and Little Harbor" (fig. 4), which accompanied his essay, confirmed his dual enthusiasms for picturesque compositions and Georgian details, as did Peabody and

1. Park Street and Hollis Street Churches, Boston, drawn by H. G. King and R. S. Atkinson *From Architectural Sketch Book* 2 (January 1875), pl. 31. Avery Architectural and Fine Arts Library, Columbia University

2. Houses in Saco, Maine, drawn by William E. Barry

From *Pen Sketches of Old Houses* (Boston, n.d.). Avery Architectural and Fine Arts Library, Columbia University

3. Washington's Headquarters, Morristown, New Jersey, drawn by Bassett Jones

From *New-York Sketch-Book of Architecture* 2 (August 1875). Avery Architectural and Fine Arts Library, Columbia University

4. Wentworth House, Little Harbor, New Hampshire, drawn by Robert S. Peabody

From *American Architect and Building News* 2 (October 1877). Vassar College Library

Stearns' design for a house on Brush Hill, Milton, Massachusetts (1877–1878).[10]

By 1878 Peabody's research led him to downplay the freedom of Georgian classicism. "The use of classical detail was universally agreed to, and the orders were naturally used by every carpenter." He discovered "a large copy of Batty Langley's classical work in an old loft in New Hampshire," which he took as firm evidence that colonial builders habitually referred to English handbooks for classical details. Further, he concluded that Asher Benjamin's *American Builder's Companion* had been influential in the detailing of early nineteenth-century houses east of the Connecticut River. Therefore he advised his fellow colonial revivalists to study these books as well as make their own sketches of old work.[11] Peabody's assumption that the colonial era in American architecture continued into the early nineteenth century was widely accepted at least through 1914.[12]

In July 1877 Peabody and Arthur Little, a draftsman in Peabody's office, studied colonial houses in Portsmouth, New Hampshire. Little's New England sketches of that summer were published in 1878 as *Early New England Interiors* (fig. 5), probably the first in the long line of books illustrating colonial buildings explicitly intended as a reference for designers and with a minimum of text. Little's career as designer of colonial revival houses began in 1879 with Cliffs, a house in Manchester, Massachusetts.[13] A reviewer found Little's drawings heavy-handed and lacking detail, but acknowledged the patriotic appeal of native models and suggested that the study of colonial architecture through measured drawings become a required part of architectural training.[14]

More than twenty years earlier, in 1854, George Champlin Mason, Sr., an artist and journalist in Newport, had published a tourist guide to the area where his family had long been prominent. Buildings were of interest for the historical events and personages connected with them, but the designs of some eighteenth-century buildings also met with his approval. In 1858 he began practicing architecture in Newport (his 1874 addition to Peter Harrison's Red-

wood Library has been called "sensitively conceived") while continuing to write local history with an architectural emphasis. Proclaiming himself "fond of antiquarian research," Mason discovered documents to help establish a chronology of eighteenth-century Newport houses. He also compared design elements such as wainscoting details as an aid to dating these houses. Peter Harrison was praised for his "fidelity to the rules of classic architecture," and his work represented "a noble protest against the shams and affectations too prevalent in modern work."[15]

George Champlin Mason, Jr., followed his father into an architectural career joined with the study of Newport's architectural history. According to David Chase, the younger Mason became a specialist in colonial restorations in the early 1870s, while at the same time referring to the colonial tradition in new work. In 1879 he published the "definitive analysis" of the controversial Old Stone Mill in Newport, which led to his appointment as chairman of an American Institute of Architects committee to study the "Practice of American Architects and Builders during the

5. Title page showing Wentworth House, drawn by Arthur Little
From *Early New England Interiors* (Boston, 1878). Avery Architectural and Fine Arts Library, Columbia University

Colonial Period and First Fifty Years of Independence."

His report, published in 1881 in the *American Architect*, admitted that the impetus for the study was the attempt to find American sources equivalent to the English Queen Anne. But he was emphatic that his architectural history was not to be "merely . . . find[ing] quaint details to copy in modern work and then unblushingly christen those works Queen Anne or Georgian." His illustrations were too small and rough to be useful to the copyist. Instead, he hoped to find "the principles that shaped and guided" early architecture by uncovering ancient documents and probing the old buildings themselves. He analyzed building contracts and bills, construction techniques, even mortar ingredients. The roles of particular builders and architects, the origins of the gambrel roof, and the general question of stylistic development were all explored. Seventeenth-century houses belonged to the first period of American colonial architecture and were "ruder erections" than their eighteenth-century successors, whose classicism he favored. Eighteenth-century houses were categorized as second (c. 1700–

1725) or third (c. 1730–?) period—differentiated by materials, construction methods, roof types, and elegance of classical ornament. Like Peabody and Little, Mason admired early nineteenth-century architecture, and he concluded his report with a description of Benjamin's *American Builder's Companion* (advertised in Newport in 1807).[16] As A. J. Bloor pointed out, Mason's report was narrowly focused on Newport, but Mason considered his essay only preliminary and suggestive for further work by others.[17]

Mason's quest for documents and principles had no appeal for Frank E. Wallis, who, as a young Boston draftsman, about 1875 followed Little as a sketcher and wanderer "in the pleasant land of Colonial architecture." While acknowledging Little's influence, Wallis was more thorough in spending seven or eight years measuring and drawing old New England buildings after office hours and on holidays. William Rotch Ware, editor of the *American Architect*, at first refused to publish Wallis' measured drawings; he had been accustomed to printing picturesque sketches. But after William Robert Ware (then at Columbia) admired them and apparently used them as models for his students' summer work, William Rotch Ware bowed to his uncle's opinion and published them in the *American Architect* in 1886. Subsequently Wallis made two trips to the South to gather additional material. These efforts resulted in his *Old Colonial Architecture and Furniture* (1887; fig. 6), sixty plates reproducing Wallis' drawings, interior and exterior details (some drawn to scale), as well as perspective sketches. The subjects ranged from Massachusetts to Virginia; most were eighteenth-century houses. Following Peabody, Wallis' short introduction assured "the student of Architecture" that American architecture from 1750 to 1800 was founded in "the classic of Palladio and Vignola."[18]

Wallis' book has been called "the first collection of measured drawings to appear in book form in this country, and as such it attracted much attention."[19] It was valued as a source for colonial revivalists (of which Wallis was one). He claimed that when he "measured, sketched, and studied

6. Stratton House, College Point, Long Island, measured drawings by Frank E. Wallis
From *Old Colonial Architecture and Furniture* (Boston, 1887). Avery Architectural and Fine Arts Library, Columbia University

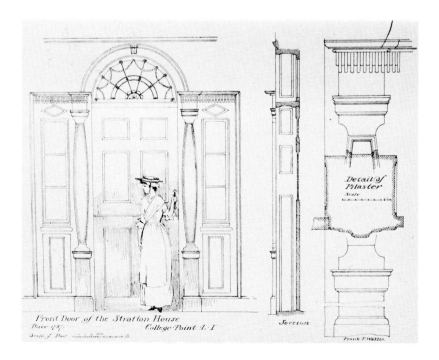

Front Door of the Stratton House
College Point L. I.
Section

the old houses," he was not calculating the profit from wide distribution of his plates, but experiencing "a strong stirring of emotion, being one generation removed from this type" of house. "I have lived in a home with a sanded floor laid out in patterns . . . and with a grandmother and her daughter who cooked in a Dutch oven."[20]

In the 1890s several variants on Wallis' publications appeared.[21] James M. Corner and Eric Ellis Soderholtz, photographers, pioneered the publication of "photographic documentation of colonial architecture in book form." In compiling *Examples of Domestic Colonial Architecture in New England* (1891) they frankly admitted their "primary object . . . was not to accumulate historical data." Instead their plates were meant to be useful to architects "in stimulating closer study [of colonial houses] in their adaptation to modern domestic work." Since seventeenth-century houses of the "Colonial Period" lacked "refinement in the way of elaborate detail," and those from the "Provincial Period" (c. 1700–1776) were only modestly enriched, the compilers emphasized "the better class of domestic edifices" from the later eighteenth century or "Federal Period" (c. 1776–1800).[22]

Charles McKim commended the compilers for the choice of material and its presentation. "It is in constant daily use in our office, and . . . we consider no Architectural Library complete without it."[23] (Another fan of photographs as design sources was Joy Wheeler Dow, who recommended photographic study as easier than traveling to see the originals, and "pictures are oftener productive of inspiration than . . . actual acquaintance with the subjects."[24]) Corner and Soderholtz were criticized in the *American Architect* for omitting color plates, but such rarely appeared in architectural publications. Lithographically tinted illustrations of "Colonial Building in New Jersey," appearing in the *Architectural Record* in 1894, were the exceptions.[25]

Like Corner and Soderholtz's volume, Joseph Everett Chandler's *Colonial Architecture of Maryland, Pennsylvania, and Virginia* (1892) was scarcely "history." Chandler, a young Boston architect later known as the restorer of the Paul Revere

house and the House of Seven Gables, presented fifty photographic plates, but no text, and the captions included no dates. The plates reflected Chandler's preference as a colonial revivalist for eighteenth- and early nineteenth-century houses: the seventeenth century was unrepresented and only two public buildings were recorded.[26]

Where Chandler ventured south as an outsider, T. Henry Randall wrote "Colonial Annapolis" for the *Architectural Record* (1892) as a member of the Annapolis aristocracy who went on to practice architecture in New York. Randall noted regional distinctions that carried over from the character of individuals to their architecture: New England was marked by puritanical "simplicity and frugality," while the South of the "Cavalier" had "the stamp of refinement [and] elegance . . . borrowed from the old homes of England." Later in the *Architectural Record*, G. A. T. Middleton took up these prototypes in his "English 'Georgian' Architecture: The Source of the American 'Colonial' Style."[27]

A broader historical overview was attempted by Montgomery Schuyler, credited by Frank Roos with writing "the first history of Colonial architecture."[28] It appeared in 1895 in the *Architectural Record*. By "colonial" Schuyler meant only English-influenced eighteenth- and nineteenth-century architecture before the Greek revival. Seventeenth-century structures, as well as Dutch and Swedish houses in New York and Pennsylvania, were "building," not architecture. Nevertheless, perhaps because of his Dutch ancestry, Schuyler did treat Dutch building in the Hudson Valley. Generally, he was concerned with chronology (the dates of the first brick kilns and sawmills; could St. Luke's, Newport Parish, be so early as 1632?), authorship (St. Michael's, Charleston, was attributed to James Gibbs), the quality of workmanship (high in the case of Independence Hall) and materials (wood should not be employed externally), the correct use of the orders (the fragmented entablatures inside Christ Church, Philadelphia, were criticized), the quality of compositions (high in the case of the University of Virginia), the rise of the architectural profession (Bulfinch was "the first educated American" to become a professional architect), and the claims of Philadelphia and Boston for "superiority in the polite arts" (Philadelphia won). Schuyler's bibliography included local histories, eighteenth-century regional descriptions, Jefferson's *Writings*, and Chandler's *Colonial Architecture.*[29]

Soon after the appearance of Schuyler's essay, a jejune survey by O. Z. Cervin, "The So-Called Colonial Architecture of the United States," originally a post-graduate thesis for the Architectural Department at Columbia College, was published in the *American Architect*. Cervin announced that colonial Philadelphia had no notable architecture because it had been ruled by "world-eschewing zealots," and "Williamsburg . . . never became important—it stands today, with a church and a court-house, almost the identical country town it was a hundred years ago." Thomas Jefferson "did many queer things."[30]

The editors of the *American Architect* did not demand much substance in the historical essays they printed. Claude Bragdon forthrightly announced that his article on colonial Salem was the fruit of one evening's "cramming at the Boston Public Library" and his drawings were based on six hours spent in Salem with his "note-books, rules, and pencils, and a kodak camera." Bragdon's essay on the Genesee Valley rambled on about fox hunting, he acknowledged, because there was "so little to be said" about its architecture that could not be found in his drawings.[31]

Between 1898 and 1902 William Rotch Ware, editor of the *American Architect*, published *The Georgian Period*, a haphazard compilation of material extending into the Greek revival, much of which had already appeared in the *American Architect*. *The Georgian Period* was composed of twelve parts with some 450 plates including measured drawings, perspective sketches (fig. 7), and Heliotype photos, along with more than 500 smaller illustrations scattered amid the short articles by authors such as Cervin and Bragdon. Ware attributed the undertaking to "the formidable attempt to bring about the destruction of the 'Bulfinch Front' of the Massachusetts State House . . . and the constant

appearance in the daily papers of accounts of the destruction by fire of this or that ancient building endowed with historic or architectural interest."

The Georgian Period served mainly as a bundle of sources for designers. Ware supposed that if his "comprehensive work" had existed twenty years earlier, architects would not have produced, out of ignorance, so many "caricatures" of " 'Old Colonial' work." Yet twenty years earlier the camera and "ever-wandering amateur photographer," so necessary for the project, were scarcely in evidence.[32]

Reviews of *The Georgian Period* were generally favorable. A laudatory review of the first three parts in the *Nation* suggested the inclusion of an appendix documenting the "less academic . . . simple clapboarded houses, with overhanging second-story pendants." Ware later added such seventeenth-century New England examples, noting their inferiority in "architectural character" to houses of "the Georgian period," but finding them still "vastly interesting and picturesque."[33] In 1915 Richard Franz Bach surveyed the bibliography on colonial architecture and concluded that *The Georgian Period* was "the best general work . . . for the detailed study of Colonial architecture," and as late as 1923 it was said that "no book of its character . . . has exercised a more profound, a more enduring or more wholesome influence."[34]

Superficiality did not mark the work of Norman Isham, an architect who approached the history of early Rhode Island and Connecticut houses as a problem to be probed "scientifically." His *Early Rhode Island Houses* (1895) and *Early Connecticut Houses* (1900; fig. 8),[35] both coauthored by Albert F. Brown, presented a collection of "scientific data" with a thoroughness previously unknown in American architectural studies. They examined the houses described, prepared measured plans, sections, and elevations, searched probate inventories to discover room names and uses. Consequently their work, they believed, would surpass in usefulness "the vague descriptions of too many of our town histories."[36] By surveying the oldest houses, they went against the tendency to concen-

The old : ROYALL MANSION : Medford : Mass :

7. Royall Mansion, Medford, Massachusetts, drawn by E. Eldon Deane

From *The Georgian Period* . . . , vol. 1 (Boston, 1898–1902). Avery Architectural and Fine Arts Library, Columbia University

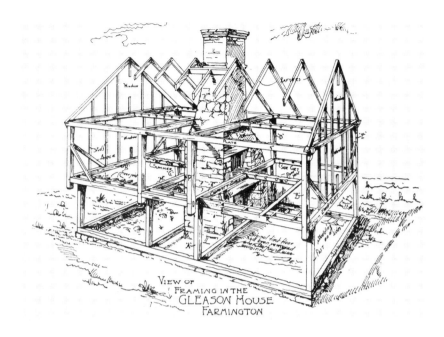

VIEW OF
FRAMING IN THE
GLEASON HOUSE
FARMINGTON

8. Gleason House, Farmington, Connecticut

From Norman M. Isham and Albert F. Brown, *Early Connecticut Houses . . .* (Providence, 1900). Avery Architectural and Fine Arts Library, Columbia University

trate on Georgian examples. In fact their work seems to have been less inspired by a desire to fulfill the needs of the colonial revivalist (although Isham designed colonial revival houses[37]) than to produce disinterested scholarly documentation of "help to the future historians of New England." Russell Sturgis lauded Isham and Brown for concentrating on buildings "handed down from father to son and for which no architect made plans," considering their Rhode Island volume "the most important contribution so far made to the history of American art."[38]

Another architect whose painstaking historical scholarship remains impressive is Glenn Brown, whose measured drawings of eighteenth- and early nineteenth-century buildings in Virginia, Maryland, and Washington were published in the *American Architect* in 1887–1888. He not only sketched and measured, but also attempted "researches or inquiries," including interviews of the oldest inhabitants. He turned up, in a Virginia warehouse, copies of Langley (1739) and William Pain (1794), which he recognized as the guides for carpenters and builders whose "free" but "refined treatment of Classical details" Brown so much admired as a designer of colonial revival houses.[39] The Oc-

tagon House in Washington by William Thornton was among the buildings Brown published in the *American Architect*, and William Bushong proposes that Brown was thereby stimulated to study other works by Thornton, notably the United States Capitol.[40]

In 1896 Brown began a series of articles on "The History of the United States Capitol," which resulted in his monumental two-volume opus with 322 folio plates, based on ten years of gathering written and drawn documentation from public and private sources. Brown's lifelong concern to document, preserve, and restore old Washington may be traced partly to ancestral piety. While most writers on colonial architecture could claim colonial ancestors, Brown took pride in the fact that his grandfather, Bedford Brown, had represented North Carolina in the Senate and his great-grandfather, Peter Lenox, had been a construction superintendent at the Capitol between 1817 and 1829. Still, in his first volume (covering the Capitol's history to 1850), Brown was not primarily concerned with glorifying his ancestors, but rather, as Bushong demonstrates, with instructing his contemporaries in government that L'Enfant's plan for the city was to be respected and that they should follow Washington's and Jefferson's example in seeking expert advice on the planning of government buildings. "Brown's *History* was a polemical study," Bushong asserts, "calculated to be the cornerstone of an AIA campaign to acquire a City Beautiful plan for Washington."[41]

The New York architect Aymar Embury II, finding New England and Virginia well studied for revival purposes, turned to the old Dutch houses near New York, which had the advantage of being "little known" yet "beautiful, and full of suggestion to both the architect and the home-builder." To Embury they seemed full of "family feeling, sturdy and virile, like the Dutchmen who occupied them," but Irving's influence still dictated that Embury should also detect "the quaintness and sly humor that we instinctively associate with the nephews of Father Knickerbocker."[42]

As a tourist-architect in search of the relatively unfamiliar in early American architecture, Embury published his impressions of "Old New Orleans"—the "exquisite faded tints" of the stuccoed walls and "delightful ironwork of the balconies"—while also writing appreciatively of Pennsylvania's old stone farmhouses with classical details "modified . . . by ignorant (although tasteful) builders." Dates and even names of buildings were of little consequence. What was important was for architects around the country to avoid the "stereotyped" colonial and to study forms that heretofore had had only a local influence on the colonial revival.[43]

Embury's *Early American Churches* (1914) was recognized as the standard reference on the topic. He traveled to old churches, perused Benjamin's handbooks, and tried to use the art historical concept of attributing authorship on the basis of style, but much of his text was drawn from a reading of *The Georgian Period* and Schuyler. He preferred the early nineteenth-century New England churches of Bulfinch, Benjamin, and Isaac Damon: the latter's church at Ware, Massachusetts (fig. 9), was "simple, extremely dignified, ecclesiastical . . . , filled with the truest architectural feeling for proportion and detail." On the other hand, Quaker meeting houses were too plain to be of architectural interest and, politically, Quakers had been "objectionable nuisances," so their buildings failed as landmarks of American patriotism.[44]

The study of American architectural history was still unsystematic in 1914. Terms such as "colonial" and "Georgian" were used with the utmost freedom.[45] The need for monographs on architects such as Samuel McIntire was recognized but not met.[46] As Fiske Kimball complained that year: "There has been too much inconsequent fantasy-spinning, in writings on the history of American architecture. The 'Georgian Period' itself feebly points to wide disagreements in its own pages as to the dates of important buildings—a confession of our historical incompetence unthinkable in any other country. Mr. Brown's painstaking and scholarly history of the Capitol . . . [is] almost the only worthy monument of our architectural history." Subsequently Kimball also hailed Isham for relating "in-

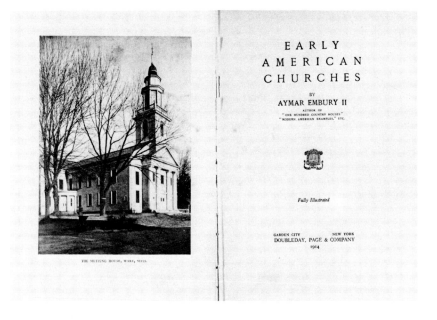

ternal and documentary evidences" in tracing the development of early houses in New England.[47]

In 1969 John Maass criticized American architectural historians for adhering to a "bourgeois standard" and "genteel tradition," which prevented them from studying buildings for the lower class and works of engineering. Earlier writers of American architectural history rarely ventured into these areas. T. Henry Randall focused on the Cavalier's grand house, while noting in passing that slaves "had to be provided for in quarters conveniently near, and yet not under his own roof." A grist mill and its construction details were not likely to interest colonial revival architects of 1889, so an article on the topic (based on an examination of the mill at Philips Manor on the Hudson) logically appeared in *Carpentry and Building*.[48]

By 1914 the American public had been bombarded with publications bringing its architectural heritage to light. In addition to those by architects and architectural critics, which have been the focus of this paper, countless local histories and magazines such as *Harper's* and *Scribner's* pre-

9. Frontispiece and title page, Aymar Embury II, *Early American Churches* (Garden City, N.Y., 1914)

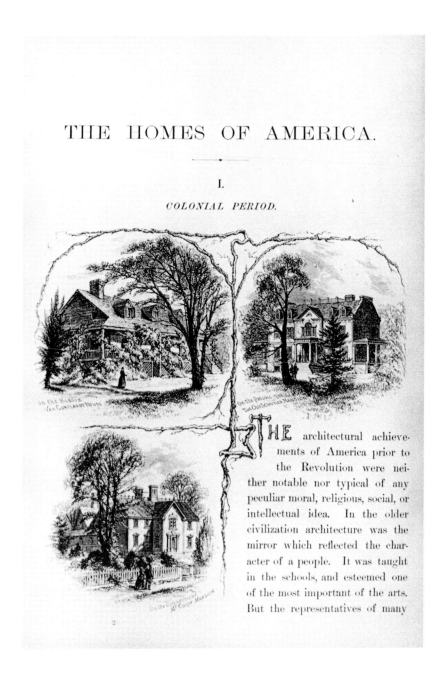

THE HOMES OF AMERICA.

I.

COLONIAL PERIOD.

THE architectural achievements of America prior to the Revolution were neither notable nor typical of any peculiar moral, religious, social, or intellectual idea. In the older civilization architecture was the mirror which reflected the character of a people. It was taught in the schools, and esteemed one of the most important of the arts. But the representatives of many

10. Martha Lamb, ed., *The Homes of America* (New York, 1879)
Avery Architectural and Fine Arts Library, Columbia University

sented illustrations of old landmarks.[49] Some local historians such as Thompson Westcott used colonial buildings as starting points for chapters on family histories.[50] Martha J. Lamb wove biography and architectural history together in *The Homes of America* (1879; fig. 10), more than a third of which covered the "Colonial Period" and such great houses as Stratford that "reveal more truthfully than any other

existing relics the life and history of the times."[51]

Preservationists used history to bolster their cause, as in the case of the *History of the Old South Church* (1876; fig. 11), where the building's history was subordinated to events in the Revolution.[52] Women were apparently the main audience for popular accounts of "social and domestic life" in colonial homes such as Anne Hollingsworth Wharton's *Through Colonial Doorways* (1893; fig. 12). Mary H. Northend found the "greatest charm" in "ancestral homes that have descended from generation to generation in the same family."[53] Genealogy was mixed with a little architectural history in Thomas Allen Glenn's *Some Colonial Mansions and Those Who Lived in Them* (1899).[54] New Americans, immigrants, might become fully Americanized by being exposed to pictures of patriotic landmarks, thought New York's blueblood-run City History Club. On the other hand, Samuel Adams Drake, the antiquarian author of *Our Colonial Homes* (1894), was angered that Paul Revere's house (fig. 13) in Boston's North End was surrounded by "dirty tenements swarm[ing] with greasy, voluble Italians."[55] Children found engravings of colonial sites and patriotic shrines in their texts, and adolescent girls could read in Kate Douglas Wiggin's *Mother Carey's Chickens* (1911), a description of the "impressive" facade of the "Colonial" Yellow House pictured on the cover (fig. 14).[56]

Guidebooks catered to the patriotic and antiquarian sentiments of their touring readers. Thus a Pennsylvania Railroad guide in 1875 featured both Independence Hall and an old mill on the Conemaugh; a 1903 trolley guide pointed out Washington's headquarters in New Jersey, while a guide for "automobile parties" in 1907 (fig. 15) directed them to "quaint inns and hostelries." Postcards of these inns and other historic sites were not only souvenirs for pilgrims, but also made a wider public aware of colonial architecture.[57]

Discoverers of colonial architecture were mobile. John Martin Hammond, a self-described "collector of old houses" with his camera, advised other would-be collectors that they must also possess "a fine power

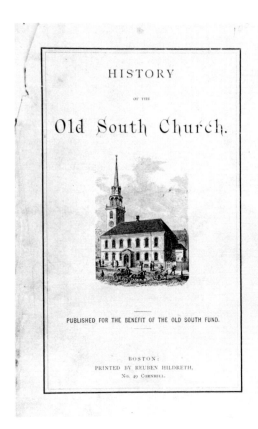

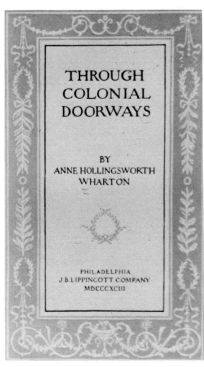

of walking." The railroad and trolley made distant sites accessible, but some found them disturbers of colonial tranquility: E. Eldon Deane sought refuge from New York in Charleston, South Carolina, where he sketched, measured, and imagined himself an eighteenth-century worshiper in St. Michael's Church (fig. 16) until his reverie was broken by the "harsh metallic grinding of the trolley-car." Yet the benefits of rapid travel by rail were recognized by the writer Richard Le Gallienne, who compared the railway to Kingston, New York, to "Mr. H. G. Wells's 'time machine,' " as it had set him down in what appeared to be a seventeenth-century town where "history . . . gazes at us dreamily from the old stone houses."

The English-born Le Gallienne supposed that "the sense of the past as a still living presence can be more fully experienced, on occasion, here in America than in Europe."[58] Many (probably most) architects and laymen who drew and described colonial architecture were attracted to it as America's own tradition, or, as Peabody wrote, "our only native source of . . . inspiration."[59] Johann Wolfgang von Goethe in the late eighteenth century had proclaimed the German roots and character of Gothic architecture, and David Watkin has shown that in early nineteenth-century Europe, "nationalism . . . was . . . often part of this new historical preoccupation" with the Gothic.[60] Americans in search of a home-grown, national mode of building would find it in the colonial.

11. Title page, *History of the Old South Church* (Boston, 1876)

12. Frontispiece and title page, Anne Hollingsworth Wharton, *Through Colonial Doorways* (Philadelphia, 1893).
Sojourner Truth Library, State University College at New Paltz

13. Paul Revere House, Boston
From Samuel Adams Drake, *Our Colonial Homes* (Boston, 1894)

14. Cover, Kate Douglas Wiggin, *Mother Carey's Chickens* (Boston, 1911)

15. Cover, Mary Caroline Crawford, *Little Pilgrimages Among Old New England Inns* (Boston, 1907)

Colonial Americans, according to Martha Lamb, had transformed foreign building forms to suit "the climate, necessities of pioneer life, and social conditions of an unformed community." Bragdon acknowledged the English Georgian origins of the colonial but insisted American eighteenth-century builders had come "as near as we have ever approached to achieving an American style of architecture." For Embury, eighteenth-century American churches represented the flowering of "our first national style," no more like English architecture than English architecture resembled Italian. Moreover, the colonial, with its modest ornament, was free of the "vulgarity and ostentation" of the European baroque.[61]

Not only was colonial architecture American, but it also embodied the virtues of the great men and women who had created the nation. Thomas Jefferson himself as an old man in 1825 advised that sites associated with the Revolution, such as the house where he lived when writing the

Declaration of Independence, might well be kept "like the relics of saints." When Bulfinch's Massachusetts State House was threatened with demolition, Boston architect Charles A. Cummings preached that its destruction "would be a lamentable concession to the modern American spirit which carries us every year farther away from the 'nobler modes of life, with sweeter manners, purer laws,' which our fathers knew."[62]

As A. W. N. Pugin decried the corruption of contemporary English society and would turn back to the Middle Ages for a model social system, so Cummings idealized America's colonial past. So did Bragdon when he proposed that "architecture . . . images at all times a nation's character . . . , is the mirror of the national consciousness. . . . The difference between Independence Hall . . . and a modern skyscraper is the measure of the difference between the men and manners of the Colonial days, and the men and manners of today."[63]

Gentility was a quality of colonial architecture identified by authors such as Stanford White's father, Richard Grant White, who saw in the houses of "Old New York" built in the early 1800s an "air of . . . large and elegant domesticity." They were the "homes of people of sense, and taste, and character," of "gentle breeding." By contrast, the "brownstone fronts" of midcentury aptly represented the vulgar mob housed within.[64] The southern plantation house was widely believed to express a "social elegance" and "aristocratic atmosphere" comparable to the houses of the English landed gentry.[65] On the other hand, a designer of middle-class houses like Embury paid tribute to the gambrel-roofed

Dutch colonial house as "never formal . . . [or] stately, yet . . . [with] a certain homely dignity eminently fitting to the homes of the courageous and determined pioneers who built them."[66]

In 1940 members of the newly organized American Society of Architectural Historians determined that their first three tours, by car, would focus on colonial houses in Massachusetts. The society has long been identified with the study of early American architecture, agreeing with an 1882 assessment in the *American Architect* that "we do have an architectural history, . . . one in which Americans may take pride."[67]

16. St. Michael's Church, Charleston, South Carolina (detail)
From E. Eldon Deane, "An Autumn Trip to South Carolina," in *The Georgian Period . . .* , vol. 3. Avery Architectural and Fine Arts Library, Columbia University

NOTES

1. Andrew A. Lipscomb, ed., *The Writings of Thomas Jefferson*, 20 vols. (Washington, 1905), 2:212; Louisa Caroline Tuthill, *History of Architecture from the Earliest Times* (Philadelphia, 1848), 242, 258, 260; James Fergusson, *History of the Modern Styles of Architecture*, 2d ed. (London, 1873), 498. Americans should not have felt Fergusson was singling out their architecture for criticism, as his writing was often vitriolic. David B. Brownlee, *The Law Courts: The Architecture of George Edmund Street* (New York and Cambridge, Mass., 1984), 249.

2. William Bentley, *The Diary of William Bentley, D.D., Pastor of the East Church, Salem, Massachusetts*, 4 vols. (Gloucester, Mass., 1962), 1:171; Abbott Lowell Cummings, *The Framed Houses of Massachusetts Bay, 1625–1725* (Cambridge, Mass., 1979), 1.

3. Joseph T. Butler, *Washington Irving's Sunnyside* (Tarrytown, 1974).

4. Thomas Tileston Waterman and John A. Barrows, *Domestic Colonial Architecture of Tidewater Virginia* (New York, 1932), 12; Charles E. Peterson, " 'Preservationism,' " *Journal of the Society of Architectural Historians* (hereafter *JSAH*) 10 (May 1951), 24; Margaret Henderson Floyd, "Measured Drawings of the Hancock House by John Hubbard Sturgis: A Legacy to the Colonial Revival," in *Architecture in Colonial Massachusetts: A Conference Held by the Colonial Society of Massachusetts, September 19 and 20, 1974* (Boston, 1979), 88–104.

5. Arthur Gilman, "Architecture in the United States, *North American Review* 58 (April 1844), 457–463; David Chase, "Notes on the Colonial Revival in Newport," *Newport History* 55 (Spring 1982), 40; Richard Upjohn, "The Colonial Architecture of New York and the New England States," *Architectural Review and American Builders' Journal* 2 (March 1870), 547–550.

6. *Architectural Sketch Book* 2 (January 1875), plate 31; William E. Barry, *Pen Sketches of Old Houses* (Boston, n.d.); for information on Barry, see Walter Knight Sturges, "Arthur Little and the Colonial Revival," *JSAH* 32 (May 1973), 151, and Margaret Henderson Floyd, "William E. Barry of Kennebunk: The Boston Years," *Maine History News* 19 (July 1983 and December 1983), 10–11, 13–14.

7. *New-York Sketch-Book of Architecture* 1 (December 1874), 1–2; 2 (July 1875); 2 (August 1875); 3 (July 1876); see Leland M. Roth, *McKim, Mead & White, Architects* (New York, 1983), 38, 44, for McKim's study and use of colonial architecture. See also Mary N. Woods, "History in the Early American Architectural Journals," in this volume.

8. *American Architect and Building News* (hereafter *AABN*) 1 (18 March 1876), 90; "American Architecture—Past," *AABN* 1 (29 July 1876), 242–244.

9. Wheaton A. Holden, "Robert Swain Peabody of Peabody and Stearns in Boston," (Ph.D. diss., Boston University, 1969), 77.

10. Robert S. Peabody, "A Talk about 'Queen Anne,' " *AABN* 2 (28 April 1877), 133–134; Peabody, "Georgian Houses of New England," *AABN* 2 (20 October 1877), 338–339; Peabody, "The Georgian Houses of New England II," *AABN* 3 (16 February 1878), 54–55. For a discussion of Peabody's writings, see Vincent J. Scully, Jr., *The Shingle Style* (New Haven, 1955), 42–45.

11. Peabody 1878, 54–55.

12. See, for example, the definition of "Colonial Architecture" in Russell Sturgis, ed., *A Dictionary of Architecture and Building, Biographical, Historical, and Descriptive*, 3 vols. (New York and London, 1902), 1:639. English architectural writers came to admire early nineteenth-century classicism only after 1914, according to David Watkin, *The Rise of Architectural History* (London and Westfield, N.J., 1980), 120.

13. Arthur Little, *Early New England Interiors: Sketches in Salem, Marblehead, Portsmouth, and Kittery* (Boston, 1878); see also Sturges 1973, 147–163, and Bainbridge Bunting, *Houses of Boston's Back Bay: An Architectural History, 1840–1917* (Cambridge, Mass., 1967), 357. In the same year, 1877, Charles McKim, William Mead, William Bigelow, and Stanford White made sketches and measured drawings of colonial houses in Marblehead, Salem, Newburyport, and Portsmouth which long remained in the office scrapbook. Charles Moore, *The Life and Times of Charles Follen McKim* (Boston, 1929), 41.

14. "Colonial Houses, and Their Uses to Art," *AABN* 3 (12 January 1878), 12–13.

15. George Champlin Mason, *Newport Illustrated, in a Series of Pen & Pencil Sketches* (New York, 1854); Mason, *Reminiscences of Newport* (Newport, 1884); David Chase, "George Champlin Mason, Sr.," in William H. Jordy and Christopher P. Monkhouse, *Buildings on Paper: Rhode Island Architectural Drawings, 1825–1945* [exh. cat., Bell Gallery, Brown University] (Providence, 1982), 222–223.

16. David Chase, "George Champlin Mason, Jr.," in Jordy and Monkhouse, *Buildings on Paper*, 223–224; Chase, "Notes," 46–52; George C. Mason, Jr., "Colonial Architecture," *AABN* 10 (13 and 20 August 1881), 71–74, 83–85.

17. A. J. Bloor in *AABN* 10 (27 August 1881), 102–103. As architect for a restoration of the Seventh-Day Baptist Church (1729) in Newport, Mason published measured drawings, a description of his work, and an analysis of the original design. Since interior details resembled those of Trinity Church, Newport, he attributed both to the same builder. *AABN* 17 (2 May 1885), 210. Such exacting studies have led Chase to describe Mason as "the most accomplished architectural historian active during the early days of the Colonial Revival." "Notes," 52.

18. Frank E. Wallis, "The Colonial Renaissance: Houses of the Middle and Southern Colonies," *White Pine Series* 2 (February 1916), 3–6; Frank E. Wallis, *Old Colonial Architecture and Furniture* (Boston, 1887).

19. Harold F. Withey and Elsie Rathburn Withey, *Bio-*

graphical Dictionary of American Architects (Deceased) (Los Angeles, 1970), 627.

20. Frank E. Wallis, How to Know Architecture: The Human Elements in the Evolution of Styles (New York, 1910), 281.

21. E.g., W. Davenport Goforth and William J. McAuley, Old Colonial Architectural Details in and around Philadelphia (New York, 1890).

22. James M. Corner and Eric Ellis Soderholtz, Examples of Domestic Colonial Architecture in New England (Boston, 1891); Henry-Russell Hitchcock, American Architectural Books (Minneapolis, 1946, repr. 1962), 27.

23. Charles McKim to James Corner and Eric Soderholtz, 17 December 1891, McKim Papers, Library of Congress.

24. Joy Wheeler Dow, "How to Make a Successful House," in The Book of a Hundred Houses: A Collection of Pictures, Plans and Suggestions for Householders (New York, 1906), 6.

25. AABN 34 (10 October 1891), 30; William Nelson Black, "Colonial Building in New Jersey," Architectural Record (hereafter Record) 3 (January–March 1894), 245–262.

26. Joseph Everett Chandler, The Colonial Architecture of Maryland, Pennsylvania, and Virginia (Boston, 1892). For Chandler as a colonial revivalist, see his The Colonial House (New York, 1916).

27. T. Henry Randall, "Colonial Annapolis," Record 1 (January–March 1892), 311; G. A. T. Middleton, "English 'Georgian' Architecture. The Source of the American 'Colonial' Style," Record 9 (October 1899), 97–108.

28. Frank J. Roos, Jr., Bibliography of Early American Architecture: Writings on Architecture Constructed before 1860 in Eastern and Central United States (Urbana, Ill., 1968), 5.

29. Montgomery Schuyler, "A History of Old Colonial Architecture," Record 4 (January–March 1895), 312–366. For Schuyler's ancestry, see Alice P. Kenney, Stubborn for Liberty—The Dutch in New York (Syracuse, 1975), 227. Schuyler also surveyed colonial architecture in his "United States, Architecture of," in Sturgis 1902, 3:895–921.

30. O. Z. Cervin, "The So-Called Colonial Architecture of the United States," AABN 48 (8, 22, 29 June 1895), 99, 115, 130.

31. Claude Fayette Bragdon, "Six Hours in Salem," AABN 39 (21 January 1893), 41; Bragdon, "Colonial Work in the Genesee Valley," AABN 43 (24 March 1894), 141.

32. William Rotch Ware, ed., The Georgian Period: A Collection of Papers Dealing with "Colonial" or XVIII-Century Architecture in the United States, Together with References to Earlier Provincial and True Colonial Work, 12 parts (Boston, 1898–1902), 1: unpaginated preface and 12: 124.

33. Nation 68 (9 March 1899), reprinted AABN 63 (18 March 1899), 86; Ware 1902, 9–12: 11.

34. Richard Franz Bach, "Books on Colonial Architecture," Record 38 (August 1915), 284; "The Georgian Period," Record 54 (August 1923), 197. A revised edition appeared in New York in 1923, edited by Charles S. Keefe.

35. Norman M. Isham and Albert F. Brown, Early Rhode Island Houses: An Historical and Architectural Study (Providence, 1895) and Norman M. Isham and Albert F. Brown, Early Connecticut Houses: An Historical and Architectural Study (Providence, 1900).

36. Isham and Brown 1895, 5–6.

37. Jordy and Monkhouse 1982, 218–219.

38. Russell Sturgis, review in Record 6 (July–September 1896), 91–92. Isham and Brown's books were in fact used by colonial revivalists: see Record 11 (October 1901), 732. Isham called Edwin Whitefield "the real pioneer in the study of New England's ancient buildings" (In Praise of Antiquaries [Boston, 1931], 9) even though Whitefield's lithographic illustrations were "not wonderful" and the first book in his series, Homes of Our Forefathers . . . , appeared in Boston in 1879, after Little's volume. Hitchcock 1962, 115.

39. Glenn Brown, "Old Colonial Work in Virginia and Maryland," AABN 22 (22 October 1887), 198–199. Charles B. Wood III recognizes George Clarence Gardner's "Colonial Architecture in Western Massachusetts," AABN 45 (15 September 1894), 99–100, as the "first serious attempt" to list colonial builders' guides. "A Survey and Bibliography of Writings on English and American Architectural Books Published before 1895," Winterthur Portfolio 2 (1965), 127. A c. 1895 reprint of Batty Langley's Examples from Ancient Masonry (London, 1733) "selected by John A. Fox, architect, Boston," has been cited as "probably the first example of the reprinting of eighteenth-century sources as models for the Colonial Revival." Hitchcock 1962, 60.

40. William B. Bushong, "Glenn Brown and the United States Capitol" [fellowship research report, U.S. Capitol Historical Society] (Washington, D.C., 1988), 12.

41. Glenn Brown, "History of the United States Capitol," AABN 52 (9 May 1896), 51–54; Brown, History of the United States Capitol, 2 vols. (Washington, D.C., 1899–1904), 1:iv; Bushong 1988, 19–24.

42. Aymar Embury II, "Three Old Dutch Roads and the Houses along Them," Country Life in America 16 (October 1909), 592. Embury's The Dutch Colonial House (New York, 1913) was a layman's guide to building new Dutch colonials.

43. Aymar Embury II, "Old New Orleans," Record 30 (July 1911), 85–98; Embury, "Pennsylvania Farmhouses," Record 30 (November 1911), 475–485.

44. Bach 1915, 379–382; Aymar Embury II, Early American Churches (Garden City, N.Y., 1914), xiii–xvi, 20, 48–52, 88, 109, 119–124, 133, 142.

45. For example, Bach 1915, 281, allowed colonial and Georgian to be used interchangeably for buildings into the 1820s, while Harold Donaldson Eberlein re-

stricted colonial to the "Pre-Georgian," before 1720. "Three Types of Georgian Architecture," *Record* 34 (July 1913), 60.

46. Joy Wheeler Dow, *American Renaissance: A Review of Domestic Architecture* (New York, 1904), 43.

47. Sidney Fiske Kimball to the editor, *Journal of the American Institute of Architects* 2 (July 1914), 330; Kimball, *Domestic Architecture of the American Colonies and of the Early Republic* (New York, 1922), xviii. Watkin credits Kimball with beginning "to apply detailed scholarship to the history of the American tradition in architecture." Watkin 1980, 37.

48. John Maass, "Where Architectural Historians Fear to Tread," *JSAH* 28 (March 1969), 3–8; Randall 1892, 311; Owen B. Maginnis, "An Old Dutch Mill," *Carpentry and Building* 11 (November 1889), 219.

49. For a discussion of the treatment of colonial architecture in popular publications, see Scully 1955, 24–30.

50. Thompson Westcott, *Historic Mansions and Buildings of Philadelphia, with Some Notice of Their Owners and Occupants* (Philadelphia, 1877).

51. Martha J. Lamb, ed., *The Homes of America* (New York, 1879), 9, 67.

52. *History of the Old South Church* (Boston, 1876).

53. Anne Hollingsworth Wharton, *Through Colonial Doorways* (Philadelphia, 1893); Mary H. Northend, *Historic Homes of New England* (Boston, 1914), vii.

54. Thomas Allen Glenn, *Some Colonial Mansions and Those Who Lived in Them, with Genealogies of the Various Families Mentioned*, 2 vols. (Philadelphia, 1899–1900).

55. Frank Bergen Kelley, compiler, *Historical Guide to the City of New York* (New York, 1909); William B. Rhoads, "The Colonial Revival and the Americanization of Immigrants," in *The Colonial Revival in America*, ed. Alan Axelrod (New York and London, 1985), 342; Samuel Adams Drake, *Our Colonial Homes* (Boston, 1894), 19.

56. Benson J. Lossing, *A Common-School History of the United States from the Earliest Period to the Present Time* (New York, 1873), 94, 128; Kate Douglas Wiggin, *Mother Carey's Chickens* (Boston, 1911), 172.

57. William B. Sipes, *The Pennsylvania Railroad . . .* (Philadephia, 1875); Cromwell Childe, *Trolley Exploring. . .* (Brooklyn, 1903), 15; Mary Caroline Crawford, *Little Pilgrimages among Old New England Inns . . .* (Boston, 1907), 158; see also William B. Rhoads, "Roadside Colonial: Early American Design for the Automobile Age," *Winterthur Portfolio* 21 (Autumn 1986), 133–135.

58. John Martin Hammond, *Colonial Mansions of Maryland and Delaware* (Philadelphia, and London 1914), v–vi; A. B. Bibb, "Old Colonial Works of Virginia and Maryland: Williamsburg—The Town," *AABN* 25 (15 June 1889); E. Eldon Deane, "An Autumn Trip to South Carolina," *Georgian Period*, 9–12: 43–44; Richard Le Gallienne, "Old Kingston," *Harper's Magazine* 123 (November 1911), 917, 920.

59. Peabody, "Queen Anne," 134.

60. Watkin 1980, 4, 25.

61. Lamb 1879, 10; Claude Bragdon, "Architecture in the United States," *Record* 25 (June 1909), 426; Embury 1914, 175–177.

62. Lipscomb 1905, 16:123; Charles A. Cummings, "The Crown of Beacon Hill," *Georgian Period*, 12:121. For Cummings, this ignoble modern spirit also gave birth to Frederick MacMonnies' *Bacchante*, which he succeeded in excluding from the Boston Public Library. *AABN* 88 (19 August 1905), 57.

63. Watkin 1980, 10; Bragdon 1909, 426.

64. Richard Grant White, "Old New York and Its Houses," *Century Magazine* 26 [n.s. 4] (October 1883), 851, 853, 859.

65. Harry W. Desmond and Herbert Croly, *Stately Homes in America from Colonial Times to the Present Day* (New York, 1903), 86; Russell F. Whitehead, "The Old and the New South: A Consideration of Architecture in the Southern States," *Record* 30 (July 1911), 1.

66. Embury 1909, 592. For more on the associations attached to colonial architecture that enhanced its popularity, see William B. Rhoads, *The Colonial Revival*, 2 vols. (New York, 1977), 1:376–551.

67. "A.S.A.H. Beginnings: A Report," *Journal of the American Society of Architectural Historians* 1 (January 1941), 20–22; *AABN* 12 (12 August 1882), 73.

LISA KOENIGSBERG
New York City

Life-Writing:

First American Biographers of Architects and Their Works

Architectural historians are devoting an increasing amount of attention to American architectural literature, yet little attention has been accorded biographical writing about architects as it appeared in the United States. This paper is a preliminary attempt to define a group of nineteenth-century American biographers of American architects and to identify their works. The writings considered comprise the small known group of nineteenth-century books and pamphlets devoted to the lives of single American architects; these works document the emergence of American biographies of architects as a distinct type of publication in the mid-nineteenth century. The publication of biographical writings about architects increased in the United States during the 1850s, most likely the result of greater interest in and increased demand for architecture, as well as the professionalization of architecture in America.

The term "life-writing," which often is employed to describe biography, here includes autobiographies as a closely related or a "specialized form" of "life-writing" authored by the subjects themselves.[1] In this paper, life-writing refers to autobiographies or to individual posthumous biographies of American architects.

Written primarily for an audience of educated laymen, these works can be divided into three groups: autobiographies, biographies by men about male architects, and biographies by women about male architects. The biographers, who were not themselves professional architects, eulogized individuals with whom they had personal, familial, professional, or organizational relationships.

In general, the books and pamphlets to be discussed were intended to right wrongs that had been done to their subjects during their careers and to depict the American architect as hero by portraying him as trained professional and virtuous man. As such, these life-writings may also have contributed to the public's increasing acceptance of the professional architect.

Biographical writing about architects, which had begun in the United States by the 1830s,[2] was published increasingly in the 1850s. Isaac Ashmead's reprint of the *Obituary Notice of John Haviland, Esq.* appeared in 1852; it was originally published earlier that year in the *Journal of Prison Reform*.[3] That year also marked the publication in New York of Shearjashub Spooner's *A Biographical and Critical Dictionary of Painters, Engravers, Sculptors, and Architects from Ancient to Modern Times*, followed in 1853 by Henry T. Tuckerman's *A Memorial to Horatio Greenough: Consisting of a Memoir, Selections from His Writings, and Tributes to His Genius*.[4] The *Annals of the Massachusetts Charitable Mechanic Association*, first published in 1853, also contain brief obituaries of housewrights, masons, and other members, including Alexander Parris.[5]

The publication of biographical writings about architects continued in the 1860s with James Gallier's 1864 *Autobiography of James Gallier, Architect* (published in Paris), William Wheildon's 1865 *Memoir of Solomon Willard, Architect and Superintendent of the Bunker Hill Monument*, Shearjashub Spooner's *A Biographical History of the Fine Arts* (essentially an 1865 reprint of his earlier work), and Edwin Martin Stone's 1869 *The Architect and Monetarian: A Brief Memoir of Thomas Alexander Tefft Including His Labors to Establish a Universal Currency.*[6]

The year 1874 appears to mark the emergence of women as authors of biographical writing about architects with the publication in New York of Clara Erskine Clement Waters' (1834–1916) *Painters, Sculptors, Architects, Engravers, and Their Works: A Handbook.* Her *Artists of the Nineteenth Century and Their Works*, which was coauthored by Lawrence Hutton (1843–1904), was first published in Boston in 1879. The emergence of women as authors of life-writing proper began with Mariana Griswold Van Rensselaer's 1888 *Henry Hobson Richardson and His Works*, followed in 1896 by both Ellen Susan Bulfinch's work on her grandfather, *The Life and Letters of Charles Bulfinch, Architect*, and by Harriet Monroe's biography of her brother-in-law, *John Wellborn Root: A Study of His Life and Work.*[7] Also during this period, Elbridge Boyden's *Reminiscences* (originally published in 1889) appeared in pamphlet form in 1890.[8]

Before 1850, building activity had also been on the upswing,[9] and the professionalization of architecture, which appears to have been a major factor in the rise of architectural biography, was well underway. It has been suggested, for example, that by 1830 a sense of professionalism was developing in Boston.[10] It has also been demonstrated that during the late 1830s architects discovered a powerful vehicle with which to assert their superiority over builders: the architectural stylebooks, which were aimed at both client and builder.[11] During the 1850s (the decade that saw the rise of biographical writing about architects in

America), opportunities for architectural training increased as a result of the intensified concern for technical education in the United States, and in 1857, the American Institute of Architects was formed.[12]

The architectural biographers working after 1850 pursued a type of writing initially made possible by the emergence of architecture as a profession distinct from the craft of building. Moreover, the biographers' pursuit of their literary endeavor may have made them agents in this professionalizing process because they celebrated their subjects' work and lives, treating them as heroes, an approach that has been seen as characteristic of nineteenth-century biography.[13]

The Biographers

Except for the autobiographies written by James Gallier and Elbridge Boyden, the books and pamphlets of this period after 1850 were written by intelligent laypeople, not members of the professional architectural establishment. Moreover, there are demonstrable relationships between subject and author.

The anonymous first biographer to be discussed here apparently knew his subject through the Philadelphia Society for Alleviating the Miseries of Public Prisons, which published the *Journal of Prison Reform*, in which the obituary first appeared. Although the 1852 *Obituary Notice of John Haviland, Esq.* is unsigned, the author—who was probably male—locates himself by informing us that Haviland "landed in this city in September, 1816." Noting that Haviland probably "scanned . . . all the resources of his profession," the author implies that he himself was not an architect.[14]

Born in Boston, where he attended the Latin School and Harvard, Henry Theodore Tuckerman (1813–1871) [fig. 1] was the author of *A Memoir of Horatio Greenough*, which is considered in this paper because of Greenough's participation in the important Bunker Hill Monument Competition.[15] A man of independent means, Tuckerman first traveled to Europe in 1833–1834 (spending most of his time in Italy), where he became engrossed in literature

1. Capewell & Kimmel, engravers, *H. T. Tuckerman*
Print Collection, Miriam and Ira D. Wallach Division of Art, Prints, and Photographs, New York Public Library, Astor, Lenox, and Tilden Foundations

2. William A. Coffin (1855–1925), *Mrs. Schuyler Van Rensselaer [Mariana Griswold Van Rensselaer]*, 1890, oil on canvas
Museum of the City of New York, 34.321

and art. According to Tuckerman, he first met Greenough on this trip; their friendship endured until the sculptor's death in 1852.[16] Tuckerman's published writings also include literary criticism, works on travel, poetry, and *Artist-Life, or Sketches of American Painters* (1847, later expanded into his important *Book of the Artists: American Artist Life* of 1867), a work that clearly fused his interests in the visual arts and in biography.[17]

Also born in Boston, the author of the *Memoir of Solomon Willard*, William Willder Wheildon (1805–1892), was a writer, editor, printer, and newspaperman. The founder and publisher of the *Bunker Hill Aurora* (1826–1871), he also wrote several books on Boston and Charlestown history.[18] Wheildon and Willard shared an organizational relationship; both were members of the Massachusetts Charitable Mechanic Association and the Bunker Hill Monument Association.[19]

The author of *The Architect and Monetarian: A Brief Memoir of Thomas Alexander Tefft*, Edwin Martin Stone (1805–1883) worked as a printer and an editor before studying for the ministry. As Unitarian minister-at-large in Providence, Rhode Island, a post he assumed in 1847 and held

for thirty years, Stone worked within the Providence community and in his annual reports offered proposals for dealing with various social ills.[20] The biographer, who, like his subject, always took "a deep interest in educational matters,"[21] also wrote several historical works. It is likely that Tefft and Stone knew one another from common organizational memberships and activities; both were involved in the Rhode Island Institute for Instruction at the same time and both also belonged to the Rhode Island Historical Society.[22]

Mariana Alley Griswold Van Rensselaer (1851–1934) [fig. 2], the author of the 1888 *Henry Hobson Richardson and His Works*, which Henry-Russell Hitchcock called "the foundation of all study of Richardson,"[23] is the first of three American women who wrote important late nineteenth-century architectural biographies. Born in New York City into a wealthy and socially prominent family, Mariana Griswold was educated by private tutors and by travel. In Dresden in 1873, she married Schuyler Van Rensselaer (1845–1884), a descendant of a distinguished family and a Harvard- and Freiburg-educated mining and metallurgical engineer. Known for her writing on architecture, art, and landscape gardening and as a historian, Van Rensselaer's important works include two series on architecture written for *Century*, one entitled "Recent Architecture in America" (1884–1886), which included discussion of Richardson's work, and the other a series of articles on English cathedrals (1887–1892, also published as a book); and *Art Out-of-Doors: Hints on Good Taste in Gardening* (1893).[24]

It has been suggested that Van Rensselaer, who was already established as a writer on art and architecture for a broad readership by 1886 when she was asked to write the biography,[25] knew Richardson well (perhaps as a result of her interest in his architecture), although it is not known how or when the two met.[26] In the biography, Van Rensselaer alludes to events at which both were present and to remarks Richardson made in her presence, such as his well-known statement that "the things I want most to design are a grain-elevator and the interior of a great river-steamboat."[27]

Harriet Monroe (1860–1936) [fig. 3], the author of *John Wellborn Root: A Study of His Life and Work*, was the daughter of a Chicago lawyer. Monroe is best known as a poet and as the editor of *Poetry Magazine*, which she founded in 1912.[28] Her formal education began in Chicago and continued in a convent boarding school in Georgetown in Washington, D.C.; also important was her extensive reading in her father's library. Returning to Chicago in the summer of 1879, she wrote poetry and prose, began participating in the city's social and cultural life, and met John Wellborn Root, her future brother-in-law (an encounter she recalled in the biography, which includes many anecdotes).[29] By this point Monroe had begun writing for the local press, and for well over twenty years she served as a correspondent and reviewer of art, theater, and other subjects for a number of Chicago and New York papers.[30]

Monroe's relationship to her subject was also clearly familial and personal. In the introduction to her biography, she lamented: "And so I, who knew him well, will turn back over the years of our intercourse, reproaching at every step the pitiful weakness of memory, longing for some

3. *Harriet Monroe. A Picture Taken When She Was in Her Thirties*
From Harriet Monroe, *A Poet's Life: Seventy Years in a Changing World* (New York, 1938). General Research Division of the New York Public Library, Astor, Lenox, and Tilden Foundations

magic lamp to illumine the path once bright."[31] In addition, Morton Zaubel has observed that Root "was influential in furthering . . . [Monroe's] artistic interests."[32] Her deep commitment to the architect is demonstrated by her inclusion of an allusion to him (although he had already died) in her ode for the dedicatory program of the World's Columbian Exposition of 1893.[33]

Little is known about Charles Bulfinch's granddaughter and biographer Ellen Susan Bulfinch (1844–1921). Born into an established family in Framingham, Massachusetts, she is listed as "an artist of Cambridge" in *A Dictionary of American Authors*.[34] The author's relationship to her subject was clearly familial. Although born after her grandfather's death,[35] she was able to draw upon his unpublished autobiographical sketch, her mother's recollections, and letters written by the architect, the architect's mother, and other family members.[36]

As architecture developed as a profession, the personal connections between the biographer and the subject appear to have shifted from relationships based on or

4. T. B. Welch, engraver,
John Haviland
From *Obituary Notice of John
Haviland, Esq.* (Philadelphia, 1852).
Library Company of Philadelphia

write biographies for those authors who had personal and family ties to their subjects, as did the women writers on architecture. Their privileged backgrounds provided an alternative to professional education upon which they could then capitalize to write about architecture in a nontechnical way.

The Biographies

The biographers glorified their subjects' pursuit of professional training and improvement, as well as their architectural practice and professional activities. Moreover, the authors seem to have viewed biography as an opportunity to right a wrong or to set the record straight on behalf of their subjects, as well as to depict the deceased man's character. This portrayal, which probably stemmed from relationships that existed between subject and biographer, is the element that transformed these glorified professionals into hero-architects, men to be admired for both their great deeds and their noble qualities. Harriet Monroe articulates this notion of the architect as hero, maintaining that by quoting extensively from Root's own writings she had "permitted . . . [her] hero to give unawares an analysis of his artistic conscience, of the motives of his work and its aims."[37]

John Haviland's (1792–1852) [fig. 4] anonymous biographer was the first of these biographers of architects to depict his subject in glowing terms. Essentially confining his comments to one aspect of Haviland's career—his role as an innovator of prison design—the biographer briefly describes the architect's schooling and his study in London with James Elmes, asserting that even as a boy, Haviland's "tastes . . . inclined him towards the profession of an architect."[38] In his biographer's eyes, the architect pursued his professional practice vigorously, familiarizing himself with his clients' conceptions and examining "all the resources of his profession" to prepare his prison designs.[39] The author praises the "generous frankness which eminently characterized him as a professional man" and which contributed to the establish-

stemming from organizational ties to those based on family and friendship (in Van Rensselaer's case, quite possibly due to her interest in Richardson's work). This shift may have resulted from the changing organizational affiliations of the architects, who had become more involved in predominantly male professional architectural associations, such as the American Institute of Architects. This suggests that authors with organizational ties to their subjects would most likely have been male and probably architects or critics for the professional journals who had been trained in a manner similar to their subjects. Thus, the professionalization of architecture can be seen as having created the opportunity to

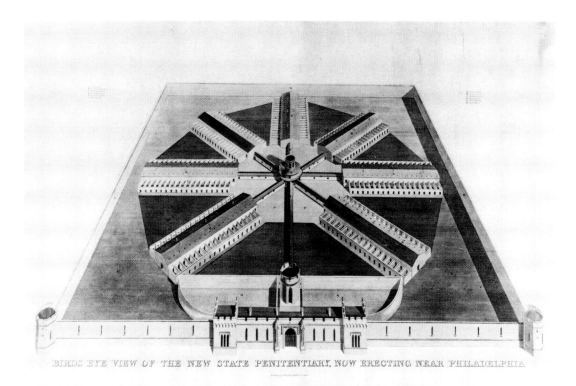

BIRDS EYE VIEW OF THE NEW STATE PENITENTIARY, NOW ERECTING NEAR PHILADELPHIA

5. John Haviland, *Eastern State Penitentiary* (1821–1837), Philadelphia, in an engraving by C. G. Childs
Historical Society of Pennsylvania

ment of his reputation "in a manner rarely exampled in the history of his profession in modern times."[40] Serving as his subject's advocate, Haviland's biographer praises the first realization of "the chief objects of prison architecture," exemplified by Haviland's Eastern State Penitentiary (1821–1837) [fig. 5], located in Philadelphia.[41] In his pamphlet, Haviland's biographer omits any reference to Haviland's financial difficulties, but rounds out his portrait by briefly mentioning positive aspects of the architect's life and personality.[42]

Tuckerman, who described Horatio Greenough's (1805–1852) entry into the Bunker Hill Monument Competition, serves as the exception to the architectural biographers because he correctly focuses on Greenough's training for and career as a sculptor. Yet even he described Greenough's early years of diligent, selfless study, which were to be rewarded by the commission to execute the monumental sculpture of George Washington. Hoping to right a wrong done to his subject, Tuck-

erman propounded the notion that Greenough was responsible for the Bunker Hill Monument's design, maintaining that although the interior was planned by another, "the form, proportions, and style . . . were adopted from Greenough's [wood] model; and the simple, majestic, and noble structure . . . is thus indissolubly associated with his name."[43]

William Wheildon presents Solomon Willard (1783–1861) as a self-taught carpenter "endowed by nature with a mind of original mechanical and artistic thought."[44] Narrating Willard's arrival in Boston, "in early life a 'rough ashlar,'" Wheildon describes Willard's work as carpenter, carver, sculptor, architect, inventor, and granite quarryman, but emphasizes his selfless involvement in the Bunker Hill Monument (1824–1842) located in Charlestown (fig. 6) as the overriding concern of the architect's life.[45] Willard's "self-education and self-elevation" revealed him as a self-made man, a member of a class "believed to be peculiar to our own country."[46] The architect avidly pursued architectural training

6. C. Cook, lithographer, *View [of the Monument]*
From Solomon Willard, *Plans and Sections of the Obelisk on Bunker's Hill with Details of Experiments Made in Quarrying the Granite* (Boston, 1843). Art & Architecture Collection, Miriam and Ira D. Wallach Division of Art, Prints, and Photographs, New York Public Library, Astor, Lenox, and Tilden Foundations

emerging architectural profession in the course of a few decades."[48] These organizations have been viewed as breeding grounds of professional consciousness.

The "wrong" that Wheildon wished to redress was the attribution of the Bunker Hill Monument to other architects. For Wheildon, clearly "the merit, . . . of the design as finally adopted and carried out, belongs chiefly to Mr. Willard. . . . In the greater merit of the work,—the construction,— . . . Mr. Willard's claims are beyond the reach of question or cavil."[49] Wheildon broadens his portrait of Willard to include the whole man, praising his "industry, economy and exemplary habits" and "his liberal, public-spirited and magnanimous conduct"[50]—but a few of the many encomia heaped upon the architect by the author.

For Stone, Thomas Alexander Tefft's (1826–1859) [fig. 7] zealous pursuit of architectural training was a demonstration of virtue and professionalism, and his brief career was an indication of the promise that might have been fulfilled. As a young schoolteacher in Richmond, Rhode Island, Tefft met Henry Barnard, then state school commissioner, who urged him to go to Providence and study architecture. Embarking on this professional course, Tefft moved to Providence in 1845 and entered the office of Tallman and Bucklin; in 1847 he enrolled at Brown University, from which he graduated in 1851.[51] He had already designed one of his most important works, the Union Depot in Providence (1847–1848, no longer extant) [fig. 8], in which, his biographer observed, he "developed a favorite idea of ornamental brick architecture and adopted the Lombardic style as best adapted to the purpose."[52]

Tefft then "opened an office for practical work," and, as a dedicated architect, involved himself in related professional activities such as the Rhode Island Art Association. Stone implied that Tefft would now reap the rewards of his sound professional preparation. Yet the architect yearned for still more knowledge, and he departed for three years of European travel in 1856.

Mourning Tefft's early death at age thirty-three, Stone wrote: "Few architects

by reading and classes, in which his progress was so impressive that he "soon ceased to be a pupil, though always a learner, and became a teacher."[47] Wheildon also mentions Willard's involvement in such associations as the Social Architectural Library of Boston, which was founded to make architectural books available to housewrights, and the Associated Housewright Society of Boston, which was established as a trade association and "became the nucleus of the

of riper age and longer experience have contributed more to the development of an aesthetic taste in Rhode Island." Had Tefft been allowed to utilize his "endowments enriched by studies abroad," he would have reached what his biographer termed "the highest rank and the surest success in his profession."[53]

The grievance that Stone hoped to redress on Tefft's behalf was not architectural in nature, but rather concerned his subject's campaign for a system of universal currency. Tefft died before an international conference on the subject was held, and although "the plan of unification" proposed there was in "nearly every particular" his, Tefft's name did not appear in the conference *Proceedings*, an omission Stone decried.[54]

7. *Thomas Alexander Tefft*
From Edwin Martin Stone, *The Architect and Monetarian: A Brief Memoir of Thomas Alexander Tefft* (Providence, 1869). Courtesy of the Rhode Island Historical Society

8. *Providence, Rhode Island c. 1875–1896. View of Exchange Place Including Tefft's Union Depot (1847–1848)*
Courtesy of the Rhode Island Historical Society

Rounding out his portrait of the young professional, Stone depicted Tefft as a perfectionist who "evidently permitted nothing worthy of notice to escape observation" and who expressed his opinions freely.[55] The architect's "whole bearing," Stone observed, "was of one who, self-conscious of native power, had made up his mind to succeed in whatever he undertook."[56] Stone revealed a tender side to the architect who "cherished a strong attachment" to his birthplace, enjoyed music, and was "not unmindful of the spiritual relations a man holds to his Creator."[57]

Portraying Henry Hobson Richardson (1838–1886) as ideally trained for the profession upon which he would embark, Mariana Van Rensselaer depicts her subject's years at Harvard, his subsequent departure for Paris, and his study at the Ecole des Beaux-Arts. Richardson is portrayed as something of a pioneer who valiantly attempted to succeed in the Parisian artistic world where few Americans had ventured.

The biographer glorifies Richardson, the European-trained American, the perfectionist who had "visibly raised the standing of the architectural profession throughout the whole country" and extolled him as "not only the greatest American artist but the greatest benefactor of American art who has yet been born."[58] Synthesizing a consideration of Richardson's practice with an examination of his role as a teacher, Van Rensselaer implies that the ultimate artist—epitomized by Richardson—was both practitioner and teacher.

Extending her consideration of the architect, who "had all the qualities which mark the born artist," Van Rensselaer presents a larger-than-life figure of "intense, immense vitality, physical as well as mental and emotional."[59] She observes that "an unusually intimate union" existed between his persona and his art, the best executed examples of which were (for her) the Marshall Field Wholesale Store (1885–1887, no longer extant) in Chicago and the Allegheny County Buildings (1883–1888) in Pittsburgh (fig. 9).[60] Van Rensselaer characterizes Richardson's nature—and therefore his architecture—as "so intensely modern, so thoroughly American" and as "robust, intensely human; in the better

meaning of the word, material," with a deeply practical aspect.[61] Van Rensselaer felt that the "fundamental qualities" of Richardson's architecture were "strength in conception; clearness in expression; breadth in treatment; imagination; a love of repose and massive dignity of aspect, and often for an effect which in the widest meaning of the word we may call 'romantic.' "[62]

Championing her architect-subject, Van Rensselaer was also concerned with setting the record straight regarding charges of "reckless extravagance and scandalous waste" that had been leveled against Richardson and the other architects during the building of the New York State Capitol in Albany (1875–1886 [1867–1899]).[63] In effect, she utilized an exoneration of Richardson's character and actions sent to her by Frederick Law Olmsted, a fellow member, with Richardson, of the Advisory Board of Architects for the project. Olmsted wrote that the architects "were not employed to superintend the work but merely to give counsel on architectural questions and prepare plans for others to carry out," a defense she employed almost verbatim.[64]

In her biography of John Wellborn Root (1850–1891), Harriet Monroe described her brother-in-law as an innovator and a leader in the spirit of "modern progressive art," whose oeuvre included many important office buildings such as the Rookery (1885–1888) and "the stern Monadnock" (1889–1892) [fig. 10], both located in Chicago; such buildings "proved his power of luring beauty to the service of commerce."[65] Monroe depicted Root as an architect who was as interested in the "engineering problems" and in "the mathematics of his profession" as he was in the art.[66] She did not see his bachelor's of science and civil engineering degree as directly relevant to his future as an architect, maintaining instead that his equipment "for the practice of his profession was rather in the quality of his mind than in its training."[67]

She wrote about business aspects of the architect's life, describing not only the creative side of Root's personality but portraying him as a competent professional in whose hands the trusting client was well placed. Monroe described Root and his

9. Henry Hobson Richardson, *Allegheny County Buildings* (1883–1888), Pittsburgh

From Mariana Van Rensselaer, *Henry Hobson Richardson and His Works* (Boston and New York, 1888). Avery Architectural and Fine Arts Library, Columbia University

partner Daniel Burnham (whom he met after arriving in Chicago while both were working for Carter, Drake, and Wight) as "pioneers of what was almost a new profession in the West," discussing Root's involvement in professional associations and elsewhere praising the firm's attitude toward its employees.[68] Monroe held the partners up as paragons of the architectural profession, noting that they fought strenuously "not only for their own place but for that of the profession as well."[69] The partners' "scrupulous regard for the rights of clients and of rival architects," were, for her, examples of consummate professionalism and of an appropriate manner of doing business.[70]

Monroe also used the biography as an opportunity to "set the record straight" by expressing her interpretation of her brother-in-law's role in the World's Columbian Exposition of 1893. She maintained that Root's vision for the Columbian Exposition differed significantly from the "White City" that resulted. Her views led her to proclaim that if "his ideas had prevailed, the Columbian Exposition would have been a City of Color; a queen arrayed in robes not saintly, as for a bridal, but gorgeous, for a festival."[71] She stated her belief that, if he had lived, Root's vision of the "progressive spirit" of architecture (which she presented fully in her book by drawing extensively from the architect's papers and lectures) would have been realized.[72]

Monroe's close familial relationship to the architect led her to include many personal anecdotes in the biography, which depicts Root as a romantic figure, "as sympathetic and intuitive as a woman . . . easily adored by men and women alike," and the consummate creative artist.[73] She pronounced him "deeply, instinctively musi-

10. Burnham and Root, *The Monadnock Building* (1889–1892), Chicago, photograph, c. 1920
Chicago Historical Society

11. Mather Brown (1761–1831), *Portrait of Charles Bulfinch*, 1786, oil on canvas
Harvard University Portrait Collection, Harvard University, Cambridge, Mass., Gift of Francis V. Bulfinch

cal," noting that he apprehended "all nature, all life . . . as harmony."[74] He was, she stated, "deeply an artist, a poet; profoundly a lover of his kind, a dreamer of God" and a man of intensely spiritual inclinations "vividly aware of the world beyond sense," whose early death "deprived us of the ripened fruit of his genius."[75]

Ellen Susan Bulfinch, who like Monroe had a familial relationship to her subject, painted her grandfather Charles (1763–1844) [fig. 11] as something of an architectural pioneer, noting that "architecture was not then recognized here as a profession." His "leisure and comparative wealth" enabled him to pursue "the field [that] was open to native talent."[76] As her quotations from his unpublished autobiography and from his letters indicate (and thus as he is revealed in her work), Bulfinch, a Harvard graduate, gained knowledge of architecture through foreign travel and observation. His familiarity with architectural books was also important. In further describing the architect as a pioneer, Bulfinch speculates about her grandfather's practice: "Personal supervision of the progress of a work, the eye of the master following each detail, possibly a drawing made upon the spot for illustration of his idea and then de-

stroyed,—such must have been his method." These, she believed, were "the simple ways of . . . working [that] . . . would be nearly inconceivable to the present generation."[77] She also linked her grandfather to American history through his design of the Beacon Hill Memorial Column (1790–1791 destroyed; replica erected 1898) in Boston, the Massachusetts State House (1795–1797) in Boston, and his tenure as Architect of the Capitol in Washington (1818–1830).

In keeping with her role as editor, Bulfinch drew much of her discussion of the Tontine Crescent in Boston (1793–1794, no longer extant) [fig. 12] from her grandfather's unpublished autobiography. Her consideration of the project that had forced the architect into bankruptcy gave Ellen Bulfinch the opportunity to state that the episode "did not imply any cause for loss of confidence on the part of his fellow-townsmen."[78]

Bulfinch also considered the whole man, discussing her grandfather's role in the Boston community as chairman of the board of selectmen and as superintendent of police. Regarding his character, she borrowed James Russell Lowell's words, which had been first applied to another, terming

Bulfinch "an aristocrat in a sense that is good even in a republic," that is, a reserved man of independence and of inherent personal dignity.[79]

The Autobiographies

In contrast to the biographers, the autobiographers, James Gallier and Elbridge Boyden, reflect on their own lives. Yet they shared the same concerns: depicting their careers, setting the record straight, and presenting themselves as virtuous and competent professionals.

Born and educated in Ireland, James Gallier, Sr. (1798–1866), worked as a builder and briefly studied architecture in Dublin.[80] After trying to make his fortune in London, he journeyed to New York in 1832, working first with James H. Dakin and then briefly with Minard Lafever. In 1834, Gallier (accompanied by a new partner, Charles B. Dakin, a successful association he dissolved in 1835) relocated to New Orleans where he became "one of the [city's] best known and most successful architects of . . . the mid-nineteenth century."[81] Gallier then executed residential and commercial commissions for which he usually served as both architect and builder. Around 1850, when his sight began to weaken, Gallier gave up his practice and traveled widely. These journeys, which are documented in his 1864 autobiography, ended in 1866 when he was lost in a shipwreck off the coast of Cape Hatteras.

Gallier portrays his early training in Ireland and England, which prompted the development of his consciousness as an architect, and his arrival in New York, at which time he already had a sense of himself as a "professional architect." His narrative of the building of the St. Charles Hotel in New Orleans (1835–1836, no longer extant) [fig. 13] is used to rectify any misconceptions about his competence as an architect that may have arisen after the building had sunk a foot more than he had originally calculated it would. Glorifying himself as a virtuous and diligent worker and as a master of all branches of architectural and building science, Gallier turns what may have been an engineer's nightmare into the architect's triumph. He also presents himself as a fair-minded employer and innovator; he discusses his introduction of the ten-hour workday and the biweekly paycheck and his use of subcontractors.

Elbridge Boyden's (1810–1898) [fig. 14] *Reminiscences* chronicle his life as a builder and architect in and around Worcester, Massachusetts. At sixteen, after limited formal education, he was apprenticed to Joel Stratton, a carpenter in Athol whose business he later purchased. After arriving in Worcester in 1844 to continue his career in building, in 1847 he formed a successful fourteen-year partnership with former mayor Phineas Ball, a

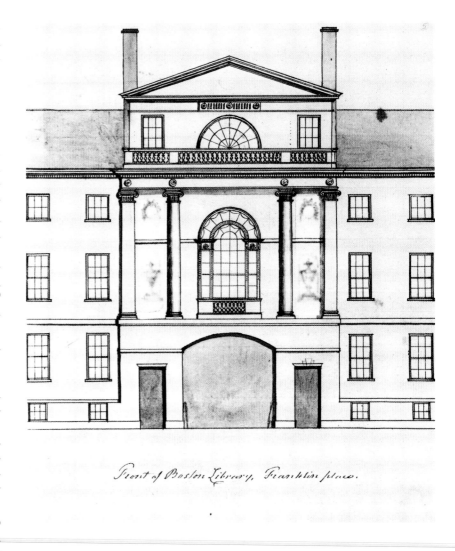

Front of Boston Library, Franklin place.

12. Charles Bulfinch, *Front of Boston Library, Franklin Place* (*Elevation of the Central Pavilion, The Tontine Crescent*) (1793–1794), Boston
Library of Congress, Washington, D.C.

13. Gallier and Dakin,
The St. Charles Hotel
(1835–1836), New Orleans,
in an engraving by
B. W. Thayer & Co., Boston,
1845
Louisiana State Museum

14. *Elbridge Boyden*
From Franklin P. Rice, ed., *The Worcester of 1898: Fifty Years a City* (Worcester, Mass., 1899). General Research Division, New York Public Library, Astor, Lenox, and Tilden Foundations

civil engineer, under the name of Boyden and Ball. It was later said that Boyden was "for many years . . . the principal designer and architect of the city."[82]

Portraying himself as a natural talent, Boyden notes that by simply reading two books by Asher Benjamin and by using his master's drawing instruments, he soon "could make a better drawing than my master, and this without teaching."[83] After enumerating his many achievements, he observes: "You can see something of what I have accomplished while laboring under the disadvantages of an inadequate school education."[84]

Boyden uses his account of the construction of Mechanics Hall in Worcester (1855–1857) [fig. 15] to show how he succeeded in having his designs carried out. He denounced the few modifications that were made in his plans by "the obstinacy and stupidity of the boss carpenter [who] . . . made the changes without counsulting either the committee or myself," thus defending the supremacy of the architect and righting a wrong that had been done to him with respect to alterations in the structure.[85]

Looking back on his career as an architect, Boyden noted that his early marriage and his "total abstinence resolution from both intoxicating liquors and tobacco, I think have contributed more to my success in life than anything else."[86] Thus, he demonstrated that as a consummate professional who through innate ability and diligence had transformed himself from builder to architect, he was also a virtuous man: in sum, the hero-architect who excelled in deed and virtue.

The Audience

The audience the autobiographers addressed were educated laypeople rather than their professional brethren. James Gallier had his *Autobiography* privately printed in Paris about fourteen years after he gave up his architectural practice,[87] thus suggesting distribution to friends rather than sale to the professional architectural community. Moreover, a substantial portion of Gallier's book discusses his travels, suggesting a possible relationship to the travel literature popular in America at mid-century.[88]

15. Elbridge Boyden,
Mechanics Hall Building
(1855–1857), Worcester

From Franklin P. Rice, ed., *The Worcester of 1898: Fifty Years a City* (Worcester, Mass., 1899). General Research Division, New York Public Library, Astor, Lenox, and Tilden Foundations

Elbridge Boyden's *Reminiscences*, first published in the *Proceedings* of the Worcester Society of Antiquity in 1889, were clearly aimed at a general audience interested in local history. His description of the Mechanics Hall project also suggests a distinction between what he termed his "brother architects" mentioned in the episode and the general readership to whom he addressed his memoirs,[89] namely the reader of the Society of Antiquity's journal.

The male biographers, like the autobiographers, addressed an audience composed primarily of educated laypeople who were generally either friends of the architect's or members of the same local organizations as both the writer and his subject. The anonymous obituary notice of John Haviland was published first in the *Journal of Prison Discipline*, a publication for an audience brought together by a shared so-cial concern. Henry T. Tuckerman, a friend of Greenough's, also addressed a general audience, remarking on the first page of his *Memoir* that Greenough's death "has caused so wide and sincere a grief that it becomes not less a sacred duty than a melancholy pleasure to trace his career, gather up the tributes to his genius, and endeavor to delineate the character of the artist who worked in a "spirit that transcended the limits of a special vocation."[90]

Wheildon's biography of Solomon Willard was published by and for the members of the Bunker Hill Monument Association, who had come together to commission and fund a monument to this important event in the nation's history.[91] Yet Wheildon also envisioned a wider audience, noting that the memoir would "furnish, in the life of an excellent and worthy man, an example of industry, perseverance, and fidelity, which would be profitable to the youth of the country and a bond of faith to the faithful."[92]

Tefft's biographer, Reverend Stone, appeared to address educated laymen, probably Rhode Island residents interested in a favorite native son. Filled with encomia to Tefft's character and discussions of his travels in Europe and his theories of universal currency, Stone's memoir can hardly have been aimed at an audience comprised solely of architects.

Like the male biographers, the women writers also addressed an audience composed primarily of laypeople. In fact, their editors and mentors often articulated their intent that these works should be or were written with a general readership in mind. While Van Rensselaer was preparing her biography of Richardson, Frederick Law Olmsted attempted to allay her fears about her lack of technical knowledge and clarify the nature of her audience, writing that "the best book would be one . . . most educative of the people—That means a book exactly in your accustomed current."[93] Harriet Monroe's editor, Horace Scudder remarked: "Your book . . . is a most sympathetic presentation of a fine subject, and I am disposed to think that you will get both the profession and the laity to read it."[94] Ellen Susan Bulfinch's work was also aimed at the general public, and its publication was perhaps related to the colonial revival then sweeping the country. Charles A. Cummings, then president of the Boston Society of Architects, in "some words by way of introduction to the memoir which is here presented to the public," pointed out what architects might find of value in the book.[95] The greater attention to the domestic realm of the architects' lives that is demonstrated by the women writers may be related to the nature of their audience and to their feminine identities.

Yet the woman writer's relationship to her audience was different. Unlike the male writers, the women biographers functioned as intermediaries between the architect and the broader general public served by the nationally known publishing firm of Houghton Mifflin, which issued the three works written by women that are considered in this paper. In this way, the women capitalized on personal or familial relationships to earn money, to write about architecture, and to address a larger readership, serving not only as advocates of a particular architect, but as champions of the architectural profession to what might be broadly termed a nation of potential clients.

These biographical books and pamphlets, published between 1852 and 1896, were written for a general audience and celebrated a group of nineteenth-century American architects. A consideration of these life-writings reveals the emergence of women as biographers of architects and an apparent shift from primarily organizational relationships to more personal or familial ties shared by authors and their subjects (even if, as might have been the case for Van Rensselaer, the relationship was founded upon the author's interest in the subject's work). Also evident is the shift in intended audience from local readers who shared an affiliation with the architect to a broader national audience.

By righting wrongs and by glorifying the architect's character, the authors not only memorialized individuals but elevated the professional architect and contributed to the public's increasing acceptance of him. At the same time, the biographers' broadened consideration of the architect mirrored the development of the architectural profession in the United States.

NOTES

1. Paul Murray Kendall, *The Art of Biography*, rev. ed., introduction by Stephen Oates (New York, 1985), iv, 4, 29; Leon Edel, *Writing Lives: Principia Biographica* (1984; repr. New York and London, 1987), 23.

2. Sarah H. J. Simpson Hamlin, "Appendix B. Some Articles of Architectural Interest Published in American Periodicals Prior to 1851. An Annotated and Selective Bibliography," in Talbot Hamlin, *Greek Revival Architecture in America* (1944; repr. New York, 1964), 365, 382. Sarah Hamlin cites the reprints in 1821 and in 1832 of an English obituary of Benjamin Henry Latrobe. William Dunlap, *History of the Rise and Progress of the Arts of Design in the United States*, 2 vols. (New York, 1834) includes discussions of Charles L'Enfant, Benjamin Henry Latrobe, Robert Mills, Ithiel Town, William and George Strickland, Maximilien Godefroy, and Alexander Jackson Davis.

3. Isaac Ashmead, *Obituary Notice of John Haviland, Esq.* (Philadelphia, 1852).

4. Henry T. Tuckerman, *A Memorial to Horatio Greenough: Consisting of a Memoir, Selections from His Writings, and Tributes to His Genius* (1853; repr. New York and London, 1968).

5. For the obituary of Parris, see Joseph T. Buckingham, comp. *Annals of the Massachusetts Charitable Mechanic Association* (Boston, 1853), 427.

6. James Gallier, *Autobiography of James Gallier, Architect* (1864; repr., introduction by Samuel Wilson, Jr., New York, 1973); William Wheildon, *Memoir of Solomon Willard, Architect and Superintendent of the Bunker Hill Monument* ([Boston?], 1865); Shearjashub Spooner, *A Biographical History of the Fine Arts; Or, Memoirs of the Lives and Works of Eminent Painters, Engravers, Sculptors, and Architects: From the Earliest Ages to the Present Time*, 2 vols. (New York, 1865); E. M. Stone, *The Architect and Monetarian: A Brief Memoir of Thomas Alexander Tefft Including His Labors to Establish a Universal Currency* (Providence, 1869).

7. Mariana Griswold Van Rensselaer, *Henry Hobson Richardson and His Works* (1888; repr., introduction by William Morgan, New York, 1969); Ellen Susan Bulfinch, ed., *The Life and Letters of Charles Bulfinch, Architect with Other Family Papers . . .* (Boston and New York, 1896); Harriet Monroe, *John Wellborn Root: A Study of His Life and Work* (1896; repr., introduction by Reyner Banham, Park Forest, Ill., 1966).

8. Elbridge Boyden, *Reminiscences of Elbridge Boyden, Architect* (Worcester, Mass., 1890). This work first appeared in the *Proceedings* of the Worcester Society of Antiquity.

9. On such expansion, see Leland Roth, *A Concise History of American Architecture* (1979; repr. New York, 1980), 22.

10. See, for example, Jack Quinan, "Some Aspects of the Development of the Architectural Profession in Boston between 1800–1830," *Old-Time New England* 68 (1977), 32–37.

11. Dell Upton, "Pattern Books and Professionalism: Aspects of the Transformation of Domestic Architecture in America, 1800–1860," *Winterthur Portfolio* 19 (Summer and Autumn 1984), 107–150.

12. Turpin Bannister, ed., *The Architect at Mid-Century: Evolution and Achievement* (New York, 1954), 95–96, 72.

13. A. O. J. Cockshut, *Truth to Life: The Art of Biography in the Nineteenth Century*, 1st American ed. (New York and London, 1974), 16; William Zinsser, introduction to *Extraordinary Lives: The Art and Craft of American Biography*, ed. William Zinsser (New York, 1986), 18.

14. Ashmead 1852, 4, 8.

15. There is debate over who should be credited as the architect of the Bunker Hill Monument, located in Charlestown, Massachusetts. Arguments have been made for Loammi Baldwin, Solomon Willard, Alexander Parris, Robert Mills, and Greenough, whose proposal (submitted in 1825 when he was a Harvard College senior) was a three-dimensional wooden model of an obelisk. For discussion, see Edward Francis Zimmer, "The Architectural Career of Alexander Parris (1780–1852)" (Ph.D. diss., Boston University, 1984), vol. 1, part 1, 522–527. In summing up the evidence, Zimmer notes that "justice awards Willard the credit as architect of the Bunker Hill Monument, with an asterisk."

16. Tuckerman 1853, 20–24, 34, 43–44.

17. *Dictionary of American Biography*, s.v. "Tuckerman, Henry Theodore."

18. "William W. Wheildon," *Annals of the Massachusetts Charitable Mechanic Association, 1795–1892* (Boston, 1892), 644–645; "Wheildon, William Wilder [sic]," *Harper's Encyclopedia of United States History* (New York and London, 1902), 10:335; *Index of Marriages in the Massachusetts Centinel and the Columbian Centinel, 1784–1840*, 8: U–Z.

19. According to the *Annals* 1892, 644, Wheildon joined the Massachusetts Charitable Mechanic Association in 1839 and Willard joined in 1825. *Annals* 1853, 198. Willard was made a member of the Bunker Hill Monument Association in 1824. Wheildon 1865, 62. Wheildon served as a director of the association from 1845, a capacity in which he was still serving when Warren's book was published. (George Washington Warren, *The History of the Bunker Hill Monument Association during the First Century of the United States* [Boston, 1877], 419.)

20. "Necrology [Edwin M. Stone]," *Proceedings of the Rhode Island Historical Society* (1883–1884), 65–68.

21. "Edwin M. Stone," *Providence Journal* (17 December 1883), 4. On Tefft's involvement in school reform, see Leslie DeAngela Dees, "The Architectural Expression of School Reform," in *Thomas Alexander Tefft: American Architecture in Transition, 1845–1860* [exh. cat., Brown University, Providence, R.I., and National Building Museum, Washington, D.C.] (Providence, 1988), 47–60.

22. Edwin M. Stone, *Manual of Education: A Brief History of the Rhode Island Institute of Instruction . . .* (Providence, 1874), 27, 50. At an 1848 meeting of the Association, Henry Barnard praised Tefft, who designed schoolhouses erected in several towns in Rhode Island, for "the taste he has displayed in the designs furnished by him, and for the elevations which he drew for plans furnished or suggested by the Commissioner." On 5 February 1849, Stone delivered addresses before that same association on "The Origin of the Public Schools of Providence" and "The Need of Evening Schools in Providence." "Necrology" 1883-1884, 68; Stone 1869, 58.

23. Henry-Russell Hitchcock, *The Architecture of H. H. Richardson and His Times*, rev. ed. (Cambridge, Mass., and London, 1981), xiii.

24. For a summary of Van Rensselaer's career, see Cynthia D. Kinnard, "Mariana Griswold Van Rensselaer (1851-1934): America's First Professional Woman Art Critic," in *Women as Interpreters of the Visual Arts, 1820-1979*, ed. Claire Richter Sherman, with Adele Holcomb (Westport, Conn., and London, 1981), 181-205.

25. On Van Rensselaer's audience, see Lois Dinnerstein, "Opulence and Ocular Delight, Splendor and Squalor: Critical Writings in Art and Architecture by Mariana Griswold Van Rensselaer" (Ph.D. diss., City University of New York, 1979), 70, 78.

26. Van Rensselaer "knew . . . [Richardson] well and, as was her style, asserts him rather than her own views." Don Creighton Gifford, ed., *The Literature of Architecture: The Evolution of Architectural Theory and Practice in Nineteenth-Century America* (New York, 1966), 439. Cynthia Kinnard states that Van Rensselaer knew Richardson well enough to visit him in Brookline in 1883. Although she is uncertain when the two met, she maintains that it was not until after the architect was well established in Brookline. Kinnard also challenges biographers of Van Rensselaer who have said that she and the architect had a close relationship. "The Life and Works of Mariana Griswold Van Rensselaer, American Art Critic" (Ph.D. diss., Johns Hopkins University, 1977), 135-136.

27. Van Rensselaer 1969 repr., 22.

28. On Monroe, see Morton Dauwen Zaubel, "Monroe, Harriet," *Notable American Women, 1607-1950: A Biographical Dictionary*, ed. Edward T. James, et. al. (Cambridge, Mass., 1971), 2:562-564.

29. Monroe 1966 repr., 48, 26.

30. For a guide to some of Monroe's newspaper articles, see "An Index to the Series of Articles on Art Written by Harriet Monroe as Published during the Years 1909 to 1914 in the Chicago Tribune," in the Manuscript Division, University of Chicago Library.

31. Monroe 1966 repr., n.p.

32. Zaubel 1971, 563.

33. Banham, "Introduction," in Monroe 1966 repr., viii.

34. Oscar Fay Adams, "Bulfinch, Ellen Susan," *A Dictionary of American Authors* (1904; repr. Detroit, 1969), 43; see also: "Miss Ellen S. Bulfinch: Resident of Cambridge for Two Score Years Was the Granddaughter of Charles Bulfinch, the Architect," *Boston Evening Transcript* (18 May 1921), 1:7.

35. Bulfinch 1896, vii.

36. Harold Kirker has noted that "of the substantial body of Bulfinch papers known to have been extant at the end of the nineteenth century, much has since been lost to scholarship other than as it was used by Ellen Susan Bulfinch." *The Architecture of Charles Bulfinch* (Cambridge, Mass., 1969), 389.

37. Monroe 1966 repr., 110.

38. Ashmead 1852, 4.

39. Ashmead 1852, 13, 8.

40. Ashmead 1852, 9, 13.

41. Ashmead 1852, 8, 13.

42. Ashmead 1852, 14; George B. Tatum, "Haviland, John," *Macmillan Encyclopedia of Architects*, Adolf K. Placzek, ed., (New York and London, 1982), 2:332-335.

43. Tuckerman 1853, 18.

44. Wheildon 1865, 20.

45. Wheildon 1865, 21. On Willard, see Jack Quinan, "Willard, Solomon," *Macmillan Encyclopedia of Architects* 4:400-401; Hamlin 1944, 102-103.

46. Wheildon 1865, 5, 20.

47. Wheildon 1865, 105.

48. Quinan 1977, 33.

49. Wheildon 1865, 84.

50. Wheildon 1865, 5.

51. Kathleen A. Curran, "Introduction" and Jenny Anger, "The Rise of the Professional Architect," in *Thomas Alexander Tefft* 1988, 6, 16.

52. Stone 1869, 10-11.

53. Stone 1869, 58.

54. Stone 1869, 42.

55. Stone 1869, 3, 52.

56. Stone 1869, 3.

57. Stone 1869, 4, 12.

58. Van Rensselaer 1969 repr., 132, 138.

59. Van Rensselaer 1969 repr., 37, 23.

60. Van Rensselaer 1969 repr., 37, 95.

61. Van Rensselaer 1969 repr., 134, 37.

62. Van Rensselaer 1969 repr., 112.

63. Van Rensselaer 1969 repr., 73.

64. Frederick Law Olmsted to Mariana Van Rensselaer, 21 December 1887, Olmsted Papers, Manuscripts Division, Library of Congress. For Van Rensselaer's version, see Van Rensselaer 1969 repr., 73.

65. Monroe 1966 repr., 130, 138, 135.

66. Monroe 1966 repr., 119, 114.

67. Monroe 1966 repr., 18.

68. Monroe 1966 repr., 60, 173, 198.

69. Monroe 1966 repr., 60.

70. Monroe 1966 repr., 61.

71. Monroe 1966 repr., 242.

72. Monroe 1966 repr., 248.

73. Monroe 1966 repr., 16, 160.

74. Monroe 1966 repr., 160.

75. Monroe 1966 repr., 159, 49, 159.

76. Bulfinch 1896, 82.

77. Bulfinch 1896, 82.

78. Bulfinch 1896, 104.

79. Bulfinch 1896, 308.

80. On Gallier, see Samuel Wilson, "Gallier, James, Sr.," *Macmillan Encyclopedia of Architects* 2:153-154.

81. Wilson, "Gallier," *Macmillan* 2:153.

82. "Elbridge Boyden," *The Worcester of 1898: Fifty Years a City*, ed. Franklin P. Rice (Worcester, Mass., 1899), 567-569; see also "Elbridge Boyden," *Worcester Daily* (26 March 1898), 124.

83. Boyden 1890, 4.

84. Boyden 1890, 12.

85. Boyden 1890, 11.

86. Boyden 1890, 5.

87. Samuel Wilson, "Introduction," Gallier 1973 repr., [v].

88. Neil Harris, *The Artist in American Society: The Formative Years, 1790-1860* (New York, 1966), 126.

89. Boyden 1890, 10.

90. Tuckerman 1853, [9].

91. Wheildon 1865, 261; Hamlin 1944, 102.

92. Wheildon 1865, 5-6.

93. Frederick Law Olmsted to Mariana Van Rensselaer, 12 June 1886, Olmsted Papers, Manuscripts Division, Library of Congress.

94. Horace Scudder to Harriet Monroe, 1 October [189]5, Pressed Letterbooks, Houghton Mifflin Archives, MsAm2030 (199), leaf 830, Houghton Rare Book Library, Harvard University; quotation used by permission of the Houghton Library.

95. Cummings, "Introduction," in Bulfinch 1896, [1].

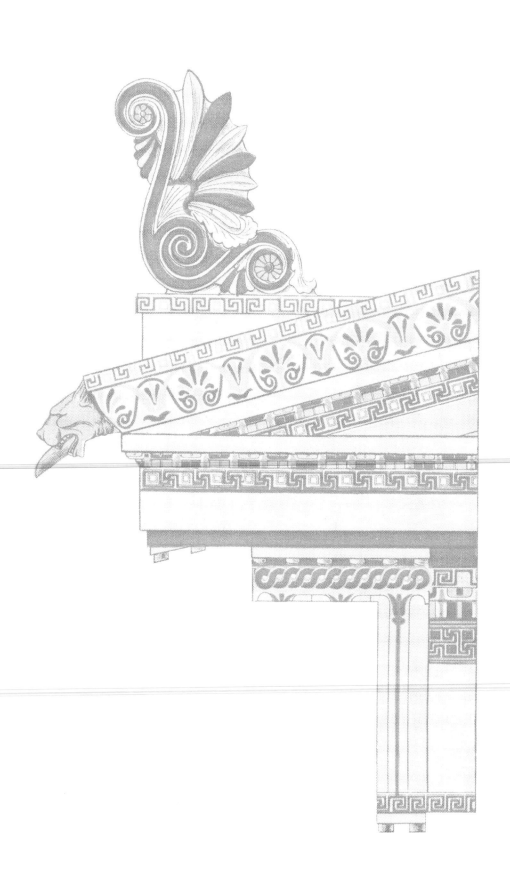

KEITH N. MORGAN
Boston University
RICHARD CHEEK
Belmont, Massachusetts

History in the Service of Design:

American Architect-Historians, 1870–1940

"We exhibit . . . the architecture of the past as a series of problems just as it appeared to the builders of its own day, showing it not as it looks from the outside, to the historian and critic, but as it looked from the inside, to the architect who designed it."[1]

William Robert Ware, 1896

A mature profession of architectural history developed in Europe and America during the decades from the 1870s through the 1930s. Leading the way in America in the late 1870s was a distinct and important new community of architectural historians—the architect-historians. In combination with amateurs, who produced the largest body of writings on architecture during these decades, and academically based architectural historians, who emerged as a small scholarly group at this time, too, the architects who wrote histories became the dominant component of American architectural scholarship for the next half century.[2]

In essence, the writing of architectural history in America was generated by the professional needs of the architect. It was the architect who determined what specific periods and styles of architecture were to be studied. It was the architect who decided which aspects or details of historic buildings were to be recorded, and it was he who did the sketching, measuring, and drawing that established the conventions of representation in the history books. As a consequence, it was the words and images of the architect-historians, not the writings of the amateur or academic historians, that influenced the course of contemporary design and criticism from the 1870s until the outbreak of World War II.

Before turning to a consideration of the basic trends in this scholarship and a discussion of the key practitioners in the architect-historian community, it would be helpful to assess briefly the general scale and evolution of writings on history from their American origins in the 1870s until World War II.[3] Approximately 1,350 books on architectural history were published in the United States from 1870 to 1941.[4] The rate of growth was dramatic. Starting with only 13 works on architectural history published during the 1870s, the number rose to 192 in the first decade of this century, and reached a crescendo in the 1920s when 358 historical treatises appeared, representing an average rate of 36 books a year for that decade. Of the 1,350 total, 256 were American imprints of books by European authors, almost exclusively British, that previously had been released abroad. Thus, the American-written production in architectural history for this period is closer to 1,100 books.

Where did American architect-historians focus their attention? First, they were interested in specific building types, most notably houses and secondarily churches. The focus on domestic architecture reflected the fact that architects were experiencing a greater demand for houses than for any other building type in the late nineteenth and early twentieth centuries. Similarly, the attention paid to the history of church building was in direct response to the large number of prestigious commissions for religious buildings that architects were receiving during this same time span.

Second, architect-historians engaged in studies of the architecture of individual nations, writing most frequently on American architecture during the colonial era. Although books on British buildings were as popular in architect's offices as works on American subjects, these studies were usually written by British authors and were subsequently republished in the United States. But regardless of the source of the literature, the demand for numerous books on prerevolutionary American architecture accompanied by studies of the British roots for colonial buildings reflects the dominant influence of the colonial revival for American architects from the 1880s until World War II.

Third, architect-historians wrote books on European buildings organized by period—antiquity, the Middle Ages, or the Renaissance. Architect-historians were not as prominent in this phase of scholarship as amateurs and academic historians, but several architects did excel in this area, especially Ralph Adams Cram.

Finally, general histories of architecture emphasizing the European and American experience became a staple in the architectural catalogues of American publishing houses from the 1880s onward. Such books were usually written by architect-educators to fulfill the needs of the expanding collegiate architectural establishment as well as to serve a growing general audience.

Within these four categories attention was focused almost exclusively on European and American architecture. The fact that until the 1930s fewer than ten books per decade were devoted to architecture

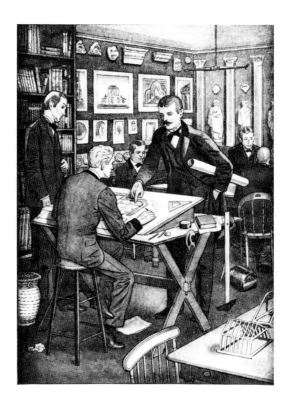

1. William Robert Ware teaching architecture at the Massachusetts Institute of Technology. One in a series of blotters featuring "Boston Firsts" issued as a promotional device by a local bank in the 1940s
Photograph by Richard Cheek

anywhere else in the world only serves to reemphasize that most architectural history was generated by the architect's need for information on design sources for their work.

The emergence of the American architect-historian coincides logically with the establishment of academic training in architecture in the United States. The educational system borrowed from the Ecole des Beaux-Arts, the French national school for training in the arts, dominated American training and produced an intellectual climate that encouraged or required architects to function as historians of their medium.[5] The founding of the first collegiate school of architecture at the Massachusetts Institute of Technology in 1865 brought Paris to Boston and architectural history to the fore.[6] William Robert Ware (fig. 1), founder of the Massachusetts Institute of Technology school of architecture, established the importance of the study of history for architecture students in his 1866 publication, *An Outline of a Course of Architectural Instruction*. In this prospectus for the school, Ware explained: "The thing

PLATE XII.

to be taught is the theory and practice of architectural design; and this is to be learned by studying its history, which everywhere illustrated its principles, and its principles, everywhere illustrated by its history."[7] The Ware program, somewhat awkwardly stated, meant that the MIT curriculum would value design and history equally, seeing the two as interdependent. Professor Ware also prescribed the training for the architect-historian, following the pattern of architectural investigation and publication that had been established by eighteenth-century European archaeologist-dilettantes and had been continued by practicing architects and by the Ecole's Prix de Rome winners in the nineteenth century.

As the key early figure in American architectural education, first at MIT and then at Columbia University after 1881,

Ware must be mentioned as the initial American model for the architect-historian. His *Greek Ornament* (1878) could be considered the first American publication by an architect with historical-archaeological intentions. Ware assembled excerpts from writings "out of the reach of the ordinary student" on Greek architecture and polychromy by Englishmen John Ruskin and Owen Jones and by Henry Van Brunt, William Robert Ware's architectural partner. He included illustrations (fig. 2) showing the recording or adaptation of Greek forms by modern European architects, including Gottfried Semper, G.-A. Blouet, and J.-I. Hittorf.

Within the Boston-Cambridge community, Ware's ideals were quickly reinforced by the publications of other architects and academics during the 1870s. For example, in 1873 architect Robert Swain Peabody published a book of the notebook sketches he made during his period of professional training in Europe, thereby announcing the value of travel, observation, and dissemination. Although his impressionistic, freehand sketches followed the more picturesque British tradition of presenting buildings as opposed to the exacting French method of measuring and drawing historic structures, Peabody shared Ware's concern for the careful study of historical forms and hoped that his book would encourage other architects and students to use their vacation time to make sketching tours.

Five years later, in 1878, the same year that Ware produced *Greek Ornament*, fellow Boston architect Arthur Little published *Early New England Interiors*, a book that established the other important vein of historical scholarship by architects, the investigation of the usable American past. Little's book lacked a text, contained only brief captions, and relied on the picturesque presentation of his vignette images to attract both a professional and a popular audience (fig. 3). Despite the relative crudeness of the sketches, the book included details as well as overall views of significant colonial interiors and was to become the grandfather of a rich and large literature.[8]

The first professor of fine arts in the country, Charles Eliot Norton, was also beginning to publish at this time his first works on architectural history since coming to Harvard in 1873.[9] Although nonarchitect-historians were not to become a significant force until the 1920s, Norton was the first academic to join his architect-historian colleagues in creating the scholarly atmosphere in Boston and Cambridge that would nourish Ware's students from the 1870s onward.

Sensing this climate, publishers began to respond directly to the growing need of the architectural profession for publications on the history of architecture. Boston publisher James R. Osgood was the first publisher to issue a series of books aimed directly at architects, beginning in the early 1870s with translations of European texts, such as E.-E. Viollet-le-Duc's *The Habitation of Man in All Ages . . .* (Boston, 1872) and *Discourses on Architecture . . .* (Boston, 1875). Osgood soon added sketchbooks and surveys of European architecture by American architects to his list, including Robert Swain Peabody's *Note-Book Sketches* (Boston, 1873) and J. Pickering Putnam's *The Open Fireplace in All Ages . . .* (Boston, 1881). His success in serving the professional and educational interests of architects soon led William Robert Ware and other Boston-area architects to urge Osgood to start a new architectural journal, using the heliotype process which he had imported from England for reproducing photographs and architectural drawings. Osgood obliged them by launching the *American Architect and Building News* in 1876, but his involvement in architectural publishing rapidly diminished in the early 1880s as bad business practices forced him to relinquish control of his publishing house.

As Osgood departed, new architectural publishers quickly moved in. George H. Polley began his publishing career in Boston by issuing two titles in 1887, Lockwood De Forest, *Indian Architecture and Ornament . . .* and Frank E. Wallis, *Old Colonial Architecture and Furniture . . .*, while William Helburn entered the field in New York in 1890 with two remarkably similar portfolios, Arne Delhi, *Selections of Byzantine Ornament . . .* and William Davenport Goforth, *Old Colonial Architectural*

3. Newel of staircase, Cabot House, Salem
From Arthur Little, *Early New England Interiors* (Boston, 1878), n. p.
Photograph by Richard Cheek

Details in and around Philadelphia. . . . Polley's and Helburn's production up until World War I was to consist chiefly of period surveys of European, Asian, and American architecture, illustrated with photographs and/or measured drawings accompanied by an introduction and little or no text. At first, most of their books on architecture abroad were assembled by foreign authors, but by 1900 American architects were doing most of the compiling. After the war Helburn devoted most of his attention to producing monographs on contemporary American architects, although he did continue to import and publish a large number of works on English architecture and period details, whereas Polley's postwar production of new books diminished rapidly in the face of increased competition from other publishers.

Most of the new rivals were located in New York, helping that city to replace Boston as the national center for architectural publishing by the end of World War I. Foremost among these new houses was the Architectural Book Publishing Company, destined to become the largest publisher of books on architecture written or compiled by American authors during the period between the two world wars. General commercial publishers, such as Charles Scribner's Sons, the Macmillan Company, E. P. Dutton Company, and G. P. Putnam's Sons, also contributed to New York's dominance in the field by greatly expanding their architectural lists after the turn of the century. In fact, Scribner's became the most prolific publisher of architectural books in the country from 1895 through 1941, although the majority of its architectural titles were of European rather than American origin.

With the leading architectural schools and the major architectural publishers located in Boston and New York, it is not surprising that two-thirds of all architect-historians practiced in one of the two cities and sometimes both. There were approximately 160 writers on architecture in America from 1870 to 1940 who were trained as architects, practiced that profession, and wrote nearly 330 books. Of these writers, most were academically trained, the largest group from the Massachusetts Institute of Technology, the next largest from the Ecole des Beaux-Arts, and the third largest group from Columbia University. Most of the architect-historians who studied at the Ecole returned to the United States to join their American-trained colleagues in either Boston or New York.

Within the Boston-New York environment, an important small contingent of architect-historians were the former recipients of the Rotch Travelling Scholarships and the McKim Travelling Fellowships. Administered by the Boston Society of Architects, the Rotch Scholarship had been established in 1883 by Boston architect Arthur Rotch and his family to allow architecture students to benefit from a period of European travel. The McKim Fellowship had been created in 1898 by architect Charles F. McKim at the Columbia University School of Architecture to serve the same purpose. Modeled on the Prix de Rome grants, which French students at the Ecole des Beaux-Arts won through competition, these fellowships allowed American students a period of independent travel and study in Europe. Like their French counterparts, the recipients of these grants were required to send home historical studies of the sites they investigated (fig. 4). Not surprisingly, this form of archaeological-architectural investigation and reporting primed these students to become future architectural historians. Rotch fellows who became architect-historians included Boston architects Clarence Blackall (the eventual historian of the fellowship program), Walter Kilham, and Louis Chappell Newhall, as well as New Yorker H. Van Buren Magonigle.[10] The local architectural clubs and societies, as well as the schools of architecture, disseminated the information sent home by these travelers through exhibitions and publications.[11]

Beyond the educational institutions and the professional organizations, the architectural history book played a central role in the daily design life of most architectural offices. In fact, the library often became the physical and symbolic core of the architectural office (fig. 5), a space useful for meetings with clients and for the continuation of the educational mission of the principal architects as they encouraged their younger colleagues to study historical models. Of course these office libraries were full of the folio volumes of European architecture, written, published, and often purchased abroad.[12] But more and more books by American architect-historians took their place on the shelves as the century progressed. Just as no office would be well equipped without the appropriate drafting tables and conference room, few architects could function without a copy of P.-M. Letarouilly's *Edifices de Rome moderne . . .* or a subscription to the White Pine Series of monographs on colonial American architecture.[13]

The histories written by American architects that were acquired for office libraries along with comparable European literature were produced by three interrelated groups of architect-historians: those who taught history and design at schools of architecture, those who practiced, and those who did both. Having audiences for their ideas inside and outside of the class-

4. Plan, section, and elevation of the Pazzi Chapel, Florence, measured and drawn by H. Van Buren Magonigle, 1894
From *Envois of the Rotch Travelling Scholarship 1891–1900 . . .* , ed. Charles Blackall, (Boston, 1902), pl. 22. Photograph by Richard Cheek

room, the teacher-historians exerted a stronger influence and thus should be approached first. As mentioned earlier, William Robert Ware had established himself as the country's first teacher-historian at MIT in the 1870s. After transferring to Columbia in 1881, Ware became an even more influential spokesman on all aspects of architecture, including history, as documented by his 1896 report entitled *The Study of Architectural History at Columbia College.*[14] This essay described an integrated, four-year program of lectures in architectural history, exercises in historical research, and projects in historical design. His most important publication was *The American Vignola* (1901), which attempted to refine and adapt the canon of classical architecture for the needs of modern American design.[15] More a codifier than an initiator, Ware used his publications to reinforce the teaching of architecture in the Beaux-Arts manner and to remind the profession of the importance of understanding appropriate precedents for modern work.

Following Ware at Columbia, but becoming more important as historians, were the two generations of the Hamlin family (fig. 6) who directed the progress of architectural scholarship at that institution through 1946.[16] A.D.F. Hamlin's influence was initially exerted through his 1896 *A Textbook of the History of Architecture* and through his 1916 *A History of Ornament*, which project a consistent emphasis on the history of style and on ornament as the carrier of style. Hamlin's theory of the "selective ideal" stressed the importance of studying the finest styles and periods of history in order to understand fully the principles of their design and their appropriateness as models for contemporary buildings. It grew directly from the pedagogy of Ware and underlay much of the best American work of the 1890s and the

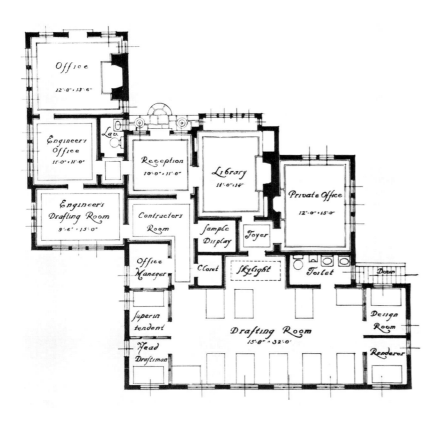

5. Plan of the architectural office of Dwight James Baum
From *The Work of Dwight James Baum, Architect* (New York, 1927), pl. 143. Photograph by Richard Cheek

studies, which were followed by A.D.F. Hamlin's general histories of Western architecture based on a more analytical and selective approach. These in turn were succeeded by Talbot Hamlin's celebration of the American past, completing the transition from European-oriented studies to histories devoted to architecture within the United States.

Indicative of the role of history in the curricula of other major architectural schools was the *Outline of the History of Architecture*, published in 1922 by Rexford Newcomb for his students at the University of Illinois. Revised and enlarged by Newcomb, it was republished in four separate parts (1931–1939) by John Wiley and Sons and distributed in England as well as the United States. Another reflection of the widespread regard for architectural history on the nation's campuses was the joint publication in 1918 of *A History of Architecture* by Sidney Fiske Kimball, formerly professor of architecture at the University of Virginia, and George H. Edgell, professor of architecture at Harvard University. This book suggests a consensus among architect-historians from disparate institutions on the centrality of history to the study of architectural design and a common voice in its writing.

Perhaps the most prolific of all the architect-historians was Ralph Adams Cram, whose wide-ranging accomplishments included his appointment as a senior professor in the school of architecture at MIT. While maintaining an active practice as a designer of churches and public buildings predominantly in a Gothic revival mode, Cram pursued a second important career as a historian of architecture, especially of the Middle Ages, and as a commentator on religion, sociology, philosophy, and architecture.[19] Although Cram was an unusually productive author (fig. 7), he was typical of most architect-historians in the practical intent of his writings. He was attracted to his projects because of a belief in the validity of those interests as models for contemporary design, philosophically and archaeologically. Thus Cram provides a useful link to the architects who wrote history outside of the academy, those for whom the needs of their design activities

first two decades of the twentieth century (fig. 8).[17]

His architect-son, Talbot Hamlin, in his role first as professor of architecture and after 1934 as the Avery Librarian, maintained his father's interest in the Western tradition while studying and celebrating the history of American architecture more specifically. Writing for a broader popular audience, Talbot Hamlin helped to mold a history of architecture with a full and legitimate role for American buildings through the publication of *The Enjoyment of Architecture* (1916), *The Trend of American Architecture* (1921), *The American Spirit in Architecture* (1926), and later books on early nineteenth-century American architecture.[18]

The evolution of the focus of architectural history at Columbia broadly represents the progression that architect-historians followed nationally in their scholarship from the 1880s until World War II. It began with Ware's reinterpretation of European archaeological and historical

6. Some of the publications produced by A.D.F. Hamlin and Talbot Faulkner Hamlin while teaching at Columbia
Photograph by Richard Cheek

8. Frontispiece and title page, J. Frederick Kelly, *The Henry Whitfield House, 1639. The Journal of the Restoration of the Old Stone House, Guilford . . .* (Guilford, Conn., 1939)
Photograph by Richard Cheek

directly informed the nature and purpose of their scholarship.

The dominant focus for the practicing architects who wrote history was the architecture of colonial America. Starting in the late 1870s, this literature constantly grew in scale and sophistication. In fact, during the 1920s, as many books were published on American architectural history as had been issued on all topics in architectural history during the first decade of this century.

To understand the evolution in scholarship on colonial architecture from the nineteenth into the twentieth century, we can briefly compare James Corner and Eric Soderholtz's important *Examples of Domestic Colonial Architecture*, published in Boston by the Boston Architectural Club in two volumes, on New England (1891) and on Virginia and Maryland (1892), with the colonial architectural histories that emerged after 1895. *Examples of Domestic Colonial Architecture*, like most of the colonial architecture studies published by ar-

chitects in the 1870s and 1880s, consists solely of illustrations (photographs in this case) of full views and details of colonial architecture. Corner and Soderholtz stated that their "primary object . . . was not to accumulate historical data, but rather to present in a form convenient for use and

reference by architects . . . some examples of the better class of domestic edifice."[20]

Indicative of the new scholarly thrust was the publication beginning in 1898 of *The Georgian Period* in twelve parts under the editorship of William Rotch Ware, nephew of William Robert Ware and editor of the *American Architect and Building News*. In his preface to the collection of essays, Ware describes the purpose and pedigree of this important work:

The desirability of making, before it should be too late, some adequate record of the architectural remains of Colonial work seemed too obvious and insistent to be longer disregarded. It remained only to determine the form and character of publication likely to prove of most value. Recalling at this point the fact that the many volumes of the AMERICAN ARCHITECT contained a large number of measured drawings and fugitive papers dealing with the selected period, it appeared evident that they might easily be made to serve as nucleus about which to gather, as they might come to hand, other illustrations and papers of various kinds.[21]

The combination of visual documentation (sketches, photographs, and particularly measured drawings) and historical narratives, although more descriptive than analytical, separated this publication from earlier studies of colonial architecture and established a more substantial base for future scholarship in this field. The desire to make a record of disappearing buildings may have been the catalyst for the series, but the increasing demand for measured drawings of plans, framing structures, and molding details of colonial work kept it rolling. Some ninety-eight architects and draftsmen contributed to the series, further swelling the ranks of professionals who are known to have been actively involved in writing or illustrating architectural histories (only four of the ninety-eight individuals cited in *The Georgian Period* are among the one hundred sixty architects who published books on architectural history independently).

Instrumental in refining colonial American architectural scholarship at this time was the Providence-based architect Nor-

9. Typical issues of the *White Pine Series of Architectural Monographs* from 1915 through 1931
Photograph by Richard Cheek

man Isham, who began his career as an architectural historian with his *Early Rhode Island Houses* in 1895, followed by *Early Connecticut Houses* in 1900, both written in collaboration with Albert F. Brown.[22] He explained the early architecture of Rhode Island and Connecticut through elaborately detailed measured drawings, but he was the first architect-historian to provide a social and economic context for the buildings he discussed. Following in Isham's path was the New Haven architect John Frederick Kelly, who published *The Early Domestic Architecture of Connecticut* in 1924 and his *Architectural Guide for Connecticut* in 1935. Concomitant with their scholarship, both Isham and Kelly were responsible for major colonial restorations in their states (fig. 8) and designed a wide range of buildings inspired by the architecture that they studied.

One of the most significant vehicles for architects functioning as historians was the series of architectural monographs sponsored from 1915 to 1924 by the White Pine Bureau, a lumber trade association, and then published privately by its architect-editor Russell F. Whitehead from 1925 until its absorption by *Pencil Points* magazine in 1932.[23] Under Whitehead's editorship, the White Pine Series (fig. 9) produced up to six monographs a year through 1940, each of which focused on a particular region, town, or building. Assessing the series' accomplishments after its first decade, Whitehead proudly observed: "We believe that *The White Pine Series* is in a small way unique, for in spite of the flood of publications of old Colonial work, nothing, not even the magnificent 'Georgian Period' has published the wealth of material we have in the past and as we aspire to do in the future."[24]

At least forty-six architects were among the eighty-eight authors who wrote for the series, which was illustrated with specially commissioned photographs throughout its run and with measured drawings from 1920 on. Among the more prominent contributors were Joseph Everett Chandler, Frank Chouteau Brown, Aymar Embury, Frank Wallis, Joy Wheeler Dow, Norman Isham, J. Frederick Kelly, and Lois Lilley

10. Representative examples of histories and guidebooks for California and Southwest missions, published from the 1890s through the 1930s
Photograph by Richard Cheek

Howe, all of whom specialized in colonial restorations or in colonial revival domestic work.[25]

During its first decade, the series was devoted exclusively to domestic architecture of wood construction, principally in New England. When the White Pine Bureau withdrew its sponsorship of the series in 1925, however, Whitehead was able to expand its scope to include "all old buildings"—public and religious buildings as well as houses—regardless of their construction material. By abandoning the exclusive white pine orientation, he was also able to extend the geographic coverage to the South and the West. Although the White Pine Series had been regional from the start, its gradual recognition of significant colonial architecture in areas of the country other than New England was symptomatic of a growing preference for regional studies and styles by historians and designers alike during the 1920s.[26]

Of all his contemporaries, Rexford Newcomb is the best example of an architect-historian who became proficient in writing about regional styles in all parts of the country as well as abroad. His first book, *Franciscan Missions of Alta California* (1916), focused scholarly attention on a subject that had been popular with travel and religious writers since the 1890s. This book was one of the first in a flood of histories and guides (fig. 10) to the missions of California and the Southwest that was precipitated by the international expositions at San Diego and San Francisco in 1915 and that would also include another work by Newcomb, *The Old Mission Churches and Historic Houses of California . . .* (1925).

As he continued to study the region, Newcomb became convinced that the Spanish colonial style in its many local variations was still the most adaptable and expressive mode of architecture for the Southwest and Florida. To promote the continued revival of the Spanish colonial and the related Mediterranean styles, he wrote three books that explored the history of the styles and their adaptation for new buildings.[27] In one of these books, he stated his belief in the national efficacy of regionalism: "What California has done, what Florida, Texas, Arizona and New Mexico are doing, a well informed and artistically inclined profession may do for other areas of the country."[28] As if to carry out his own dictum, Newcomb moved his studies eastward, publishing *The Colonial and Federal House* in 1933 as part of Lippincott's Home-Maker Series and *Old Kentucky Architecture* in 1940. With the exception of his *Outlines of the History of Architecture*, mentioned previously, all of Newcomb's publications seem to have had a regional revival thrust, including the series of pamphlets on the historical uses of ceramic tiles entitled *Architectural Mono-*

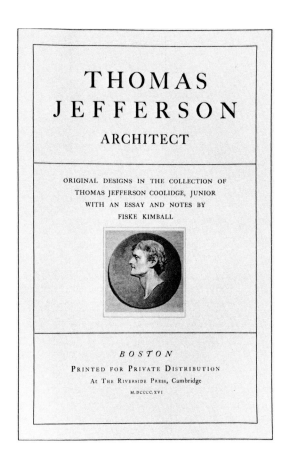

THOMAS
JEFFERSON

ARCHITECT

ORIGINAL DESIGNS IN THE COLLECTION OF
THOMAS JEFFERSON COOLIDGE, JUNIOR
WITH AN ESSAY AND NOTES BY
FISKE KIMBALL

BOSTON

PRINTED FOR PRIVATE DISTRIBUTION
AT THE RIVERSIDE PRESS, CAMBRIDGE
M.DCCCC.XVI

11. Title page, Fiske Kimball, *Thomas Jefferson, Architect* . . . (Boston, 1916) Courtesy of the Massachusetts Historical Society. Photograph by Richard Cheek

12. Table of contents, *The Significance of the Fine Arts* (Boston, 1923), vii Photograph by Richard Cheek

graphs on Tiles and Tilework, which he wrote for the Associated Tile Manufacturers between 1924 and 1929.

Without question, the most notable publication on American colonial architecture, one that remains a valuable resource for continuing scholarship, is Fiske Kimball's *Domestic Architecture of the American Colonies and the Early Republic*, published in 1922. As an architect who specialized in colonial restorations and as one of the earliest Americans to submit a doctoral dissertation in architectural history, Kimball presented the first comprehensive and analytical history of colonial buildings, even if it was limited to domestic architecture.[29] This book was groundbreaking in its synthesis of both structural and documentary information on approximately two hundred carefully selected buildings and for its segregation of vernacular and academic strains in American colonial architecture. Kimball bracketed this book with his two biographical mono-

graphs (fig. 11) on colonial and federal designers, *Thomas Jefferson, Architect* (1916) and *Mr. Samuel McIntire, Carver, The Architect of Salem* (1940).

Later nineteenth-century architecture was almost totally overlooked by architect-historians until after World War II. From the mid-1880s onward, American architectural criticism had relegated most of the buildings of the last half of the nineteenth century to outer darkness. The architect-historians essentially drew the line for their interests at the end of the classically influenced traditions of the early nineteenth century.

Not only individual architects, but the profession of architecture at large, through organizations such as the American Institute of Architects, attempted to spread the gospel of history, both to educate clients and to elevate American cultural awareness. The most conspicuous example of these efforts was the publication in 1923 of *The Significance of the Fine Arts* (fig. 12), an anthology of essays on the history of architecture and the other arts, sponsored by the education committee of the AIA and the committee on architecture and art of the Association of American Colleges. In introducing articles on the history of architecture by C. Howard Walker, Ralph Adams Cram, H. Van Buren Magonigle, and Paul P. Cret, committee chairman George C. Nimmons commented:

History reveals the fact that those nations in the past which were leaders in commerce and the industries were also the leaders afterwards in the fine arts, and it is significant that many of the people of America are descendants of those who excelled in the arts of Europe. . . . With all this in mind, the architects of the country as represented by the American Institute of Architects . . . have undertaken to arouse popular interest in the subject, and to make art instruction an integral part of all education.[30]

No clearer indication of the central position of architectural history for the work of contemporary architects need be found, but by the time that publication appeared, the history-rejecting forces of international modernism were beginning to spread across the Atlantic.

From Ware forward, American architect-historians joined in a common belief that a history of architecture recording the linear chronology of styles should be the base for contemporary design. Although their research focused increasingly on American subjects and their methods of analysis became more detailed and sophisticated, their intention remained the same: the artistic achievements of builders and architects from the past were to be documented and sympathetically interpreted in order that they might serve as the foundation for future creativity in the art of architecture. While contemporary criticism in the 1930s would eventually challenge both the validity of the history-focused form of architectural education borrowed from the Ecole and the legitimizing of contemporary buildings through allusion to historical precedent, the writing of architectural history by architects reinforced the pedagogy and the design philosophy of the American architectural establishment throughout the six decades from 1880 to 1940. For this crucial period in the emergence of architectural history in America, it is impossible and inappropriate to separate the building and the book. And the important thing to remember is that the architect wrote the book.

NOTES

1. William Robert Ware, *The Study of Architectural History at Columbia College* (New York, 1897), 61. This report was written for the Committee on Education of the American Institute of Architects and was originally published in the *School of Mines Quarterly* 17 (1896), 56–67.

2. It is important to remember that we are discussing only the work of architects who wrote histories. A great many other architects wrote criticism of contemporary design, but they did not contribute to documentation and analysis of historic buildings.

3. Our observations are based on Henry-Russell Hitchcock's *American Architectural Books . . .* (1938–1939; repr. New York, 1976) and on a bibliography of American architectural books published from 1895 to 1941 that we have been compiling with the aid of a grant from the National Endowment for the Humanities.

4. The number is approximate because we are still attempting to verify that certain authors were trained as architects. We wish to thank Lora McDonald for assistance with biographical information on architect-historians in this essay.

5. Richard Chafee provides an excellent description of the educational system of the Ecole des Beaux-Arts. See "The Teaching of Architecture at the Ecole des Beaux-Arts," in *The Architecture of the Ecole des Beaux-Arts*, ed. Arthur Drexler (New York and Cambridge, Mass., 1977), 61–110.

6. For a thorough analysis of William Robert Ware and the formation of the school of architecture at the Massachusetts Institute of Technology, see John Andrew Chewning, "William Robert Ware and the Beginnings of Architectural Education in the United States, 1861–1881," Ph.D. diss., Massachusetts Institute of Technology, 1985, and "William Robert Ware at MIT and Columbia University," *Journal of Architectural Education* 33 (November 1979), 25–29.

7. William Robert Ware, *An Outline of a Course of Architectural Instruction* (Boston, 1866), 19. Ware was hired in 1865 to establish a school of architecture at MIT and went to Europe in 1866–1867 to observe academic training practices in architecture, especially in England and France. The school of architecture opened in 1868, and Ware remained its director until he was hired to establish a school of architecture at Columbia University in 1881. Chewning 1979 and 1985. In a history of MIT, its program was described: "At MIT, the education in architecture differed from the Ecole chiefly in a planned curriculum with scheduled classes, including courses in construction, and in Ware's insistence on the need for a broad and general background not only in the history of architecture but of the entire realm of the fine arts." Caroline Shillaber, *Massachusetts Institute of Technology School of Architecture and Planning, 1861–1961: A Hundred Year Chronicle* (Cambridge, Mass., 1963), 8.

8. Architect William E. Barry's *Pen Sketches of Old Houses* had appeared in Boston in 1874, four years before *Early New England Interiors*, but because it was published privately in a small edition, its influence was limited to Barry's friends and professional acquaintances.

9. See Michael Brooks, "New England Gothic: Charles Eliot Norton, Charles H. Moore, and Henry Adams," in this volume. Following Harvard's example, other universities began to hire professors of fine arts, but the concept of training doctoral candidates for careers in scholarship and teaching did not emerge until the end of the century. Only in the mid-1920s did a significant number of doctoral candidates appear in the history of architecture. Refer to the list of American doctoral dissertations in architectural history compiled by Peter Kaufman and Paula Gabbard, published as an appendix to this volume.

10. For information on the Rotch Scholarship, see Clarence H. Blackall, *A History of the Rotch Travelling Scholarship, 1883 to 1938* (Boston, 1938) and Shillaber 1963, 23. For a discussion of the McKim Fellowship, consult Steven M. Bedford and Susan M. Strauss, "History II: 1881–1912," in *The Making of An Architect, 1881–1981: Columbia University in the City of New York*, ed. Richard Oliver (New York, 1981), 34.

11. Typical examples would be Boston Society of Architects, *Envois of the Rotch Travelling Scholarship 1891–1900 . . .* (Boston, 1902); Boston Architectural Club, *Boston Architectural Club Year Book, Containing Reproductions from the Various Exhibitions Held in the Club Building during the Year 1911* (Boston, 1911), and The Architecture Society, *Annual of the School of Architecture, Columbia University* (New York, 1918).

12. Representative examples of these collections can be seen in the Memorial Library of the Boston Architectural Club, housed at the Boston Architectural Center, or the office library of Charles A. Platt, now held by the Century Association in New York City. Some professional libraries of this period are still in use, such as the one in the offices of Shepley, Bulfinch, Richardson, and Abbott in Boston.

13. Pierre Marie Letarouilly, *Edifices de Rome moderne . . .* (Paris, 1818). See note 24 for a discussion of the publication record of the White Pine monographs.

14. For a discussion of the teaching of architectural history at Columbia under the influence of William Robert Ware, see Oliver 1981, especially chapter 2, David G. De Long, "William Robert Ware and the Pursuit of Suitability, 1881–1903."

15. William Robert Ware, *The American Vignola; Part I, the Five Orders* (New York, 1901); later editions by various publishers in 1902, 1904, 1905, and 1925. *The American Vignola; Part II, Arches and Vaults, Roofs and Domes, Doors and Windows, Walls and Ceilings, Steps and Staircases* was issued in 1906, revised in 1913, and republished in 1925. The numerous editions of both parts testify to the popularity and three-decade influence of the work.

16. The writings and influence of both generations of Hamlins have been analyzed in Peter Kaufman, "American Architectural Writing, Beaux Arts Style: The Lives and Works of Alfred Dwight Foster Hamlin and Talbot Faulkner Hamlin," Ph.D. diss., Cornell University, 1986.

17. An excellent discussion of A.D.F. Hamlin's philosophy and influence can also be found in Richard Longstreth, *On the Edge of the World: Four Architects in San Francisco at the Turn of the Century* (Cambridge, Mass., 1983), chapter 1.

18. Kaufman 1986, chapter 7; and Kenneth Frampton, "Slouching toward Modernity: Talbot Faulkner Hamlin and the Architecture of the New Deal," in Oliver 1981, 149–166. Talbot Hamlin continued writing until mid-century, publishing his more encyclopedic *Architecture through the Ages* (New York, 1940), his important study, *Greek Revival Architecture in America* (New York, 1944), and his biography, *Benjamin Henry Latrobe* (New York, 1955).

19. For further information on Cram's career and publications see Peter Fergusson, "The Middle Ages: Ralph Adams Cram and Kenneth Conant," in this volume.

20. James M. Corner and Eric E. Soderholtz, *Examples of Domestic Colonial Architecture in New England* (Boston, 1891), foreword.

21. *The Georgian Period, Being Photographs and Measured Drawings of Colonial Work with Text* (New York, 1923), iii. The book was originally issued in twelve parts from 1898 to 1902, then gathered into a three-volume set that was issued in 1902 and again in 1908. A reduced students' edition containing only 100 of the original 451 plates was published in 1904 and again in 1922. A revised edition of the full set appeared in 1923.

22. Norman Isham published two later books, *Early American Houses* (1928) and *A Glossary of Colonial Architectural Terms* (1939). He frequently worked as a restoration architect; for example, he served as the consultant for the colonial rooms of the American Wing at the Metropolitan Museum of Art, New York. Refer also to Dell Upton, "Outside the Academy: A Century of Vernacular Architecture Studies, 1890–1990," in this volume.

23. The White Pine Bureau initiated the series in order to make architects aware of the continued availability of white pine and its historical usages as a building material. The bureau was but one of many trade associations and building product manufacturers in the early twentieth century that sup-
ported architectural history publications that suggested the importance of their material in the past and its usefulness for the present. Although many books and pamphlets were published on the history of particular building materials or equipment, the historical trade journal was the preferred vehicle for promoting a product for its past associations and architectural heritage. In addition to the *White Pine Series* and the *Architectural Monographs on Tiles and Tilework* mentioned in the text, other prominent journals included *The Tuileries Brochures*, published by the Ludowici-Celadon Company to highlight the use of roofing tiles during past periods of architecture, and *Atlantic Terra Cotta*, a monthly pamphlet published by the Atlantic Terra Cotta Company on historic buildings that featured terra cotta.

24. Russell F. Whitehead, "A Review and A Forecast," *White Pine Series Monographs on American Colonial Architecture* 10, no. 6 (1924), 4.

25. Only two American women architects published architectural histories in this period. Lois Lilley Howe, who worked in Cambridge, published *Details from Old New England Houses, Measured and Drawn* with Constance Fuller (New York, 1913) and wrote a White Pine Series monograph, *An Architectural Monograph: The Col. Robert Means House at Amherst, New Hampshire* (New York, 1927). Eleanor Raymond, also of Boston, published *Early Domestic Architecture of Pennsylvania, Photographs and Measured Drawings* (New York, 1931).

26. Mark A. Hewitt, *American Country Houses of the Eclectic Era. Architects, Patrons and Domestic Ideals, 1890–1940* (New Haven, forthcoming) contains an excellent discussion of the issue of regionalism for domestic architecture in chapter VII.

27. Rexford Newcomb, *The Spanish House for America; Its Design, Furnishing and Gardens* (Philadelphia and London, 1927); *Mediterranean Domestic Architecture in the United States* (Cleveland, 1928); *Spanish-Colonial Architecture in the United States* (New York, 1937).

28. Newcomb 1928, first page of unpaginated text.

29. For Kimball, see Lauren Weiss Bricker, "The Writings of Fiske Kimball: A Synthesis of Architectural History and Practice," in this volume. Kimball's *Domestic Architecture* served as the foundation for Hugh Morrison's more expansive *Early American Architecture*, published in 1951.

30. *The Significance of the Fine Arts* (Boston, 1923), xxviii.

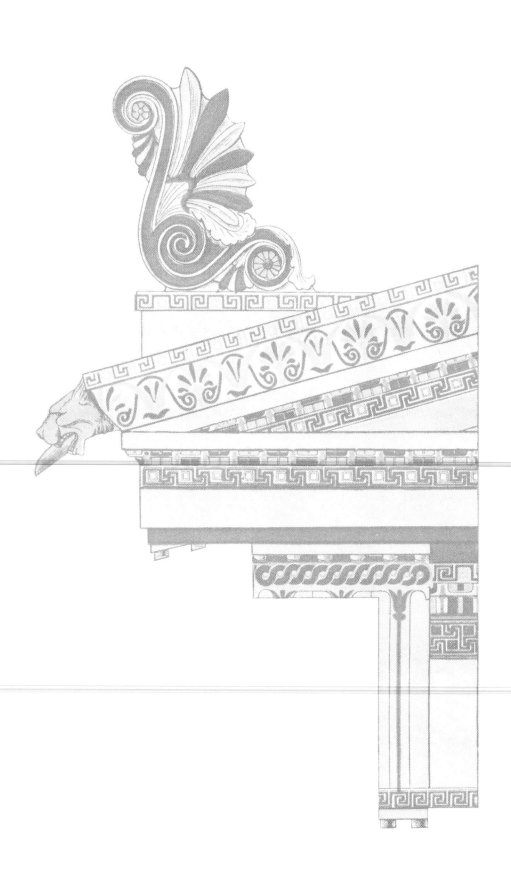

MARY N. WOODS
Cornell University

History in the Early American Architectural Journals

Henry Van Brunt, an eminent critic and practicing architect in late nineteenth-century America, was acutely conscious of the relationship between architectural history and contemporary design. He saw the dynamic between architecture's past and present as the central issue confronting his generation of architects. Travel, professional education, publications, and photography, Van Brunt believed, gave the late nineteenth-century architect in this country an unprecedented knowledge of architectural history. "All the past is ours," Van Brunt wrote. "The question is not whether we shall use [it] but how we shall choose . . . and to what extent shall such choice be allowed to influence our modern practice."[1]

Van Brunt approached architectural history from the perspective of a practitioner, not a scholar. Although he did advocate the comprehensive study of architectural history in professional schools, he also believed that too slavish a devotion to precedent crippled the contemporary designer.[2] The architect's "greatest privilege and greatest danger," Van Brunt wrote, were the study of architectural history.[3]

The editors of the first architectural journals published in the United States seemed to share Van Brunt's attitudes toward architectural history. An examination of the articles and illustrations published in the early periodicals reveals, I will argue, that the editors felt far more comfortable when history served only a limited function as handmaiden to design. Furthermore, it seems that some editors found architects and architectural critics better qualified than scholars to write on history for a professional audience.

This paper will examine the treatment of history in five early architectural journals during the late nineteenth and early twentieth centuries: *Architects' and Mechanics' Journal* (New York, 1859–1861); *Architectural Review and American Builder's Journal* (Philadelphia, 1868–1870); *American Architect and Builder's Monthly* (Philadelphia, 1870–1871); *American Architect and Building News* (Boston and New York, 1876–1938); and *Architectural Record* (New York, 1891–). Apart from their primacy, the first four journals are important in a consideration of the coverage accorded history in the American architectural press because they were models in both form and content for the regional periodicals that proliferated in the 1880s and 1890s.[4] *Architectural Record* is included because as a journal of commentary and criticism it was a conscious departure from the periodicals that preceded it.

Architects' and Mechanics' Journal

Alexander Harthill, a New York publisher of travel books, brought out the first issue of the *Architects' and Mechanics' Journal (AMJ)* in the fall of 1859.[5] He took as his model the mechanics' magazines of the early nineteenth century in the United States and Great Britain. The dissemination of "useful knowledge" to all workingmen was the common cause of the periodicals and institutions associated with the mechanics' movement.[6]

The "useful knowledge" that Harthill regularly published in the *AMJ* consisted of contract announcements and construction news from major American cities. Lists and descriptions of inventions patented by the federal government as well as essays on such technical subjects as stone and iron construction, steam engines, and electric lighting also appeared. A full-page wood engraving was reproduced each week and illustrated rather generic details of decoration and construction. These plates, the editors wrote, were intended as a "perfect encyclopedia of practical workmanship connected with building."[7]

Yet the *AMJ* was not simply a magazine for building mechanics; it was also the first periodical for professional architects to be published in this country. Although Harthill never identified his editors, he wrote that they were members of the "architectural and engineering profession."[8] It is evident from the editorials that the *AMJ* was edited by architects trying to distinguish themselves from builders and mechanics. The editors wrote extensively on such aspects of professionalization as the architect's unique qualifications for design and supervision of construction, his control of architectural drawings, professional education, the justice of the percentage fee, and reform of competition procedures.

These editorials on the profession were similar to the concerns voiced by members of the American Institute of Architects (AIA). Founded by Richard Upjohn in 1857, the institute was the first successful professional society for architects in the United States.[9] Given the common agenda of the *AMJ* and AIA, it is not surprising that institute members voted to give Harthill their meeting minutes for publication beginning in January 1860.[10] Some AIA members further supported the *AMJ* by contributing drawings of their work for

publication. Although the editors failed to make the *AMJ* a pictorial review of current American architecture, they did publish a few works by such AIA members as James Renwick (fig. 1), Calvert Vaux, and F. C. Withers.[11] In view of these connections between the *AMJ* and the institute, it is conceivable that Harthill recruited some of his editorial staff from the membership rolls of the AIA.[12]

What was the attitude of the *AMJ* editors toward architectural history? No article that they ever published dealt with past styles as its principal subject. The oldest building that the editors illustrated was Ammi B. Young's Boston Customs House of 1837. The discussion of architectural history in the *AMJ* only arose when the editors discussed the future direction of American architecture and whether precedent should play a role.

Harthill's emphasis on "useful knowledge" for the builder and mechanic would not have necessarily precluded some attention to the history of architecture. The editor of the *Mechanics' Magazine* (New York, 1833–1837) published an account of ancient and medieval architecture in 1834.[13] Architectural history was also a topic of discussion at the early meetings of the institute. Before Harthill began publication of the *AMJ* in October 1859, several AIA members presented lectures on history. Leopold Eidlitz spoke on Gothic architecture, Detlef Lienau on romantic and classic structures, and Charles Babcock on the architecture of the past and present. These speeches, along with the discussion they sparked, were then printed in the *Crayon* (New York, 1855–1861), a fine arts review, between January 1858 and March 1859.[14] The *AMJ* editors, however, apparently did not solicit articles on architectural history.

Accounts of these early AIA meetings may help to explain the absence of architectural history from the pages of the *AMJ*. The institute lectures on history usually became the occasion for divisive arguments over whether the classic or medieval styles should serve as the basis for contemporary design. The discussion that followed J. Coleman Hart's remarks, ironically entitled "Unity in Architecture," at the 15 February 1859 meeting revealed the

THE GALLERY OF ART, WASHINGTON.—RENWICK & AUCHMUTY, ARCHITECTS.

1. James Renwick, Gallery for W. W. Corcoran, Washington, D.C.
From *Architects' and Mechanics' Journal*, October 1859. Avery Architectural and Fine Arts Library, Columbia University

deep divisions between the medieval and classic camps within the AIA. Praising Hart's discourse on the superiority of medieval styles, Eidlitz called for their revival. He then launched an attack on Renaissance architecture, claiming that such architects as Michelangelo had done great harm. Richard M. Hunt, an Ecole *élève*, retorted that "Gothic architecture should give way to another style" for contemporary design. Upjohn, an eminent Gothic revival architect, tried to end the fractious meeting on a note of harmony by recommending the "study of all styles, for the purpose of adapting the beauty contained in them."[15]

Van Brunt later recalled that such "ensanguined" disputes between the proponents of classic and medieval architecture were common during the early years of the AIA. "Finally a vote was passed," he stated, "excluding this dangerous subject from the discussions of the Institute."[16] The editors of the *AMJ* may have concluded, like the institute members, that articles on architectural history might embroil the magazine in pointless stylistic debates and deflect attention from the campaign for professional recognition and rights.

Whatever their reasons, the editors maintained a neutral stance between the classic and medieval camps of American architecture in the second half of the nineteenth century. The few illustrations of contemporary work that appeared in the journal were examples of both the Second Empire and Gothic revival. While the editors did not condemn architects who invoked traditional forms, they clearly hoped that a novel American architecture would gradually evolve as new materials and new building types were melded with past styles. Yet the editorial writers were careful never to advocate any particular period of architectural history as the most appropriate point of departure for this new style.

"If we work simply, neither copying nor striving for originality," one editor insisted," the feeling of our age and country . . . will give an impress to our work." The hope for an American architecture rested not so much on adherence to any one past style, he continued, but on "a higher aim and the recognition of the dignity of our art."[17]

Architectural Review and American Builder's Journal

Seven years after Harthill suspended publication of the *AMJ* in April 1861, Samuel Sloan, a Philadelphia architect, established a monthly periodical, the *Architectural Review and American Builder's Journal*. The *Review* was the first American architectural journal with extensive coverage of architectural history in its pages. Sloan, who began his career as a carpenter, believed that a knowledge of architectural history distinguished the architect from the mere draftsman. Young men ignorant of history, Sloan wrote in the *Review*, were nothing more than "mere office machines . . . putting others' ideas, mixed with their own prettily on paper."[18]

Sloan's own interest in history was first evident in *The Model Architect*, a house pattern book that he published in 1852. He introduced each of his residential designs in the Norman, Italian, and "Hindoo" modes with an account of that style's history. In the preface to the book, Sloan wrote that he had originally intended to publish "a matter of fact business like book on cottages and country residences" for the builder and mechanic. He ultimately decided, however, to include discussions of "the various styles, historical, descriptive, and critical" as "would render it [the book] interesting and desirable to the general reader."[19]

Sloan's belief in the appeal of architectural history for the lay reader may have affected the composition of the *Review*. Since he wished to attract "a noble column of educated amateurs and admirers" to the *Review* subscription list, Sloan may have chosen to emphasize articles on the history of architecture.[20]

Coverage of architectural history in the *Review* was broad. Sloan published articles on Greek and Roman dwellings, Vitruvius and the architect's character, origins of Gothic architecture, the life of Michelangelo, the Palladian style, pre-Columbian structures, and "Hindoo" architecture. The authors of these essays, usually anonymous, tended to emphasize the given period's general historical background, the formal traits of a style, and biographical details from the architects' lives. The exception to this rule was George Wightwick's contribution on Sir Christopher Wren. Wightwick, an English architect and prolific writer, provided a detailed analysis of Wren's buildings as well as his life in this essay, which was awarded a RIBA medal in 1858, eleven years before Sloan published it.[21]

The essays on architectural history Sloan presented in the *Review* were not illustrated. He complained in 1869 that architects refused to submit drawings for publication.[22] In order to reduce the production costs of the magazine, Sloan apparently depended on generous and gratuitous contributions of architectural drawings for publication. Although Sloan was clearly interested in architectural history, he was evidently unwilling to go to the expense of purchasing plates or hiring draftsmen to illustrate *Review* articles on the subject.

Sloan's decision not to publish illustrations of architectural history may have been dictated by professional as well as economic considerations. In an editorial entitled "Novelty in American Architecture," he lamented his countrymen's imitation of "bygone modes and styles, limiting ourselves in all things to the very letter of the composition we take for our guide."[23] Sloan may have feared that illustrations of architectural history in the *Review* would further encourage this tendency toward imitation. He had previously complained that few young architects and draftsmen bothered to read about the history of architecture. "They may subscribe to the monthly issues that have much that is valuable in their pages," Sloan wrote, "but, it is the illustrations alone that receive their attention and then merely to steal an occasional idea from, in order to help out some meagre crochet of their own."[24]

Sloan's views on just how architects should use historical precedent are elusive. He refused to publish criticism of individual designs in the *Review*.[25] While Sloan called for "an independent position with regard to the past," his own interest in history as *Review* editor and as a practicing designer belies a desire for an absolute break with tradition.[26]

American Architect and Builder's Monthly

Sloan discontinued the *Review* with the October 1870 issue. During the last months of its publication, he had a local competitor, *American Architect and Builder's Monthly*. Benjamin Linfoot, a former delineator for Sloan, published the *Monthly* beginning in March 1870. Linfoot won the support of Philadelphia architects who had been unwilling to contribute work to the *Review*.[27] John McArthur, Frank Furness, Napoleon LeBrun, and others submitted drawings of their current work for publication in the *Monthly*. As a result, the *Monthly* was the first American architectural periodical to provide a pictorial review of this country's contemporary architecture. Five to eight full-page photolithographs, usually perspective views, were reproduced in each issue by Linfoot's own commercial press. While these plates were depictions of such building types as banks, city halls, country houses, and churches, there were no illustrations of historical buildings.

The *Monthly* editors, as usual unidentified, were not too interested in the history of architecture. They did not believe that a study of past styles would elevate taste. Exposure to a true architect's buildings, the editors wrote, would "go further toward improving the taste of the masses than all the books written on the subject and all the teaching can ever accomplish."[28] While the editors published Second Empire, Queen Anne, and Gothic revival designs that interpreted architectural traditions for contemporary building types, they did not expound on the dynamic between history and current design (fig. 2).

Only a few feature articles on architectural history were published in the *Monthly*. The most extensive treatment of the subject was an eight-part series on English Gothic architecture by J. H. Chamberlain, a British architect and RIBA fellow. Chamberlain approached the Gothic style as the result of a straightforward adaptation of form to function and structure and as an expression of national life and feeling.[29]

Chamberlain's contention that English Gothic architecture gradually evolved through the fulfillment of certain fundamental needs must have soothed those American architects who were anxious to create a national style. It may also be significant that the *Monthly* editors chose an architect rather than a scholar to provide the only lengthy discourse on history in the journal. The implication of such a decision might have been that only a professional practitioner could isolate those aspects of history most useful to an audience of architects and builders.

American Architect and Building News

Five years after Linfoot ended the *Monthly* James R. Osgood, a prominent Boston publisher, brought out the first issue of the *American Architect and Building News (AABN)*, a weekly journal for the architectural profession. Before publishing the *AABN*, Osgood had experimented with two monthly periodicals, the *Architectural Sketch-Book* and the *New-York Sketch-Book of Architecture*. While Henry Richards and Francis Chandler, two Boston architects, edited the *Architectural Sketch-Book*, H. H. Richardson and Charles F. McKim supervised the New York publication.[30]

The two periodicals were essentially portfolios of Eastern architects' current work. There was no text apart from brief descriptions of the projects and buildings that were illustrated. The editors certainly were aware of such similar publications as *Architektonisches Skizzenbuch* (Berlin, 1852–1886), *Croquis d'architecture* (Paris, 1866–1898), and the *Architectural Association Sketchbook* (London, 1867–1923). Despite the emphasis on the visual in the journal's format, McKim used the New York *Sketch-Book* to promote an interest

in the colonial buildings of New England through illustrations and brief, but impassioned, editorial statements (fig. 3). McKim believed that a study of American colonial architecture could improve contemporary residential design. The old New England houses, in particular, possessed a charm and comfort all too frequently absent in late nineteenth-century American residences. These early structures were "always reasonable, simple in outline," he wrote, and had "great beauty of detail." "Now let somebody write about them as *Architecture*," McKim wrote of the colonial buildings. "The architects are their true historians."[31] McKim looked to practitioners to analyze early American buildings as architecture and provide a more substantive account than had appeared in newspaper articles on the subject.

Osgood discontinued the two periodicals at the end of 1876; he did not believe the market could support them and the *AABN*.[32] He conceived of the new weekly journal as a counterweight to his literary list, which included works by Charles Dickens, Henry James, Mark Twain, and Henry W. Longfellow. Osgood used the *AABN* to excerpt and promote the architectural books that he published. He hoped that the *AABN* illustrations, reproduced as photolithographs, would attract business to the Heliotype Company, his photomechanical printing concern. Architectural journalism was always a commercial matter for Osgood. He later confessed that he never found the contents of the *AABN* to be of any real interest.[33]

Fortunately, supporters of the *AABN* such as William Robert Ware, founder of architectural education at the Massachusetts Institute of Technology in 1868 and Columbia University in 1881, did regard the journal as a professional undertaking and personal mission. As early as 1867, Ware had argued that a professional periodical was necessary in order to elevate architecture in the United States.[34] Ware's friends,

2. John McArthur, Philadelphia City Hall
From *American Architect and Builder's Monthly*, March 1870. Avery Architectural and Fine Arts Library, Columbia University

3. Bishop Berkeley House,
Middletown, Rhode Island

From *New-York Sketch-Book* 1
(December 1874), pl. 45. Avery
Architectural and Fine Arts Library,
Columbia University

relatives, and colleagues served on the *AABN* editorial staff: William P. P. Long-fellow, a Boston architect and lecturer in Ware's MIT program; William Rotch Ware, his nephew; and Van Brunt, the elder Ware's architectural partner. Ware himself also wrote occasional editorial statements.[35] When Osgood wanted to cease publication of the *AABN* after the first year, Ware orchestrated a publicity campaign, solicited new stockholders, and even invested his own money in the journal.[36]

Ware's attitude toward architectural history as revealed in the curricula he devised at MIT and Columbia is relevant to a discussion of the coverage of past styles in the *AABN* because of the editors' close ties to him. Ware wanted the student to approach precedent "not in the spirit of the historian or connoisseur . . . but like the men who first invented it . . . , as problems to be solved."[37] Although he did not believe that a study of history would lead to a new

style, Ware hoped it would endow his students with "temperance and refinement."[38] At the very least an understanding of historical principles was "the most efficient safeguard against the wild and wanton tendencies in American architecture.[39]

The *AABN* editors, like Ware, believed contemporary design in this country, as exemplified in the Second Empire, Queen Anne, and High Victorian Gothic styles, was excessively romantic and picturesque; American architects failed to endow their work with "sobriety, balance, subordination, and refinement."[40] These academic principles were best taught at the Ecole des Beaux-Arts or at American university programs like those of Ware. Yet the editors, who considered themselves "part educators of the young men who are to be the architects of the future," advised those unable to matriculate to study Italian Renaissance architecture and American colonial and federal buildings as exemplars of academic precepts.[41] Illustrations and discussions of these periods of architectural history would appear in the magazine.

Despite their enthusiasm for Italian Renaissance and early American architecture, the editors did not advocate the wholesale revival of those two styles. Instead, they believed that an architect conversant with academic principles could imbue any given style with "freedom, correctness, grace, and elegance." As proof of this contention, the editors cited the success of Hunt and Richardson, both trained at the Ecole, in interpreting such disparate styles as the French Renaissance, Romanesque, and Gothic for modern building types.[42] The *AABN* editors stood for academic training and professional practices, not the revival of any one style. As Longfellow wrote in 1876, "we are not going to fight the battle of the styles."[43]

Nevertheless, one period of architectural history, eighteenth- and early nineteenth-century American architecture, did receive the lion's share of coverage in the *AABN*. The editors were obviously in favor of colonial and federal precedents for late nineteenth-century American domestic design. As a response to indigenous conditions and an example of an American classicism, this country's early architecture was an especially apposite model for current residential work, in the editors' opinion.[44]

Articles on colonial and federal architecture were written by architects such as Robert S. Peabody, Claude Bragdon, and Glenn Brown. These contributions, with the exception of Brown's rather scholarly essays, focused on the visual, anecdotal, and descriptive aspects of early American architecture.[45] The authors provided extensive visual documentation through their own sketches, measured drawings, and photographs (fig. 4). This material on the colonial and federal periods proved so popular that it was published separately as *The Georgian Period* (Boston, 1899–1902), a multivolumed series, under the editorship of William Rotch Ware.

Other periods of architectural history received far more limited coverage in the *AABN*. The authors of these essays were frequently architects. The editors' publi-

cation of selections from Viollet-le-Duc's *Habitations of Man in All Ages*, an Osgood title for 1876, is a case in point. In the spring of 1876, the editors presented Viollet-le-Duc's discussions of Aryan, Chinese, and Egyptian dwellings and his illustrations of the buildings, their sites, and construction techniques.[46]

The excerpts from Viollet-le-Duc's text doubtlessly appeared because the editors were obliged to promote a new Osgood

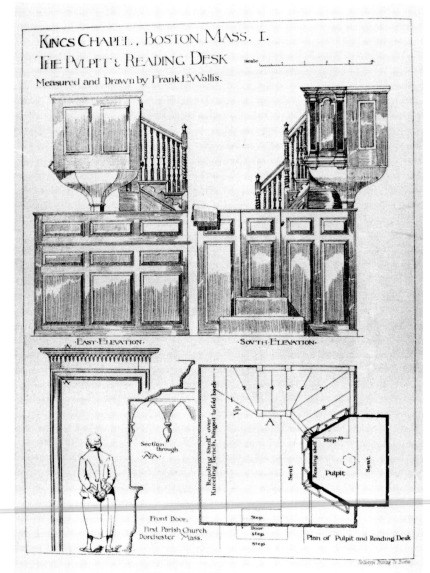

OLD COLONIAL WORK.

4. Frank E. Wallis, Pulpit and Reading Desk, King's Chapel, Boston
From *American Architect and Building News*, 20 November 1886. Avery Architectural and Fine Arts Library, Columbia University

publication in the *AABN* columns. Yet the editors may have felt that Viollet-le-Duc's simple discussion, originally written for laymen with an emphasis on built form as a response to climate, materials, and indigenous traditions, was a useful object lesson for American architects who strained after novel effects.[47] Furthermore, the editors respected Viollet-le-Duc as a professional practitioner whose rational approach to design was a welcome antidote to the sentimental cant and arbitrary judgments of John Ruskin. The English critic was a misguided amateur, the editors wrote, who discussed art and architecture as if they were the result of moral homilies rather than the product of the artist's instincts and training. Throughout the late nineteenth century, the *AABN* editors continued to attack Ruskin as a baneful influence on American architecture.[48]

Perhaps the editors' dislike of Ruskin and resentment of the layman's interference in what they saw as professional matters explain why Charles Eliot Norton and Charles H. Moore, two of the most eminent American scholars of art and architecture in the late nineteenth century, never contributed writings to the *AABN*. Both historians were especially concerned with medieval architecture and were close friends of Ruskin. Before his death in 1908, Norton wrote extensively on past and present architectural issues for the literary journals. His criticism was often pointed, and a published attack on Ware and Van Brunt's Memorial Hall at Harvard (1865–1878) would not have endeared him to the *AABN* editors.[49] If the staff of the journal were also wary of Moore, his subsequent writings for *Architectural Record*, it will be shown, would have confirmed their suspicions.

The *AABN* editors seemed to feel more comfortable with contributors on architectural history like A. D. F. Hamlin, W. H. Goodyear, and Mariana Van Rensselaer. Hamlin, a practicing architect and member of Ware's faculty at Columbia, published articles on ancient and Renaissance architecture in the *AABN*. His most extensive contribution on history was a fifteen-part series on the evolution of decorative motifs that appeared between 1898 and 1901.

Illustrated with many drawings, Hamlin's articles on ornament were, as he wrote, a synchronic rather than a diachronic examination of specific motifs such as the palmette.[50] Goodyear, an archaeologist and curator at the Brooklyn and Metropolitan museums, published a series on the lotus in ancient art in 1889. Although a more scholarly account than Hamlin's, Goodyear's articles could also be used as a reference source for architects or draftsmen in search of an ornamental motif.[51] Van Rensselaer was a lay critic who wrote sympathetic reviews of contemporary American architects' designs and buildings for journals like *Scribner's* and the *Century*. After Richardson's death, his friends enlisted her to write the architect's biography. She contributed a few pieces on architectural history to the *AABN*. Her essay on English cathedrals of 1892 is interesting because she chose not to deal with architectural issues, but with the "sociological" (economic and political) aspects of these religious structures.[52]

William Rotch Ware, an editor of the *AABN* from 1876 until 1907, once wrote that he routinely turned down articles for publication that he considered too scholarly or technical.[53] Judging from the limited number of essays on history that were published in the *AABN*, the staff seemed to believe that discussions of past styles had to be carefully tailored for a weekly professional journal. Contributions on history, preferably written by an architect, should stress academic principles of design or provide a reference source for decorative motifs.

Architectural Record

Scholarly articles on architectural history, William Rotch Ware believed, belonged in a monthly review rather than the "ephemeral columns of a weekly journal."[54] *Architectural Record*, first established as a quarterly publication in 1891, was just such a review. Clinton W. Sweet, the publisher of *Record*, envisioned it as a magazine for the layman as well as the architect. Henry W. Desmond and Herbert Croly, Sweet's editors, were not architects but journalists and writers.[55] In his inaugural editorial, Desmond wrote that his aim was to occupy the "higher ground" left open by the other architectural journals that were merely "record[s] of the current scene."[56]

Although many of the subjects of *Record* articles (the profession, education, colonial architecture, and the search for an American style) were familiar from the earlier journals, Desmond and Croly encouraged a more lengthy and thoughtful treatment, a luxury of the longer deadlines of a quarterly. Montgomery Schuyler's "The History of Old Colonial Architecture" of 1895 is representative of the *Record* approach. Although Schuyler was an architectural critic and journalist, he presented a rather scholarly examination of early American buildings. He was attentive to matters of chronology, attribution, and primary source material. Schuyler even appended a bibliography to his discussion.[57]

Yet Schuyler still allowed current design considerations to shape his view of early American architecture. He omitted any discussion of the New England meetinghouse because "not even the most bigoted observer suggests it as the basis for contemporary ecclesiastical work."[58] The importance of architectural history was still evaluated in terms of its application to current practice.

Jean Schopfer reiterated Schuyler's viewpoint in a 1905 essay on Greek and Roman architecture. The ancient buildings selected for discussion, Schopfer wrote, all exemplified certain design precepts "which hold good now as firmly as they did twenty-five centuries before. . . . We shall extract rules of present value to ourselves—rules which might guide an architect entrusted with the erection of a skyscraper on Fifth Avenue or a national monument in Washington, D.C."[59]

The *Record* editors not only published more articles on architectural history than their colleagues at the other journals, but they solicited contributions from scholars as well as architects and critics. Goodyear regularly published his researches on optical refinements in ancient and medieval architecture beginning in 1894. After World War I, Charles H. Moore and Arthur Kingsley Porter also contributed to *Record*.[60]

The articles that Moore wrote for *Record* and the controversy they caused perhaps explain why his work never appeared in the *AABN*. Moore considered a variety of topics in *Record*: medieval and Renaissance architecture, Ruskin, Viollet-le-Duc, and architectural education.[61] He also brought the passion and moral commitment of Ruskin to his writings on architectural history and the profession. In a 1918 article on Renaissance architecture, Moore attacked the style on grounds of structural illogic and moral detachment. Seven years later, he announced that there was no greater obstacle to current architectural progress than the Italian Renaissance style and the commitment of American design programs to academic principles.[62]

A. D. F. Hamlin published a rebuttal to Moore's arguments of 1918 in *Record*. The Harvard professor's views on Renaissance architecture, Hamlin wrote, were typical of the narrow and intolerant writings of the English Gothic revival. The laymen who initiated this movement in Great Britain, like Ruskin, "focused attention first on the details and dressings of art, conceiving that if one kind and system of forms was right and logical, all others must be fundamentally wrong."[63] As long as architectural history in the United States was allied with figures like Moore, committed to the Gothic and opposed to the Renaissance tradition, the editors of some professional journals would not publish these scholars' articles. It is significant that the first architectural journal to provide Moore with a forum was *Record*, a publication of criticism edited by writers rather than architects.

Conclusion

Architectural history was never extensively discussed or illustrated in the pages of the first American architectural periodicals. The editors of these journals emphasized articles on professional and technical issues and illustrations of contemporary American architecture. The published essays on architectural history were considerations of how the current practitioner should use precedent or how design principles from past styles might correct unfortunate tendencies in contemporary work. The editors also seemed to prefer contributions on history from architects and critics rather than scholars. Some editors, such as William Rotch Ware, considered scholarly articles inappropriate for a weekly professional journal. It is significant that history was most extensively discussed in Sloan's *Review*, a monthly, and *Record*, a quarterly, which were both intended for the layman as well as the architect and builder.

Architectural history also seemed a dangerous topic to some editors. It could potentially inhibit the contemporary designer in the search for a modern expression, or it could divide the professional community into warring stylistic factions. While the editors of the first architectural journals never called for a complete rejection of precedent, and many stressed the value of academic principles derived from past styles, they seemed more concerned with what Van Brunt described as the dangers rather than the privileges of history.

NOTES

Works frequently cited have been identified by the following abbreviations:

AMJ   *Architects' and Mechanics' Journal*
Review   *Architectural Review*
Monthly *American Architect and Builder's Monthly*
AABN   *American Architect and Building News*
Record   *Architectural Record*

1. Henry Van Brunt, "Translator's Introduction" to Eugène-Emmanuel Viollet-le-Duc, *Discourses on Architecture*, in *Selected Essays of Henry Van Brunt*, vol. 1 (1875; repr. in *Architecture and Society*, ed. William Coles [Cambridge, Mass., 1969]), 147.

2. Report of the Education Committee, *Proceedings of the Annual Convention of the American Institute of Architects* (1894), 27–28.

3. Henry Van Brunt, review of *The Nature and Function of Art*, by Leopold Eidlitz, *Nation* 33 (29 December 1881), 515–516.

4. These regional journals included: *California Architect and Building News* (San Francisco, 1879–

1900), *Western Architect and Building News* (Denver, 1889–1891), *Inland Architect* (Chicago, 1883–1908), *Northwestern Architect and Improvement Record* (Minneapolis, 1882–1894), *Architect and Builder* (Kansas City, 1886–1907), and *Southern Architect* (Atlanta, 1889–1932).

5. Prospectus, *AMJ* 1 (October 1859), 14. After he discontinued the *AMJ* in 1861, Harthill became a stockbroker. *Trow's New York City Directory* (1864, 1865), 373, 380.

6. Information on the history of the mechanics' movement and the conception of "useful knowledge" can be found in Howard B. Rock, *Artisans of the New Republic: The Tradesmen of New York City in the Age of Jefferson* (New York, 1979), 15 n.5 and Bruce Sinclair, *Philadelphia's Philosopher Mechanics: A History of the Franklin Institute, 1824–1865* (Baltimore, 1974), 4–20.

7. *AMJ* 1 (January 1860), 94. The plates in this series were illustrations of door frames and linings, framing of a bay window, and mouldings for a Romanesque window.

8. Prospectus 1859, 14.

9. The American Institute of Architects was preceded by the American Institution of Architects, founded in 1836 by T. U. Walter, Alexander J. Davis, and William Strickland. The American Institution held only two meetings, but it still was the first professional association of American architects. For more information on both organizations, see my "The First American Architectural Journals," *Journal of the Society of Architectural Historians* 48 (June 1989), 119 and 123-125.

10. "The AIA," *AMJ* 1 (February 1860), 150.

11. Prospectus 1859, 14.

12. Van Brunt and Leopold Eidlitz were AIA members with literary talents. In 1857 Van Brunt would write for the *Atlantic Monthly* (Boston), and from 1863 to 1865 Eidlitz would write for *The New Path* (New York). Compare Van Brunt's conception of stylistic evolution in his "Cast Iron in Decorative Architecture," *The Crayon* 6 (January 1859), 15-20, with similar ideas in "Gradual Formation of Styles," *AMJ* 3 (29 December 1860), 121. Also compare Eidlitz's thoughts on the Gothic in "Cast Iron in Decorative Architecture," *The Crayon* 6 (January 1859), 20-24, with those expressed in "Common Sense in Architecture," *AMJ* 3 (16 February 1861), 191. Both the Eidlitz and Van Brunt essays in *The Crayon* were based on lectures they gave at a 7 December 1858 AIA meeting.

13. "Compendium of Civil Architecture," *Mechanics' Magazine* 4 (12 July 1834, 9 August 1834), 17-24, 67-72.

14. *The Crayon* 5 (January 1858, May 1858, July 1858), 53-55, 168-169, 199-200.

15. *The Crayon* 6 (March 1859), 84-89.

16. "Richard M. Hunt," *Proceedings of the Annual Convention of the American Institute of Architects* (1895), 76-77.

17. "True Source of Progress in Architecture," *AMJ* 3 (9 February 1861), 181.

18. The editorials that appeared in the *Review* were not signed. Since Sloan was identified as editor on the title page, these statements were presumably his work. Thus I attribute this editorial and others from the *Review* to Sloan until further evidence comes to light. "Important to Young Men," *Review* 1 (May 1869), 717.

19. Preface, *The Model Architect* (1852, repr. New York, 1975), 7-8.

20. "The New Year," *Review* 1 (January 1869), 417-418. Elisabeth Blair MacDougall discusses the American belief that the arts and architecture provided intellectual and moral uplift in "Before 1870: Founding Fathers and Amateur Historians," in this volume.

21. "Sir Christopher Wren," *Review* 2 (September 1869), 159-164. Wightwick's essay, titled "On the Architecture and Genius of Sir Christopher Wren," appeared in *Transactions of the RIBA* (1858/1859), 119-128.

22. "A Word to Our Brethren," *Review* 2 (February 1870), 433-434.

23. "Novelty in American Architecture," *Review* 2 (January 1870), 370-371.

24. "Important to Young Men," 717.

25. *Review* 1 (July 1868), 2-3.

26. "Novelty in American Architecture," 370-371.

27. Sloan's abrasive personality and aggressive business practices alienated many in the Philadelphia architectural community. John McArthur was the only local architect to submit a drawing for publication in the *Review*. For more on Sloan's relations with Philadelphia architects see Harold N. Cooledge, *Samuel Sloan: Architect of Philadelphia, 1815-1884* (Philadelphia, 1986), 47-48, 71-73, 91-92.

28. *Monthly* 1 (May 1870), 33.

29. The Chamberlain series appeared in the June 1870 issue of the *Monthly* and concluded with the magazine's final number in January 1871.

30. While the title page of the *Architectural Sketch-Book* lists the members of the Boston Portfolio Club as its editors, Roger Reed of the Maine Historic Preservation Commission has identified Henry Richards and Francis Chandler as the editors, based upon his examination of Richards' papers in the Gardiner Public Library, Gardiner, Maine. I am grateful to Mr. Reed for sharing this information with me. The identification of Richardson and McKim as the New York editorial staff occurs in A. J. Bloor, "Annual Address," reprinted in *AABN* 2 (24 March 1877), xi and "Charles Follen McKim," *Architectural Record* 26 (November 1909), 381. McKim, however, was the real editor of the *New-York Sketch Book* because Richardson left the city for Boston in the spring of 1874 to work on Trinity Church.

31. *New-York Sketch Book of Architecture* 1 (December 1874), 1-2, pl. 45.

32. *AABN* 1 (9 December 1876), 394.

33. James R. Osgood to Benjamin H. Ticknor, 9 August 1887, Benjamin H. Ticknor Collection, Manuscript Division, Library of Congress, Washington, D.C.

34. William Robert Ware, "On the Condition of Architecture and Architectural Education in the United States," *Sessional Papers of the RIBA*, (1866-1867), 37.

35. Longfellow was editor from 1876 until 1880. William Rotch Ware was associate editor from 1876 until 1880, when he and T. M. Clark, the elder Ware's successor as head of the MIT program in 1881, became coeditors. Van Brunt and the elder Ware contributed editorials in the late 1870s and early 1880s. This information on the editors comes from William Rotch Ware's annotated copies of the *AABN*, now in the collection of Loeb Library, Harvard Graduate School of Design, Cambridge, Mass. I am grateful to J. A. Chewning, University of Cincinnati, for telling me about Ware's annotated *AABN*.

36. Undated manuscript biography of William Robert Ware, MIT Archives, Cambridge, Mass. While this manuscript is unsigned, the handwriting seems to be William Rotch Ware's.

37. Education Commitee Report, *Proceedings of the AIA*, (1894), 133-134.

38. Education Committee Report, 33-34.

39. Education Committee Report, 33-34.

40. "American Architecture—Present," *AABN* 1 (5 August 1876), 250. Ware's copies of the *AABN* at Harvard list Longfellow as the author of this essay.

41. "Retrospect," *AABN* 18 (16 December 1888), 303, and "American Architecture—Past," *AABN* 1 (29 July 1876), 242. The latter article is by Longfellow, according to the Ware *AABN*, Harvard.

42. "American Architecture—Past," 242, and "Delicacy of Perception Dependent upon Study," *AABN* 2 (11 August 1877), 254. Van Brunt wrote the latter essay, according to the Ware *AABN*, Harvard.

43. William P. P. Longfellow, "In Search of a Style," *AABN* 1 (12 August 1876), 259.

44. "American Architecture—Past," 242.

45. Peabody, "Georgian Houses of New England," *AABN* 2, 3 (20 October 1877, 16 February 1878), 338–339, 54–55; Bragdon, "Colonial Work in the Genesee Valley," *AABN* 43, 45, 46 (24 March 1894, 21 July 1894, 13 October 1894), 141–142, 26–27, 11–12; and Brown, "Old Colonial Work in Virginia and Maryland," *AABN* 22 (22 October 1887), 198–199.

46. *AABN* 1 (26 February, 1876, 4 March 1876, 11 March 1876, 1 April 1876), 68–70, 77–78, 85–86, 107.

47. "Originality in American Architecture," *AABN* 3 (5 January 1878), 3.

48. "Doctrinaire in Art," *AABN* 2 (22 December 1877), 407–408. See also "Some Trials of English Architects" and "Architectural Retrospect," *AABN* 21, 70 (30 April 1887, 20 December 1900), 206, 98.

49. Norton wrote that Memorial Hall lacked unity, simplicity, and originality. See *Nation* 5 (1867), 34–35. Both Norton and Moore taught at Harvard. See Charles Moore, "Charles Eliot Norton" and Arthur Pope, "Charles Herbert Moore," *Dictionary of American Biography*, vol. 13 (New York, 1934), 569–572, 116–117.

50. *AABN* 59 (29 January 1898), 35.

51. *AABN* 25 (9 February 1889, 29 June 1889), 66–69, 308–310.

52. *AABN* 37 (17 September 1892), 180–181.

53. William Rotch Ware to Glenn Brown, 14 May 1894, Glenn Brown Papers, American Institute of Architects Archives, Washington, D.C.

54. Ware to Brown, 14 May 1894.

55. See "Clinton W. Sweet," *National Cyclopaedia of American Biography* 20 (New York, 1929), 353; David Levy, *Herbert Croly of the New Republic* (Princeton, 1985), 72–76, 84–86; and "Henry W. Desmond," *Record* 33 (May 1913), 469.

56. "By Way of Introduction," *Record* 1 (July–September 1891), 3–6.

57. Montgomery Schuyler, "The History of Old Colonial Architecture," *Record* 4 (January–March 1895), 312–366.

58. "Old Colonial Architecture," 332.

59. Jean Schopfer, "The Greek Temple," *Record* 17 (June 1905), 441–442.

60. See, for example, Goodyear, "Optical Refinements in Medieval Architecture," 6 (July–September 1896), 1–19; Porter, "The Case against Roman Architecture," *Record* 43 (January 1918), 23–36; and Moore, "Church of Santa Sophia," *Record* 52 (August 1922), 156–159.

61. See Charles Moore, "Character of Renaissance Architecture," *Record* 43 (January 1918), 46–51, "Ruskin as Critic of Architecture," *Record* 56 (September 1924), 117–122, "The Writings of Viollet-le-Duc," *Record* 59 (February 1926), 128–132, and "University Instruction in Architecture," *Record* 50 (November 1921), 407–412.

62. "Character of Renaissance Architecture," 466–467, and Charles Moore, "Conditions Conducive to Architecture," *Record* 58 (September 1925), 213–214.

63. A. D. F. Hamlin, "Renaissance Architecture and Its Critics," *Record* 42 (August, September 1917), 266, 272, 116–118, 125.

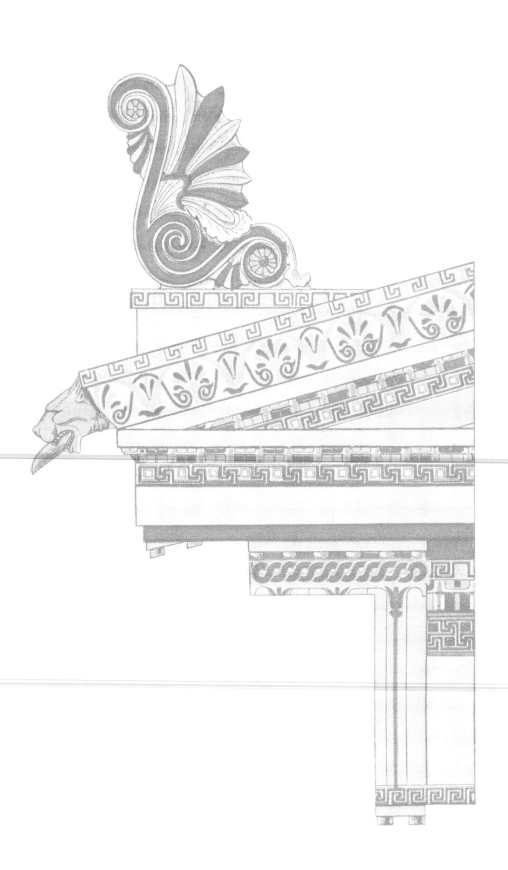

DAVID VAN ZANTEN
Northwestern University

Chicago in Architectural History

C hicago" in twentieth-century history has always been as much the name of some cause as the designation of a place at the southwestern corner of Lake Michigan. Just what cause, however, has varied widely over the span of its evocations. Its examination raises the double problem of what misinterpretations say about the objectives of its interpreters and what sort of reality might lie there to inspire such constant and partisan attention.

The idea of a distinct "Chicago school of architecture" became convincing and significant in Sigfried Giedion's *Space, Time and Architecture* of 1941, the publication of the Charles Eliot Norton Lectures at Harvard given in 1938–1939. While critics had always recognized the genius of Louis Sullivan and Frank Lloyd Wright and foreign observers had noted something special about the city, only midwesterners previously had believed that Chicago harbored its own actual "school" of architecture.[1] It took this lucid Swiss brought to Harvard in the wake of Walter Gropius to convince the world of the existence of a special Chicago genius in design and to define it precisely.

Starting from a methodological introduction in which he insists on the parallel evolution of art and science, Giedion distinguishes between "constituent facts" of history, which constitute "recurrent and cumulative tendencies," and "transitory facts," which are merely "spasmodic trends." Within this structure he identifies in recent art and architectural history eight threads, or "traditions," in which he perceives a continuous interrelationship of art and science or technique. Among them is building in Chicago from the balloon frame through the skyscraper to Frank Lloyd Wright. These traditions he presents as culminating during the 1920s in the International style of Le Corbusier, Ludwig Mies van der Rohe, and Walter Gropius.

Giedion's Chicago chapter is one of his longest and in America the most influential. He reestablished the local catchphrase "Chicago school." Considering the argument in which Giedion embeds the phrase, it seems inevitable that what he presents as the core of his "Chicago school" is its accommodation with technique, most dramatically displayed in the city's supposed invention of the skyscraper frame. His central images are William Le Baron Jenney's Second Leiter Building set next to Le Corbusier's Maison Clarté in Geneva, Daniel Burnham's Reliance Building set next to Mies' glass tower project of 1921, and finally Sullivan's Carson Pirie Scott Store set next to Gropius' Chicago Tribune competition entry of 1922. He implies not only continuity from the Chicago skyscraper of the 1890s to the International style of the 1920s, but equality between the Chicagoans Jenney, Burnham, and Sullivan by his standard of technical frankness rather than that of decorative or compositional subtlety.[2] Wright, however, Giedion analyzes not just as a frank engineer, but as an artist of scientific revelation, that is, an artist who uses pure geometric shapes to create a continuous, flowing space like that later broached in European cubist painting. "He [Wright] is impelled unconsciously by the same forces that worked in Europe about ten years later,"[3] Giedion writes, and mentions the "temporal coincidence" of cubism and Einstein's 1905 Theory of Relativity.[4]

As a result of Giedion's analysis of 1938–1941, two American architects once seen as the leaders of a provincial school emerged as unconscious heroes of a force of history: Sullivan, significant not for his luscious ornament but for the minimalism of his facades, and Wright, not for his interest in locality and symbolism but for his simple forms and his treatment of space.

An uneasiness with Sullivan's ornament and Wright's romanticism, however, had already appeared among the first American proponents of the International style: Henry-Russell Hitchcock in his 1928 *Cahiers d'art* monograph on Wright and his 1929 *Modern Architecture: Romanticism and Reintegration*, as well as Hitchcock and Philip Johnson in their 1932 "International style" catalogue.[5] What was significant in Giedion's formulation was its positive rather than its negative treatment of Sullivan and Wright: he saved them both for modernism by submerging them in a broader technical tradition and by giving that tradition vast importance. Hitchcock presented Sullivan as a provincial equivalent of Victor Horta or Hendrik Berlage; Giedion made him the poet of Chicago's special union of science and art.

Giedion's volume was also remarkable for its incisiveness and its readability. Kenneth Conant, reviewing it in the *Journal of Aesthetics and Art Criticism* in 1941, wrote: "It reads like a detective story, and architectural students say that once started on it, they read it the night through—unable to put it down."[6] Giedion's writing style and use of illustrations was almost as important as his message, especially since his faltering English made the actual lectures

of 1938–1939 a disappointment.

The idea that the West was different, more innovative, and better organized, is a fundamental motif of American self-analysis. As Oscar Hammerstein has a character say in *Oklahoma* of 1943, "Everything's up-to-date in Kansas City." From its steel mills and its gangsters to its schools, Chicago (like Detroit, St. Louis, or Kansas City) was the up-to-date place around the time of the two world wars.[7] Interestingly, in the case of Chicago this distinction was most generally perceived in its monumental urbanism, already broached in the Court of Honor of the 1893 World's Columbian Exposition, sketched more concretely in Burnham's 1909 plan, and partially realized in Michigan Avenue facing toward the lake across Grant Park, which was finally finished during the depression.[8] Giedion, judging art by its reflection of technique and heroicizing the practical pioneer, dismissed the legacy of the Columbian Exposition as "Eastern mercantile classicism." But with Grant Park spanking new and awe inspiring in 1941, the locals must have been disappointed when a Swiss critic announced that the city's achievement lay in the crowded old loft buildings of the South Loop. Indeed, one of the first preservationist crises occasioned by *Space, Time and Architecture* resulted from the demolition in 1940–1941 of the cast iron lofts on the St. Louis riverfront to make way for that city's equivalent of Grant Park, the Jefferson National Expansion Memorial Park, eventually graced by Eero Saarinen's huge arch.[9]

Confronting the self-image of Chicago as the monumental city was its claim to stylistic progressivism, usually contrasted to a perceived East Coast conservatism. Sullivan, of course, had fired the first shot with his Wainwright Building in St. Louis of 1890–1891, his Transportation Building at the Columbian Exposition, designed in 1891, and his Schiller Building in Chicago of 1891–1892. In its January–March 1892 issue the New York *Architectural Record* published a mock debate between architects in which a western practitioner is made to rise and declare, "In the West, you will be interested to know, several of our brainiest architects are now engaged in the creation of an original 'American style' and what with the Chicago system of construction on the one hand, and the inventive genius of our people on the other, the copying of effete forms is about ended."[10] An illustration of the Schiller Building is on the facing page. (The speaker sits down and is not heard from again in the debate.)

Already by 1893 the younger progressive designers of Chicago had made a system of Sullivan's innovations, as in Wright's Winslow House of that year or Richard E. Schmidt's Montgomery Ward Building on Michigan Avenue of 1897–1899. By 1900 they constituted a large and vocal group noticed in the national journals.[11] In 1908 one of their number, Thomas Tallmadge, formally named the movement the "Chicago school" in the Boston Architectural Review, at the same time, however, questioning its focus and longevity. Tallmadge's hesitance contrasted with a continuing faith in western architectural progressivism on the part of Irving K. Pond, Claude Bragdon, and especially Emil Lorch—with the aging Sullivan still at his guns until his death in 1924 and Wright hovering over the horizon in Wisconsin.

Pond and Bragdon were prolific popular architectural writers as well as respected designers who were proposing in the teens and twenties a modern American architecture marked by Sullivan-like ornament and modulated massing.[12] Lorch was more positive still. He was a Detroiter trained at MIT and employed as assistant director in charge of architecture at the Art Institute of Chicago in 1899–1901.[13] In that position he was an active partisan of Sullivanism, teaching a kind of "Chicago" design in the School of the Art Institute and proselytizing through the Chicago Architectural Club and the newly founded (1899) Architectural League of America. In 1906, after studying the abstract compositional rules of "pure design" under Arthur Wesley Dow at the Museum of Fine Arts, Boston, Lorch was named the head of the architectural program at the University of Michigan and put his progressive ideas into action. Beginning in 1889 Dow and Denman W. Ross of Harvard developed a method of geometric analysis of painting and design, which Lorch transformed into a process of functional (rather than historicizing) architec-

tural design. He formulated a new curriculum based on "pure design," had Sullivan visit, and employed as design critics first Albert Kahn's designer Ernest Wilby and then, in 1923, Eliel Saarinen. In 1926 Lorch, Pond, and Tallmadge helped mount an exhibition of American architecture in Berlin and Vienna. The central room was devoted to Sullivan's work. There was included a display of student projects from the University of Michigan, and the catalogue contained essays by Pond and Tallmadge as well as Sullivan's 1906 essay, "What Is Architecture?" from the Craftsman.[14] Giedion must have known the Berlin-Vienna exhibition and may have been reacting directly against its presentation of western American progressivism as a sort of Saarinenesque expressionism.

Sullivan's, Pond's, and Lorch's faith in the ultimate triumph of progressive design was belied by Burnham's successes and by Grant Park. Less partisan historians of the 1920s tended to depict the "Chicago school" as a brave failure of two decades before, flawed by its dependence on artistic genius and its intractability to systematization. Fiske Kimball in 1925 argued that Sullivan, just dead, was now only an "Old Master." In his authoritative and elegantly written American Architecture of 1928, he treats Sullivan and Wright in a chapter entitled "Crosscurrents," calling them "romantic" individualists and going on to praise the unity of McKim's and Burnham's classicism. The Chicagoan Tallmadge in his Story of Architecture in America of 1927 also treats Sullivan and Wright in a moving chapter entitled "Louis Sullivan and the Lost Cause."[15] Lewis Mumford in his lyrical Brown Decades (1931) praised Sullivan and Wright unstintingly but avoided subsuming them in any provincial "Chicago school" and blended them in his analysis with H. H. Richardson and the critic Montgomery Schuyler.[16]

Giedion's accomplishment in 1938–1941 was to redefine this "Chicago school" in such a broad manner that the decorative signature formerly insisted upon so ineffectually by Pond, Bragdon, and Lorch was deemphasized so that the romantic isolation of Sullivan and Wright that Kimball denigrated was overcome, and they emerged as far more significant for world architecture than locally suspected. But, to an extent, the "expressionist" reading of Sullivan and Wright was simply replaced by an International style interpretation. A disinterested, historical interpretation had not yet been presented.

One of the proofs of the weakness of the older, parochial idea of a "Chicago school" was its immediate collapse before Giedion's onslaught. With *Space, Time and Architecture* a new framework for architectural historical research appeared. The history of the skyscraper as proof of the American ease with technology became a general enterprise pursued with thoroughness and enthusiasm on many fronts, most especially by Carl Condit, originally an English and history professor at Northwestern University with experience in engineering. In 1948 he published a short essay developing Giedion's history of the skyscraper in *Art in America*, in 1952 his *Rise of the Skyscraper*, and finally in 1965 a lengthened version of that pointedly entitled *The Chicago School of Architecture*.[17] Contemporaneously Winston Weisman studied the skyscraper in a broader context, embracing East Coast contributions and questioning whether it was really a Chicago invention.[18] There were more modest parallel studies of the history of the "balloon frame," prefabrication, and cast iron architecture.[19] This, of course, gave impetus to the study of minor members of this "Chicago school," especially the more exotic Sullivan and Wright imitators. David Gebhard, Allen Brooks, and Mark Peisch set the type with their doctoral dissertations, all subsequently published as books. Individual monographs appeared as doctoral dissertations and as articles in the *Prairie School Review*.[20] Somewhat more slowly, the work of the early skyscraper architects Jenney, John Wellborn Root, William Holabird and Martin Roche, and S. S. Beman has been explored.[21]

Giedion's analysis, however, put the study of Sullivan and Wright themselves in a problematic situation: they had been saved from Tallmadge's and Kimball's historic graveyard of romanticism at the price of their individuality. Was it really convincing to Americans to base their exegesis of these two artists on their typicality? Could one really overlook Sullivan's ornament? Is it really convincing to imagine Wright as a cubist before the fact?

In the case of Sullivan, denied the admiration of the artistic *virtù* in his ornament, historians turned to the poetry of his writings and to the tragic heroism of his biography. From Hugh Morrison's aptly titled *Louis Sullivan: Prophet of Modern Architecture* of 1935 through Willard Connely's touching biography of 1960 to Sherman Paul's *Louis Sullivan: An Architect in American Thought* of 1962, his towering personality was depicted, but through his words and stoicism more than through his designs.[22]

Distantly parallel in the case of Wright was the almost exclusive focus of historical research on his work before 1910, where a consistent abstract vocabulary could be recognized. The variety and symbolic force of Wright's later work has proven less tractable to conventional analysis in spite of its obvious brilliance. Furthermore, one of the basic analytical tactics has been the attribution of his spatial gymnastics to childhood training with Froebel blocks (as if other great architects had not played with blocks as well). Wright himself mentioned this experience in his 1932 *Autobiography*, and it was explored in detail by Grant Manson in his Harvard doctoral dissertation of 1940, in his article "Wright in the Nursery" of 1953, and in his book *Frank Lloyd Wright to 1910* of 1958. Edgar Kaufmann, Stuart Wilson, Richard Mac-Cormac, and Joseph Connors have extended this analysis.[23] The attraction of the Froebel reading of Wright seems to lie in its provision of a direct, concrete source for his aesthetic, while avoiding the implausibility of the cubist parallel.

One final result of Giedion's influence and of the whole International style reevaluation of architecture led by his friend Walter Gropius was the dismissal of Chicago's monumental urbanism as merely a "transitory fact" of history. Edward Bennett's contract with the Chicago Plan Commission had been terminated in 1930, and after World War II there emerged such "urban renewal" schemes as that of the

South Side Planning Board, sketched out between 1945 and 1953 by Gropius himself in collaboration with his former pupil Reginald Isaacs, now established in Chicago.[24] Mies van der Rohe, of course, had been teaching in Chicago since 1938 at the Illinois Institute of Technology, together with the Berlin planner Ludwig Hilberseimer.

Into this pleased but puzzled aftermath of the neat formulations of *Space, Time and Architecture*, Vincent Scully emerged during the 1950s. He was not so quick as his contemporaries to give up Sullivan's ornament, Wright's sense of locality and symbolism, or Burnham's urban vision.[25] More important, he could see Sullivan and Wright not just as leaders of a provincial school, as had Lorch or Tallmadge; not just as typical contributors to a movement they themselves could not grasp, as did Giedion; but as truly great artists, self-contained and justified by their works. Sullivan he recognized as a humane classicist, a designer trying to perfect the articulation of the new steel-framed office tower in terms of empathetically expressive ornament. "He was the great, perhaps the only, humanist architect of the late nineteenth century, as he brought into the mass metropolis . . . a dignified image of human potency and force."[26] Scully was able to recognize and enjoy the symbolic power of Wright's designs and to understand their relation to their sites as more than sentimental or "picturesque." Neil Levine has greatly expanded on this in his own Wright research.[27] Scully could also accept Burnham as the architect of urban order. In a sense, Scully was correcting Giedion in the spirit of Lewis Mumford in his *Brown Decades* and even Hitchcock in his 1942 *In the Nature of Materials*. While they could not accept Sullivan's ornament or Wright's cinematic image-making, they could appreciate their sense of materials and locality.

During these same years, Colin Rowe proved the wishfulness of Giedion's equation of the "Chicago school" and the International style in "The Chicago Frame" and other essays, while William Jordy explored the "symbolic essence" of modern architecture, confronting Giedion's functional abstraction.[28]

More recently, several different aspects of Chicago architecture have come into focus through the efforts of scholars, many outside the immediate field. An awareness of the social significance of building and of architects has brought us to acknowledge that around 1900 Chicago produced a tightly organized professional community with distinct standards and procedures.[29] This in part responds to recent economic studies of real estate in the Loop, which have illuminated skyscraper construction from the perspective of profit and loss.[30] Researchers exploring the origins of corporate self-celebration—such as Alan Trachtenberg in *The Incorporation of America* (1982), Robert Rydell in *All the World's a Fair* (1984), and Stuart Culver's study of L. Frank Baum—have been led to the Columbian Exposition as one of the pivotal monuments of American culture, as well as to the Chicago Tribune Tower—John Mead Howells' and Raymond Hood's built design, not Gropius' competition project.[31] The so-called postmodern reevaluation of architectural expression has attracted designers and critics like Alan Greenberg to Burnham's simple classicism instead of Sullivan's and Wright's modernism. Feminism and the psychohistorical study of the heroes of twentieth-century culture have caused us to recognize the suburb as a cultural entity, particularly in Gwendolyn Wright's *Moralism and the Model Home* (1980). On the general plane there are Kenneth Jackson's *Crabgrass Frontier* (1985), Dolores Hayden's *Grand Domestic Revolution* (1985), and Robert Fishman's *Bourgeois Utopias* (1987).[32] For all the scholarship on Frank Lloyd Wright, it is Kenneth Lynn's *Hemingway* (1987) that explores Oak Park as a cultural force and brings forward such fundamental personalities as Dr. William E. and Bruce Barton, the former the leading clergyman of Oak Park in Wright's day, the latter a founder of Batton, Barton, Durstine, and Osborn and author of *The Man Nobody Knows* (1925).[33] Surprisingly we still lack any serious study of Wright's uncle, Rev. Jenkin Lloyd Jones,[34] tremendously active in Chicago social and intellectual causes and influential upon Wright.

The social historians have made important proposals. Claude Massu, in an attractive if simplified analysis, reads the "Chicago School" skyscrapers socially—as open, antihieratic, and democratically transparent. From this perspective he sees the crisis of the school around 1900 as a reflection of the rejection of pioneer openness and community before the onslaught of hieratic corporate capitalism abetted by Burnham and the East Coast aesthetes.[35]

In sum, we have come to think in terms of a Chicago culture rather than merely a "Chicago school of architecture."

Giedion formulated his ideas fifty years ago, in 1938. He was analyzing events fifty years before that, of around 1890. We stand today as far removed from Giedion as he did from the inception of the "Chicago school" and must see him in the same historical perspective in which he envisioned Sullivan, Burnham, and Wright.

On the practical plane, his impetus has failed: the public housing programs his friends Isaacs and Gropius outlined for Chicago have collapsed due to factors never acknowledged in *Space, Time and Architecture*, among them race. The example of another, more present hero, Mies van der Rohe, has likewise lost its force. The question today with fifty years' perspective is, how did we ever mistake things so dated for a universal panacea? What was the psychopathological history of the Modern Movement?[36]

But more than a critique of the projection of a "Chicago school of architecture," we need an effort toward a synthesis to replace it. Every generation has gotten the "Chicago school" it deserved—Pond and Lorch's, Giedion and Condit's, Scully and Rowe's—and we today need our own.

Recently, T. J. Jackson Lears has attempted a broader, if more worrisomely eclectic, synthesis in his *No Place of Grace* of 1981. Where Giedion tried to accept nineteenth-century mechanization, Lears frankly sees its dehumanization. Lears traces not accommodation, but disguise and rejection as America's reaction. He sets up consumerism and antimodernism

as responses paralleling avant-garde modernism, all of these seeking what Lears characterizes as heightened experiences of "authenticity," taking off from Philip Rieff's self-involved culture of the "therapeutic" or Christopher Lasch's "Culture of Narcissicism."[37]

This is a dreary vision, but a historical rather than a partisan one. It is too simple, as a comparison with the less cosmic but more focused analyses of Philip Fisher or Stuart Culver makes clear.[38] But this perspective begins to permit us to acknowledge in the case of Chicago architecture the centrality of the Columbian Exposition as the point where corporate culture switched emphasis from production to consumption and where the fantasy world of imaging and streamlining emerges that leads on to William Rainey Harper's University of Chicago as well as to Colonel McCormick's Chicago Tribune organization. It also makes us aware of the theatrical quality of progressivism as presented in Sullivan's Transportation Building at the Columbian Exposition and of the prophetic crusading engaged in by Wright in the suburbs and finally at Taliesin, East and West. The point in the study of Chicago architecture is not dichotomy—Sullivan "good," Burnham "bad"—but parallelism: that is, the story of human responses in the new American city of industrial organization to forces much larger than what any single architect could master. The point is not to consider whether Sullivan's romantic classicism was tighter than Burnham's or Burnham's conventional classicism more comprehensible, nor is it to elevate Wright as a cubist before the fact or to denigrate him as a kindergarten block builder. Instead, I think the point is to acknowledge the compensatory oblivion that visual imagery—both "progressive" and "conservative"—has come to inspire in American twentieth-century culture and to look beyond that to examine its significance.

NOTES

1. Sigfried Giedion, *Space, Time and Architecture: The Growth of a New Tradition* (Cambridge, Mass. 1941), with five later editions. See also Eduard Sekler, "Sigfried Giedion," in this volume. On European reactions generally, see Arnold Lewis, "Evaluations of American Architecture by European Critics, 1875–1900" (Ph.D. diss., University of Wisconsin, 1962). See also Paul Bourget, *Outre-Mer: notes sur l'Amérique* (Paris, 1894) and Paul Scheerbart, *Das graue Tuch und zehn Prozent weiss: ein Damenroman* (Berlin, 1914).

2. Giedion 1941, 381–393.

3. Giedion 1941, 413.

4. Giedion 1941, 436. Compare Linda Henderson, *The Fourth Dimension and Non-Euclidean Geometry in Modern Art* (Princeton, 1983), especially 355.

5. Henry-Russell Hitchcock, *Frank Lloyd Wright* (Paris, 1928); Hitchcock, *Modern Architecture: Romanticism and Reintegration* (New York, 1929); Hitchcock, Philip Johnson, Alfred Barr, and Lewis Mumford, *Modern Architecture* (New York, 1932) especially 29–30 and 37. Compare Philip Johnson, "Is Sullivan the Father of Functionalism?" *Art News* 85 (December 1956), 44–46, 56–57. See also Helen Searing, "Henry-Russell Hitchcock: The Architectural Historian as Critic and Connoisseur," in this volume.

6. Kenneth J. Conant, *Journal of Aesthetics and Art Criticism* 1 (Fall 1941), 128–129. See also the reviews by Henry-Russell Hitchcock, *Parnassus* 13 (May 1941), 179–180; Sir John Summerson, *Architectural Review* 91 (May 1942) 125–126; and Turpin Bannister, *Art Bulletin* 26 (June 1944), 134–138.

7. Hugh D. Duncan, *The Rise of Chicago as a Literary Center from 1885 to 1920: A Sociological Essay in American Culture* (Tatowa, N.J., 1964); Carl Smith, *Chicago and the American Literary Imagination, 1880–1920* (Chicago, 1984). This was especially true in the literary depictions of the Columbian Exposition: David Berg, *Chicago's White City of 1893* (Lexington, Ky., 1976).

8. Daniel H. Burnham and Edward H. Bennett, *Plan of Chicago* (Chicago, 1909); Joan Draper, *Edward H. Bennett: Architect and City Planner, 1874–1954* (Chicago, 1982).

9. "Jefferson National Expansion Memorial," *Architectural Record* 81 (March 1937), 34d; "Riverfront Reconstruction, St. Louis, Mo.," *Architectural Forum* 80 (April 1944), 111–116; "Jefferson Memorial Competition Winners," *Architectural Record* 103 (April 1948), 92–95. See Giedion 1941, 200–204.

10. Harry Desmond, "Modern Architecture—A Conversation," *Architectural Record* 1 (January–March 1892), 276–277. My analysis here is a slight revision of the current analysis of Sullivan, which I explain in my essay "Sullivan to 1890," in *Louis Sullivan: The Function of Ornament*, ed. Win de Wit (New York, 1986) 13–63, and in "Schooling the Prairie School: Wright's Early Style as a Communicable System," in *The Nature of Frank Lloyd Wright*, ed. Carol R. Bolon, Robert S. Nelson, and Linda Seidel (Chicago, 1988), 70–84.

11. Thomas Tallmadge, "The Chicago School," *Architectural Review* (Boston) 15 (April 1908), 69–76.

12. Irving K. Pond, "Autobiography," MS in the American Academy of Arts and Letters, New York; Pond, *The Meaning of Architecture: An Essay in Constructive Criticism* (Boston, 1918). Claude Bragdon, *More Lives than One* (New York, 1938); Bragdon, *Projective Ornament* (New York, 1915); Bragdon, "Letters from Louis Sullivan," *Architecture* 64 (July 1931), 7–10. Emil Lorch's papers are in the Bentley Historical Library, University of Michigan, Ann Arbor.

13. See Lorch's papers, Bentley Historical Library, University of Michigan. Also Narciso G. Menocal, "Frank Lloyd Wright and the Question of Style," *Journal of Decorative and Propaganda Arts* 2 (1986), 4–19.

14. Akademie der Künste zu Berlin, *Ausstellung neuer Amerikanischer Baukunst* (Berlin, 1926).

15. Fiske Kimball, *American Architecture* (Indianapolis, 1928); Kimball, "Louis Sullivan—An Old Master," *Architectural Record* 57 (April 1925), 289–304; Thomas E. Tallmadge, *The Story of Architecture in America* (New York, 1928). Tallmadge ends with Saarinen but does not depict him as Sullivanesque. See also Lauren S. Bricker, "The Writings of Fiske Kimball: A Synthesis of Architectural History and Practice," in this volume.

16. Lewis Mumford, *The Brown Decades: A Study of the Arts in America, 1865–1895* (New York, 1931), 113ff. Compare his earlier *Sticks and Stones: A Study of American Architecture and Civilization* (New York, 1924), especially 169–172. Hitchcock never speaks of Sullivan and Wright as part of a "Chicago School" in *Modern Architecture: Romanticism and Reintegration*. However, in 1933 the Museum of Modern Art in New York organized a traveling exhibition entitled "Early Modern Architecture: Chicago, 1870–1910." Hugh Morrison in his *Louis Sullivan: Prophet of Modern Architecture* (New York, 1935) cites the "Chicago School" only as the immediate Sullivan-Wright circle (270). See also Robert Wojtowicz, "Lewis Mumford: The Architectural Critic as Historian," in this volume.

17. Carl Condit, "The Chicago School and the Modern Movement in Architecture," *Art in America* 36 (Spring 1948), 19–36; Condit, *The Rise of the Skyscraper* (Chicago, 1952); Condit, *The Chicago School of Architecture: A History of Commercial and Public Building in the Chicago Area, 1875–1925* (Chicago, 1964). He will soon publish in collaboration with Sarah Landau a study of the origins of the skyscraper in New York.

18. Among Winston Weisman's numerous essays and articles see especially "Commercial Palaces of New York, 1845–1875," *Art Bulletin* 36 (December 1954), 285–302 and "A New View of Skyscraper History," in

The Rise of an American Architecture, ed. Edgar Kaufmann, Jr. (New York, 1970) 115–162.

19. The most recent study of the "balloon frame" question, summarizing earlier research, is Paul E. Sprague, "The Origin of Balloon Framing," *Journal of the Society of Architectural Historians* 40 (December 1981), 311–319. See also Daniel Boorstin, *The Americans: The National Experience* (New York, 1965), 148–152, with extensive bibliography.

20. David Gebhard, *The Work of Purcell and Elmslie, Architects* (Palos Park, Ill., 1965); Mark Peisch, *The Chicago School of Architecture: The Early Followers of Sullivan and Wright* (New York, 1964); H. Allen Brooks, *The Prairie School: Frank Lloyd Wright and his Midwest Contemporaries* (Toronto, 1972). Walter Burley Griffin has an extensive bibliography of his own due to his larger stature: James Birrell, *Walter Burley Griffin* (Brisbane, Australia, 1964); David Van Zanten, *Walter Burley Griffin: Selected Designs* (Palos Park, Ill., 1970); Donald Leslie Johnson, *The Architecture of Walter Burley Griffin* (South Melbourne, Australia, 1977); and Monash University, *Walter Burley Griffin, A Review* (Clayton, Australia, 1988).

21. Donald Hoffmann, *The Architecture of John Wellborn Root* (Baltimore, 1973); Thomas Hines, *Burnham of Chicago, Architect and Planner* (New York, 1974); Theodore Turak, *William Le Baron Jenney: A Pioneer of Modern Architecture* (Ann Arbor, Mich., 1987); and Thomas Schlereth, *Solon S. Beman*, forthcoming.

22. Morrison 1935; Willard Connely, *Louis Sullivan: The Shaping of American Architecture, A Biography* (New York, 1960); and Sherman Paul, *Louis Sullivan: An Architect in American Thought* (Englewood Cliffs, N.J., 1962). Hugh D. Duncan, *Culture and Democracy: The Struggle for Form in Society and Architecture in Chicago and the Middle West during the Life and Times of Louis H. Sullivan*, (Tatowa, N.J., 1965). This depiction of Sullivan as an idea and a story still informs more recent detailed studies: Narcisso Menocal, *Architecture as Nature: The Transcendentalist Idea of Louis Sullivan* (Madison, Wisc., 1981); David Andrew, *Louis Sullivan and the Polemics of Modern Architecture* (Chicago, 1985); and Robert Twombley, *Louis Sullivan: His Life and Work* (New York, 1986). This view of Sullivan also reflects Frank Lloyd Wright's depiction of his "Lieber Meister" in his *An Autobiography: Frank Lloyd Wright* (London and New York, 1932) and in his *Genius and the Mobocracy* (New York, 1949).

23. Robert C. Spencer, "The Work of Frank Lloyd Wright," *Architectural Review* (Boston) 7 (June 1900), 61–72; Wright 1932, 11–12; Grant Manson, "Wright in the Nursery, The Influence of Froebel Education on the Work of Frank Lloyd Wright," *Architectural Review* (June 1953), 349–351; Manson, *Frank Lloyd Wright to 1910: The First Golden Age* (New York, 1958), 6–7. Richard MacCormac, "The Anatomy of Wright's Aesthetic," *Architectural Review* (London) 143 (February 1968), 143–146; Joseph Connors, *The Robie House of Frank Lloyd Wright* (Chicago, 1984); Edgar Kaufmann, Jr., "'Form Becomes Feeling': A New

View of Froebel and Wright," *Journal of the Society of Architectural Historians* 40 (May 1981), 130–137; Kaufmann, "Frank Lloyd Wright's Mementos of Childhood," *Journal of the Society of Architectural Historians* 41 (October 1982), 232–237; Jeanne S. Rubin, "The Froebel-Wright Kindergarten Connection: A New Perspective," *Journal of the Society of Architectural Historians* 48 (March 1989), 24–37.

24. Reginald Isaacs, *Walter Gropius: der Mensch und sein Werk*, vol. 1, (Berlin, 1983–1984), 935–939. Walter Gropius et al., *An Opportunity for Private and Public Investment in Rebuilding Chicago* (Chicago, 1947).

25. Vincent Scully, Jr., "Louis Sullivan's Architectural Ornament: A Brief Note Concerning Humanist Design in the Age of Force," *Perspecta: The Yale Architectural Journal* 5 (1959), 73–80; "Modern Architecture," *College Art Journal* 17, (1958), 140–159; *Frank Lloyd Wright* (New York, 1960); *Modern Architecture: The Architecture of Democracy* (New York, 1961); and *American Architecture and Urbanism* (New York, 1969).

26. Scully 1961, 19.

27. Neil Levine, "Abstraction and Representation in Modern Architecture: The International Style of Frank Lloyd Wright," *AA Files* 11 (Spring 1986), 3–21; "Landscape into Architecture: Frank Lloyd Wright's Hollyhock House and the Romance of Southern California," *AA Files* 3 (January 1983), 22–41; "Frank Lloyd Wright's Diagonal Planning," *In Search of Modern Architecture: A Tribute to Henry-Russell Hitchcock*, ed. Helen Searing (Cambridge, Mass., 1982), 245–277; "Frank Lloyd Wright's Own Houses and His Changing Concept of Representation," in Bolon et al. 1988, 20–69. Compare Norris Kelly Smith, *Frank Lloyd Wright: A Study in Architectural Context* (Englewood Cliffs, N.J., 1966) and Leonard Eaton, *Two Chicago Architects and Their Clients: Frank Lloyd Wright and Howard Van Doren Shaw* (Cambridge, Mass., 1969).

28. Colin Rowe, "Chicago Frame," *Architectural Design* 40 (December 1970), 641–647. William H. Jordy, "The Symbolic Essence of Modern European Architecture of the Twenties and Its Continuing Influence," *Journal of the Society of Architectural Historians* 22 (October 1963), 177–187. See Jordy's subsequent *American Buildings and Their Architects*, vols. 3 and 4 (New York, 1970–1978) and "The Tall Buildings," in de Wit 1986, 65–164.

29. Sibel Bozdogan, "Towards Professional Legitimacy and Power; An Inquiry into the Struggle, Achievements and Dilemmas of the Architectural Profession through an Analysis of Chicago 1871–1909" (Ph.D. diss., University of Pennsylvania, 1982).

30. Gerald Larson in particular is pursing this ("The Iron Skeleton Frame: Interactions between Europe and the United States," in *Chicago Architecture, 1872–1922: Birth of a Metropolis*, ed. John Zukowsky [Munich and Chicago, 1987], 39–55). See Homer Hoyt, *One Hundred Years of Land Values in Chicago: The Relationship of the Growth of Chicago to the Rise in Its Land Values, 1830–1933* (Chicago, 1933),

and David Van Zanten, "The Nineteenth Century: The Projecting of Chicago as a Commercial City and the Rationalization of Design and Construction," in *Chicago and New York: Architectural Interactions*, ed. John Zukowsky (Chicago, 1984), 30–49.

31. Alan Trachtenberg, *The Incorporation of America: Culture and Society in the Gilded Age* (New York, 1982), especially chapter 7; Robert W. Rydell, *All the World's a Fair: Visions of Empire at American International Expositions, 1876–1916* (Chicago, 1984), especially chapter 2; and Stuart Culver, "What Mannikins Want: *The Wonderful World of Oz* and *The Art of Decorating Dry Goods Windows*," *Representations* 21 (Winter 1988), 97–116.

32. Gwendolyn Wright, *Moralism and the Model Home: Domestic Architecture and Cultural Conflict in Chicago, 1870–1913* (Chicago, 1980); "Architectural Practice and Social Vision in Wright's Early Designs," in Bolon et al. 1988, 98–124; Delores Hayden, *The Grand Domestic Revolution: A History of Feminist Designs for American Homes, Neighborhoods, and Cities* (Cambridge, Mass., 1981); Kenneth T. Jackson, *Crabgrass Frontier: The Suburbanization of the United States* (New York, 1985); and Robert Fishman, *Bourgeois Utopias: The Rise and Fall of Suburbia* (New York, 1987).

33. Kenneth S. Lynn, *Hemingway* (New York, 1987), 15–27. Bruce Barton, *The Man Nobody Knows: A Discovery of the Real Jesus* (New York, 1925).

34. A biography is promised by Thomas E. Graham.

35. Claude Massu, *L'Architecture de l'école de Chicago: architecture fonctionnaliste et idéologie americaine* (Paris, 1982), and Giorgio Ciucci, Francesco dal Co, Mario Manieri-Elia, and Manfredo Tafuri, *La Città americana dalla guerra civile al New Deal* (Rome, 1973).

36. The burst of anger at modern architecture of the last decade has still not produced carefully considered analysis. See Peter Blake, *Form Follows Fiasco: Why Modern Architecture Hasn't Worked* (Boston, 1977); Tom Wolfe, *From Bauhaus to Our House* (New York, 1981); and Klaus Herdeg, *The Decorated Diagram: Harvard Architecture and the Failure of the Bauhaus Legacy* (Cambridge, Mass., 1983).

37. T. J. Jackson Lears, *No Place of Grace: Antimodernism and the Transformation of American Culture, 1880–1920* (New York, 1981); Christopher Lasch, *The Culture of Narcissism: American Life in an Age of Diminishing Expectations* (New York, 1978); and Philip Rieff, *The Triumph of the Therapeutic: Uses of Faith after Freud* (New York, 1966).

38. Philip Fisher, "Democratic Social Space: Whitman, Melville, and the Promise of American Transparency," *Representations* 24 (Fall 1988), 60–101 and Culver 1988.

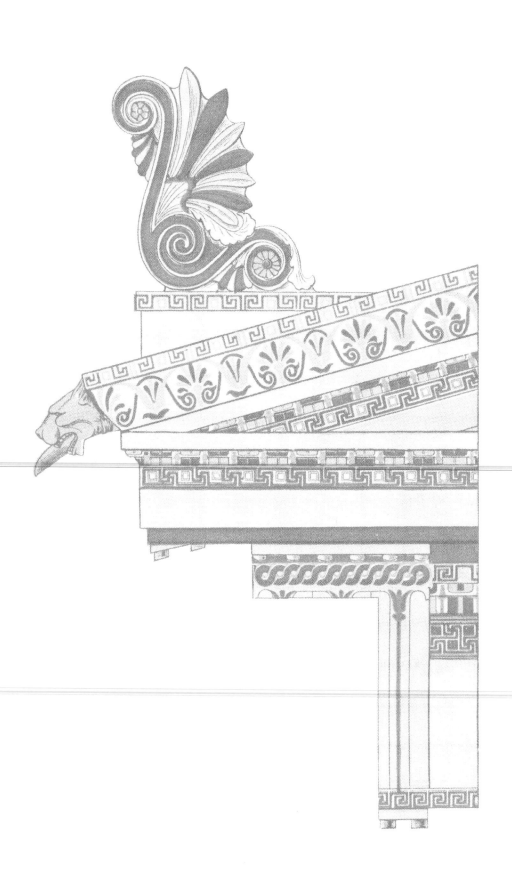

J. A. CHEWNING
University of Cincinnati

The Teaching of Architectural History during the Advent of Modernism, 1920s–1950s

The decades on either side of the year 1940—the year of the founding of the Society of Architectural Historians—were a time of recurrent reflection in architecture, as important figures, identified variously as traditionalists and modernists, passed from the scene. Obituaries of the 1930s and 1940s became occasions for muted polemics on the old and the new. The death of traditionalists, such as Cass Gilbert, John Russell Pope, Ralph Adams Cram, and Paul Cret, reminded many of the last attempts of eclecticism to accommodate itself to modern society. The passing of leaders of the Arts and Crafts movement, such as C. F. A. Voysey, C. R. Ashbee, and Edwin Lutyens, reminded others of the ideals of a union between art, craft, and modern life. The death of some of the pioneers of modernism, such as H. P. Berlage, Raymond Hood, Bruno Taut, Gunnar Asplund, Peter Behrens, Albert Kahn, and Laszlo Moholy-Nagy, reminded still others of the pluralism and the mortality of modernism itself.[1]

During the 1940s, schools of architecture felt the successive impacts of the lingering depression, the war, and the postwar recovery. Enrollments and faculties, which had grown slowly from a low point in the mid-1930s, fell sharply again as students and young instructors went into the service, then soared to unprecedented levels as the veterans returned to school.[2] In addition to responding to these disruptive fluctua-tions, schools were also trying to come to terms with shifts in curriculum from four-year to five-year programs and with shifts in architectural ideology from traditionalism to modernism. Both areas of change had implications for how history was taught, what history was taught, and when history was taught. Looking back over the decades before and after 1940, one sees a particularly widespread experimentation in schools of architecture in the years between 1935 and 1945. In the late 1930s a greater sense of confidence about economics, modernism, and standards for professional education gave new impetus to revision and innovation in the architectural curriculum. The war years, with reduced faculties and enrollments, brought an end to some of the experiments, but the deliberations continued even more insistently, as a way of maintaining hope for a postwar world and faith in the continuity of educational values.

This widespread interest during the 1930s, 1940s, and 1950s in revitalizing architectural education had several manifestations. One of these was the founding of the Society of Architectural Historians (SAH) by a group of educators, many of whom taught in schools of architecture.[3] During these decades, schools began to benefit from new organizations committed to standards and coordination of efforts, such as the National Architectural Accrediting

Board (established in 1940) and the American Institute of Architects' Department of Education and Research (established in 1946). New journals appeared for the exchange of ideas generated by research and teaching, such as the *Journal of the Society of Architectural Historians* (begun in 1941) and the *Journal of Architectural Education* (begun in 1947 as the official publication of the Association of Collegiate Schools of Architecture, or ACSA, which had been founded in 1912).[4]

In the spring of 1941, Leopold Arnaud, then president of the ACSA, proposed inviting SAH members to conduct a session at the next ACSA annual meeting on the role of architectural history in schools of architecture. SAH members who delivered papers at the session included outgoing president Turpin Bannister, then at Rensselaer Polytechnic Institute, who spoke on "The Contributions of Architectural History to the Development of the Modern Student-Architect"; Carroll Meeks of Yale, who discussed his recent survey of approaches to teaching history; and Henry-Russell Hitchcock, then at Wesleyan, who talked about the interpretation of modern architecture.[5]

This paper will examine the development of architectural history education, with emphasis on the decades from the 1920s through the 1950s as the period when the architectural profession, the architectural press, and architecture schools came to adopt modernism in its many varieties. Architectural history and modernism were not inherently opposed to each other. Indeed, many of the leading historians of fifty years ago were modernists in their attitudes toward architecture, history, and education. It is more reasonable to say that a growing awareness of modernism coincided with a growing awareness of the need for change in schools of architecture. Changes in the teaching of history were but one aspect of a larger transformation of architectural education. Issues to be considered in this paper are the training of teachers of history; the chronological coverage of history courses; the core and periphery of the history curriculum; the amount of time devoted to history; and changing views of the purpose and value of history.

Architectural Historians in Schools of Architecture

Well into the first half of the twentieth century, there were professors of architectural history whose sensibilities had been shaped by direct contact with William Robert Ware and Nathan Clifford Ricker, two of the pioneers of architectural education in America.[6] Students of Ware who went on to become influential historian-educators include Herbert Langford Warren, who taught at Harvard until 1917; A. D. F. Hamlin, who taught at Columbia until 1926; and Nathaniel C. Curtis, who taught at Tulane until the mid-1940s. Best known of the historian-educators trained by Ricker is Rexford Newcomb, who taught at Illinois until the late 1940s and served as the second president of the SAH. These men of the second generation of historian-educators had several things in common. First, as administrators of departments, schools, and colleges, they had an opportunity, like their mentors Ware and Ricker, to serve as advocates and coordinators for history in the overall curriculum. Second, as perennial lecturers on the history of architecture, they accomplished something their mentors had not. They all published textbooks and outlines that extended their impact on the teaching of history and theory well into the 1940s. And third, they themselves became mentors to still another generation of historian-educators.[7]

Most of the leaders in architectural education since the 1920s have had a multidisciplinary education. By the 1920s and 1930s, it was becoming less common for someone with only an undergraduate professional education to have regular responsibility for architectural history courses in a school of architecture.[8] Until the 1950s, but rarely after that, there were still a few teaching historians who had received their undergraduate preparation in arts and sciences, followed by an undergraduate professional degree but no more than that. Among these architect-historians with liberal educations were Leopold Arnaud, Nathaniel C. Curtis, Donald Drew Egbert, A. D. F. Hamlin, and Talbot F. Hamlin. Through the decades, relatively few people with only an undergraduate followed by a graduate professional degree have pursued careers as teaching historians. Joseph Hudnut was one of these. From the 1920s onward, most of the leading historians teaching in schools of architecture had done some postgraduate work in the history of art or architecture. Of these, the majority would continue to have a professional education in architecture. As early as the time of World War I and into the 1950s, some had undergraduate or graduate professional degrees followed by master's-level studies in art history. Among them were Alan Laing, Rexford Newcomb, and Buford Pickens. Individuals who held undergraduate or graduate professional degrees in architecture were also beginning to earn doctorates in art history. Noteworthy examples include Turpin Bannister, Kenneth Conant, Fiske Kimball, and Carroll Meeks. Finally, among the leading historians working as both teachers and critics, some had no professional training, only an undergraduate liberal arts degree followed by graduate studies in art history, such as Henry-Russell Hitchcock. Thus, since the 1920s, there has been a growing recognition of the importance of graduate work in the history of art and architecture for the teacher of these subjects in professional schools. This recognition has been both cause and effect of the interest historians have shown in formulating a cultural history of architecture grounded in the humanities as well as in professional studies.

Chronological Scope of the History Survey Course

The typical architectural history survey course from the 1890s well into the 1930s was divided according to the major eras and styles, with one year devoted to ancient through early medieval and a second year devoted to Gothic and Renaissance and post-Renaissance architecture. By the 1940s, some architectural historians active in the SAH were beginning to suggest that schools could make history both more complete and more immediate by devoting more time to the modern period, particularly the past two hundred years. Carroll Meeks conducted a survey in 1942 that showed that schools gave the period since

1750 widely varying emphasis. Meeks found that as little as six weeks in a typical four-semester survey course might be devoted to the past two hundred years, with eighteen weeks (or a little more than a semester) being about average.[9] Early leaders of the SAH were quick to point out that the textbooks of the first decades of the twentieth century were woefully obsolete.[10] While the leading historians took pride in supporting the development of the Pelican History of Art series through the next three decades, not until the 1980s did still another generation of historians finally develop the much-needed history survey texts. To fill the void in the meantime, teaching historians had to make uneasy pedagogic choices among the successive editions of Talbot Hamlin's *Architecture through the Ages* (1940), Sigfried Giedion's *Space, Time and Architecture* (1941), Nikolaus Pevsner's *Outline of European Architecture* (1943), and the old standard, Banister Fletcher's *History of Architecture*.[11]

As an alternative to the chronological approach during the late 1930s and early 1940s, the typological approach was sometimes tried. In 1942, about one-third of the twenty schools responding to a questionnaire about their history courses indicated that their surveys were organized according to building type.[12] Shortly after the arrival of Mies van der Rohe at Armour (later Illinois) Institute of Technology, for instance, the standard period survey was replaced in 1939–1940 by a survey of selected building types. A yearlong course on "the historical development of the human habitation and its expression in domestic architecture" was followed by a yearlong course on "the influence of material and construction on the form of public and ecclesiastical buildings and their historical development."[13]

The most ambitious nonchronological approach to history was at Yale during the early 1940s, when the typological approach affected the entire curriculum. Under the "Yale Plan," the whole department would spend five or six weeks (about one-third of a semester) on a single building type. The work in all courses, including design, history, construction, mechanical systems, and city planning, would be coordinated, so that by the end of the allotted period "each student and each faculty member is saturated with a profound comprehension of all the aspects of the problem studied" and for the curriculum, there is a noticeable "gain in coherence and efficiency."[14]

Most historians, however, remained committed to the chronological approach. Through their teaching and research, some began to take a real interest during the 1930s and 1940s in exploring the origins of contemporary architecture in the eighteenth and nineteenth centuries. Courses variously called the philosophy or history of modern or contemporary architecture began to appear in the schools, offering graduate students and upper-level undergraduates the opportunity to engage in more demanding research and discussions, often in a seminar setting. In these culminating courses of the history curriculum, the interrelationships among a variety of subjects, including the history of the design fields and the other visual arts, the theory of architecture, and intellectual and cultural history, finally became visible.[15]

Relation of Architectural History to Other Subjects

The subject matter of architectural history in schools of architecture can be divided between a core of courses on the history of the visual arts and a periphery of courses in which references are made to architectural history, such as architectural design and theory. The core history subjects through the decades have been the history of architecture and the history of art (i.e., the other visual arts). The history of painting and sculpture has seldom been ignored entirely. The subject has, from time to time, been incorporated with the history of architecture in one comprehensive survey of the visual arts. By mid-century, history of art courses were becoming either introductions to the visual arts offered before the history of architecture survey or upper-level cultural analysis courses following the history of architecture survey. As the profession of architecture during the 1930s became less concerned with decorative detail, the history of ornament faded

in importance as a core history subject. As the profession became more concerned during the 1940s and 1950s with social context, the history of planning became more prominent as a core history subject.[16]

From the standpoint of architectural history, architectural design and theory have constituted a periphery of courses in which the attention to historical architecture has varied widely from decade to decade and from school to school. Toward the beginning of the century, the historical sensibility provided much of the discipline and the inspiration in the design studio. By mid-century, the bond between history and design had weakened considerably, as studio projects calling for the use of specific historical vocabularies were becoming a rarity. Architectural theory has had the most complex relation to the core history courses and the courses in architectural design. Toward the beginning of the century, theory, like history, existed to serve design. By mid-century, the design-theory linkage was still present, but another linkage, between theory and cultural history, had begun to form. Courses concerned with interpreting the history of architecture—in fact, all the visual arts—as an expression of civilization began to be regarded more as theory than as history courses.

Several examples will serve to illustrate the more innovative approaches to coordinating core and peripheral subjects. While the enthusiasm for the new cultural history of architecture became widespread during the 1940s, attempts at integrating the history of architecture, the history of art, and the history of civilization can be found even earlier. At the Massachusetts Institute of Technology, from the first decade of the century until the 1940s, the approach was to teach a series of "European Civilization and Art" courses in the upper years, following a two- to four-semester survey of the history of architecture in the lower years. The "Civilization and Art" courses occupied six semesters and counted for about 60 percent of a student's exposure to history in the broadest sense, including the architectural history survey taken first. The emphasis was on literature, sculpture, and painting, with some consideration also given to philosophy and the history of science.

An appreciation of the unities within the culture of an era, including architecture, the other fine arts, and literature, could also be encouraged by structuring a sequence of parallel courses on successive eras in the history of civilization. The University of Cincinnati was unique in sustaining such an approach from the founding of its architecture program in the 1920s well into the 1960s. A yearlong course in the arts of a historical era was taught concurrently with a yearlong course in the history of that era and a yearlong course in the literature of that era. Over a period of three years, a student was exposed to a comprehensive survey of "Ancient and Early Medieval Civilization," followed by "Later Medieval and Renaissance," followed by "Post-Renaissance and Contemporary." To assure coordination among these courses, the art history and even literature instructors all taught within the School (later College) of Applied Arts (now Design, Architecture, Art, and Planning). The system did make the study of art, history, and literature more integral to the curriculum. From an administrative point of view, however, the independent existence of humanities instructors in a college of design raised questions of redundancy and accountability. While other departments in the college maintained the multiyear sequence of three parallel courses through the 1950s, the architecture department accepted the full coordination only in the freshman year and in 1943–1944 developed its own courses in "Architectural Analysis" for second- and third-year students. These courses were described as "an analytical study of architecture of selected historical periods in relation to human requirements, resources, and motivation." By the early 1960s, these courses had evolved into a two-year survey of the "History of Architecture and City Planning"— among the first courses in the country to acknowledge this affiliation.[17]

Amount of Time Devoted to Architectural History

The spirit of history was undeniably present in much of the architectural curriculum for the first four decades of the twentieth century. Many students and instructors would have conceded readily that history was inherently the subject of the design and drawing studios and even the courses in architectural theory. Today we need to remind ourselves that it was not architectural history as such that was discredited in architectural education at midcentury, but the too-casual use of history, particularly in the design studio. If we look at the total presence of history in the curriculum—both the core of history courses and the accessory uses of history in the studio—we see that the amount of time devoted to history in all its manifestations did decline in the 1930s, as historicism lost its hold on architecture and architectural education. What happened to the core of courses explicitly concerned with the history of the visual arts is still being examined. A look at survey data from the files of the ACSA confirms that, at least through the early 1930s, there was no significant overall decline in the average amount of time spent on the core history subjects. Comparable sets of data for a large sample of schools have yet to be assembled for that critical period beginning in the 1930s.[18]

More informative than such survey data, in which schools emphasizing fine arts are averaged together with schools emphasizing architectural engineering, are the profiles on individual schools. I have done a more detailed survey of curricula in sixteen schools of architecture associated with the leading historians of the period from the 1920s to the 1950s, with the intention of examining their impact on history curricula wherever they taught.[19] This smaller sample admittedly has a bias toward history. For the broader purposes of this study, however, this selection of schools has the advantage of allowing us to follow the fortunes of history in curricula where this subject has had an acknowledged importance, across many decades or for a shorter span of time associated with a particular educator. My findings for the average amount of time devoted to history in these schools are still tentative, but it appears that the core history courses amounted to 10.8 percent of the professional curriculum in 1920–1921, 11.9 percent in 1930–1931, 9.0 percent in 1940–1941, 9.1 percent in 1950–1951, and 8.8 percent in 1960–1961.

The closer study of this smaller sample of schools has led to three conclusions. First, the percentage of time devoted to history within any one school remained fairly constant. If not much history was taught at the end of our time period, then we can look back through the decades and see that not much history was being taught at the beginning. Second, the percentages of time spent on design and construction fluctuated more widely from decade to decade than the percentages for history, undoubtedly because in these areas of the curriculum, not in history, schools carried out revisions that were expressive of fundamental shifts in philosophy.[20] Third, there have been important changes in approach within the history part of the curriculum that are qualitative, not quantitative. These changes of approach have generally involved an exploration of the relations between history and theory and other subjects within the specifically architectural curriculum, as well as an exploration of the relations between architectural history and the history of civilization within the wider general studies curriculum.

Changing Attitudes Toward Architectural History

The question of the importance of architectural history in the professional curriculum ultimately goes beyond the questions of who taught history, what time periods were emphasized, how much history was taught in a core of explicitly historical courses and in a periphery of other courses, and how much time was allowed for these core courses. Educators of fifty years ago were keenly interested in the fundamental question: What approach does one take toward history? This question, in turn, provoked others: When is the most opportune time in the curriculum to teach history? Why is history valuable to the student of architecture?

The dilemma of the teacher of architectural history in the twentieth century has been the selection of an approach or point of view. If one is committed to an internal history of architectural form, can this be more than a history of styles? If one is committed to an external, contextual history of architecture, can this be more than a history of civilization, in which the architecture is explained as characteristic or expressive of a succession of periods and cultures? Certainly the trend in architectural history teaching and research in this century has been toward a more inclusive contextual history, in which the core of a distinctively architectural history has become as large as our perception of the activities of conceiving and constructing buildings and environments.

Justifications for the teaching of architectural history during the 1930s and 1940s placed less emphasis on precedent as a source of forms for design and more emphasis on precedent as a source of problems relating design to other aspects of culture. Catalogue descriptions of history survey courses are one indication of this trend. Particularly informative is the case of four decades of history teaching at Armour Institute of Technology (which became IIT in 1940). Descriptions of the four-semester course called "History of Architecture and Research Work," taught by Thomas E. Tallmadge into the mid-1920s, are typical of history courses of this period in several ways. First and foremost, there was an emphasis on style. Second, there was a close association between the history of architecture and the history of ornament. Third, there was an acknowledged but weakly articulated relation between architectural and general history. And fourth, there was coordination between the history lecturer and the studio instructor. Descriptions of the second-year architectural design course at Armour Institute indicate that the coordination worked both ways. In conjunction with their studio projects, students were expected to do a series of historical readings and to attend public lectures and exhibitions in Chicago.[21]

During the 1930s, the history courses at Armour were still being taught with an emphasis on style and drawing. Ornament had faded from prominence, and a more vivid background of cultural context was being highlighted in order "to present architecture in its true light as the resultant of a given time and place, and in its relation to the history of the people whose deeds it records."[22] One of the most resounding statements concerning the contextual, critical, theoretical history that would become the ideal of the 1940s and 1950s can be found in the introduction to the new architecture curriculum prepared by Mies van der Rohe, who directed the program at Armour/IIT from 1938 to 1958:

In conjunction with the curriculum there is a clarification of the cultural situation today so that the student may learn to recognize the sustaining and compelling forces of his times, and to comprehend the intellectual and spiritual environment in which he lives. The material, intellectual and cultural aspects of our era are explored to see wherein they are similar to those of former epochs and wherein they differ from them. The buildings of the past are studied so that the student will acquire from their significance and greatness a sense for genuine architectural values, and because their dependence upon a specific historical situation must awaken in him an understanding for the necessity of his own architectural achievement.[23]

Thoughtful architectural historians in the 1940s and 1950s hoped that the student could be introduced to the intellectual, social, economic, and technological context in which a building of the past was created and thus better appreciate that building as a design solution in the context of its time. Carroll Meeks, historian and design professor at Yale, speaking in 1942, represented the point of view that a broadly contextual history should make possible something far more vital than a history of styles and periods:

The concept of style is stifling most teachers' imagination. It was a superficial thing and led to a misplaced emphasis on orders and ornament. The reality was overlooked. For instance, the plans found in most books ignore the drains and pipes; poché conceals intricate structural systems. No effort is made to determine the original functions of the interior spaces, or to relate them with the furniture that made them usable, or the habits of life that called them into being.[24]

During the late 1930s and early 1940s, there was an increasing amount of discussion concerning the most opportune timing and sequencing of the courses that made up the chronological history survey. Whatever changes were implemented during these years were in response to fundamental concerns about the way in which history functioned in a curriculum increasingly committed to modernism in a wide range of professional courses. First, there was the perennial problem of not getting around to recent developments until the last week of the typical survey course. Second, there was the assertion that beginning students are better able to grasp ideas based on contemporary architecture than on architecture of the more distant past. Finally, there was the corresponding assertion that students should *not* be exposed to history early in their studies, either because they are better able to deal with it later, or because too early an exposure might stifle their creativity.

Turpin Bannister, then professor of architectural history and other subjects at RPI, spoke at the ACSA meeting in 1942 in favor of easing into history from the present:

The introducing of students to principles by means of history alone involves the danger that they might not grasp fully the difference between a specific historical application of a principle, and the principle, as origin and truth, as active today as in ages past. To guard against any such confusion, it is strongly urged that a general introductory survey of contemporary architecture be given early enough to encourage the formation of a positive, even if tentative, point of view which can serve both as a background for early problems in design and a vital frame of reference when history is undertaken.[25]

Speaking at the ACSA meeting in 1948, Dean Leopold Arnaud of Columbia, who had started on the faculty there teaching history in the late 1920s, sounded even more passionate on the imperative of the present:

The student should begin his studies with a survey of architecture in its fullest sense: building as an art, a science and a social expression. He should, therefore, see what is being done today, for he will understand the present better than the past. Contemporary needs and problems should be analyzed, modern methods and materials should be investigated in all their potential applications; and the important relation of engineering to architecture should be seriously studied. Only after the general introduction through current history should the student begin the study of the past.[26]

Three compromise solutions responded to the issue of the students' analytical maturity. One was to postpone the entire history of architecture survey until the upper years. The second solution was to offer a more compact chronological survey course early in the curriculum, followed by a more analytic history-theory course or sequence of courses in the upper years. The third solution (really a variant of the second) was to offer a compact introductory survey, followed by history and theory electives in the upper years.[27]

Beginning with Turpin Bannister's first exposition of the reasons for teaching architectural history in his talk at the 1942 ACSA meeting, a great deal of thought has been given to the value of history in the education of the modern architect. While the lists offered by educators have varied, almost all of them have contained these basic ideas:

• First, the study of architectural history helps to sharpen a student's critical ability. Specifically, the study of history is the best way of counteracting either the complacency or the conviction that the recent past has a greater importance than the rest of the past.

• Second, the study of history allows the student of today to identify with the problem-solvers in architecture of the past and to have a better sense of his or her own professional heritage.

• Third, the study of history liberates rather than inhibits the imagination, particularly the "spatial imagination," and shows the importance of the "quest for meaning" in architecture, beyond the resolution of programmatic and structural requirements.

• Fourth, the study of architectural history helps to promote an attitude of scholarly curiosity and the willingness to take an interest in

a subject in itself, without regard for where it might lead.[28]

With the first and second reasons, the apologists for history answered a challenge that was more generally felt than articulated by the academic modernists of the 1930s and 1940s, who still were driven by the manifestos of the early twentieth century. This was the contention that, if historicist architecture was irrelevant in modern society, then the architectural history that had supported historicism was also irrelevant and unnecessary. With the third reason, the apologists for history answered the most often repeated challenge of the modernists (including Walter Gropius), that history, especially if taught too early, limits the imaginative freedom of students by placing before them precedents they are too likely to mimic without understanding. With the fourth and final reason, the apologists for history in an age of modernism chose simply to stand by the belief that the most enduring justifications for architectural history are the least pragmatic ones. This position shifts the burden of finding relevance from the teacher to the student and is consistent with attitudes present in twentieth-century psychologies and philosophies of education.

From the time of the founding of the SAH in 1940, architectural historians have generally managed to respond to those skeptical of the value of history without appearing to be on the defensive. Whenever justifications have been offered, these have provided history teachers the opportunity to clarify their own pedagogical assumptions as much as to maintain the already modest position of history in a crowded curriculum. The discipline of architectural history has been enriched during the past fifty years by the thought that historians have given to understanding the nature and scope of this subject. Architectural education has been enriched, as well, by the ever-widening awareness that historians have shown of everything that constitutes the activity of architecture.

NOTES

1. Gilbert died in 1934, Pope in 1937, Cram in 1942, Cret in 1945. Voysey died in 1941, Ashbee in 1942, Lutyens in 1944. Berlage and Hood died in 1934, Taut in 1938, Asplund and Behrens in 1940, Kahn in 1942, Moholy-Nagy in 1946.

2. Total enrollments in architecture reached a low point of 3,151 in 1935–1936 and another of 1,382 in 1943–1944. They leveled off at about 11,400 between 1947–1948 and 1950–1951. Figures are taken from *The Architect at Mid-Century: Evolution and Achievement*, ed. Turpin C. Bannister (New York, 1954), table 56.

3. Articles on the history of the society appear in the March 1990 issue of the *Journal of the Society of Architectural Historians.*

4. Educators also gained an appreciation for the contemporary and historical context of their concerns from such comprehensive studies as Francke Huntington Bosworth, Jr., and Roy Childs Jones, *A Study of Architectural Schools* (New York, 1932), for the ACSA and the Carnegie Corporation; Arthur Clason Weatherhead, *The History of Collegiate Education in Architecture in the United States* (Los Angeles, 1941); *The Architect at Mid-Century: Conversations across the Nation*, ed. Francis R. Bellamy (New York, 1954); and Bannister 1954. The Bannister and Bellamy reports were prepared for the AIA's Department of Education and Research.

5. Papers from the SAH session at the ACSA meeting in Detroit in June 1942 were printed in the *Journal of the [American] Society of Architectural Historians* 2 (April 1942).

6. Ware taught at MIT from 1868 to 1881 and at Columbia from 1881 to 1903. Ricker taught at the University of Illinois from 1873 until 1916.

7. Hamlin published *A Text-Book of the History of Architecture* (New York, 1896), the first American textbook on the subject. His *History of Ornament* was published in two volumes (New York, 1916 and 1923). Warren's *Foundations of Classic Architecture* was published posthumously (New York, 1919), with an introduction by his student Fiske Kimball. Curtis first published his theory text, *Architectural Composition*, in 1923. Newcomb was the most prolific and original scholar of the group, writing 18 books and about 250 articles, mostly on American regional topics. His "Outlines of the History of Architecture" (1922–1939) were the privately printed syllabi for his courses at Illinois. Among Hamlin's students at Columbia were his son Talbot Hamlin, Joseph Hudnut, Turpin Bannister, and possibly Leopold Arnaud. Among Warren's students at Harvard were Fiske Kimball and Kenneth Conant. Among Curtis' students at Tulane was Bernard Lemann. Among Newcomb's students at Illinois were Harley McKee and Buford Pickens.

8. Early in the century, John Galen Howard, Thomas Eddy Tallmadge, and Herbert Langford Warren were typical of this group of architect-historians. In this discussion I am including only individuals born before 1910.

9. Carroll L. V. Meeks, "The Teacher of Architectural History in the Professional School: His Training and Technique," *Journal of the [American] Society of Architectural Historians* 2 (April 1942), 14–23, 17.

10. Meeks 1942, 19. The four most commonly used textbooks until the 1940s were Hamlin 1896; Banister F. Fletcher, *History of Architecture for the Student, Craftsman, and Amateur . . .* (London, 1896); Frederick Moore Simpson, *A History of Architectural Development* (London and New York, 1905–1911); and Fiske Kimball and George Harold Edgell, *A History of Architecture* (New York and London, 1918). These texts, as well as those from mid-century, appeared in numerous revised editions. Comparative data for the coverage of various periods will be presented in my expanded study of architectural history education in the twentieth century.

11. Sigfried Giedion's *Space, Time and Architecture: The Growth of a New Tradition* devoted 70 to 80 percent of its coverage to the nineteenth and twentieth centuries. As Eduard Sekler has shown elsewhere in this volume, Giedion's book was probably the most influential book on the history of architecture for a whole generation of students, from the 1940s through the 1970s.

12. Meeks 1942, 17–18.

13. Armour Institute of Technology catalogue for 1940–1941, 54, 56.

14. The curriculum is described in Carroll L. V. Meeks, "Training and Technique of the Teacher of the History of Architecture" (Unpublished transcript of the 29th ACSA Annual Meeting, Detroit, June 1942, in *ACSA Minutes*, vol. 5; copy at ACSA headquarters, Washington, D.C.).

15. Among the earliest courses on contemporary architecture were those taught by George Edgell and Kenneth Conant at Harvard during the early 1930s. Joseph Hudnut took responsibility for these courses between the time of his arrival at Harvard in 1936 and the early 1940s. Other early ventures into contemporary architecture were the fifth-year seminar on the philosophy/history of modern architecture, taught by Marion Dean Ross at Tulane for about six years beginning in 1937–1938; the graduate seminar on contemporary architecture taught by Ralph Winslow and Turpin Bannister at RPI from about 1940–1941 to 1943–1944; and the similar course introduced by Bannister at Auburn after the war. According to catalogue descriptions, these courses involved broadly integrated discussions of design and contemporary culture.

16. Other subjects with variable importance in the historical core include the history of landscape architecture, the history of interiors, the history of decorative arts, the history of industrial design, and the history of technology.

17. University of Cincinnati catalogue for 1930–1931, 294, 296; catalogue for 1950–1951, 42.

18. In 1898, a survey of nine of the thirteen schools showed that history amounted on the average to 9.1 percent of the time spent on architectural courses. In 1913, a survey of twenty-five of the thirty-three schools showed the percentage for history down a little, at 7.5 percent of the time spent on architectural courses. In 1929, a survey of twenty-five of the fifty-five schools showed that history now amounted to an average of 12.3 percent of the professional curriculum. The official Bosworth-Jones study (see note 4) of forty-nine of fifty-eight schools, conducted during 1930–1931, found a slightly lower figure for history, about 9 percent. In 1943, an ACSA survey of thirty-two of the sixty-three schools grouped history with an odd assortment of subjects and found that these constituted 13.3 percent of the professional curriculum, yet this figure tells us very little.

19. These are the historians who published numerous books and articles on scholarly and pedagogical subjects. The sixteen schools are Auburn University (formerly Alabama Polytechnic Institute), University of California at Berkeley, University of Cincinnati, Columbia University, Cornell University, University of Florida, Harvard University, Illinois Institute of Technology (formerly Armour Institute of Technology), University of Illinois at Champaign-Urbana, Massachusetts Institute of Technology, University of Pennsylvania, Princeton University, Rensselaer Polytechnic Institute, Tulane University, University of Virginia, and Yale University. Except for Columbia, Harvard, Penn, Princeton, and Yale, college catalogues containing course descriptions and curriculum requirements have been published almost yearly. A sampling of these catalogues has been examined for the decade intervals 1920–1921, 1930–1931, 1940–1941, 1950–1951, 1960–1961, and 1970–1971, as well as for most of the years when one of the historians featured in this study was teaching at the school. In addition to the further research being done on the five Ivy League schools, nine schools are being added to the larger study: Carnegie-Mellon University, Cranbrook Academy, Georgia Institute of Technology, University of Michigan, University of Minnesota, University of Oregon, Syracuse University, University of Texas, and Washington University.

20. The amount of time devoted to history in individual schools rarely fluctuated from decade to decade below 8 percent or above 12 percent of the curriculum. The amount of time devoted to design in individual schools fluctuated from decade to decade in a range between 30 and 60 percent of the curriculum. The amount of time devoted to construction and practice fluctuated in a range between 15 and 35 percent of the curriculum.

21. Tallmadge taught the history of architecture from 1908 until 1926. The course description is found in the Armour Institute of Technology catalogue for 1920–1921, 105.

22. Report of Earl H. Reed, head of the Department of Architecture, to John Holabird, chair of a visiting committee of architects organized by the president of Armour, Willard Hotchkiss. Reed's report is dated December 19, 1935. I am grateful to Kevin Harrington for bringing this reference to my attention.

23. This version of the statement is taken from the Armour catalogue for 1940–1941, 47. About 1942, the center of gravity of history shifted to the upper years, to the four-semester sequence called "Analysis of Art" (later "History and Analysis of Art"). The course description for this sequence, which grew out of the senior-year Architectural Theory course of 1939–1942, reads like an abstract of Giedion's *Space, Time and Architecture:* "Growth and significance of Architecture, representing the artistic and spiritual efforts of a specific civilization. Development of architectural space concepts, corresponding to the development of the means of architectural construction. Architecture as the expression of original unity of construction and form. Interdependence of Architecture, Sculpture, and Painting. History of the Arts as an experience in aesthetic appreciation and judgment." IIT undergraduate catalogue for 1949–1950, 78.

24. Meeks 1942, 21. See also Carroll L. V. Meeks, "The New History of Architecture" *Journal of the [American] Society of Architectural Historians* 2 (January 1942), 3–7, and the response by John Coolidge, "Preliminary Steps towards 'The New History of Architecture,' " *Journal of the [American] Society of Architectural Historians* 3 (July 1943), 3–11.

25. Turpin C. Bannister, "The Contributions of Architectural History to the Development of the Modern Student-Architect," *Journal of the [American] Society of Architectural Historians* 2 (April 1942), 5–13, 11.

26. Leopold Arnaud, "History and Architecture," *AIA Journal* 10 (October 1948), 149–154, 153; also published as "History of Architecture," *Journal of Architectural Education* 3 (Fall 1948), 59–66.

27. The idea of a progressive sequence of architectural history courses, beginning with a survey course and culminating in a variety of topical elective courses, did not become common until the 1960s. As early as the 1930s, however, some individual elective courses were available. These courses typically dealt with a specific building type, an allied design field, non-Western architecture, American architecture (especially regional or nineteenth-century), or contemporary architecture.

28. I have synthesized these four reasons from ones articulated by Bannister and others during the 1940s and 1950s. The third point is derived from the articles by Sigfried Giedion and Alan Gowans in the *Journal of Architectural Education* 12 (Summer 1957), a special architectural history issue. Bannister would refine his own 1942 list of justifications in an address to the southeast regional meeting of ACSA schools in 1948–1949. See "The Functions of Architectural History in the Education of Modern Architects," *Journal of Architectural Education* 4 (Winter 1949), 23–30. This listing, with a few modifications, became part of his discussion of architectural history in his 1954 *Architect at Mid-Century* report, 173.

MICHAEL W. BROOKS
West Chester University

New England Gothic:

Charles Eliot Norton, Charles H. Moore, and Henry Adams

Americans began to write scholarly works on Gothic architecture in the 1870s. Since they came late to the subject, it is not surprising that their first books and articles developed ideas already current in England and France. Charles Eliot Norton adapted John Ruskin's views on the morality of art; Charles H. Moore developed the functionalist theories of Eugène Emmanuel Viollet-le-Duc; and Henry Adams drew on both Ruskin and Viollet-le-Duc. But these men did not merely adopt the ideas of others, nor did they study medieval architecture in a vacuum. A.W.N. Pugin and Ruskin had shown that a love of Gothic architecture led inevitably to a study of the relation between architecture and the society that produced it and then to a corrosive critique of the spiritual failings of the nineteenth century. In the same spirit, Norton, Moore, and Adams used architectural history to explore their anxieties about America's Gilded Age. They studied St. Denis and Chartres because they were appalled by Boston and New York. They shared the Victorian hope that the past would help resolve the crisis of the present, and they used architectural history to preach a mission for the educated mind in an age of industrial turbulence and mass democracy.

Charles Eliot Norton (fig. 1) was John Ruskin's friend, disciple, and eventually his executor.[1] He was also, Henry James

said, a man who conducted "a great and arduous mission" against the materialistic tendencies of American life.[2] Norton's sense of social purpose, moreover, preceded by some years both his devotion to Ruskin and his interest in architecture.

Norton's first book, *Considerations on Some Recent Social Theories* (1853) was a response to the radical theories of popular sovereignty made glamorous by the revolutionary wave of 1848. It revealed a social outlook that is at once democratic and elitist. It was democratic in its assumption that "liberty depends not on forms, but on the personal character of the individuals who compose them, that it rests on the virtue, the power of self-government, of each one of the people."[3] It was elitist in that one essential mark of a virtuous people was the ability to look to the few for enlightened leadership. Members of Norton's family had played leading roles in New England society since the 1630s. His father, Andrews Norton, had been the Dexter Professor of Sacred Literature at Harvard Divinity School and a leading figure in the Unitarian church. All the Nortons belonged to a class that rested its claim to authority on sound learning and moral probity.

In Charles Eliot's view, this class was in a state of crisis. Its cultural authority was weakened from within by its neglect of the aesthetic aspects of life. It was threatened from below by immigration and the growth of large cities. It was menaced from above by a new ruling class of flamboyant, tasteless millionaires.

Norton sought ways to respond to all three challenges. He spread the gospel of beauty by writing for the *Crayon* on art and architecture of Italy and by keeping readers of the *Atlantic Monthly* informed about the pleasures of the Oxford Museum and the 1857 Manchester Art Exhibition. He tried to meet the challenge from the working classes by supporting night schools, model housing for the poor, and, less attractively, by expressing sympathy for the Know-Nothing Party.

But while the rowdy democracy of the working classes was troublesome, the newly wealthy posed the most difficult challenge. E. L. Godkin, Norton's admired friend and editor of the *Nation*, described the problem with characteristic bluntness: "Who knows how to be rich in America? Plenty of people know how to get money; but . . . to be rich properly is, indeed, a fine art. It requires culture, imagination, and character." America's new rulers seemed to have none of these things, and yet they were overrunning the globe. Godkin recalled that "Norton and I used at one time to have such gloomy talks over the future of modern society late at night in his library that the story got about Cambridge that the dogs used to howl in sympathy with us."[4]

Norton was thus profoundly anxious about the future of culture in American democracy. Ruskin helped him turn those anxieties to positive use. The two men first met in 1855 when Norton called at Ruskin's London home with a letter of introduction from the art collector James Jackson Jarves. They met again in Europe the following year and began a friendship that lasted—allowing for a period of strain during the Civil War—until Ruskin's death in 1900.

Ruskin was never an admirer of American democracy. His social views united a radical protest against industrialism with a paradoxical Toryism. But Ruskin did provide Norton with certain key ideas that helped Norton orient himself within the cultural crisis of the nineteenth century.

1. Charles Eliot Norton (1827–1908)
Courtesy of the Harvard University Archives

Ruskin's belief that the splendor of medieval architecture testified to the moral greatness of those who built it was profoundly liberating to Norton, though he felt the need to restate it in American terms. The medieval cathedrals, Norton decided, represented "the prevalence of the democratic element in society," but, unlike the democracy of his time, it was redeemed by moral virtue and common civic purpose.[5]

Norton therefore became an admirer of the Catholic Middle Ages. Not that he could ever completely surrender to medieval enthusiasms. Nineteenth-century Protestants always felt anxiety before the power of the medieval church and the worship of the Virgin Mary. Norton, a Calvinist by descent, a Unitarian by birth, and an agnostic by inclination, held Catholic fervor at arm's length. He worried that the men who built medieval cathedrals were moved by the fear of hell rather than any positive religious vision. He regarded the miracles of the carts, in which the pious townsmen who dragged building stone to Chartres were cured of deafness, blindness, and paralysis, as primarily psychological phenomena susceptible to rational explanation: "The enthusiasm of the moment, the nervous tension, the excitement of the imagination, the confident expectation of miraculous intervention, the perfect faith in the power of the agency invoked to accomplish the desired end—all furnish an effective combination of the conditions most favorable to what is not ill termed the 'mind cure.' "[6] Medieval carvings of the torments of the damned reminded him unpleasantly of the terrifying descriptions of Hell in the sermons of Jonathan Edwards.

Nevertheless, Norton used the medieval cathedrals as a standard by which to judge the moral weaknesses of his age. "We are," he lamented, "incompetent to execute and indifferent to attempt such buildings." To ask why we cannot build a cathedral, he said, is to address a question "touching the very foundations of the spiritual development and civilization of modern Europe."[7]

Norton's writings include his book, *Historical Studies of Church Building in the Middle Ages* (1880), and his articles "The Building of the Church of St. Denis" and "The Building of the Cathedral at Chartres," which appeared in *Harper's New Monthly Magazine* in October and November of 1889. These, however, may not represent his greatest achievement. Ruskin complained that he felt a chill in the *Historical Studies* that he didn't feel in Norton's conversation, and we must assume that his personality was more appealing than his writings. Norton found his vocation in the fall of 1874 when he became Harvard's first professor of fine art.

Norton's appointment was part of President Charles W. Eliot's effort to expand and liberalize the Harvard curriculum. For Norton, it was also an opportunity to follow in Ruskin's footsteps. Ruskin had been Oxford's first Slade Professor since 1870, and he had combined lectures on the history of art with searching social criticism. Anticipating his Harvard appointment, Norton had traveled to England in 1872 and heard Ruskin lecture. Admiring Ruskin's collections for the use of students, Norton also set out to gather photographs, plaster casts, and original art works. Norton's courses were small at first. In 1874 he had only thirty-four students. By 1895, however, he had 446. A term of fine arts with Norton was regarded as an essential part of the Harvard experience.

Norton's lectures were both lively and topical. Oswald Garrison Villard recalled that he "deliberately included in his lectures discussions of the events of the day, of every phase of manners and morals and social happenings, [and] called politicians by their right names." More skeptically, Josephine Preston Peabody wrote of one of his lectures at Radcliffe in the 1890s: "The dear old man looks so mildly happy and benignant while he regrets everything in the age and the country—so content, while he gently tells us it were better for us had we never been born in this degenerate and unlovely age."[8]

We do not have transcripts of Norton's lectures, but copies of his final examination questions are preserved in the Harvard University Archives."[9] An 1882 examination is typical. Norton posed a series of questions that were to be answered in order. He asked the student to begin by speculating broadly "on the causes of the intellectual activity and moral energy displayed in the greater part of Europe during the twelfth century, and on their chief manifestations in thought and action." He next called for a description of different vaulting systems, an account of a typical scheme for a cathedral facade in the north of France, and detailed information about the sculpture on the west front of Amiens. Norton then asked his student to describe Italian Gothic and explain why the principles of the Gothic style were not consistently carried out in Italy. That led to a comparison of the French and Italian schools of sculpture, with an account of Giotto's Campanile in Florence. The student was then asked to describe the place of art in private life during the twelfth and thirteenth centuries and comment on a favorite Ruskinian theme: the merits of handicrafts as compared with manufactured goods. He would end by speculating broadly "on the decline in the arts of architecture and sculpture in modern times, and the significance of this fact as regards the moral ideas of the modern civilized world." Thus, the student was asked to begin by commenting on the relation of art to morals in the twelfth century and end by speculating on the relation between them in the nineteenth.

Two essential points will be noticed in this exam. One is that Norton was more concerned with structure than might be expected of such a fervent admirer of Ruskin. He had concluded as early as 1870 that Ruskin tended to underestimate the importance of Gothic construction. After visiting the cathederal of Pisa with Ruskin, Norton had written to his wife that "he likes the Gothic used merely as a decoration without regard to its essential principles as in S. Maria della Spina,—I, while admitting that it is very pretty and picturesque, think the building bad from the want of proper construction, and believe that a much prettier, more picturesque and more pleasing building could have been erected had the essential laws of Gothic construction been followed. But the Italians never understood Gothic."[10] Norton's students could be sure that they had to know the difference between northern and southern Gothic and should be prepared to give solid information on vaulting systems and the construction of domes.

The second point is that Norton always taught architectural history in a heavily ideological context. "What," he asked in an 1878 examination, "is the value of [the fine arts] as testimony concerning the conditions, moral and social, of the races who have practiced them?" "Why," he asked in 1895, "is the culture of the poetic imagination especially needful in America?" Norton's students were constantly reminded of the vulgarity of their own age. An 1881 question asked them to describe the decline of handicrafts and to speculate on the possibility of their renewal. Norton then added: "*N.B.* In answering this last question, do not fall into the error of assuming the fashionable art of the present day—the art of the bric-a-brac shops, and of so-called decorators—to be art that is a joy to maker and user." Always Norton insisted that the study of architectural history was only a means to some nobler end. In 1890 he

2. Charles H. Moore (1840–1930)
Courtesy of the Harvard University Archives

ended an examination by simply asking: "What is the use of the knowledge requisite for answering the preceding questions?"

Norton's ultimate goal was to produce an elite that might redeem the disorder of late nineteenth-century American life. He wanted a graduate who was critical, urbane, genteel, someone who would look on the Gilded Age with disdain but would also work to transform it.

Charles H. Moore (fig. 2) commands our attention as a follower of Viollet-le-Duc, but he began as a disciple of Ruskin.[11] He was a landscape painter in the 1860s, one of the American pre-Raphaelites, a man who could assure readers of the *New Path* in 1863 that "by the mercy of God, Ruskin has been sent to open our eyes and loose the seals of darkness."[12] Not surprisingly, Norton saw in him a congenial collaborator and encouraged him to come to Cambridge. Moore first taught as an instructor in freehand drawing and watercolor at the Lawrence Scientific School, beginning in 1871. Three years later Norton, now firmly appointed to his professorship, asked him to teach a course in Harvard College on "Principles of Design in Painting, Sculpture, and Architecture."

Moore was less concerned with the state of society than was Norton, but he enthusiastically accepted Ruskin's views on the need for the study of art in universities. In 1876 and 1877 Moore traveled abroad, observing Ruskin's teaching methods at Oxford and traveling with him on the continent. He sent back Ruskin's folio *Examples of Venetian Architecture*, copies of Ruskin's educational materials, and all the photographs that Ruskin had arranged to have published, as well as casts from St. Mark's and the Ducal Palace. After commenting unfavorably on most of the art instruction in Europe, Moore wrote to Norton: "I have seen nothing at all good except Ruskin's school. That is supremely good."[13]

In 1885 Moore traveled to Europe again. This time Ruskin was too ill for extended contact. Moore found himself concentrating on architecture, especially French architecture. He came across a book entitled *La filiation généalogique de toutes les écoles gothiques*, by a Belgian author named Jean François Colfs.[14] Since Moore's response to this book conditioned all his future researches, his comments on it to Norton should be quoted at length:

To my surprise the author maintains that French Gothic is the latest and least excellent of all Gothic styles. He thinks that the English invented the style and the Germans perfected it—the cathedral of Cologne being the "chef-d'oeuvre de cette école." The book seems to me one mass of misapprehension and errors, and yet it is, the author affirms, the result of forty years study of the subject. The fact is, I think, that he entirely misunderstands the essential principles of Gothic architecture and that he has little aesthetic perception. He affirms that the Gothic style was completely understood in England as early as 1180, and that it was derived by the French from that source, but that it was never really understood or consistently employed by them. He makes no account of the enormous French influence which has been brought to bear upon all matters of taste in England by the Norman conquest, and of the fact that so much was actually done there by French workmen. He even refers to

Canterbury as illustrating certain important principles without making any reference whatever to William of Sens.[15]

Moore set out to prove that all of this was wrong, and as he did so he found himself leaning less and less on *The Stones of Venice* and more and more on Eugène Emmanuel Viollet-le-Duc's *Dictionnaire raisonné de l'architecture française du XIe au XVIe siècle.* This is not surprising. The replacement of Ruskin by Viollet-le-Duc as an authority on Gothic architecture was a common phenomenon in American architectural thought.[16] But this replacement was no gradual process for Moore. It was a dramatic conversion. Rejecting an old master, he embraced a new one.

Moore's new view led him to insist that the greatest Gothic architecture was to be found in France. This was still a view that required defense when Moore published his *Development of Gothic Architecture* in 1890. Two years later Barr Ferree, writing on "French Cathedrals" in the *Architectural Record*, complained that "the average tourist is consumed with amazement when it is intimated there are finer and grander cathedrals in France than in England, and the person bold enough to make such a statement runs the risk of being looked upon as most singularly misinformed indeed."[17] Moore not only shifted attention from England to France, but also encouraged the tendency to value the earlier and transitional phases of Gothic more highly than the fully achieved style, a preference that will be marked in Henry Adams. Moore wrote Norton from Paris on 25 December 1885: "The more I study the art of the middle ages here, the more impressed I am with the superior character of that of the earlier times. The best I think is about all included in what was done between 1160 and 1220. After 1220 no new principle is developed, and the effort to achieve daring feats begins to be too apparent, while the strict subjection of sculpture to architectural effect is less constant."[18]

Had Moore only claimed that French Gothic was greater than English Gothic he would have been persuasive. But Moore was not a man to shrink from a conclusion, and his researches convinced him that there were few examples of Gothic architecture at all in England. Moore believed that William of Sens attempted to introduce the style at Canterbury but it did not take. The English cathedrals, in Moore's view, rarely showed the sense of structure, the dynamic equilibrium between opposed thrusts, which was crucial to Moore's definition of Gothic. And if they did not show it, it could not be the definition which was at fault. In his book on *The Medieval Church Architecture of England* (1912), Moore insisted that the great English cathedrals were not Gothic. They were only medieval.

This view, which struck Moore's contemporaries as quixotic, should not be allowed to obscure his real importance in the development of American architectural history. He domesticated Viollet-le-Duc's functionalism in America, and he ensured that questions of structure would be at the forefront of American discussions of Gothic. A.D.F. Hamlin, who disliked the rigorous functionalism of both Viollet-le-Duc and Moore, nevertheless conceded that Moore had "no valid rival" until the 1915 publication of the Sturgis-Frothingham *History of Architecture*.[19] Frank Jewett Mather testified that Moore's books on architecture "had been almost required reading for the art-loving intelligentsia."[20]

The elements we have seen in Norton and Moore reappear in Henry Adams (fig.3) but in a more complicated form.[21] Like Norton, Adams wrote out of a sense of cultural crisis. Like Moore, he kept Viollet-le-Duc's *Dictionnaire raisonné* close at hand. But his sense of crisis was more anguished than Norton's and his use of Viollet-le-Duc was more paradoxical than Moore's.

Like Norton, Adams was a member of New England's elite. Both his great-grandfather, John Adams, and his grandfather, John Quincy Adams, had been presidents of the United States; his father was minister to Great Britain during the Civil War; and his brother was president of the Union Pacific Railway. But again like Norton, Adams felt that the proper leaders of American society had been replaced by shortsighted, graceless, unprincipled men. His father had been pushed aside during the

3. Henry Adams (1838–1918)
Courtesy of the Harvard University Archives

Grant administration. His brother fought a losing battle with Jay Gould for control of the Union Pacific. And Adams' autobiography was to be filled with laments for the failure of his generation of Harvard men to achieve their full promise.

Adams built his own career as a scholar and man of letters. Adams' period on the Harvard faculty was shorter than Norton's or Moore's, but, like theirs, it was a result of President Eliot's educational reforms. Adams taught medieval history from 1870 to 1877. He served as editor of the *North American Review*, America's major intellectual quarterly, from 1870 to 1878 (Norton had edited it from 1863 to 1868). He wrote for E. L. Godkin's crusading weekly, the *Nation*. He caused a stir by attacking the spoils system in Congress and the scandals of the Erie Railway wars, and he achieved great prestige as the author of the multivolume *History of the United States during the Administrations of Thomas Jefferson and James Madison* (1884–1891). Thereafter, he abandoned any attempt at a public role and lived the life of a wealthy member of America's leisure class. Though he always returned to the home that H. H. Richardson had designed for him opposite the White House on Lafayette Square, Adams traveled to Samoa, Cuba, Mexico, Italy, England, and, most frequently, to France.

Adams had wide and varied interests, but architecture was not large among them until the 1890s. He was sixty-four years old in 1904 when *Mont-Saint-Michel and Chartres* first appeared in a limited edition of only one hundred copies.[22] The origins of this book can be traced back to the late spring, summer, and early fall of 1893, when Adams felt first hope and then despair at America's future. The hope was prompted by a visit to the World's Columbian Exposition in Chicago. The despair was provoked by a massive crisis in the nation's banking system, which directly threatened the Adams family trust.

Adams toured the fair in May and was startled to find a vision of aesthetic harmony appearing in a city that he associated with chaotic energy and social disorder. "Even you [he wrote to his host Franklin MacVeagh on 26 May] who are of it, must admit that no matter-of-fact human being could have imagined that Chicago would suddenly, without apparent cause or consequence, lavish millions on millions of money, and infinite effort, in order to produce something that the Greeks might have delighted to see, and Venice would have envied, but which certainly is not business."[23] Norton, it may be noted, had a similar reaction. He thought the fair reflected the tastes of a wealthy and immature people, but still felt he was witnessing the pledge of a hopeful future.[24] At first sight, the Columbian Exposition suggested that America's commercial civilization might yet be redeemed.

In June Adams set off on a tour of England and Europe. In July he was abruptly summoned home. Banks were failing, the Adams family trust was threatened, and, as Adams said later, "the entire nervous system of Boston seemed to give way."[25] Adams managed to preserve a tone of slightly deranged gaiety as he awaited the impending destruction. "I have made up my mind to finding myself in a universal mess a week from today," he wrote to his dear friend Elizabeth Cameron on the voyage home. "I only hope I have pocket-money enough to reach Quincy. If obliged to tramp, I shall be too late to sign my certificate of insolvency."[26] "I am furious," he wrote to John Hay on 12 August, "and in no frame of mind to be judicial or historical. I am intensely curious, too, for I think we may be on the verge of a general collapse of the social fabric in Europe."[27] "I am in a panic of terror about finance, politics, society, and the solar system, with ultimate fears for the Milky Way and the nebula of Orion," he wrote Elizabeth Cameron on 9 September. "The sun-spots scare me. Ruin hangs over the Pole Star!"[28]

The nation recovered and Adams' own investments had been conservative, but his thoughts were still unreservedly pessimistic when he visited the Columbian Exposition for a second time in October.

Now it was even more difficult than it had been the first time to reconcile the cultural aspirations of the fair with the commercial push of Chicago and the dreamlike beauty of the architecture with the cheap dazzle of the midway. The fair, Adams now concluded, "was just as chaotic as my own mind . . . , a pure white temple, on the pure blue sea, with an Italian sky, all vast and beautiful as the world never saw it before, and in it the most astounding, confused, bewildering mass of art and industry, without a sign that there was any connection, relation or harmony or understanding of the relations of anything anywhere."[29] The financial panic had made Adams even more preoccupied than before with the nature of American society, and suddenly architecture seemed the crucial index of that society's moral condition. "I want to talk among other matters about the architecture," Adams wrote John Hay on 18 October, "and discuss the question of the true relation between Burnham, Attwood [sic], McKim, White, Millet &c, and the world."[30]

Confronted by chaos, Adams wanted an explanation. He was delighted to find his brother Brooks Adams offering one in a bitter, pessimistic, and polemical book entitled *The Law of Civilization and Decay.*

Brooks Adams interpreted history in terms of currency manipulation and an eternal warfare between the soldier and the artist on one side and the merchant on the other. "The mercantile mind," he tells us, "had always the same characteristic: it was unimaginative. . . . All commercial communities have rebelled against paying for miracles, and it was the spread of a scepticism already well developed in the thirteenth century among the manufacturing towns which caused the Reformation of the sixteenth."[31] The monopolists and the currency manipulators—the "gold bugs," as Henry and Brooks Adams called them—choked off civilization's most glorious period and were now approaching their final triumph.

These grandiose historical speculations were in Henry Adams' head when he toured France in 1895. He was hoping to escape from the crisis of his own times, but in one sense he felt that he was returning home. The Normandy landscape reminded him of New England, and he soon felt, against all genealogical probability, that his ancestors were undoubtedly Norman. "Caen, Bayeux, St Lo, Coutances and Mont St Michel," he wrote to John Hay, "are clearly works that I helped to build, when I lived in a world I liked."[32] Adams is known as a lover of Gothic, but, as we shall see, he had a certain suspicion of the fully achieved Gothic. It was really the transition that he loved, the buildings in which Gothic had not yet fully separated itself from Romanesque. Here he found a point of greatness from which the decline of the nineteenth century could be measured.

Mont-Saint-Michel and Chartres indeed grows out of crisis and fevered speculation about the rise and fall of civilization, but the reader's first impression is one of pure sunshine. The book is extremely deceptive. It seems at first to be only loosely put together. It is, in fact, an extraordinarily intricate piece of work.

Adams begins by focusing on two works of architecture—Mont-Saint-Michel, which to him represented the supremacy of the male spirit in the eleventh century, and Chartres, which he interpreted as the triumph of the Virgin Mary and the female

principle in the twelfth. Adams portrays the age in terms of sharp contrasts—the passion of St. Bernard against the skepticism of Abelard, the brutality of warriors against the civilizing grace of Eleanor of Aquitaine. The Virgin, in his view, holds these forces together and makes the twelfth century an age of unity, but she does this only so long as men accept her as the center of their culture. Once they cease to do this, the unity of the twelfth century is dissolved and the decline to nineteenth-century chaos has begun. When Adams leaves Chartres at the end of chapter 10, he looks back at Mary in her great window, still in majesty, still calm and confident, but "looking down from a deserted heaven, into an empty church, on a dead faith."[33]

Like most nineteenth-century writers on Gothic, Adams drew a line between a period of cultural greatness and a subsequent decline. Unlike most others, however, he located the beginning of the downward slope not in the Renaissance but within the medieval period itself. The crucial error, he concludes, was the effort by scholastic philosophers to replace the Virgin and faith by masculine rationality. But he saw a secondary error, just as disastrous in its long-term effects, in the intrusion of commerce into the temple of the imagination. Adams, the *rentier* who despised capitalism, could never quite separate the fully achieved Gothic of Amiens and Rheims from the taint of money. A thirteenth-century cathedral was, he wrote Elizabeth Cameron, "a Chicago Exposition for God's profit."[34] He told his brother that "the Gothic always looks to me a little theatrical and false. . . . It is always restless, grasping and speculative, it exploits the world and makes profits."[35]

We are now in a position to ask what role Ruskin and Viollet-le-Duc play in *Mont-Saint-Michel and Chartres.* Ernest Samuels, Adams' great biographer, writes that the book can be regarded as a companion to Ruskin's *Bible of Amiens*, the study of Chartres for which Ruskin made elaborate notes but never wrote.[36] This seems to me true but only in a general way. Ruskin was a major presence in Adams' culture, and several of his friends—notably Clarence King and John La Farge—went through periods of great enthusiasm for Ruskin's work. But references in Adams' letters suggest that Ruskin was only one of several Victorian thinkers who had engaged his attention and not one to whom he turned anew when he was exploring French architecture.

Nevertheless, there is a Ruskinian tradition in American architectural writing, and Adams belongs to it in three general but quite important ways. First, he assumes that architecture above all expresses an emotion, and he uses literature to define that emotion. Thus, Ruskin had used passages from Edmund Spenser's *The Faerie Queene* to interpret the capitals of the Ducal Palace in Venice, and Norton's Harvard course had actually been entitled "The History of the Arts of Construction and Design, and their Relation to Literature." Adams interprets Mont-Saint-Michel in the second chapter of his book by reading *The Song of Roland*, and he studies Chartres in the thirteenth chapter with the aid of poems celebrating the miracles of the Virgin. Second, Adams shares the key Ruskinian conviction that if you want to understand the moral nature of an age, you must first turn to its architecture. Third, and perhaps above all, Adams uses medieval architecture to create a powerful myth of cultural decline. His version is not identical with Ruskin's, since it involves a critique of High Gothic architecture, and he avoids Ruskin's tone of prophetic urgency. Unlike Ruskin, but much like Norton, Adams assumes that the best stance a gentleman can adopt toward the modern age is one of pessimistic detachment.

With Viollet-le-Duc the case is even more complicated. At first it looks simpler. The French architect is cited more than twenty times and is sometimes quoted at considerable length. Adams refers to the ten volumes of the *Dictionnaire raisonné* as "sacred sources,"[37] consults "the inevitable Viollet-le-Duc" (446), and pictures himself examining the Tree of Jesse window with a volume of the *Dictionnaire* in one hand and a binocle in the other (462).

And yet there is a sense in which Adams is temperamentally much closer to Ruskin than to Viollet-le-Duc. The French architect was precisely the sort of nineteenth-century positivist that Adams had learned to distrust.[38] Interpreting the cathedrals in terms of structural rationality, he leaves little room for Adams' Virgin. By making the cathedral builders early manifestations of urbanism, secularism, and nationalism, he makes them ancestors of Adams' hated gold bugs.

Accordingly, Adams treats Viollet-le-Duc in an extremely complicated way. He uses the French architect's authority when examining parts of Chartres and undercuts it when considering the whole. He does this most obviously in his chapter on "Roses and Apses."

The crucial issue is that of vaulting. In view of its obvious importance, and considering that Adams is attempting to describe a Gothic cathedral in all of its aspects, his treatment of this topic is exceedingly curious. "The subject of vaulting is far too ambitious for summer travel," he announces airily; "we must not touch it" (374). "The problem of the permanent equilibrium of arches" is a technical matter, he says elsewhere (442), one that need not trouble ignorant tourists. Such comments as these presumably made Paul Frankl dismiss Adams' book lightly in his *The Gothic: Literary Sources and Interpretations through Eight Centuries*.[39] Even Robert Mane, in his *Henry Adams on the Road to Chartres*, seems to accept Adams' claim that he avoids a discussion of vaulting because he is only an ignorant tourist.[40] Adams himself, however, gives us warrant for setting aside that interpretation: "We," he says, "whose pose is ignorance" (419). For we clearly are dealing with a rhetorical posture, and Adams in fact does not ignore the question of vaulting. He treats it gingerly, however, because a full acceptance of the rationalist interpretation of Gothic vaulting would conflict with Adams' stress on the irrational force of Mariolatry.

For Viollet-le-Duc, "la construction commande la forme."[41] For him the essential structure of the Gothic vault was the framework of transverse and diagonal ribs. They made it possible to eliminate the heavy Romanesque wall but required the provision of flying buttresses. Accept this account, and it will be difficult to see Chartres as anything except a masterpiece of rational calculation constructed by scientifically skilled, forward-looking, secular-minded architects.

Adams therefore subverts Viollet-le-Duc's authority by accepting what he calls the Beaux-Arts account of vaulting. Viollet-le-Duc taught that every aspect of a Gothic cathedral was justified by its structural function. The Beaux-Arts teaching, as Adams summarizes it, was that Gothic vaulting actually had two inherent structural weaknesses. One was in the flying buttress needed to support the vault, which was apt to give way. The other was in the false wooden roof over the stone vault, which was apt to burn.

Adam raises the issue of vaulting near the beginning of his chapter on "Roses and Apses." Avoiding the technicalities of the matter, which would lead to a long discussion indeed, he nevertheless makes it clear that he accepts the Beaux-Arts view of the matter rather than Viollet-le-Duc's. It is not likely that he is prompted by a disinterested interest in architectural statics. His real interest is in persuading us to regard the Gothic cathedral as an expression of emotions and its vault as a magnificent piece of stage decoration.

Once he has established that Chartres is not a piece of rational construction, Adams can go on to insist that it is precisely, magnificently an expression of the irrational. At this point in his chapter he begins to develop the conceit that the Virgin rather than the architect was responsible for the planning of her cathedral.

He is aided in this by the fact that Viollet-le-Duc seemed to regard Chartres as an imperfect achievement on the way to the structural masterpiece of Amiens. Adams dwells on the awkwardnesses of Chartres—the lack of strict alignment between the rose window and the lancets of the west front and the abrupt collision of the nave arches with the western towers. He accepts Viollet-le-Duc's judgment that the vaulting of the apse "ne fait pas grand honneur a son architecte."[42] He shares Viollet-le-Duc's admiration for the older of the two towers, and perhaps in a way would even agree that "la beauté de sa construc-tion contraste avec la negligence et la grossièreté de celle de l'eglise."[43]

Chartres is imperfect architecture when judged in strictly structural terms because the Virgin consistently disregarded the architect's preferences. "In his western front," Adams tells us, "the architect has obeyed orders so literally that he has not even taken the trouble to apologize for leaving unfinished the details which, if he had been responsible for them, would have been his anxious care" (444). In the apse, the Virgin herself saw to "the lighting of her own boudoir" (454). Chartres becomes an embodiment of female willfulness. Mary issues her commands and the architect listens "like the stone Abraham . . . while he caresses and sacrifices his child" (449).

As the result of this elaborate literary strategy, by the end of the chapter on "Roses and Apses" structural rationalism has become only one more sign of the feebleness of the nineteenth-century imagination. The reader understands that the *Dictionnaire* is to be consulted, but that it is necessary to "paraphrase Viollet-le-Duc's words into a more or less emotional or twelfth century form" (457).

Explicit concern with architecture is confined to the first nine chapters of *Mont-Saint-Michel and Chartres*, but architecture returns as metaphor when Adams characterizes scholastic rationalism in his final chapters. "These great theologians," he tells us, "were also architects, who undertook to build a Church Intellectual, corresponding bit by bit to the Church Administrative, both expressing—and expressed by—the Church architectural" (664). In many ways, Adams' image of the Middle Ages—with its careful balancing of Mont-Saint-Michel and Chartres, Pierre de Dreux and Queen Blanche, Saint Bernard and Saint Thomas—resembles Viollet-le-Duc's view of a Gothic cathedral: It is a dynamic equilibrium of opposed thrusts.

But clearly there is one last problem here. Viollet-le-Duc insists that the Gothic cathedral is a structure that stands. Adams insists that the equilibrium was lost. Therefore, it remains necessary to undercut Viollet-le-Duc, and Adams once again invokes the Beaux-Arts view of architecture. William of Champeaux was sure that realism was the Roman arch—"the only possible foundation for any Church" (619). Abelard's opponents were sure that "conceptualism was a device, like the false wooden roof, to cover and conceal an inherent weakness of construction" (621). Ultimately, "scholastic science and the pointed arch proved to be failures" (625).

In thought as in architecture, Adams' heart belongs not to the High Gothic period but to the transition where the love of God and the logic of God, the round arch and the pointed, are held in an exquisite equilibrium:

One may not be sure which pleases most, but one need not be harsh toward people who think that the moment of balance is exquisite. The last and highest moment is seen at Chartres, where, in 1200, the charm depends on the constant doubt whether emotion or science is uppermost. At Amiens, doubt ceases; emotion is trained in school; Thomas Aquinas reigns (638).

By balancing Viollet-le-Duc with the Beaux-Arts, Adams maintains his own equilibrium. He presents the Gothic world view as a massively intricate structure, a triumph of rationality, a dynamic equilibrium of thrust and counterthrust which is nevertheless under greater and greater danger as its builders grow more and more heroic. Henry Adams' final image for the late Middle Ages is that of a collapsing Gothic cathedral. That is why his book is mistitled. It ought to be called not *Mont-Saint-Michel and Chartres,* but *Mont-Saint-Michel, Chartres, and Beauvais.*

NOTES

1. The best general account of Norton will be found in Kermit Vanderbilt's *Charles Eliot Norton: Apostle of Culture in a Democracy* (Cambridge, Mass., 1959). Norton's relation to Ruskin is discussed in Roger B. Stein's *John Ruskin and Aesthetic Thought in America, 1840–1900* (Cambridge, Mass., 1967). T. J. Jackson Lears' *No Place of Grace: Antimodernism and the Transformation of American Culture, 1880–1920* (New York, 1981) contains important interpretations of both Norton and Henry Adams. One aspect of Norton's cultural context is treated in David E. Shi's *The Simple Life: Plain Living and High Thinking in American Culture* (New York, 1985), 154–175. John Lewis Bradley and Ian Ousby have prepared a new edition of *The Correspondence of John Ruskin and Charles Eliot Norton* (Cambridge, 1987).

2. Quoted in Leon Edel, *Henry James: The Untried Years* (Philadelphia, 1953), 206.

3. [Charles Eliot Norton], *Considerations on Some Recent Social Theories* (Boston, 1853), 38.

4. Quoted in Shi 1985, 166–167.

5. Charles Eliot Norton, *Notes of Travel and Study in Italy* (Boston, 1859), 105.

6. Charles Eliot Norton, "The Building of the Cathedral at Chartres," *Harper's Magazine* 79 (November 1889), 946.

7. Norton 1859, 106.

8. Quoted in Vanderbilt 1959, 133–134.

9. Norton's examination questions are quoted by permission of the Harvard University Archives.

10. Sara Norton and M. A. DeWolfe Howe, eds., *Letters of Charles Eliot Norton*, 2 vols. (Boston, 1913), 392–393.

11. There is no general biography of Moore, but a valuable account of one side of his career can be found in Frank Jewett Mather, Jr., *Charles Herbert Moore: Landscape Painter* (Princeton, 1957). A short biographical article by Arthur Pope appears in the *Dictionary of American Biography*, s.v. "Moore, Charles Herbert."

12. Quoted in David W. Dickason, *The Daring Young Men: The Story of the American Pre-Raphaelites* (Bloomington, Ind., 1953), 117.

13. Charles Moore to Charles Eliot Norton, 27 July 1876, Houghton Library, Harvard University (4772). Quoted by permission of Houghton Library.

14. Jean François Colfs, *La filiation généalogique de toutes les écoles gothiques* (Paris, 1883).

15. Charles Moore to Charles Eliot Norton, 21 August 1885, Houghton Library, Harvard University (4772). Quoted by permission of Houghton Library.

16. I have discussed one aspect of this process in chapter 13 of Brooks, *John Ruskin and Victorian Architecture* (New Brunswick, N.J., 1987).

17. Barr Ferree, "French Cathedrals," *Architectural Record* 2 (October–December 1892), 125.

18. Charles Moore to Charles Eliot Norton, 25 De-cember 1885, Houghton Library, Harvard University (4787). Quoted by permission of Houghton Library.

19. A.D.F. Hamlin, "Gothic Architecture and Its Critics—The Definition of Gothic," *Architectural Record* 39 (May 1916), 424. Hamlin gives his reasons for rejecting Moore's definition of Gothic in this article. Moore replied in "The Definition of Gothic," *Architectural Record* 40 (September 1916), 274–278.

20. Mather 1957, ix.

21. The literature on Adams is extensive. The standard biography is in three volumes by Ernest Samuels: *The Young Henry Adams* (Cambridge, Mass., 1948), *Henry Adams: The Middle Years* (Cambridge, Mass., 1958), and *Henry Adams: The Major Phase* (Cambridge, Mass., 1964). William H. Jordy's *Henry Adams: Scientific Historian* (New Haven, 1952) treats Adams' evolving theories of history. Adams' concern with architecture is discussed in Ernst Scheyer's *The Circle of Henry Adams: Art and Artists* (Detroit, 1970) and Robert Mane's *Henry Adams on the Road to Chartres* (Cambridge, Mass., 1971). Michael Ann Holly's article "Cultural History as a Work of Art: Jacob Burckhardt and Henry Adams" appeared in *Style* 22 (Summer 1988), 209–218.

22. The one hundred copies of the 1904 edition of *Mont-Saint-Michel and Chartres* were given away to friends. The book's reputation soon spread beyond the Adams circle, and, responding to requests from medievalists, Adams prepared the revised edition of 1911. This was limited to five hundred copies, which were given to friends and libraries. Ralph Adams Cram urged Adams to permit an edition for the public. Adams then authorized the American Institute of Architects to publish a trade edition, which appeared in 1913 with an "Editor's Note" by Cram. All royalties from this edition were donated to the AIA.

23. J. C. Levenson, Ernest Samuels, Charles Vander-see, and Viola Hopkins Winner, eds., *The Letters of Henry Adams*, vol.4 (Cambridge, Mass., 1988), 103.

24. See Vanderbilt 1959, 201–204.

25. *Letters of Henry Adams*, 4:215.

26. *Letters of Henry Adams*, 4:115.

27. *Letters of Henry Adams*, 4:119.

28. *Letters of Henry Adams*, 4:126.

29. *Letters of Henry Adams*, 4:133.

30. *Letters of Henry Adams*, 4:134.

31. Brooks Adams, *The Law of Civilization and Decay: An Essay on History* (New York, 1943), 182–183.

32. *Letters of Henry Adams*, 4:319.

33. Henry Adams, *Novels, Mont-Saint-Michel, The Education* (repr. ed., New York, 1983), 522.

34. *Letters of Henry Adams*, 4:326.

35. *Letters of Henry Adams*, 4:321.

36. Samuels 1964, 265.

37. Henry Adams, 393. Further references to the Library of America 1983 edition of *Mont-Saint-Michel and Chartres* will be incorporated into the text.

38. My view of Viollet-le-Duc as a positivist is influenced by Jerzy Frycz's "Viollet-le-Duc, créateur romantique ou positiviste?" in *Actes du Colloque International Viollet-le-Duc* (Paris, 1980), 21–28.

39. Paul Frankl, *The Gothic: Literary Sources and Interpretations through Eight Centuries* (Princeton, 1960), 662–663.

40. Robert Mane, *Henry Adams on the Road to Chartres* (Cambridge, Mass., 1971), 128–130.

41. Eugène Emmanuel Viollet-le-Duc, *Dictionnaire raisonné de l'architecture française du XIe au XVIe siècle* (Paris, 1882–1885), 1:146.

42. Viollet-le-Duc 1882–1885, 1:235.

43. Viollet-le-Duc 1882–1885, 3:365.

PETER FERGUSSON
Wellesley College

Medieval Architectural Scholarship in America, 1900-1940:

Ralph Adams Cram and Kenneth John Conant

The first forty years of the twentieth century saw the establishment of medieval architecture as a scholarly discipline in America. Yet what is understood as the study of medieval architecture now bears only small resemblance to that discipline. It is inextricably connected nonetheless. The English historian Maitland remarked that one of the problems of establishing historical truth was that we forget that things now in the past were once in the future. As for history, so for historiography. For medieval architecture, as for other periods, historiography is part growth, part mutation; today's pioneers are tomorrow's ancestors—names on a map whose frontiers have moved. Two men typify this process in the early twentieth century: Ralph Adams Cram (1863-1942) and Kenneth John Conant (1894-1984). Both seem strangely distant in time, more so than is justified by the years that separate us from them. Neither is widely read; at best their work is regarded with curiosity, at worst it is ignored or even belittled. What was their contribution? How may the themes and qualities in their writings be assessed?

Of the two, Cram was vastly the more famous. Born the son of a poor Unitarian clergyman in Hampton Falls, New Hampshire, and lacking a university education, Cram's long life was nonetheless filled with academic achievement: chairman of the Department of Architecture at the Massachusetts Institute of Technology for seven years, honorary degrees from Harvard, Princeton, Yale, Williams, and Notre Dame, trustee positions on the boards of East Coast colleges and universities, a charter member of the Medieval Academy of America and its president in 1933.[1] And it was as an academic that he more than once presented himself (fig. 1). Yet the academic accomplishments pale beside the professional: founder of Cram and Ferguson, one of the most prestigious architectural firms in America in the first three decades of the twentieth century; architect of more than one hundred churches and cathedrals scattered across the continent; designer or consulting architect for university buildings at Bryn Mawr, Yale, Princeton, Williams, Notre Dame, Wheaton, Wellesley, Rice, Sweet Briar, and other campuses; the architect (with Bertram Goodhue) of West Point; first chairman of the Boston City Planning Board; founder and editor of five journals, including *Commonweal*; and, the reason for this paper, the author of nearly thirty books and about four hundred scholarly and polemical papers.[2] The man's energy and brilliance leave one breathless—as, too, do his eccentricities. Some were endearing, like his penchant for dressing in period or ecclesiastical costume, a habit he continued into old age (fig. 2), or his published designs for the beautification of Boston, in which he envisioned an island in the Charles River Basin to be called St. Botolph's, modeled on the Ile de la Cité in Paris, complete with a new city hall, cathedral, and open-air theater. Others were less so, like his interests in eugenics, his abrasive antimodernism, or his sometime espousal of Mussolini. When he died in 1942 much of the last was forgiven, however, and obituaries characterized him as "one of the truly great men in America."[3]

Conant was younger by thirty years (fig. 3). While his career lacked the glittering accents of Cram's, it was marked nonetheless by considerable prestige. Regarded by World War II as the leading medieval archaeologist in North America, his important work at Cluny in eastern France already extended through nearly fifteen seasons; he also had excavated at Kiev in the Soviet Union and Chichén Itzá in Mexico.[4] Although edged out of the Graduate School of Design at Harvard by the doctrinaire and ahistorical Walter Gropius, Conant remained an important and inspiring teacher within the university, his well-filled courses ranging across the spectrum of architectural history from ancient Greece to the modern day. In fact, it was a group of his colleagues and students who gathered in the summer of 1940 at the Harvard Faculty Club to form the Society of Architectural Historians, hailing Conant as their "academic Godfather" and electing him the society's first honorary president. Not only, as John Coolidge has written, was he the catalyst who made the society possible, but in his role as a scholar-teacher he inspired most of the articles that appeared in the early issues of its journal.[5]

The historiographical quest for Cram begins with one great advantage. In his seventies he set down an account of his career—*My Life in Architecture*—which stands as one of the most readable and honest autobiographies written by an American architect.[6] While ostensibly addressed to his wife, children, and grandchildren, no one probably believed that Cram had anyone else in mind but the public at large. Rich in information, generous to colleagues and friends, largely free from the dated philosophizing that marks much of his writing, brimming with en-

1. Ralph Adams Cram
From Ralph Adams Cram, *The Substance of Gothic* (Boston, 1917), frontispiece

thusiasms, self-aware (within the limits of the genre), and good humored, the book blocks out the main episodes of his event-filled life. The reader quickly faces a polymath: an architect first, but not always foremost, compulsive writer, playwright, social reformer, religionist, philosopher, political commentator and pamphleteer, utopian. All these identities are Cram's—and he wrote extensively about each. To organize this formidable output I propose to look at Cram under three headings: Cram as traveler, as political idealist, and as Goth.

Cram loved travel, traveled well and intelligently, and traveled with a focus on architecture. He was abroad most years, his tolerant office somehow weathering the absences. From these prodigious journeyings came knowledge, the stimulus for his architecture, and books. An early example of the last and, in some ways, the best illustration of his travel gifts is *Impressions of Japanese Architecture.* Published

2. Ralph Adams Cram, age 72
From *Time*, 6 January 1936, 33

tween intensive meetings with government officials, Cram plunged into Japanese culture, history, and art.

Cram responded sensitively to what he could still see of old Japan. In describing early buildings like the eighth-century monastery of Horiuji and the Temple of Yakushiji in the old capital of Nara, Cram not only used comparisons with Western architecture, but astutely characterized their indigenous qualities. Here, he describes the setting of the Ashikaga temples:

As the castles and abbeys of England blend with her landscape and her air, as the nacreous palaces and shrines of Venice grow out of the opal sea, as the hot sandstone fortresses of Hindustan rear their blistered walls from the desert sands, or the marble miracles of tomb and pleasure house flash above still pools and in the midst of tropical gardens, so, and with equal intimacy, do these brown and weathered temples rest in the purple shadow of gnarled cryptomeria or lift themselves from the shoulders of deep-wooded hills. With infinite craft, priests and artists and gardeners have wrought a perfect setting for their shrines, piling long flights of stone steps up the broken hillsides, raising ramparts and terraces, training the willing trees into strange architectural forms, blending the whole as a painter blends his col-

in 1905, the book originated in his firm's 1898 commission to rebuild the Parliament House in Tokyo (fig. 4), which took Cram to the Japanese capital for a four-month stay; the commission subsequently was scrapped when the government fell. Be-

3. Kenneth John Conant
From *GSD News* (Harvard Graduate School of Design), Fall 1984, 15
Photograph by Barry Donahue

4. Cram, Ferguson, and Goodhue, Design for Houses of Parliament, Tokyo
From *Bertram Grosvenor Goodhue— Architect and Master of Many Arts*, ed. Charles Harris Whitaker (New York, 1925), pl. 65

ours, *composing the lines and masses as he builds his pictorial masterpiece.*[7]

If this passage reveals Cram's personal response to place and monument and his openness to different cultures, it also shows the unmistakable influence of Ruskin, whose books he had devoured as a teenager.[8]

But if this book showed Cram's openness to different cultures, his *Ruined Abbeys of Great Britain* reveals a different side. Although sparkling with Ruskinian flourishes, the images nonetheless become burdened. At Lindisfarne he begins: "[Here] . . . where the wild and windswept northern cliffs that frown on the German ocean . . . break down into the ever-thundering sea and crabbed islands lift bravely out of tempestuous breakers. . . . [Here] . . . lashed by tumultuous winds and drenched by sea-spume and swirling fog . . . were established the first outposts of the Catholic Faith in the North."[9] As the passage suggests, the historical context woven around the buildings is a history

with a purpose. The ruins trigger reveries on past monastic greatness, to be sure, but they also become the means by which Cram confronts wider matters, such as the greed of Henry VIII and the corruption of his henchmen, notably Thomas Cromwell, who Cram insists throughout on calling Crumwell. In his reassessment of the Reformation, Cram was no groundbreaker—Lenoir and Montalembert in France, Cardinal Gasquet in England, and others had preceded him[10]—but his tone is more ascerbic and his implications more moralizing. Behind the events in England, Cram informs us, lies a more sinister force, the Renaissance, which "first debauched the world it had come to destroy, then assailed it for the very faults and vices it had instilled into its being."[11] From the Renaissance sprang absolutism, demoralization, the loss of liberty, revolt against Divine law.

Some of these same preoccupations had, in fact, already been anticipated, although in different guise and under different topics. Cram's earliest writing when he was working as a journalist on the *Boston Evening Transcript* had concentrated on political matters, and this interest formed the subject of his first book, *The Decadent*, published in 1893 when he was thirty.[12] Using the form of a novel, this volume launched a stinging critique of political systems, a subject to which Cram would frequently return. In literary images that bring to mind the visual images in the etchings of Pugin's *Contrasts*, Cram blasts both social and political structures, comparing rural innocence to industrial, meaning urban, debasement. Democracy Cram defines as "the government of the best, by the worst, for the few." If such phrasing carries the ring of the tabloids, Cram's remedy is anything but populist. He urges a return to monarchy, albeit a monarchy of strongly Jacobite cast. These views had already led Cram somewhat earlier to found a monarchist society in Boston with his friend Fred Day and to establish a short-lived serial called *The Royalist*.[13]

Reactionary as this sounds, Cram's utopian views reveal a figure who was much more a rebel than a reactionary, a passionate critic of the status quo. These qualities explain other causes he pushed with equal ardor. Some appear directly antithetical to his monarchist views, like the strong advocacy of "socialistic ideas," as he called them. If *The Decadent* examined this theme at the start of Cram's career, at least five books dealt with it during his middle years, their pitch discernible from such titles as *The Nemesis of Mediocrity* (1917) and *The Sins of the Fathers* (1918); he returned to it again in his last book at the close of his life, *The End of Democracy* (1937).[14] All of these volumes are marked by a pervasive pessimism and a sense of imminent cultural crisis. Democracy has failed, big government is evil, bureaucracy intolerable, modernism corrupting, Roosevelt imperial. The short-term solution lies in the amendment of the American constitution through the reconfiguration of the then forty-eight states into five or six provinces or commonwealths. The long-term ideal remains a constitutional monarchy, complete with orders of knighthood.[15]

These prolonged forays into political

theory are particularly hard to digest today. But they are important. Underlying Cram's ideology was a profound commitment to designing, social as well as architectural. Cram began with the premise that manifestations of cultural decay lay everywhere and that modern society was doomed. Since art reflects culture, it follows that a morally corrupt culture can not produce good art. Only a return to the values of the Middle Ages, meaning the twelfth and thirteenth centuries, could save society. Likewise, only a return to Gothic art would restore Cram's socialistic commonwealth based on the guilds. Cram used this argument with an urgency, intellectual subtlety, and careful theological, even Thomistic, reasoning that are essential to grasp for their own intrinsic qualities, but also as clues to why contemporaries found the articulation of such views persuasive. In fairness, his consistent critique of culture and the political theorems he proposed to mend it need to be seen in the context of American politics in the decades of World War I and specifically to Wilsonian democracy. Princeton is in many ways a key to Cram. In its president, Woodrow Wilson, Cram found both a figure whose social idealism matched his own and a supporter of his architectural style.[16] Social and architectural reforms in America were to be advanced not so much through socialism as through medievalism.

Cram's ideology also needs to be seen as much in relation to the past as to that of his contemporaries. He was raised on the books of John Ruskin and William Morris. Like the pre-Raphaelites, Cram deplored the callousness of industrialism and urged a new social order. Cram acknowledged these associations and did little to discourage references to himself as the American Pugin or American Ruskin. Pre-Raphaelite influence extended to other areas. Following Morris, for instance, Cram was deeply interested in hand-printed books, in typesetting, and, aided by his brilliant partner Bertram Goodhue, in the design of typefaces.[17] In his own work these interests can best be seen in his successful *Black and White Spirits: A Book of Ghost Stories* of 1896 and in the launching of the short-lived quarterly publication, *The Knight Errant* (fig. 5). Among contributors to the first issue were Goodhue, F. Holland Day, Charles Eliot Norton, and Francis Watts Lee. Other authors whom Cram drew into the quarterly from his wide circle of friends included Bernard Berenson, Walter Crane, and Ernest Fenollosa.[18]

Unlike Morris, however, Cram had no personal fortune to bankroll his brand of elitist socialism or highbrow monarchism. By 1890 the need for money had driven him first to interior decorating, including the design of wallpaper (perhaps another Morris influence) and then back to architecture. He poured his immense energy into establishing a firm that for some years consisted of just two men, Cram and Charles Wentworth, plus a white Boston bull terrier, who were squeezed into a shoebox-size office at Park Square. Commissions trickled in with painful slowness. The first were almost exclusively domestic houses, which were executed in English half-timber work, and it was three to five years before the firm turned to churches. At the start, the choice of churches as a special area of interest was determined by entrepreneurial opportunism as much as by high moral motives; put simply, Cram informs us in an unexpected admission in his autobiography, they were something no one else was working on.[19]

In approaching Cram the Goth it is necessary to distinguish first between his views as a historian of Gothic and as a Gothic practitioner. They are by no means the same, and it is difficult to determine whether the views of the historian preceded those of the architect or vice versa. Cram wrote five books as a historian of Gothic, of which the most interesting are *The Ministry of Art* (1914) and *The Substance of Gothic* (1916).[20] In both, as in his previously mentioned *Ruined Abbeys*, the reader needs to pass quickly over Cram's potted church history, his views on medieval society, politics, the guilds, and, alas, race (discourses on the virtues of northern blood occur on more than one occasion). As suggested earlier, the lessons of history preoccupy Cram as much as, if not more than, history itself. Monasticism is given a preeminent role: in fact, Cram views all of history in the light of the rise and fall of

5. *The Knight Errant*
Whitaker 1925, pl. CCLXVII

monasticism (fig. 6). Of the renewal in the eleventh century Cram writes, "Never was such an upheaval, such a rattling of the dry bones of wide decrepitude by militant monks hot with the zeal of reform,"[21] only to ignore the severely modified role of monasticism in the thirteenth and fourteenth centuries, for instance, that resulted from the changed bases of funding and patronage.

Turning to architecture, Cram credits monasticism as both the agent of civilization and the patron of the arts. When it comes to architecture, his historical divisioning is eccentric, however. In *The Substance of Gothic*, given as the Lowell lectures in 1916, Cram promises coverage from Charlemagne to Henry VIII. Yet not until the fifth of his six lectures does he reach Abbot Suger's St. Denis. For the development of Gothic, Cram employs the biological metaphor of birth, maturity, and decline.[22] Having been alerted in lecture five to "the inevitable decline" of architecture from 1300 forward, the reader anticipates a suitable lament from the title of the last lecture, "Decadence and the New Pagan-

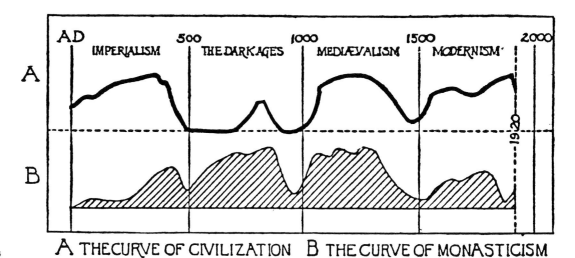

6. Ralph Adams Cram
From *Walled Towns* (Boston, 1920), 33

A THE CURVE OF CIVILIZATION   B THE CURVE OF MONASTICISM

ism." But confusion now sets in. If society, ethics, philosophy, government, and religion degenerate after the age of St. Louis, Cram is forced to conclude that architecture is somehow nonsynchronous; this, even though the preceding chapters had demonstrated their congruence. By 1400 Cram sees architecture revealing a "sudden, novel . . . and captivating" vigor.[23] If late Gothic could initially be faulted for "the isolation of the decorative and artistic forms from their structural context" in England, at least in Perpendicular, the whole nature of architecture was transformed "to produce a completely articulated system."[24] For its time this was a bold approach for which Cram deserves credit.[25] What cut this new flowering in mid-growth, however, was the Renaissance. Earlier Cram had warned that "inch by inch the virus engendered in Italy . . . [had] crept though the veins of Europe," but now "its poison began to work" in earnest.[26] We can leave Cram to tell us why in what is by now a familiar litany, and turn instead briefly to Cram writing about his use of Gothic in his own architecture.

Ironically, Cram rejects the biological metaphor he had employed as a historian to explain the development of Gothic and champions as a practitioner the architecture of the period 1300–1500. This about-face was disguised by adopting a model for late Gothic as a process very much in pro-

gress when the Renaissance terminated its still-promising growth. Unlike Pugin, who saw the fourteenth century as a golden age that could not be surpassed but only copied, Cram saw the architect's role as continuing the fifteenth- and sixteenth-century development where it had been interrupted. Far from being a dead style worthy of imitation, Gothic was a living force with a potential that awaited release.[27] For Cram this construct firmly separated him from the early nineteenth century. He lambastes the Gothic revival for being archaeological and retrograde. Indeed, far from being a fuddy-duddy antiquarian or archaeologist—a word loaded with opprobrium for Cram—he saw himself first and last as an innovator, as the assimilator and inventor using modern principles, as a figure analogous to H. H. Richardson.[28]

Compared to reading his history, reading Cram on architecture—old and new but particularly new—is like night and day. In scattered writings, often in articles rather than books, or in the introductions he was constantly called upon to write for the books of others, Cram takes on many of the big questions of architecture and architectural theory in the twentieth century: the role of structure and function, the relation of style to typology, the purpose of decoration, issues of restoration and preservation, the implications of materials and technology for style, and urbanism.

Cram's architecture and its extraordinary impact on contemporaries—Kingsley Porter called St. John the Divine in New York City "a tenth symphony"—are matters that lie outside this paper; Tucci has elucidated the churches, Turner the campus buildings.[29] Of the writings, however, one book in particular deserves attention: *Church Building*, published in 1901. Reissued in two editions (1914, 1925), it remains indispensable to an understanding of church architecture for the subsequent half century. With an authority reminiscent of the Ecclesiological Society of sixty years earlier, Cram sets out the qualities of an ideal church: the need to distinguish choir from nave, the creation of an all-encompassing mood for the interior, the representation of Christian history in sculpture and glass, the visibility of both pulpit and altar.[30] Pugin's interests keep emerging, as does something of his method, as when Cram offers the reader beguiling comparisons of good and bad design. Of country chapels, for instance, the reader is confronted with illustrations of "false picturesque," "affectedly picturesque" (fig. 7), and "vicious design." Cram also includes something much harder—examples of good design, his own firm's for the most part, often illustrated by his brilliant partner Goodhue with the use of restrained linear accents, evocative splashes of reflected light, and distinct Arts and Crafts vocabulary for surrounding trees, ivy, or foregrounds (fig. 8). The book's confident judgments and advocacy of good taste served as a bible of design for many an anxious vestry member or insecure patron. Furthermore, since his clients included an amazing range of Protestant denominations—from Baptists and Swedenborgians to Presbyterians and Episcopalians—Cram, under the guise of taste, accomplished the unthinkable, the catholicization of Protestantism. Remarkably, architecture embraced pluralism long before theology.[31]

From his voluminous writing and from this survey of him as traveler, political idealist, and Goth, Cram emerges as a complex, even contradictory, personality. Excluded for financial reasons from academe as a youth, he spent much of his career

I. EXAMPLE OF FALSE "PICTURESQUE."

II. EXAMPLE OF THE AFFECTEDLY PICTURESQUE.

(and made much of his money) in the highest academic circles. Born an austere New Hampshire Yankee, he lived among and worked with Boston brahmins. He espoused monarchism yet advocated socialism. He championed the guild system but despised unions. He embraced technology and at the same time pushed for a machine-free urbanism. He dabbled endlessly in politics but rejected political parties. By birth and upbringing a liberal Unitarian,

7. Ralph Adams Cram
From *Church Building* (Boston, 1901), figs. I, II

he practiced a fervent Anglo-Catholic piety, albeit with brief flirtations in the direction of Buddhism and Judaism. He proposed Gothic in his architecture and will always be associated with it, but he practiced other styles with a refreshingly undoctrinaire freedom.

Turning from Cram to Conant brings one down to earth. This is literally the case in the archaeological sense, but it is true in the literary sense as well, because Conant never shared Cram's writing ambitions (or gifts), indulged in his flights of imagination, or sympathized with his evangelizing bent. Conant was rooted in academe, a patch Cram successfully cultivated for commissions, but which was far too constraining of his energies. In some areas the careers of the two men overlapped. They knew each other and saw themselves in a line of descent from Ruskin (for Conant via Herbert Langford Warren, his undergraduate teacher and founder of Harvard's School of Architecture, H. H. Richardson and Charles Eliot Norton).[32] They shared the profession of architecture and even interlocked on one or two commissions: Conant claimed a role in Cram's design of

the west facade of St. John the Divine in New York and also in his Cowley Fathers monastery in Cambridge.[33]

But it is the differences between the two men that are interesting, and important. Conant's archaeological interests and academic career were completely different from Cram's. His world was university based and university disciplined, meaning Harvard. Furthermore, Conant's approach lay at the furthest extreme from Cram's. It was object oriented; it sought some solid grounding in the past; it substituted objective systems of stylistic classification for Cram's vague substances; and it focused on Romanesque—that "stern realm of simple walls and vaults," in Eduard Sekler's phrase[34]—and France, rather than late Gothic and England.

Conant's name will always be linked with his lifelong work and publications on Cluny in Burgundy in eastern France, the center of the greatest monastic movement of the Middle Ages. His interest began before the completion of his doctoral dissertation on Santiago de Compostela, published in 1926. At the suggestion of his thesis advisor, the charismatic Arthur

Kingsley Porter, Conant appraised the site of the largely destroyed abbey and grasped its potential for archaeological investigation.[35] Work began in 1927, funded through the newly founded Medieval Academy of America, and preoccupied Conant for the next fifty years, culminating only in 1968 with the publication of his monograph on the monastery.[36] Conant began in the east parts of the monastic church, digging the first of a series of what would eventually become ninety "pits" (to use Conant's own blunt term) [fig. 9]. A stream of reports soon emerged; while largely straightforward accounts of work, they served to reawaken interest in Cluny and to establish Conant's reputation.[37]

But the Cluny work was always somewhat isolated from Paris. In part this was due to Conant's 1930 articles, in which he entered the fraught and sometimes chauvinist debate over the date of the Cluny ambulatory capitals, championing "proof" of his mentor Porter's early dating.[38] Watertight as Conant believed his arguments to be, they won few converts among traditional French scholarship in Paris, which closed ranks behind Paul Deschamps, who dated the capitals and thus the church a good twenty-five years later. Despite being excluded by Paris, Conant enjoyed an august status in Burgundy. A certain provincialism now hung over his work, however. Whether Conant was a victim or to some extent an agent of this is hard to know. In any event, once the archaeology paused, Conant's subsequent publications on Cluny were also marked by a certain "loner" quality. He turned to the less-frequented and even esoteric areas of architecture, such as setting out, symbolism, metrology, and, through induction, to other generative processes. In fairness, Conant was drawn to them by his heroic endeavor to leave no stone unturned in the quest of uncovering the lost masterpiece.

Driving Conant's archaeology (and his writing) was the passionate conviction that Cluny marked the culmination of the artistic revival of the eleventh and twelfth centuries. This conviction led Conant to make large claims, not all of which were capable of proof: Cluny was the summation of Romanesque; it synthesized multi-

ple international sources; it introduced the pointed arch and initiated the fashion for monumental doorway sculpture; it pioneered the use of flyers; it foreshadowed Gothic.

While it has become fashionable to criticize Conant—to see him as archaeologically suspect, Cluny-obsessed, and a pencil-happy inventor rather than the reconstructor of medieval architecture—

9. Kenneth Conant at Cluny, 1931
Courtesy of Graduate School of Design Library, Harvard University

the eye-rolling that normally follows mention of his name has recently abated. In marked contrast to Conant's patient labors, the Office of the Monuments Historiques in Paris cleared the narthex of Cluny in July 1988 using a bulldozer, which bladed up more than two thousand sculptural fragments, their archaeological record now permanently destroyed, before horrified international reaction could halt its work. For their time, Conant's day books and the hundreds of drawings preserved in the Musée Ochier in Cluny are models of sound recording and serve as the basis for the valuable inventory of the more than ten thousand labeled fragments now being conducted by a team from the British Museum.[39]

Apart from the Cluny work, Conant's views on Romanesque center around certain themes that emerge most clearly in two small but influential books published in the 1940s.[40] In both Conant focused on a select number of prominent, lost monuments—Old St. Peter's in Rome, St. Benigne at Dijon, St. Martin at Tours, and Cluny, the last three stressed by Cram in the Lowell lectures in Boston, which Conant almost certainly heard in 1916 during his first year in graduate school at Harvard.[41] A second theme, also central to Conant's Pelican volume, *Carolingian and Romanesque Architecture 800–1200* (1959), asserted the unity of particular techniques of building or structure, vaults especially, and certain habits of design or decoration. This risked reductionism. Thus, the achievement of Romanesque in three of the most seminal areas—Normandy, England, and the Ile-de-France—is defined by "the creation of a new structural unit, . . . the ribbed groin-vaulted bay."[42] A third theme stressed monasticism, which Conant, like Cram, saw as the central, even the dominant force in the period. Romanesque reached its major accomplishment in the monastic church, and at Cluny and Cîteaux it achieved a synthesis of traditional forms. Innovators outside monasticism—as in Romanesque cathedrals like Durham, Winchester, and Lincoln in England or S. Ambrogio in Milan—Conant blandly explains as a "foil [to] . . . the many varied regional styles."[43] Had the typological tension between the monastic and nonmonastic solutions been elaborated, Romanesque would be better understood, but Conant plunged into a dissection of styles which, when scrutinized, turn out to be an anthology of architectural and structural elements and enumerated details. Disentanglement of these features creates a complex picture: within the modern frontiers of France, for instance, Conant identified no fewer than twenty-two stylistic regions.

Surprisingly, Conant's approach is often narrower than Cram's or, for that matter, than that of his somewhat earlier counterpart in England, William Lethaby.[44] If Cram read nearly everything, consuming books with the unfettered enthusiasm of the autodidact, Conant gave small concern to what others had written, as John Coolidge has pointed out.[45] On the other hand, Conant's books provided a far wider acquaintance with monuments and a much sounder historical base. In the last analysis Conant's was an architectural history of the physical properties of buildings, object oriented rather than intellectually oriented. What architecture meant, what it symbolized or expressed, who its patrons or clients were and what effects mattered to them, how it related to the society that created it were matters that held scant interest for him.[46] These more inclusive readings of medieval architecture had already been introduced into North America in the late 1930s by German scholars such as Richard Krautheimer at Louisville and Vassar and Paul Frankl at Princeton, and French scholars such as Marcel Aubert and Henri Focillon at Yale. Conant was not, therefore, unacquainted with other approaches, but he believed firmly in his own.

In many ways Conant had a greater influence as a teacher than as a writer. For a number of years he taught everything Harvard offered in architectural history, an indication of his often overlooked breadth and openness and his immense knowledge.[47] His popularity derived in part from his teaching style, which was brisk and authoritative, gentlemanly, often good humored, and notably unstuffy. For instance, to illustrate the resonance of certain East-

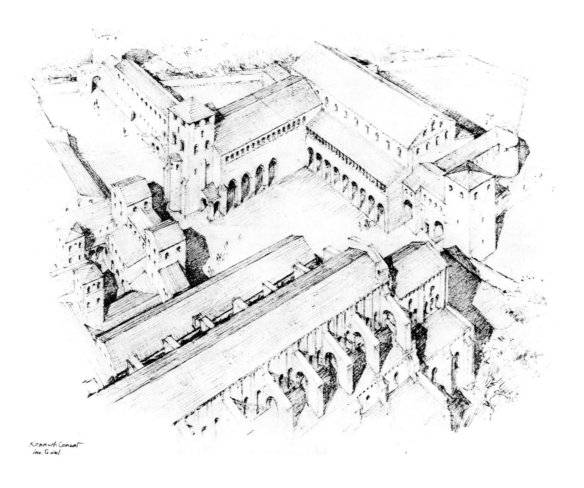

Kenneth Conant
inv. G del.

ern church forms, Conant would unself-consciously intone a few bars of Byzantine chant, filling Robinson Hall with a fine bass-baritone, or he would leap from stage to floor when carried away by excitement.[48]

In keeping with the strong technical and design emphasis of his history, Conant's courses included a final assignment that involved the construction of a model, such as two or three bays of a Romanesque or Gothic church. Making conditioned seeing. Ironically, Conant's own gifts lay in drawing (fig. 10), his numerous reconstructions bringing to life destroyed buildings. Most important of all, what came through in his lectures time and again was a love of buildings, their physical presences and characters, no matter the period. Students were deeply influenced. Even after Gropius' arrival at Harvard and the removal of

architectural history from the required curriculum (involving Conant's sideways shift from the Graduate School of Design to the Fine Arts Department), his classes remained filled.[49] In time the students became architects, scholars, or influential figures in the professions. And, as already mentioned, his students established the Society of Architectural Historians in 1940.

In concluding, one might ask why Cram and Conant's importance in the period 1900–1940 differs from their reputation today. For Conant one clue may be his brand of history. Along with histories that focused on matters such as the priority of the rib vault, or the pointed arch, or the morphology of mouldings and ornament, Conant's was left high and dry by the more inclusive histories established in the 1940s and the methods practiced since by Richard Krautheimer, Charles Seymour, Earl

10. Drawing by Conant of the reconstruction of the outer court at Cluny
From *Cluny—Les églises et la maison du chef d'ordre* (Macon, 1968), pl. 30, fig. 50

Baldwin Smith, Sumner McK. Crosby, Robert Branner, Jean Bony, Walter Horn, and others.

If Conant focused on reconstructing the past, Cram constructed a living present from the past. Yet understanding Cram's eclipse is more complex. By the 1930s the demand for the firm's work declined rapidly. College and church had been mainstays of the firm, whose historical vocabulary suited institutions that were, as Lewis Mumford pointed out, tradition oriented[50] (as also, it could be pointed out, was the military academy). The Depression now bit deeply into the collegiate Gothic boom, however, and, similarly, into ecclesiastical commissions. Economic catastrophe forced America in the 1930s to look inward, not outward to Europe. For this reason, in part, the Anglophilia that marked the early decades of the twentieth century no longer held strong appeal. Gothic, as a paradigm for a threatened social order, looked empty as a source for architecture, and it no longer spoke a language with much meaning for its patrons or users. By the 1920s colonial revival—brick Georgian—then art deco, and finally modernism became more important architectural idioms. From this perspective Cram looked not just out of place, but

hopelessly out of date, a figure whose thunderings and moralizings represented the last gasp of a movement originating a hundred years earlier with Pugin. It is perhaps thus easier to grasp why Cram's demotion was so much more complete than that of his English contemporary, Edwin Lutyens, and why any revival lies on a distant horizon. It was the same with Cram's political ideologies. Even the staunchest supporter of monarchism was forced to see in the abdication of Edward VIII not just moral weakness but constitutional limitation; the New Deal had not led to Armageddon; and the nation's vigor remained unimpaired by emigration and southern Mediterranean blood.

Despite their divided modes of knowledge and production, Cram and Conant structure the study of medieval architecture in the period 1900–1940. They form a paradoxical whole, oppositionally linked. If we think today of Cram more as practitioner than thinker, as a figure whose work graces city, suburb, and college, Conant's reputation resides in academe and in the effect his teaching had in countless professional offices, in historical commissions, and not least in the impetus that led to the creation of the society whose semicentennial we honor.

NOTES

In the preparation of this paper I gratefully acknowledge the help of friends and colleagues, while in no way implicating them in the shortcomings of content or writing. Of particular assistance were: James O'Gorman, John Coolidge, Caroline Bruzelius, Arnold Klukas, Patricia Berman, John Rhodes, Anne Higonnet, Neil Stratford, David Walsh, William MacDonald, Elizabeth Pastan, and Lilian Armstrong.

1. In two recent books Douglass Shand Tucci has dealt boldly and effectively with Cram's life, philosophy, and architecture; see *Church Building in Boston, 1720-1970s*, with an Introduction to the Work of Ralph Adams Cram and the Boston Gothicists (Concord, Mass., 1974) and *Ralph Adams Cram: American Medievalist* (Boston, 1975).

2. Tucci 1974, 49 lists "two dozen books and hundreds of scholarly and polemical articles." No bibliography of Cram's writings has been published, however. The British Library catalogues thirty books, and the number for his papers needs to take account of such contributions as reviews, prefaces, and introductions to the books of others.

3. For instance, see "Memoir: Ralph Adams Cram," *Speculum* 18 (1943), 388-389, an appreciation signed by John Nicholas Brown, C. R. Coffman, and E. K. Rand.

4. Like Cram, Conant has not been the subject of a complete study, nor have his writings been collected. For a biographical sketch see Peter Fergusson, "Necrology—Kenneth John Conant (1895-1984)," *Gesta* 24, no. 1 (1985), 87-88.

5. John Coolidge, "Kenneth Conant and the Founding of the American Society of Architectural Historians," *Journal of the Society of Architectural Historians* 43 (1984), 193-194.

6. Ralph Adams Cram, *My Life in Architecture* (Boston, 1936).

7. Ralph Adams Cram, *Impressions of Japanese Architecture and the Allied Arts*, 3d ed. (Boston, 1930), 102.

8. While not intended as a history, *Japanese Architecture* remained a standard work for more than thirty years and in three editions, the last published by the Japan Society in 1930. The originality of Cram's treatment, with its heavy emphasis on characterization and interpretation, needs to be seen in the context of earlier books on Japanese architecture, like that of Edward S. Morse, *Japanese Homes, and Their Surroundings* (Boston, 1885). One of the only influences of the journey on Cram's own architecture is found in his design in 1909 of the Japanese garden and gallery at the Boston Museum of Fine Arts. This remained until it was replaced by the present, austere gallery in the renovations of 1978-1982.

9. Ralph Adams Cram, *The Ruined Abbeys of Great Britain* (New York, 1905), 46. The book was again the product of a remarkably short visit. In the context of the Lindisfarne evocation, it is worth recalling

Cram's revelation in his autobiography that the goal of his first trip to Europe in 1886 was not Chartres or the Gothic cathedrals, but Bayreuth and the Wagner festival; see Cram 1936, 50.

10. See Alexander Lenoir, *Architecture Monastique* (Paris, 1852); Comte de Montalembert, *Les moines d'Occident*, vol. 4 (Paris, 1877); and Cardinal Francis Gasquet, *Henry VIII and the English Monasteries* (London, 1889).

11. Cram 1905, 215.

12. Ralph Adams Cram, *The Decadent: being the Gospel of Inaction wherein are set forth in romance form certain reflections touching the curious characteristics of these ultimate years and the divers causes thereof* (Boston, 1893).

13. First published in 1891, the quarterly went through only two issues.

14. Ralph Adams Cram, *Nemesis of Mediocrity* (Boston, 1917); *The Sins of the Fathers* (Boston, 1918); *The End of Democracy* (Boston, 1937).

15. See Cram 1937, 201-211.

16. Princeton was decisive for Cram in the political, educational, and architectural sphere. For Wilson, buildings in the Tudor Gothic style "not only added a thousand years to the history of Princeton, [but] point everyman's imagination to the historic traditions of learning in the English speaking race." Donald Drew Egbert, "The Architecture and the Setting," in *The Modern Princeton*, ed. Charles G. Osgood (Princeton, 1947), 86-121, 94. Arnold Klukas kindly drew my attention to this quotation.

Cram was appointed supervising architect at Princeton in 1909 and held the post for the next twenty-two years, an association he described in his autobiography as "a sort of cumulative joy that was one of the greatest experiences of my life." Cram 1936, 118. Cram designed the university's master plan and was the architect of three important buildings: Campbell Hall, the Graduate College complex, and the chapel. However, as supervising architect he exercised strong additional influence on the design of two other firms active at the university: Day and Klauder, and Cope and Stewardson.

17. See James O'Gorman, " 'Either in books or [in] architecture': Bertram Grosvenor Goodhue in the Nineties," *Harvard Library Bulletin* 35 (1988), 165-183.

18. The first issue appeared in 1892; there was a total of four issues before the magazine collapsed.

19. Cram 1936, 72.

20. Ralph Adams Cram, *The Ministry of Art* (Boston and New York, 1914); *The Substance of Gothic* (Boston, 1916).

21. Ralph Adams Cram, *The Substance of Gothic: Six Lectures on the Development of Architecture from Charlemagne to Henry VIII, given at the Lowell Institute, Boston, in November and December, 1916* (Boston, 1917), 71.

22. Cram 1917, 137-157.

23. Cram 1917, 166.

24. Cram 1917, 173.

25. For the general literary context for the recognition of late Gothic, see Paul Frankl, *The Gothic: Literary Sources and Interpretations through Eight Centuries* (Princeton, 1960), 641–650.

26. Cram 1917, 162, 186.

27. This view surfaced even in Cram's preface to Henry Adams, *Mont-Saint-Michel and Chartres* (Boston, 1913), viii. It was Cram who persuaded Adams to allow commercial publication of the book. With a true patrician's disdain, Adams calmly handed the text to Cram to do with as he wished.

28. Cram 1936, 37. Elsewhere Cram would write, "From the past, not in the past, . . . we must return, but we may not remain. It is the present that demands us." Ralph Adams Cram, *Church Building: A Study in the Principles of Architecture in their Relation to the Church* (Boston, 1901), 13.

29. Tucci 1974; Paul Venable Turner, *Campus: an American Planning Tradition* (Cambridge, Mass., 1984), 217.

30. It might be pointed out that research by medievalists would severely qualify these qualities as characteristic of the Middle Ages.

31. Lest this place Cram in too prophetic a light, it needs emphasizing that in using Gothic for Protestant denominations, Cram saw his architecture carrying a distinctly, even mischievously, evangelizing side—good Gothic would convert. Interestingly, Roman Catholics were at first slow to employ Cram, a delay that clearly rankled. Long after this might have been forgotten, Cram in his autobiography gives this reason, expressed in characteristically trenchant fashion: "The [Roman Catholic] church was still submerged in an artistic barbarism comparable only with that of the Methodist and Baptist denominations." Cram 1936, 97.

32. Conant specified this line of descent in the preface to his *Carolingian and Romanesque Architecture 800–1200* (Baltimore, 1959), xxv.

33. It may be inferred that Conant's estimate of Cram the architect was a lot higher than of Cram the writer. Nowhere do Cram's books appear in Conant's bibliographies, and they were not even on the shelves of his extensive library given to Harvard in 1979.

34. Eduard Sekler's tribute to Conant delivered in Harvard's Memorial Church is quoted in *GSD News* (Harvard Graduate School of Design), Fall 1984, 16.

35. Porter was more than just Conant's doctoral supervisor. He effected Conant's conversion to the Middle Ages, became friend and mentor, and steered Conant's early career. The closeness of the two men emerges in a touching tribute by Kingsley Porter in his review of Conant's first book (and doctoral dissertation); see Arthur Kingsley Porter, "Santiago Again," *Art in America* 15 (February 1927), 96–113.

Conant liked to explain why the permission to excavate had been given to an American by noting that in French eyes he had shed blood for France when wounded in World War I at the Second Battle of the Marne. Prime as Cluny now appears to us as a site, it needs to be pointed out that few realized its potential in 1926. In part, taste and restoration efforts were directed in the 1920s toward the war-damaged Gothic cathedrals in the northeast.

36. Kenneth John Conant, *Cluny—Les églises et la maison du chef d'ordre* (Macon, France, 1968). At the start of the Cluny excavation the academy's secretary was Ralph Adams Cram, who enthusiastically supported Conant's proposal (another inconsistency, given his dislike of archaeology) and mentioned it warmly in his autobiography. Cram 1936, 226. Nearly all of the funding, however, came from the personal support of the academy's president, John Nicholas Brown, as well as through the assistance of three Guggenheim fellowships.

37. Conant's publication on the abbey culminated only in 1968 with the publication of his monograph; see note 36.

38. Kenneth J. Conant, "Medieval Academy Excavations at Cluny—The Date of the Ambulatory Capitals" and "The Iconography and the Sequence of the Ambulatory Capitals of Cluny," *Speculum* 5 (1930), 77–94, 278–287.

39. Conant's archaeological methods have been analyzed recently by a member of that team; see David Walsh, "The Excavations of Cluny III by K. J. Conant," *Le Gouvernment d'Huges de Semur à Cluny, 1988* (Mâcon, France, 1990), in press.

40. Kenneth John Conant, *A Brief Commentary on Early Medieval Church Architecture, with Special Reference to Lost Monuments* (Baltimore, 1942) and *Benedictine Contributions to Church Architecture* (Latrobe, 1949).

41. A history based on lost monuments was eccentric, and Conant even proposed a similar approach for his volume in the Pelican series, *Carolingian and Romanesque Architecture 800–1200* (Baltimore, 1959) until overruled by Pevsner. It is worth observing that for other scholars, like Krautheimer, the lacunae of lost monuments can be filled by building a picture through what remains of related buildings and through documentary and archaeological work. But Conant never employed this method in his general writing, although he used it in his Cluny monograph; see note 36.

42. Conant 1956, xxv. It is debatable whether development of this structural component was more critical than, say, the developing conception of the Great Church with the conscious evocation of themes drawn from Christian antiquity, as Peter Kidson pointed out in his review of the book, "The Literature, Art: Carolingian and Romanesque Architecture," *Burlington Magazine* 102 (1960), 414–415.

43. Conant 1959, xxv.

44. As in, for example, William Richard Lethaby, *Westminster Abbey and the King's Craftsmen, a Study of Mediaeval Building* (London, 1906) or *Westminster Abbey Re-Examined* (London, 1925).

45. Coolidge 1984, 193.

46. For a graphic example of the difference in ap-

proach compare the treatment of Durham by Conant 1959, 288–290, where the building's qualities are flatly enumerated, to that by Jean Bony, "Durham et la tradition saxonne," in *Etudes d'art medieval offertes à Louis Grodecki*, eds. Sumner McK. Crosby et al. (Paris, 1981), 79–92. In the latter, the vocabulary of forms and of style used in the cathedral are interpreted as a conscious fusion of Saxon and Norman traditions and related to the history of the building and site at the end of the eleventh century.

47. Even in his first year of teaching (1924) he offered three history courses that ranged from ancient Greece to modern America. His capacity for travel in pursuit of this information was formidable. It is worth noting that in an age before air travel Conant claimed in his twentieth reunion class book to have traveled 150,000 miles since graduation.

48. Professor William MacDonald kindly provided these memories of Conant's lectures.

49. Conant was as adventurous in his religious tastes as Cram. Apparently raised as a Unitarian in Wisconsin, he was baptized as an Episcopalian while an undergraduate at Harvard, the ceremony taking place in Romanesque Trinity Church with no less a person than Isabella Stewart Gardner standing as godparent (an anecdote confirmed to me by Rollin van N. Hadley, director of the Gardner Museum). Conant converted to Greek Orthodoxy in the mid-1930s.

49. Outside Harvard, Conant's teaching also drew wide audiences, as on his foreign lectureships to France, Argentina, and Mexico. His *Tres conferencias sobre arquitectura moderna en los Estados Unidos* (Buenos Aires, 1949) became one of the rare books available on the subject in the southern continent.

50. Lewis Mumford, *Sticks and Stones: A Study of American Architecture and Civilization* (1924; rev. ed., New York, 1955), 52–53.

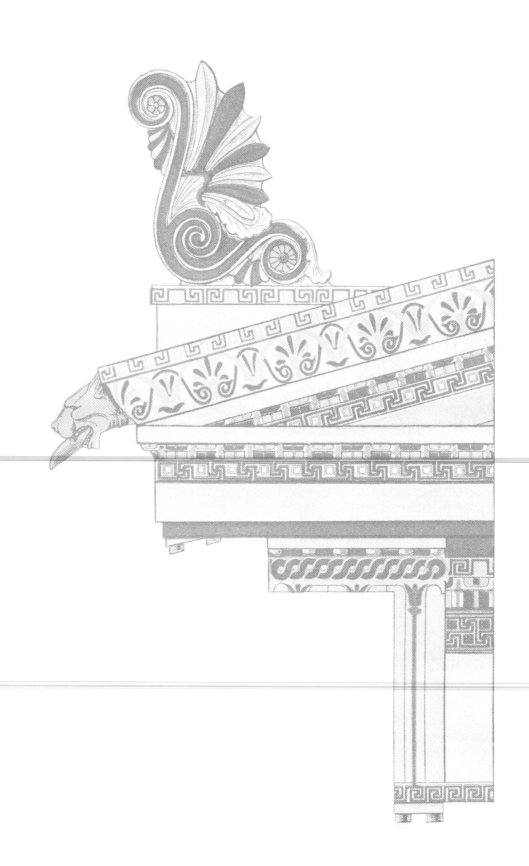

LINDA SEIDEL
University of Chicago

The Scholar and the Studio:

A. Kingsley Porter and the Study of Medieval Architecture in the Decade before the War

When Kingsley Porter disappeared in the summer of 1933 at the age of fifty, a news item announced the event on the front page of the *New York Times*. The story reported that Porter, the William Dorr Boardman Professor of Fine Arts at Harvard, had been spending his summer vacation in Ireland "conducting archaeological work with his wife Lucy Bryant Wallace of New York." A small boat in which Porter had set out from shore overturned in a severe thunderstorm, and he was presumed drowned off his beloved Donegal coast.[1] Porter's body was never recovered. A few days later, a different version of the story of his disappearance was published. It was claimed that Porter, while on a walk to meet his wife, had slipped on wet rocks, fallen into the sea below and vanished in a "swift outgoing tide."[2]

The revision of the death notice added a sense of mystery to the aura of idiosyncrasy and boldness that attended Porter throughout his scholarly life. His written work, like his final adventure, always held an element of the unexpected. An obituary on the editorial page of the *Times* for Sunday, 16 July, called his books

so many deeds of derring-do edifying, appalling or delighting his peers according to their temper. No time or territory was quite the same after KINGSLEY PORTER had traversed it. He illuminated it through a vast and often new documentation; he enlivened it through new

and at times startling theories and interpretations. His scholarship offered a paradoxical blend of solidity with a penchant for living dangerously.[3]

Although the attention the New York press paid to Porter's demise may well have had more to do with the prominence of his wife's family than with his own reputation as a "valued exotic" at Harvard, the editorial provided serious evaluation of a scholarly production that was, by any measure, singleminded and innovative. Porter, in numerous publications, took up subjects European nationals ordinarily addressed, attacking such issues as the dating of medieval monuments and putting forward new theories about the origins of Gothic architecture, Romanesque sculpture, and Irish iconography. He blazed a trail that no American scholar had trod before. The editorial of 16 July argued that Porter's accomplishments should not be measured solely by their correctness:

In the long run it may not greatly matter whether theories of this sort are right or wrong; they will have in any case done their work in ventilating a fusty branch of knowledge and in challenging archaeological vested interests. No such qualification attaches to KINGSLEY PORTER'S immense contribution to the published body of medieval architecture and sculpture. Its value is permanent.

Indeed, Porter's contributions to the literature on medieval art and architecture have stood the test of time even though all of his ideas have not always been fashionable in academic circles. In several instances, his definition of a problem established the paradigm within which research is still pursued and scholarly discourse advanced. Students continue to turn, for example, to his model of artistic movement in analyzing the pilgrimage art and architecture of southern Europe in the eleventh and twelfth centuries. At the same time, suggestions he made long ago about the material motivations of Cluny in developing churches along the pilgrimage roads have only recently resurfaced in the work of Karl Werckmeister.[4]

One of the things that energized Porter's inventions and may well have helped sustain his formulations over time was the attention he paid to ideas and evidence from other areas of inquiry. Throughout his life, Porter saw art and architecture in terms of societal circumstances and not in relation to either historical events or problems of form alone. Thus his radical approaches to medieval buildings seem less arbitrary when they are understood in the context of work in other disciplines. His theory of the distribution of sculptural decoration in the churches pilgrims visited in pursuit of salvation is derived from notions about how medieval epic poems circulated and developed in the same society.[5] His examination of the emergence of the ribbed vault as the enclosure of choice in the early twelfth century likewise reached into daily life in its search for explanations. Confronting both the rusticity of the earliest efforts and their geographical location, Porter noted that the first examples were so clumsy and so lacking in both aesthetic and structural advantage that one was pressed to explain why builders adopted the form. "It is absurd to suppose that the masons were gifted with prophetic foresight," he wrote in a little pamphlet of 1911.[6] To his mind, the only explanation was that the rib vault was less expensive or somehow easier to build. He concluded that "the desire to economize wood led to the introduction of the rib vault, not only in France, but in Lombardy as well."[7] Porter's assertion that "this process of construction is of the gravest

importance for the history of art, and is one with which the student of medieval architecture must seriously reckon,"[8] alerts the reader to Porter's sense that there was something amiss in the study of architecture in his own time.

When Porter's career is viewed retrospectively, his repeated search for a practical aspect or explanation as opposed to a theoretical one—be it chronological, stylistic, or developmental—draws renewed attention. For that reason Porter's work was criticized by his peers across the sea. Marcel Aubert, the doyen of French archaeology, criticized Porter for his unmethodological manner; he characterized the beloved American colleague who had helped save ruined monuments at the end of World War I in a condescending fashion in an obituary written for the *Revue archéologique*:

Son of a young race, where the science of archaeology was still in formation, he hasn't our certitudes . . . especially our need of logic, of clarity, our sense of deduction, which departing from a precise point, establishes well determined frames, topographically and chronologically, following a rigorous order, where everything ought to fit and be methodically classified.[9]

In the decades after his death, Porter's pragmatic approach to medieval art and architecture was implicitly disavowed by a modernist discourse in which art was disengaged from the claims of its times; in that environment, seemingly rigorous methods of disinterested analysis, such as those brought over by newly arrived immigrant European scholars, readily took root on American soil. Only now, eighty years after the appearance of Porter's first scholarly work, when the offshoots of those intervening art historical approaches have faded in their allure, can his early study of medieval monuments be appreciated as something other than the personal idiosyncrasy it has too often seemed to be.[10]

Porter established his reputation with a two-volume work entitled *Medieval Architecture: Its Origins and Development*. I shall suggest in this paper that the book should be viewed as authentic response to the ideology and practice of the professional architectural community in which

Porter had briefly trained after graduating from Yale College in 1904. Examination of Porter's work in the context of actual disputes about architectural training and practice and the role of art in an industrial society, rather than in regard to an abstracted history of architectural style, allows us at once to understand the forces that shaped Porter's intellectual outlook and evaluate his contribution to the development of architectural history in America in new ways.

In the preface to the book, Porter appeared to identify the audience for which he was writing. He says that the work was "designed primarily with the view to putting the general reader in possession of such knowledge as is indispensible for the appreciation and enjoyment of the great masterpieces of Gothic architecture." At the same time, he allows that what he has written "may not be altogether without value to the more advanced student." Porter goes on to say that he has also tried to "supply the tourist with a *vade mecum* of somewhat larger scope than had hitherto been attempted."[11] Such imagined readers make curious, if not impossible, companions, especially since there was no advanced study of architectural history or of medieval art on American campuses in 1909, when *Medieval Architecture* was published. For whom else, then, might Porter have assembled the illustrations, compiled long lists of dated monuments, and arranged and annotated a bibliography of hundreds of books?

If we proceed on the assumption that there is an audience to which a product of scholarship, like a work of art, is addressed, and that it is both explicit and implicit—part of the production of the piece—then Porter's first published work invites inspection in terms of the context in which it was written and into which it was received. It demands that we go beyond the audience Porter identified and construe a larger public circumstance, inferred from Porter's movements, his background, and his schooling, as well as from the teaching and practice of medieval studies and medieval art around the turn of the century.

Porter's widow Lucy provided an outline of his life in the brief biographical note that prefaced the two volumes of papers, to which colleagues and students contributed, that were published in Porter's memory in 1939.[12] The facts of Lucy's account appear to be unalloyed, even if the whole picture she presents is one we might not choose to call unvarnished. Porter is presented in her words as a man of destiny: a Connecticut boy who was sent to Yale as a matter of course but whose career brought him to Harvard where he sometimes wished he had originally matriculated in order to have studied with Charles Eliot Norton. We are introduced to a future law student whose "conversion" at the cathedral of Coutances, when there suddenly shined a light around him, convinced him that he could never stand before the bar. Instead, on his return to New York in the fall of 1904, he entered the Columbia School of Architecture and made his home on the northern edge of Central Park.[13] The text of Lucy's tribute celebrates someone whose first scholarly effort was a history of medieval architecture, which he completed at the age of twenty-five, "secretly and alone." This brilliant achievement, Lucy's account continues, proved to his family that he was justified in again changing his life work, this time from architecture to archaeology, for which he knew his scholarly type of mind better fitted him. Hindsight allows us, even encourages us, to follow Lucy in reading Kingsley's career as a natural, independent, serpentine progression, but that is not the way things happen. Porter's books, like his life, are analogous to the monuments about which he wrote: all are framed by the discourses of the communities in which they took shape. Of necessity, they are all in dialogue with these communities from the moment of their invention. Examination of Porter's early life and writing discloses perspectives that appear to be eccentric and mythic only when, as in Lucy's memoir, his career is decontextualized.

While an undergraduate, Porter took classes at the Yale School of the Fine Arts, the first professional art school to have been founded at an American college.[14] Disputes within the art school between John Weir and Daniel Cady Eaton over the proper role of studio work, the subordination of one medium to another, the relation of studio work to history, and the appropriate leadership such an institution should have, left their mark on Porter. Throughout his life he remained a staunch advocate of the study of art in a liberal arts setting.[15] In 1916, Porter wrote the president of Yale of his desire to leave a sizeable bequest, around half a million dollars, to his alma mater for "establishing a Faculty of the History of Art in the College." But because of perceived resistance to such instruction, Porter wondered whether his gift would be accepted.

The problems were substantial. The Yale History Department, where Porter had recently taken up a lectureship in order to teach art history, viewed such pursuits as "so-called cultural work" and thought they might interfere with the "hard-work of men who are studying history and not playing with it." The Yale Art School, dedicated at the time of its founding to technical instruction, would, according to the president, be obligated to apply additional endowment monies—should any be received—to such courses and not to the study of art history, "however important that might be."[16] Still, Porter wished to have art history taught in the Art School, where the atmosphere would be "an extremely valuable asset for a course of this kind." Whether Porter foresaw or wished to forge a link between history, theory, and practice cannot be determined; nor is it known whether the coeducational character of the Art School played any part in his decision—not because of any incipient feminism, but because by 1916 women had long been the major consumers of art history education on American college campuses.[17]

Porter wished to see the art history course he proposed made available to all college students and to count for the bachelor of arts degree. He anticipated that it would arouse the interests of academic students, attract them to the study of architecture, and thereby help the Art School, which otherwise attracted merely technically competent students. Above all, Porter's project of 1916 involved a critique of contemporary education: "The adequate study of the history of art would tend to raise rather than lower the present loose standard of scholarship," he noted in another letter to the president of Yale, and for that reason, too, he was "anxious to see it added to the curriculum.[18]

Porter's regard for hands-on training was reinforced, in his formative years, in another way. After finishing Yale, Porter moved to New York to study architecture as a special student at Columbia. Barely a decade had passed since the Architecture Department's relocation to the light, spacious top floors of McKim, Mead, and White's Havemeyer Hall on the new Upper West Side campus. When Porter arrived, drafting students could easily look up from their work and gaze through the windows down sparsely developed slopes beyond Broadway to the Hudson River and the newly built Grant's Tomb. In these relatively open spaces of the growing city, they were confronted with opposing architectural ideals: Ralph Adams Cram's Gothic design for St. John the Divine, which was planned for an adjacent site southeast of the campus, and, at the heart of the new academic quadrangle, McKim's classicizing monument to Seth Low, the president of Columbia who in 1901 had become the city's mayor.[19]

In the early years of the school, the study of architecture had been under the stewardship of William Robert Ware. He was recruited from the Massachusetts Institute of Technology to direct the program and was assisted by A. D. F. Hamlin, whose specialty was the history of ornament. Under them, conflict between engineering and design in the study of architecture was momentarily resolved. Ware had studied architecture in 1859 in the atelier of Richard Morris Hunt, the first American graduate of the Ecole des Beaux-Arts. It was not surprising, then, for him to introduce a modified Beaux-Arts curriculum to the department at Columbia. But insofar as his program deemphasized competitive judgment of studio work, tempered the study of classical orders with medieval ones, and, in general, stressed historical scholarship at the expense of technical skills, it was criticized for its dilution of professionalism in students. Ware's preference for an academic rather than a purely professional curriculum ultimately strained his relations with Hunt and gave rise to dissatisfaction among the faculty.[20]

Ware's lasting contribution to the curriculum was the union of the study of architectural history with the development of drawing skills. Students were required to produce illustrated reports on a historical subject or monument at regular intervals throughout the spring term in a sequence of years, a procedure that allowed students to "learn the aspects of the great monuments of the various styles" as they developed skills of draftsmanship. Ware laid out his program in a paper published in 1897.[21] He described how students would first trace from prints and photographs to develop techniques without worrying about form. And, since the material to be copied represented a variety of historical periods, students "accumulated valuable memoranda for future reference." After tracing, attention turned to shapes, shades, and shadows, then the development of freehand techniques for both ornament and elevations, followed by brushwork and outdoor sketching. Although the curriculum was intended to prepare the student specifically for professional work in design, some of its aspects in the early steps—attention to shapes, shades, and shadows, for example—were not so different from the course in studio art that Charles Moore had begun to teach at Harvard in the 1870s as a complement to Charles Eliot Norton's undergraduate lectures there on art history.[22] Rendering was seen, in this case, as a form of discipline that elevated the student and enhanced his moral and intellectual growth along the lines espoused by Ruskin, whom Norton and Moore knew and admired. Awareness that Porter was himself exposed to this gentlemanly tradition during the two years he spent at Columbia prepares the reader of his books for the extraordinary sensitivity to visual form that characterizes his writing. It may equally help to explain the attention he paid, beyond that of his contemporaries, to visual aids other than photographs in the construction of his first book.

When Ware was forced to resign the leadership of Columbia's architectural school in 1903, purportedly over a combination of events—disagreements concerning McKim's new master plan for the campus along with personal and administrative problems—the opportunity to reorganize the school and revamp the curriculum presented itself to his successors. Revision, spearheaded by McKim, sought to replace Ware's ideal of a liberally conceived, aesthetically oriented training from which anyone might benefit with a program of rigorous professional preparation. A return to the atelier system of instruction, the introduction of juried competitions in the fourth year of study, and renewed attention to the importance of rendering in the training of young architects converted Ware's curriculum into an American alternative to the Ecole des Beaux-Arts rather than a prelude to it. Attention shifted from "Beaux-Arts baroque" to the original Roman roots of the style; in opposition to an adulation of either English aesthetics or French practice, McKim urged Italian study.[23]

This American controversy, with its tension between Beaux-Arts principles and Ruskinian tradition, helps to explain aspects of Porter's initial approach to the study of architecture; attitudes toward the study of architectural history in professional training programs may account for others. In particular, review of the role to be played by architectural history in the curriculum of the newly re-formed architecture school was being debated in the years in which Porter attended Columbia.[24] Because the study of history detached from creative design was thought to lead to conventional imitative work, it was deemed dangerous in some quarters at the time Porter wrote. Yet history was intimately implicated in Ware and Hamlin's classes in the development of theory, since these teachers had students take as their point of departure the elevations and orders of the past. The extent to which the initial illustrations in Porter's volume present the reader with renderings of the sort that architecture students in Columbia's revamped program were required to do throughout their training demonstrates the degree to which *Medieval Architecture* can be seen to be taking a position on an especially stressful issue in current campus discourse: the importance of the study of history for the understanding of planning and design at the introductory level.

Ware had illustrated his 1897 treatise on architectural drawing with examples of the kind of work students could be expected to produce under such a curriculum. *A Doric Porch*, plate 18 in that pamphlet (fig. 1), belonged to the Brush Work section of the first-year program (28); plate 21, a *Diagram of the Corinthian Order*, showing both plan and elevation of a Corinthian capital and entablature, was a project in the section called Graphical Construction; plate 20, *Measured Work*, represented a second-year exercise. Similar material was included in the annual *Year-Book* that the department published. The publication for 1905–1906, the year in which Porter is listed as a special student, used examples of the work of students—many of whom, like Porter, were not regular degree candidates—as a record of the program.[25] J. N. Reid contributed drawings of a triumphal arch and a capital (75, 76); H. M. Seabury was represented in the *Year-Book* by a photo of modeled ornament (66) and a "frontispiece" (fig. 2), which had received "mention" in the Elementary Design section (67). This last plate is virtually indistinguishable from the second illustration in Porter's *Medieval Architecture*: a tipped-in plate on which *The Greek Ionic Order* is elegantly represented. Illustration 3 in Porter's book shows a variety of Greek ornaments; such forms were the focus of interest for A.D.F. Hamlin, the interim director of the Architecture School after Ware stepped down.[26] Illustration 3a is a pencil sketch of a *Corinthian Capital*, the sort of drawing that had been included in the 1904–1905 and 1905–1906 *Year-Books*; illustration 18, a watercolor of a Roman entablature, belongs to the same genre (fig. 3). Comparisons of this kind demonstrate the way in which the illustrations in the opening chapter of Porter's first book would have established a direct visual link with architectural school practice for its prepared readers.

Renderings emphasize how contemporary students were taught to see ancient monuments—as models of planning, composition, structure, and ornament. They do not necessarily convey what a building actually looked like. Yet Porter asserted in his preface that "for illustrations I have preferred photographs whenever available as being more accurate and as presenting architectural forms as they actually appear" (viii). A single photograph in *Medieval Architecture*—illustration 5, *The Theseion, Athens*, "from a Carbon by Braun Clement & Cie"—suffices for a descriptive view of a complete Greek structure even though Porter had words of praise for such monuments: "Entirely suitable for the needs of the time and adorned with a refinement and beauty of detail the world has not equaled" (11). For the Roman section of his chapter on "The Heritage of Antiquity," Porter used a few more photographs—the arch at Orange (31), the amphitheaters at Nîmes and Arles (28, 29), and the Pont-du-Gard (24). For the most part, however, the illustrations are diagrams, elevations, and renderings of the sort that students would have been required to make in the course of their training. The identification of the source of a few of the illustrations as "From a French Drawing," (e.g., ill. 17, *Corinthian Pilaster of the Portico of Octavia, Rome*), further secures the association of this part of his project with another Beaux-Arts interest—on-site study of ornamental details.

Porter acknowledged the significant advances that the Romans had made in the area of planning and construction, and he had considerable praise for this activity. According to Porter, the Romans first treated the arch architecturally even if they had not invented it. Being "thrifty," they devised a scheme in which the use of transverse arches both reduced the amount of centering necessary to erect a vault and permitted the reuse of the same centering along the length of a ribbed-barrel vault (15–16). For the vault, he concluded, "we owe to Rome unqualified admiration and gratitude. Unfortunately, no such unstinted praise can be given the architectural ornament of the Romans," he continued (24). Porter lamented the colossal edifices and debased secondhand versions of ornament that the Romans first adopted from Asia Minor and then employed in a wholly decorative, rather than constructively integrated, manner. He failed to un-

1. *A Doric Porch*
From William R(obert) Ware, "The Study of Architectural Drawing in the School of Architecture," pl. 18

·PLATE X·

A

DORIC PORCH.

derstand, he said, "how so great a difference of opinion prevails to-day" in regard
to the use of Roman ornament: "Nothing
that human art has devised is more dreary,
monotonous, and uninteresting than the
Roman order," he wrote (26). Porter focused on the "wholesale character" of Roman architecture as the ultimate root of
its evil, since from it came the machine-
made qualities he abhorred (31).

*Roman art has a ready-made, exotic quality; it
lacks originality, and is, in fact, little more
than an adaptation of Greek models to suit the
pomposity and vulgarity of Roman taste. Under Rome, magnificence was substituted for
refinement.*

Porter's disdain for Roman decoration did
not diminish his praise for Roman construction, however, a point to which he
returned throughout his book.

The format of this chapter is modified in
subsequent parts of the book and is ultimately abandoned. Renderings, elevations,
and diagrams continue to dominate the
section on Carolingian architecture, to
which Porter drew unprecedented attention, as well as the chapter on Lombard
work. Photographs, which play such an
important role in the second volume of
Medieval Architecture, provide only exceptional illustration throughout most of
the first volume. They are used for the
Lorsch Gatehouse (98), the facade of San
Zeno in Verona (118), and the interior of
San Ambrogio in Milan (119). The chapter
on Norman architecture opens with two
picturesque photographs of the ruined abbey of Jumièges, seen in the midst of its
foliage, and continues with the abbeys at
Caen—interior and exterior views—and the
facade of St. Georges de Boscherville. Supplementing these images are technical
drawings Porter borrowed from scholarly
studies by Ruprich-Robert. These nonphoto-
graphic illustrations parallel Porter's use in
the earlier sections of the book of drawings
from the works of Dartein, De Rossi, Dehio,
Butler, and Rivoira. The absence in this
latter part of the volume of student renderings is, however, noteworthy. Through the
choice of illustrations, Porter identified
both his intellectual lineage for the reader,
as an author may explicitly attempt to do

2. H. M. Seabury, *A Frontispiece*
From *Year-Book of the Columbia
University School of Architecture,*
1905–1906, 67

in the preface to a book, and his argumen-
tative strategy: in this case attention to
design ceded place to concern for construction. The only acknowledgments Porter
included contained appreciation of individuals who helped to make and secure illustrations and of the Avery librarian who
located books for him and whose bibliographies he incorporated into his own.[27]

3. Entablature of the Temple of Castor, Rome, by Covell
From A. Kingsley Porter, *Medieval Architecture* I, ill. 18

into the study of medieval architecture the kind of scientific standards that would put it on a footing with the then-dominant disciplines in the study of the Middle Ages. Intellectual history, romance languages, and English literature were the preferred subjects in the schools at which medieval studies were flourishing, institutions such as Johns Hopkins, Yale, and Columbia.[29] Apart from Harvard and a few women's colleges in the Northeast, art and architectural history were seldom addressed as courses in their own right.

Only in Europe had works on related subjects and of comparable erudition to Porter's appeared. Porter knew of these, either directly or through the bibliographic work of the Avery librarian whom he acknowledged in his book. He provided his own reader with a "ranked" list of works. Among foreign publications, Porter singled out Auguste Choisy's recent *Histoire de l'architecture*, which had appeared in Paris in 1899, as "an excellent general history, treated from the point of view of construction"; he was critical of James Fergusson's *Illustrated Handbook of Architecture*, then on the brink of its fourth edition, finding it "too replete with errors of fact and judgment to be worth resuscitation." Porter called the work of F. M. Simpson and A. D. F. Hamlin "elementary"; other books he described as "mediocre," "unimportant," "out of date," or "not recommended." Russell Sturgis' work was praised for the quality of its illustrations, in contrast to a book by E. A. Freeman, which, though "valuable historically . . . has no illustrations and is not consulted." Porter's preferential listing concluded with general histories deemed to be "of little value" or those that lacked illustrations. The last three on his list he called worthless.[30]

In a section headed "Desultory and Miscellaneous," Porter included books he admired despite any number of problems, such as Rivoira's *Le origini della architettura lombarda*, which he called "a book of great value notwithstanding that its thesis is somewhat questionable," and others, such as Charles Eliot Norton's *Historical Studies of Church Building in the Middle Ages*, which, cited without publication information, engendered no comment (343).

Porter wrote *Medieval Architecture* at a time when academic inquiry into the Middle Ages was in its infancy in this country. Although nearly forty years had passed since Henry Adams first lectured on medieval history at Harvard, and nearly as much time had elapsed since Charles Eliot Norton initiated his course on the history of art for undergraduates on the same campus,[28] the study of the subject was in no way as systematic, as sweeping, or as venerable as a glance at Porter's book might lead a reader to imagine. If anything, Porter's book was to make it so: to introduce

The final section of the general bibliography was devoted to criticism, philosophy, and aesthetics. William Morris' "stimulating little essay," *Gothic Architecture*, published in 1893, headed the list (351). Three references to John Ruskin came next. His work was described as "'Transcendental estheticism' abounding in all manner of errors of fact and judgment, and yet of undeniable value" (325). He described Gottfried Semper's *Der Stil in den technischen und tektonischen Künsten* of 1878 as "a philosophical treatise characterisically German," and notation of an English language synopsis of Semper by Laurence Harvey followed. The book that was possibly best known and most influential on this side of the Atlantic in the decades preceding the one in which Porter wrote was Viollet-le-Duc's *Dictionnaire raisonné de l'architecture française*. Porter placed it at the head of a category called "Dictionaries, Encyclopedias and Works of Reference," and he described it as "a book whose immense reputation was doubtless deserved at the time it was written, but which is somewhat out of date at the present time" (349). Viollet's *Entretiens sur l'Architecture* were listed under "Histories" (341), but Porter did not mention Henry Van Brunt's translation of the first volume, in the 1870s, with which professional architectural audiences in America were familiar.[31] Was he ignorant or was he not telling?

The bibliography provided Porter with a coded way of identifying his authorities. In reviewing the extensive list of works he cited—more than he may actually have read—we see him in courteous exchange with a number of writers who preceded him and in stern judgment of others. His bibliography indicates not just what books he knew and what he thought of them; it overwhelms the reader with a mass of documentation of its claims. In this way, Porter's book differentiates itself from contemporary American works that employed verbal or visual rhetoric rather than erudition to argue their points. The American supporter of French Gothic, Charles Moore, had been a distinguished watercolorist and studio assistant to Norton at Harvard.[32] Converted to Gothic through his associa-

tion with Ruskin, he illustrated his book with his own elegant drawings. Ralph Adams Cram, the Boston architect who sought in Anglo-Gothic style the alleviation of society's ills, wrote impassioned defenses of those spiritual forms. Neither had been formally educated. Porter, in contrast to both, had a B.A. from Yale (even though Lucy said he wished it had been from Harvard); by emphasizing primary as well as secondary sources in his book, Porter made scholarship a palpable part of both volumes' organization. Compared to the more personal record of others who were writing on architecture, Porter's voice was endowed with the authority of external reference.

Porter's preferred sources, like the illustrations he used, helped to reinforce the subtext of his book: a critique of current architectural practices both in schools and in the profession. Choisy's work on vault techniques, which underlies Porter's discussion of eleventh-century work, had appeared in translation in the mid-1890s in installments in the magazine the *Brick Builder*, a trade journal for practitioners.[33] Even if Porter was familiar with the original publication, it is more likely that his readers would have known the recent, popular presentation. Porter's focus on building technology pointed to the materiality and concern for workmanship that was to remain an interest, in one way or another, throughout his life. It equally addressed the needs of the architectural audience for which he was writing and for whom the shift from structure to construction may well have signaled a movement away from Viollet-le-Duc, the work of Moore, and Beaux-Arts tradition—in short, a rejection of French taste and values. At the same time Porter played down discussion of Anglo-Norman buildings, a point that his English critics did not fail to note. One reviewer of *Medieval Architecture* observed that there was little to be said about the first volume, "for it is only by way of working up to the second," and then he faulted the latter for its attention to "the subject of Mr. Porter's prepossessions—the Gothic of France. Indeed had we not the prospectus to herald a third volume covering English architecture, we should have supposed Mr. Porter was ignorant of its existence."[34] Yet all Porter had said in the preface to *Medieval Architecture* was that he hoped someday to be able to "supplement the present volumes with others dealing with those styles that I have here left untouched" (v). An English reader of 1910 seemed to feel that at least one of those works was forthcoming; the sense that *Medieval Architecture* was prolegomenon to further work may well have facilitated the reception of the book in certain quarters.

Porter, however, was carefully providing his readers with a new view of the medieval development, one that enhanced the role of Italian tradition. No longer would it be a wasteland between Rome and the Renaissance; rather, Porter celebrated the architecture of northern Italy, with its clever and efficient building techniques, as the cradle of necessary invention. He located the turning point in the architecture of the Middle Ages in the Carolingian period, which he rightly noted had been little studied up to that date. The rise of capable masons who traveled, such as the famous Comacini, and the energy generated by the emergence of the Holy Roman Empire invited concentration, according to Porter, on the buildings of the Carolingian rulers. Change had been slow and subtle, Porter agreed, but significant nonetheless. "It is an era of great, of almost revolutionary changes, carried out, however, on so small a scale and so quietly as to be barely perceptible" (130). The chapel at Aachen (with what Porter saw to be its Italianate plan), the return of the Latin basilica, and even the Roman ornament of Lorsch (which is illustrated in an academic rendering, ill. 98), characterized the art of this era and set the stage, in Porter's mind, for the development of Lombard vaulting. By validating the architecture of the ninth and tenth centuries as neither degenerate Roman form nor tentative Gothic yearning, Porter transformed and latinized the previously argued sequence of medieval style. He reinforced his message in the first volume of *Medieval Architecture* by using the pictures of architectural renderings to evoke the preparation and technical training of the Beaux-Arts student in the period before true design began, that is, the transitional or Gothic style, the subject of volume two. In

part, Porter's English critic had been correct!

The practice of architecture had been divided in late nineteenth-century America between advocates of Beaux-Art tradition and enthusiastics of the Gothic. Even in the barren outcroppings of upper Manhattan island, McKim's Beaux-Arts plan for Columbia's new main campus rose alongside Cram's Gothic St. John; the styles competed for a voice as the architecture of the new age in building as well as in books. What Porter succeeded in doing, with words and images, was to introduce as an alternative something that was other to them both. Lombard Romanesque, in assuming this role, took the place of Middle Eastern monuments which, in earlier surveys of art and architectural history, such as those by Goodyear and Hamlin, had been employed to bridge the spatial and chronological gap between Roman and Anglo-Norman building.[35] They would remain absent from work that followed Porter's for several decades thereafter; Kenneth Conant's study of *Carolingian and Romanesque Architecture* illustrates this point.[36]

A lengthy review of *Medieval Architecture* appeared in the *Bulletin monumental* in 1910, entitled "A Manual of French Archaeology in English."[37] The author, Louis Serbat, noted that Porter placed archaeological facts in a historical and social framework and followed Rivoira for his arguments about Lombard architecture, Enlart for his discussion of the flamboyant, and Mâle for his remarks on iconography; in other words, he was familiar with continental scholarly writing. But while Porter may have read much, the French reviewer faulted him for not having seen enough, a flaw Porter was to rectify in the course of his travels throughout his remaining years. The reviewer also cautioned Porter to check his quotes from medieval authors; their medieval Latin may have been bad, Serbat noted, but do not add to it crimes the monks and clerics did not commit. Above all, the book, the reviewer observed, had been written simply, too simply and clearly, perhaps, since one does not notice the controversies as one reads.

That had been Porter's project, I believe: a deliberate disguise of the disputes he was addressing. The plates in his book, which ostensibly document the text, actually develop an alternate and not always so subtle conversation, one that engages a reader familiar with certain classes of pictorial material, in particular professional architectural students. Through a carefully arranged mixture of drawings and photographs, Porter (the former special student) communicated to that knowledgeable reader a preference for certain forms over others in a developmental system. By attending to image, apparatus, and text and by considering all three in the context of what we know about the decade in which Porter worked, it becomes possible to suggest for whom *Medieval Architecture*, the first scholarly history of that material to be written by an American, was conceived. It was not simply a much-needed survey, and it was not exclusively addressed to the international community of scholars. The text is relentlessly critical of the Beaux-Arts sources it has visually employed to seduce the reader; it warns against the symptoms of gigantism that ruined Rome and that could be seen everywhere in New York in the early twentieth century. At the same time, the text seeks to neutralize the nationalist fervor that led French practitioners on one side and English on the other to their own theories about the emergence of the Gothic. Into this partisan field, Porter interposed the alternative of Italy as the place where significant developments in construction, not merely in design, were made in the late eleventh and early twelfth centuries; he would develop these ideas in subsequent publications.[38]

In utilizing Porter's books, generations of historians have misconstrued them, as did his first reviewers. They have fallen into the trap of focusing on and revising his neat lists of evidence and chronology in the name of rigorous scientific scholarship, and they have alternately dismissed or celebrated as idiosyncratic bursts of light his novel but "undocumentable" insights. But by seeing the way in which his book suppresses controversy and appropriates familiar images to another discourse, the reader gains a different perspective on the young Porter. *Medieval Architecture* was not written for scholars to come. It was created instead to promote a dialogue with the powerful institutions of its time and should be seen as a challenge to the contemporary architectural hierarchy and a confrontation with the gentlemen practitioners and educators of urban America. It is, of course, also a plea for status for its author within an emerging academic community.

NOTES

1. "A. Kingsley Porter Drowned Off Ireland . . . ," *New York Times*, 10 July 1933, sec. 1, p. 1.

2. "Porter Death a 'Mishap' . . . ," *New York Times*, 15 July 1933, sec. 1, p. 12. The article noted that this version of the accident was the one that had been reported to relatives via cable. The coroner accepted this account as the probable cause of Porter's disappearance according to a brief notice that appeared two months later in the *New York Times* of 15 September 1933, 12. Martha MacFarlane, who sought out the earliest obituaries for her own work on Porter's photographic illustrations, generously brought them to my attention along with numerous insights of her own.

3. *New York Times*, 16 July 1933, sec. 4, p. 4.

4. Frances Terpak, "Pilgrimage or Migration? A Case Study of Artistic Movement in the Early Romanesque," *Zeitschrift für Kunstgeschichte* 51 (1988), 414–427 and O. K. Werckmeister, "Cluny III and the Pilgrimage to Santiago de Compostela," *Gesta* 27, 1 and 2 (1988): 103–112. Werckmeister's assertion of a "Cluniac takeover attempt" on the pilgrimage roads (103, 104) embraces the current language of the marketplace that Porter also employed: "Surely no capitalist of the XIX century ever promoted more shrewdly . . . than the Cluniac monks. . . . The rulers of the great abbey were quick to realize the success of the pilgrimage and far-sighted in driving, at an early date, their fingernails firmly into the carrot of St. James." A. Kingsley Porter, *Romanesque Sculpture of the Pilgrimage Roads*, 10 vols. (1923, repr. New York, 1966), 1:174.

5. Porter 1923, 1:171, 178, 180.

6. A. Kingsley Porter, *The Construction of Lombard and Gothic Vaults* (New Haven, 1911), 1. Porter fully acknowledged the importance of Auguste Choisy's ideas in the formulation of his own (3, n. 1).

7. Porter 1911, 3.

8. Porter 1911, 16–17.

9. Marcel Aubert, "A. Kingsley Porter (1883–1933)," *Revue archéologique*, 6 sér. (1933), 327.

10. Noureddine Mezoughi, in an analysis of "le dogme portérien," concluded that Porter's work on medieval sculpture was less revolutionary than its author claimed, since its abiding concern was really the rebirth or renaissance of an art form, the same theme that guided his European colleagues in the first decades of the century. Yet Mezoughi viewed Porter idiosyncratically and apart from his context, calling him "un catalyseur d'idées (plus) qu'un inventeur. 'Reformiste' de nature, . . . révolutionnaire un peu malgré lui." "A. Kingsley Porter et la sculpture préromane," *Histoire de l'art* 3 (1988), 29–36; quotations from 34.

11. A. Kingsley Porter, *Medieval Architecture: Its Origins and Development*, 2 vols. (New York, c. 1908), 1:v. Subsequent references are cited in the text.

12. "Arthur Kingsley Porter," in *Medieval Studies in Memory of A. Kingsley Porter*, ed. Wilhelm R. W. Koehler, 2 vols. (Cambridge, Mass., 1939), I:xi–xiii. I have discussed, in a general way, the biographic aspects of Porter's career in a forthcoming paper entitled "Arthur Kingsley Porter: Life, Legend, and Legacy," to appear in a history of the teaching of art history (Princeton University, Department of Art and Archaeology).

13. Porter noted his address, 320 Central Park West (just above 91st Street) in the preface to *Medieval Architecture*, 1:x.

14. The school was founded in 1869. For information and references about the teaching of art at Yale in the decades before the establishment of an art department, I am indebted to Betsy Fahlman, from whose research on this material I have learned much.

15. The best-known published evidence of Porter's attitudes toward education in general appeared in an article entitled "Problems of the Art Professor," *Scribners' Magazine* 65 (1919), 125–128.

16. I cite, with permission, from unpublished letters written in 1916–1917 by President Arthur Twining Hadley of Yale to Porter and Dean William Sergeant Kendall of the Yale School of the Fine Arts. Records of President Arthur Twining Hadley (YRG 2-A-14), Yale University Archives, Manuscripts and Archives, Yale University (hereafter cited as Hadley Records). Porter's original offer appears in a letter dated 28 January 1916; Hadley's response was swift, since Porter answered it a week later; see below and n. 18. My thanks to Betsy Fahlman for bringing this material to my attention.

17. See the abstracts of talks by Claire Richter Sherman and Mary Ann Stankiewicz in Donald Preziosi's session "Institutionalizing Art History: The Early Discipline in the United States," *Abstracts and Program Statements*, 77th Annual Meeting of the College Art Association, San Francisco (New York, 1989), 204–205: to appear in a history of the teaching of art history (Princeton University Department of Art and Archaeology).

18. Porter to Arthur Twining Hadley, 3 February 1916, Hadley Records.

19. The study of architecture had been incorporated in 1881 into the School of Mining and Engineering at the urging of Frederick Schermerhorn, whose concern for New York's inadequate housing and hygiene had led to its initial organization. See the history of the school edited by Richard Oliver, *The Making of an Architect 1881–1981* (New York, 1981), specifically the essay by Steven M. Bedford, "The Founding of the School," 5–12. For a discussion of the political context of McKim's work at Columbia see Francesco Passanti, "The Design of Columbia in the 1890s: McKim and His Client," *Journal of the Society of Architectural Historians* 36 (1977), 69–84. On Cram, in general, see the studies by Douglass Shand Tucci, *Ralph Adams Cram, American Medievalist* (Boston, 1975) and Ann Miner Daniel, "The Early Architecture of Ralph Adams Cram 1889–1902" (Ph.D. diss.,

University of North Carolina, 1978). Cram committed his views to print as well as to mortar. See "On the Religious Aspect of Architecture," *Architectural Record* 2 (1892-1893), 351-356 and "The Case Against the Ecole des Beaux-Arts," *American Architect and Building News* 53 (26 December 1898), 107-109. See also Michael Brooks, "New England Gothic: Charles Eliot Norton, Charles H. Moore, and Henry Adams," in this volume.

20. Ware's problems are summarized by David G. DeLong, "William R. Ware and the Pursuit of Suitability: 1881-1903," in Oliver 1981, 13-21. For later developments in the training of architects see J. A. Chewning, "The Teaching of Architectural History during the Advent of Modernism, 1920s-1950s" in this volume.

21. William R(obert) Ware, "The Study of Architectural Drawing in the School of Architecture," *School of Mines Quarterly*, Columbia University (1897). Subsequent references to Ware's article are cited in the text.

22. Frank Jewett Mather, Jr., *Charles Herbert Moore: Landscape Painter* (Princeton, N.J., 1957), 47-48.

23. For a discussion of McKim's founding of the American Academy in Rome in 1894 see the essay by Steven M. Bedford and Susan M. Strauss, "History II: 1881-1912," in Oliver 1981, 34-35.

24. Bedford and Strauss 1981, 42-43.

25. *Year-Book of the Columbia University School of Architecture, published by The Architectural Society* (1905-1906). Among the individuals Porter acknowledged in his preface to *Medieval Architecture* for their help in providing architectural drawings were students at Columbia in the years he was studying there. MacDonald Mayer, a member of the class of 1907, was an undergraduate and president of the executive committee of the Architecture School. *Year-Book 1905-1906*, 5, 7. Franklin J. Walls had been an undergraduate the year before. *Year-Book* 1904, 7. W. E. Covell was identified as an alumni member of the school in the *Year-Book* of 1905-1906, 7.

26. Oliver 1981, 38-40.

27. Porter 1908, 1:x. For a brief note on Smith, "a sculptor of prominence," see Theodor K. Rohdenburg, *A History of the School of Architecture, Columbia University* (New York, 1954), 76-77. Porter might find the plates in a work to be valuable even if the text were not. See his comments on F. de Dartein, *Etude sur l'architecture lombarde et sur les origines de l'architecture romano-byzantine*, 2 vols. (Paris, 1865-1882), in Porter 1908, 1:429.

28. See Michael Brooks, "New England Gothic: Charles Eliot Norton, Charles H. Moore, and Henry Adams," in this volume.

29. See William J. Courtenay, "The Virgin and the Dynamo: The Growth of Medieval Studies in North America, 1870-1930," in *Medieval Studies in North America: Past, Present and Future*, ed. Francis G. Gentry and Christopher Kleinhenz (Kalamazoo, Mich., 1982), 5-9.

30. "General Histories of Architecture," in Porter 1908, 1:339-341.

31. For H. H. Richardson's knowledge of the *Dictionnaire* see Henry-Russell Hitchcock, *The Architecture of H. H. Richardson and His Times* (New York, 1936; rev. ed. 1961), 48, 60. David Van Zanten has made relevant comments in "Viollet-le-Duc's Impact Upon American Architecture During the Nineteenth Century," in Françoise Bercé and Bruno Foucart, *Viollet-le-Duc, Architect, Artist, Master of Historic Preservation* (Washington, D.C., 1988), 21-22.

32. Mather 1957.

33. Compare Porter's dicussion of vaulting techniques and the accompanying diagrams in Porter 1908, 1:11-24.

34. "An American Historian of Gothic," *Architectural Review* 27 (1910), 242-244.

35. W. H. Goodyear, *Roman and Medieval Art* (New York, 1893), and A.D.F. Hamlin, *A Textbook of the History of Architecture* (New York, 1896). Bannister Fletcher included a chapter on Saracenic architecture in a section on "Non-Historical Styles," in his *History of Architecture on the Comparative Method*, 4th ed. (London, 1901), 473-496.

36. Kenneth Conant, *Carolingian and Romanesque Architecture* (Harmondsworth and Baltimore, 1959). Conant had been Porter's student at Harvard and acknowledged his debt to "his mentor, colleague, and friend" in the foreword, xxv. Conant also identifed himself as "academically the heir of Herbert Langford Warren and his teachers Henry Hobson Richardson and Charles Eliot Norton, the latter an intimate friend of John Ruskin." Conant's intellectual lineage as he constructed it is worth our attention.

37. Louis Serbat, "Un manuel d'archéologie française en anglais," *Bulletin monumental* 74 (1910), 291-303.

38. Porter 1911. See also Porter's grander work, *Lombard Architecture*, 4 vols. (New Haven, 1915-1917). The fact that similar interests already informed continental, especially French, architectural writing, as Katherine Taylor has so kindly pointed out to me, does not seem to have affected Porter; he appears to have proceeded from a personal and local rather than a professional and international perspective. My thanks to Dr. Taylor for her careful reading of my manuscript.

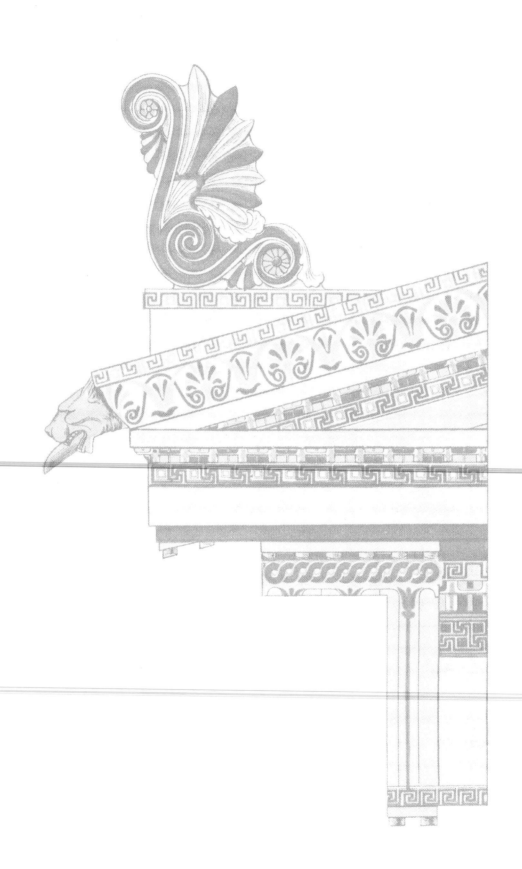

TOD MARDER
Rutgers, The State University of New Jersey

Renaissance and Baroque Architectural History in the United States

Fifty years ago the notion of a significant American contribution to the history of Renaissance and baroque architecture in Italy would have seemed but a distant possibility. These fields were still dominated by foreign scholars. The literature in English upon which to build enthusiasm was sparse; and while significant work had been done by American authors on the painting and sculpture of the Renaissance, they had contributed little to architecture and almost nothing to seventeenth-century studies. Out of this unpromising situation has come one of the most vital traditions of architectural scholarship in the country and one of the most important contributions to the international study of architecture in Italy. This paper is devoted to charting the course of an increasing tide of publications and interest in Italian Renaissance and baroque architecture in America and to demonstrating how this scholarly activity has appropriated most of the essential topics in the field.

By way of introduction, something must be said of the German tradition that shaped much of this interest, for the study of architectural history as a scholarly discipline separate from the practice of architecture and independent of aesthetics is largely a German development. The development arguably can be traced back as far as Winckelmann, but a tradition of dispassionate analysis of historic architecture re-ally stems from the work of Franz Theodor Kugler (1808–1858), the first person who could properly be called an art historian and professor of art history.[1] He occupied an academic chair in art history at the Academy of Art in Berlin and organized the publication of a four-volume history of architecture, the *Geschichte der Baukunst* (Stuttgart, 1856–1872). Part I of the fourth volume of Kugler's *History* was written by Jacob Burckhardt (1818–1897) and entitled *Geschichte der Renaissance in Italien* (1867). Burckhardt suggested that architectural style has a life and historical trajectory of its own quite apart from the development of the society that produced it. It was he who had first used the term *baroque* to refer to a style period rather than as a pejorative adjective.[2] In turn, his most famous student Heinrich Wölfflin (1864–1945) altered the course of Renaissance and baroque studies in his time by attempting to construct a theoretical and formalist approach to the discipline that would be valid for all periods of art.

In his *Renaissance und Barock* (Munich, 1888) Wölfflin presented the concept of the growth, maturation, and decay of an architectural style according to contrasting formal attributes such as "linear" and "painterly," "unity" and "multiplicity," and so forth.[3] The concept was made famous in his later *Kunstgeschichtliche Grundbegriffe* (Munich, 1915, translated as

Principles of Art History), which applied the notion to painting and sculpture as well. His stylistic analysis of fifteenth- and early sixteenth-century architecture led him to conclude that the period from the late sixteenth and seventeenth centuries on represented a serious decline, and it was left to Cornelius Gurlitt (1850–1938) to rehabilitate the baroque with his monumental *Geschichte des Barockstiles in Italien* (Stuttgart, 1887), an "objective" compendium of the period beginning around 1560 and ending around 1730.[4] (Whereas Burckhardt identified the "baroque" much as we do, with the seventeenth and early eighteenth centuries, Wölfflin argued that it really began with Michelangelo, and his view held sway in many quarters up to World War II.) In any case, the positivist tradition made concrete by Gurlitt's encyclopedic account maintained its hold over the research and publication of the scholars who most influenced American research in the late twentieth century.

The lack of a concurrent tradition in the United States in the study of Renaissance and baroque architecture should not obscure some of the early achievements by American pioneers in these fields. Charles Eliot Norton's *Historical Studies of Church-Building in the Middle Ages—Venice, Siena, Florence* (New York, 1880) offers a surprisingly comprehensive grasp of the art historical literature of his time. Thus, while making the obligatory bow to Ruskin's *Stones of Venice*, Norton (1827–1908) produced citations from Sanudo, Sansovino, and Dandolo in the discussion of St. Mark's in Venice.[5] Norton also made wide use of the contemporary literature in German, French, and Italian.[6] Moreover, in research for the discussion on the cathedral at Siena, Norton had delved into the archives as early as 1870 and had transcribed Latin and Italian documents dating from the thirteenth and fourteenth centuries.[7] For his section on the Florence cathedral Norton consulted the documents from Gaye's *Carteggio* (1839), Guasti's books on the facade (1863) and the dome (1857), and, of course, Vasari and other Renaissance sources. Indeed Norton's account of the construction of the dome is hardly different in substance or detail from what one might glean from a late twentieth-century handbook for the period.[8]

Similarly, in the study of garden design, the United States could boast of major accomplishments in both scholarly and critical realms in the early years of the twentieth century. Best known to a general readership is Edith Wharton's *Italian Villas and Their Gardens* (New York, 1904). In seven chapters Wharton (1862–1937) presents the villas region by region, from Genoa, Lombardy, and the Veneto to Siena, Florence, Rome, and Latium. This material had originally appeared as a series of articles in *The Century Magazine* between 1903 and 1904.[9] Others participated in the same interest at about the same time. Rose Standish Nichols (died 1960), whose uncle and advisor was Augustus Saint-Gaudens, wrote an early article on "Italian Villa Gardens" for the Brochure Series of Architectural Illustration in May 1899; she continued her interest in a series of "elaborate, scholarly, well-written guidebooks" on the subject of gardens, which culminated with her volume on *Italian Pleasure Gardens* (New York, 1928).[10]

Such activities were not entirely outside the established academic curricula, as the work of James Sturgis Pray would illustrate. Pray, a professor at the Harvard School of Design, wrote a series of articles entitled "The Italian Garden" for the *American Architect and Building News* in 1900. But the essential point from our perspective is that these enterprises had only modest repercussions in American academic programs. Indeed, not until 1942 was a doctoral program in landscape architecture established at Harvard.[11] To be sure, one might have followed an interest in architectural history in a graduate program in fine arts and art history departments by this time, such as those established at Harvard, Yale, Princeton, Columbia, or New York University's Institute of Fine Arts. But these programs had no leaders in the fields of Renaissance and baroque architecture who could attract or convert students or inspire graduate research.

Indeed, for the American student of the turn-of-the-century there was little to read, at least in English, for synthetic accounts of Renaissance or baroque architecture in

Italy. From 1896, students might have availed themselves of the college-level survey of architecture written by A.D.F. Hamlin, *A Text-Book of the History of Architecture* (New York, 1896) in the "College History of Art Series."[12] In it Hamlin (1855–1926) encompassed the Italian architecture that we call Renaissance and baroque in two chapters, one devoted to the "early Renaissance" and the other to the "advanced Renaissance and decline."[13] This conception of the period 1400–1700 is reflected in the periodization he proposed as follows: the early Renaissance or formative period (1420–1490), "characterized by the grace and freedom of the decorative detail, suggested by Roman prototypes"; the high Renaissance or formally classic period (1490–1560) when "there was increase of stateliness but some loss in freedom and delicacy of design"; and finally the baroque and decline (1560–1700), "a period of classic formality characterized by the use of colossal orders, engaged columns and rather scanty and heavy decoration, followed by increasing poverty of invention in the composition and a predominance of vulgar sham and display in the decoration."[14] These developments were followed, Hamlin thought, by the classic revival, which was "a reaction from these extravagances, showing itself in a return to the imitation of classic models, sometimes not without a certain dignity of composition and restraint in the decoration." In this scheme the influence of Wölfflin was everywhere evident. Of the baroque style, almost no pejorative was adequate for Hamlin's discussion. He saw the seventeenth century as a reaction, manifest in "lawless and often tasteless extravagances," to the classicism of the later sixteenth century. He identified the chief culprit in "the wealthy Jesuit order"—"a notorious contributor to the debasement of architectural taste"—and to the buildings that followed its "pernicious example . . . [in] monuments of bad taste and pretentious sham."[15]

The chief rival to the "College History of Art" was the "Harper's Fine Arts Series," which must have been conceived in response to the success of its predecessor. The Harper's books were written by au-

thors drafted mainly from the ranks of Harvard University professors. Interestingly, the first volume was *A History of Architecture* (New York, 1918), written by Fiske Kimball, then assistant professor at the University of Michigan, and George Harold Edgell, assistant professor at Harvard.[16] For our purposes their contribution was summed up in an authors' preface in which it is clear that the organic metaphor of the historical growth and decay of styles had been left behind. "The idea of an analogy," they wrote, "between the history of styles and the growth and inevitable decay of organic life is now generally abandoned, and it is understood that the material must not be forced into conformity with any other misleading analogy." Thus they disposed of the Wölfflinian underpinnings that appeared so prevalent in historical writing in the other arts. "Most important of all," they state, "it is recognized that in the history of art, as in other branches of history, subjective criticism must give way to the impartial study of development—in which historical influence is the criterion of importance."[17]

With regard to periodization Kimball, who was responsible for all but the medieval section of the book, set out a scheme that included an early Renaissance (1420–1500) and a high Renaissance (1500–1540), which comprised a single chapter, and a style he called post-Renaissance architecture, which was served by a separate chapter to cover the multiple developments carrying the story into the eighteenth century. Between 1540 and 1580 Kimball discerned the establishment of "academic and baroque tendencies" in the works of Michelangelo, Palladio, Vignola, Vasari, Alessi, and Ammanati. These were succeeded by a period of "baroque supremacy," c. 1580–1730, which includes the work of Giacomo della Porta, Domenico Fontana, Maderno, Bernini, Borromini, Guarini, and Longhena. And finally came the "compromise," c. 1730–1780, established by Juvarra, Galilei, and Vanvitelli.[18]

In the introduction of the "post-Renaissance" chapter Kimball explains that, in English, the term *baroque* had been generally applied to buildings whose compositions eschew classical disposition and theory and employ the orders for sculptural effects. On the other hand, he informs us, the word in German and Italian was used as the name of a period style and was applied to all works of the period 1540–1750, including those he himself preferred to characterize as "academic" because of their classical features and mathematical canons of proportion. What Kimball recognized is the diversity of later sixteenth- and seventeenth-century architecture, which could not be encompassed by a single term. It was a realization about the diversity of style over a given span of time that would arise much later in the discussion of mannerism.[19]

American textbooks must have played a significant role in shaping our perception of Italian Renaissance and baroque architecture, but a series of books published in London by the presses at B. T. Batsford, beginning in 1893, would have been equally influential and far more detailed. In particular, William J. Anderson's *The Architecture of the Renaissance in Italy* (London, 1896) provided a fulsome, positive account even if there remained backwaters (seen in retrospect) as represented by C. H. Moore's *Character of Renaissance Architecture* (London, 1905) that still preferred to see the superiority of the Gothic.[20] (Geoffrey Scott sought finally to overthrow this attitude in *The Architecture of Humanism*, London, 1914.) Yet these backwaters were neap tides compared to attitudes about the period after 1550 and especially the seventeenth century. The new awakening was heralded in English by Martin S. Briggs, *Baroque Architecture* (London, 1913), and contemporaries would soon follow his lead in reassessing these periods. In this regard the introduction to the fifth edition of Anderson, revised by Arthur Stratton (London, 1927) is instructive. Stratton explains the addition of a last chapter dealing with seventeenth-century material as follows: "The architecture of the seventeenth century in Italy can no longer be dismissed as wholly decadent, and there is much to be learnt from that of the eighteenth century, which saw many a versatile Baroque architect at the height of his power." And Stratton adds, "This later and more riotous expression of Renaissance vitality has now been dealt

with in an entirely new concluding chapter, and the most difficult part of a difficult undertaking has been to graft this additional branch on to the old stem in such a way that it grows naturally out of it and in its luxuriance endangers not the root."

It would be a mistake to assume that Kimball's gesture of inclusionism and historical relativism for the later material was more than a mere beginning: Della Porta, Maderno, Bernini, and Borromini receive two paragraphs and Borromini himself just two sentences! But the flood gates had been opened. By 1942 Talbot Hamlin (1889–1956) could be numbered among the converted: in a special issue of the *Journal of the American Society of Architectural Historians* devoted to the theme of history in architectural education he discussed the need for "still unwritten architectural histories."[21] Among them Hamlin cited "one of the great current needs—a good book on Baroque architecture, as a great international movement." So far had he come along with the currents of historiographic taste that Hamlin—extolling its free planning, spatial development, movement, and "free inventiveness"—could call the study of baroque architecture "especially valuable to the architectural student today." By this time, Wittkower's extensively detailed article on the Roman baroque architect Carlo Rainaldi had appeared in English in the *Art Bulletin* 29 (1937); T. H. Fokker, *Roman Baroque Art: The History of a Style* (Oxford, 1938) would have been well known; and Briggs' book would have been considered out-of-date. Sigfried Giedion's Charles Eliot Norton Lectures for 1938–1939 at Harvard, published as *Space, Time and Architecture* (Cambridge, 1941), had material on Borromini and Guarini but would not contain the sections on Sixtus V's Rome until the third edition of 1954.

Hamlin's statement in 1942 is pregnant with the conflicts within the profession by the time of World War II. On one hand was the old guard, of which he was a distinguished representative, teaching in a school of architecture and espousing the study of history for the purposes of an architectural education: history at the service of practice. On the other hand was an increasingly catholic and relativistic view of the field of architectural history, represented by Kimball and Edgell, which grew from the field of art history and which had a more broadly humanistic mission as its goal. When the Nazi era resulted in the emigration of major scholars of architectural history to the United States, it was not by accident that they were welcomed and absorbed completely by the art historical establishment rather than by schools of architecture. Certainly the hegemony of modernism, with its skeptical attitude toward history, took its toll in schools founded on the principles and practices of the Beaux-Arts tradition. But the wariness and guarded hostility between the two programs in many universities had, and in some cases still have, roots deeper than the modernist influence.

Thus it was that distinguished contributions to the history of architecture were made by individual American scholars before mid-century without developing a dominant school or tradition of rigorous research that might have sustained the energies of a few dedicated writers. The importance of this phenomenon can hardly be overemphasized. With strength of numbers in the camp represented by the architectural schools, the torch of history could be passed but fitfully to succeeding generations. With the development of architectural history within art history curricula, the situation would change dramatically after World War II. Among the notable contributions between the world wars, one example will stand for many. W. W. Kent, *The Life and Work of Baldassare Peruzzi* (New York, 1925) took as its subject one of the most admired heroes of the High Renaissance and treated his work in a fully illustrated, monographic style. Although brief, Kent's book provided a handy, well-informed summary of knowledge about the artist and his drawings, painting, and architecture, including bibliographic materials in French, German, and Italian as well as in English. Kent's purpose was to summarize, and this he did well, but subsequent research put his generalizing treatment seriously out of date within two decades. Missing was a penetrating analysis of evidence and argumentation to support or challenge current views in order to make a more durable contribution to the literature.

Just such a contribution was made in 1942 to the literature on Sebastiano Serlio by the archaeologist William Dinsmoor (1886–1973). Already famous for his edition of Anderson and Spiers' *Architecture of Ancient Greece* (London, 1927), Dinsmoor, a professor at Columbia University, had begun research in 1920 on Serlio's unpublished sixth book, a copy of which had been deposited on campus at the Avery Memorial Architectural Library. Twenty-two years later, his two articles appeared in the *Art Bulletin*, and they are still regarded as fundamental to the literature on Serlio.[22] In these articles the author displays a command of previous literature and original sources that had scarcely been equaled in American scholarship. His staggering erudition was such that only fifty years later has there been significant progress on the subject.

In the same year, 1942, John Coolidge (born 1913) had published his study of Lowell, Massachusetts, when his brilliant work on the little domes of St. Peter's appeared in *Marsyas*, the student journal of the Institute of Fine Arts, New York University.[23] To be sure, his thesis on Giacomo Vignola was written under the supervision of Richard Krautheimer and Karl Lehmann, but the sustained logic of the argument in *Marsyas* and the originality of the conclusions about Vignola had no European precedent. Similarly, the article on the Villa Giulia in the *Art Bulletin* in 1943 and on Vignola's personality in the *Journal of the Society of Architectural Historians* in 1950 had anticipated to a large extent Lotz's more widely recognized generalizations on style in the later sixteenth century.[24] Coolidge's deductive reasoning in the piece on the little domes remains a model of critical analysis, and the elegant writing of these articles still ranks among the most compelling in the field in any language.

The contributions of Dinsmoor and Coolidge demonstrated that American scholarship in Renaissance architecture had to be treated with the utmost seriousness, but they were distinguished in part for being rarities of their time. There simply was no great school of architectural history, nor was one in the making until the early 1950s. At that time Richard Krautheimer began a full-time teaching appointment at the Institute of Fine Arts, New York University, and Rudolf Wittkower was appointed to the Department of Art History and Archaeology at Columbia University. Both of these men brought from Europe a wide range of interests in architecture, both of them continued to write in the United States with apparently boundless energy, and both had a special ability to attract and inspire the students who became the leading scholars of the next generation in our country. Great teachers cannot produce great students, but they can excite and involve the minds of those whose intellects and dispositions are best equipped to continue the journey; for this task Krautheimer and Wittkower were ideally suited. Their presence during the years that witnessed a rapid growth of academic departments of art history and the development of a strong identity for the profession helped to propel research along the path it has taken over the last forty years, as their students—and the succeeding generation of students—created both the ambience and the opportunities to promote their scholarly pursuits.

Richard Krautheimer (born 1897) emigrated in 1935 to the United States, where he took a teaching position at the University of Louisville in Kentucky. Two years later and for fifteen years after that, he taught at Vassar College. In 1952 he moved to the Institute of Fine Arts, New York University, where he had been a visiting lecturer for many years. Krautheimer's life work had been established as early as 1933, with his commitment to the publication of the *Corpus Basilicarum Christianarum Romae* under the auspices of the Pontifical Institute for Christian Archaeology. The first of five volumes of the *Corpus*, published in English by the Vatican Press in 1937, established the author as one of the premier archaeologists of our time. Subsequent articles on the Carolingian revival of early Christian architecture and on the iconography of medieval architecture, both published in English in 1942, signaled a mind as attuned to broad themes and speculative notions as to dirt archaeology and literary reconstructions.[25]

In the field of Renaissance architecture Krautheimer's fascination with the relationship to antiquity is manifest in his lecture on Alberti and Vitruvius.[26] In it the author argues that Alberti's *De re aedificatoria* was written as both an interpretation and a critique of Vitruvius' *De architectura*, and not in simple emulation of it. Krautheimer points out that the two writers had different points of departure: Alberti wrote as a humanist, a "counsellor-at-antiquity" whose prescriptions would create the buildings of an ideal social order; Vitruvius wrote as a craftsman advising craftsmen, a knowledgeable builder whose theory was founded on practice rather than an ideal conception of the art.

The interrelationships of fifteenth-century theory, practice, and the influence of Roman remains are themes that Krautheimer dealt with in other contexts as well. Most memorable is the account of Brunelleschi's invention of perspective discussed in the monograph on Ghiberti, written by Krautheimer in collaboration with his wife Trude.[27] In this passage the Krautheimers give new, visceral meaning to Brunelleschi's panel depicting the Florentine Baptistery, explaining how Brunelleschi created a perspective based on the Florentine *braccia* and then beheld the illusion at arm's length, from the back, through a hole in the vanishing point, with the help of a mirror. The sky was rendered with burnished silver to reflect real, moving clouds so as to vivify the pictorial rendering of the Baptistery before which the viewing would take place. The Krautheimers also explain how the invention of a perspective method may have derived from a method invented to record and reconstruct ancient ruins, which Brunelleschi thought had been designed, like his own buildings, according to repeating modular proportions. This explanation of the invention of perspective thus accounts for Brunelleschi's interest in antiquity, his desire to make records of it on graph paper (recounted by his biographer), his adherence to simple proportional schemes in his own buildings, and the reasons why a revolutionary pictorial invention was the product of an architect rather than a painter.

Beginning a lecture some years ago,

Krautheimer explained his interest in the Rome of Pope Alexander VII Chigi (1655–1666) with the excuse that "old men need new toys." For the audience familiar with Krautheimer's love of Rome and his long interest in baroque architecture, his new hobby was hardly a surprise. For decades his imaginative teaching in early Christian, medieval, and Byzantine architecture had been complemented by his courses in baroque.[28] In fact, the class notes for his baroque architecture lectures, written up by students and made into dittos, had a wide and quite unauthorized circulation in many programs, particularly among candidates for doctoral exams. His book on *The Rome of Alexander VII, 1655–1667* (Princeton, 1985) is, more than anything else, a testament to Krautheimer's affection for the city and his fascination with the Chigi pope.

In some sense *The Rome of Alexander VII* can be seen as developing the long-neglected subject of A. E. Brinckmann's *Platz und Monument als künstlerisches Formproblem* (1908). But where Brinckmann was concerned with the visual analysis of space—as were Edmund Bacon and Sigfried Giedion—Krautheimer considers matters of patronage, politics, and the quotidian realities that have always shaped the urban environment. Thus, we learn about the widening of squares and the creation of new streets for the purpose of accommodating coach traffic, the reorientation and systematization of squares to satisfy the outspoken but disenfranchised and disorganized lobbies of greengrocers, fishmongers, and cobblers. Relationships between stage design and planning are considered but cautiously, for the dynamics of urban design are not the result of ideal constructs drawn from literary sources but of mundane realities colliding with exalted programs of a personal nature. Thus, too, political policies are seen to be reflected in architectural commitments, and the general importance of the renewal of Rome is emphasized in light of the economic benefits of increased tourist trade.

The importance of this book lies in Krautheimer's interest in suggesting broad-ranging connections between architecture and seventeenth-century life. He explains how the vast space of Piazza San Pietro was to be used for parking, and the enormous expense of the enterprise was justified as a stimulus to the local artisan economy—"to keep such a large number of poor artisans at work," says an anonymous memo. The systematization of Piazza della Rotonda has as much to do with banishing the flower vendor from the steps of the Pantheon as it does with organizing the marketplaces of the city. None of these interesting facts in themselves explain the creation of great architecture, of course, but they put the process of designing and constructing impressive monuments into a perspective remote from the usual discussions of baroque grandeur and power. Moreover, monuments were not the only method to glorify the city: there were also the avenues of elms planted in the Roman Forum to provide an elegant promenade in the midst of the glories of Rome's antiquity. Such avenues of shade trees had appeared earlier in the seventeenth and even the sixteenth century; Alexander VII was the first to make a consciously planned network of them, taking the visitor from one ancient or Christian monument to the next, along the outskirts of the populated center.

By contrast with Krautheimer's early arrival, Rudolf Wittkower (1901–1971) came much later to the United States. Krautheimer spent only a handful of his forty-three teaching years outside of the American situation.[29] Wittkower, who had spent more than twenty years at the University of London (Warburg Institute and University College) and some years as an *assistente* at the Bibliotheca Hertziana before that, settled permanently in the United States in 1955. He had taught in the Harvard University Summer Session in 1954 and again in 1955, before taking a position at the Department of Art History and Archaeology at Columbia University in 1955. Wittkower served as chairman of the department from 1956 until his retirement in the spring of 1969. His impact on American scholarship was therefore in large part made even before his arrival.

In the fields of Renaissance and baroque architecture, Wittkower's most influential writings were the early studies of Rainaldi and Bernini, the articles on Michelangelo, and the book entitled *Architectural Principles in the Age of Humanism* (London, 1949). *Architectural Principles* was based on an investigation of proportion and number theory, primarily in the work of Alberti and Palladio. Wittkower sought to show that these architects (and others such as Francesco Giorgi) used ancient forms and "harmonic" proportions in order to capture what they believed to be celestial harmonies that governed the cosmos. For them beauty was achieved by the rational integration of proportions and components according to simple ratios derived from music, such as the octave (1 to 2), the fifth, and so forth. This notion refuted Geoffrey Scott's conclusion that beauty in Renaissance architecture "is not a matter for logical demonstration," and this Wittkower pointed out in the first page of his book.[30]

Wittkower's work on Michelangelo began with the collaboration on Ernst Steinmann's *Michelangelo—Bibliographie, 1510–1926* (Leipzig, 1927), and continued in the famous articles on Michelangelo's dome for St. Peter's and on the Laurentian Library. In the extensive article on the dome, Wittkower attempted to demonstrate that its elevated profile was due to the work of Giacomo della Porta, who built the dome from the drum to the lantern in 1585–1590, long after Michelangelo's death.[31] In the article on the Laurenziana, Wittkower sought not only to clarify the building history of the library but also to establish principles for identifying mannerist buildings and hence for rethinking the Wölfflinian notion of Michelangelo as a "baroque" architect.[32]

When Wittkower arrived at Harvard for his first summer session, he was also well known for his work in baroque architecture, both from the monumental edition of Bernini's drawings, published in collaboration with Heinrich Brauer, and from the extensive article on Carlo Rainaldi, published in the *Art Bulletin*.[33] The piece on Rainaldi was a painstaking effort to trace the design process through an analysis of drawings, documents, and corollary evidence, and then to extend this effort to formulate some principles to characterize the architect's style. The corpus of Bernini drawings had a more limited intention, following as it did Fraschetti's weighty monograph of 1900, a work much indebted to the archival investigations of the late nineteenth century. Interestingly, Brauer and Wittkower's book on Bernini, complemented by numerous subsequent articles and a book on his sculpture, had a greater impact on American students for its broadly based evidence and its narrowly argued building histories than did the more complex issues of style and typology in the contribution on Rainaldi. Indeed, Brauer and Wittkower's work on Bernini's drawings set an enviable example of precision and thoroughness for the entire field of Italian baroque studies.

Wittkower's awesome command of Italian baroque subjects was consolidated in his volume of the Pelican History of Art series, *Art and Architecture in Italy, 1600–1750* (Baltimore, 1958) which, if not truly an American contribution—he had begun dictating it in 1950—nevertheless influenced a great number of students in the United States. By imposing a reasoned scheme on a vast amount of apparently disparate material, Wittkower made the field accessible and even inviting. Great artists and architects are given their due, balancing a narrative that embraces leading schools and styles without neglecting regional developments and typological themes. The essays on Bernini, Borromini, and Pietro da Cortona presented a completely new picture of Roman baroque architecture, and the sections on the Piedmontese architects Guarini, Juvarra, and Vittone opened vast new scholarly territory. The same could be said for eighteenth-century architecture in Rome and Venice. So commanding indeed is Wittkower's summation of baroque architecture that his view of the period seems almost inescapable despite its failure to discuss garden architecture, ephemeral design, or even town planning.[34]

Among the possibilities for new research that Wittkower opened during his American years were those announced in *Born under Saturn: The Character and Conduct of Artists: A Documented History from Antiquity to the French Revolution* (New York, 1963), written in collaboration with his wife Margot. Here genius and madness, celibacy and suicide, nobility and melancholy in the lives of artists are considered as part of the art historian's preserve. The notion that the character of an architect has much to tell us about buildings is in fact a throwback to early nineteenth-century attitudes about morality and art; but psychoanalytic methods and Freudian analysis in the late twentieth century seemed to suggest a newly profitable approach to the personality of the artist. In a later essay on Borromini's life and character, Wittkower uses contemporary accounts to draw distinctions between the dispositions of the architect and his rival Bernini, revealing in the process how the usually despondent Borromini lived in smug assurance that time, rather than contemporary recognition, would reveal his qualities as an architect.[35] Where Wittkower uses evidence of Borromini's actions and opinions to reveal the architect and, by extension, the nature of his work, the procedure is reversed in an essay on Guarini. Disputing Guarini's reputation as a tormented genius, Wittkower analyzes Guarini's *Architettura civile* and other books, as well as his buildings, concluding that he consistently exercised measured judgment and was methodical in his pursuit of the "art that pleases," but open to the subjectivity that accounts for the differing tastes in architecture over the ages.[36]

The presence of Richard Krautheimer and Rudolf Wittkower in leading American graduate programs in art history in the mid-1950s marked a distinct watershed in the study of Renaissance and baroque architecture in our country. Both of these men taught, inspired, and continued to encourage the study of architectural history with apparently boundless energy, and it is largely they who spawned the leaders of the next two generations of scholars. In 1940 one could have imagined a major gathering of Renaissance and baroque architectural historians without a single American representative. Twenty years later this situation would have been inconceivable. By that time, first John Coolidge and later James Ackerman (both students of Krautheimer) had been teaching at Harvard for a number of years. Howard Hibbard, who

had earned his degree under Coolidge at Harvard, was teaching at Columbia, having also been a protegé of Wittkower since the first summer seminar at Harvard in 1954. In 1952 Wolfgang Lotz, the German scholar of Renaissance architecture, came to teach at Vassar in Krautheimer's place and in 1959 followed him to the Institute of Fine Arts. At that time David Coffin, who had begun a dissertation on Pirro Ligorio's Villa d'Este with Erwin Panofsky, was teaching at his alma mater, Princeton. These names, dates, and institutions—incomplete as they are—give an appropriate indication of the change in Renaissance and baroque architectural history that took place in the United States by 1960. By 1980 the situation had developed to the extent that there was hardly a period or an approach not represented by an older or younger member of the profession.

James Ackerman set a new standard of thoroughness and precision in the gathering and interpretation of archival materials in the dissertation written under Krautheimer's aegis, *The Cortile del Belvedere* (Vatican City, 1954). His work on the Belvedere and in related articles demonstrates an interest in pursuing the intellectual and cultural framework of history explored by Krautheimer. In Ackerman's monograph on the architecture of Michelangelo the subject is larger and the approach narrower, as the author's understanding of the architect's work derives not as much from the finished buildings as from their resolution out of seemingly insurmountable challenges recorded in mountains of drawings, documents, and contemporary sources.[37] In the little book on Palladio, Ackerman provides a masterful synthesis of an architect whose style and opportunities were created by the economic and social forces of his time.[38] As Ackerman proposes, the mercantile patriciate of Venice required villas whose cultural allusions would ennoble the effort to cultivate land as trade possibilities declined.

Howard Hibbard's early work was dominated by an interest in archival evidence, and his book on Carlo Maderno is perhaps the most scrupulously documented monograph on a single architect ever written.[39] Its archival apparatus leads in many directions forward and back in time, from the late Renaissance in Rome to the later seventeenth century. Hibbard's interest in matters of style and periodization is evident in an essay ostensibly on Michelangelo and Maderno, but the substance of which deals with the question of mannerism and alternative characterizations of the later sixteenth century.[40] This essay takes its cue from the articles of Lotz, who believed that the term, in order to be useful, had to be restricted to certain architects and buildings of the second quarter of the century.[41] Hibbard demonstrated that mannerist traits could be discerned in Raphael's Palazzo Branconio dell'Aquila, while Michelangelo's use of columns partly embedded in a wall is a motif found in ancient architecture, so that chronological definitions of mannerism (Raphael died in 1520) or characterizations of the style as "anticlassical" would have to be rethought.

It is evident from these examples that the great teachers of Renaissance and baroque architecture had a measurable impact on their students, but there are distinct limits to a genetic explanation of research methods and approaches. Howard Saalman, another student of Krautheimer, emphasized an archaeological rather than cultural approach to Renaissance architecture in his early articles on Brunelleschi and Michelozzo and in his recent book on the dome of the Florence Cathedral.[42] Ackerman's work on the Belvedere owed much to Wittkower's pioneering efforts in the Vatican archives. Hibbard's debts to Krautheimer and Lotz have already been mentioned, and his interest in psychological approaches to art probably had less to do with Wittkower's influence than a personal interest in Freud and psychoanalysis.[43] Richard Pommer, a student of Krautheimer at the Institute of Fine Arts, and Henry Millon, a student of Coolidge at Harvard, began dissertations on Piedmontese architecture after a student trip through the region led by Wittkower in 1958.[44] Moreover, Millon developed Wittkower's interest in studies of proportion, extending it to the work of Francesco di Giorgio, whose writings and drawings could be demonstrably related to his most

famous church, Santa Maria del Calcinaio in Cortona.[45] Coffin's book on the Villa d'Este at Tivoli, written with the encouragement of the art historian Panofsky, introduced the whole study of gardens with the same seriousness of purpose and method that Ackerman had brought to the Cortile del Belvedere.[46] Elisabeth Blair MacDougall, a student of both Krautheimer and Wittkower, has also brought the former's interpretation of iconography in architecture to the analysis of allegorical programs in Roman sixteenth-century gardens and the latter's interest in Piedmontese architecture to the study of the royal gardens of the seventeenth century in Turin.[47] Finally, the arrival of the German-trained Hellmut Hager, who has had so much to do with encouraging the study of eighteenth-century architecture in Rome, occurred only in the 1970s.[48]

What, finally, accounts for the growth of scholarly interest in the United States in the fields of Italian Renaissance and baroque architecture? To this question various answers must be given. In part the development is due to a more general interest in architectural studies of all periods and an increasing concern after World War II for the built environment. This interest coincided with structural changes in the American educational system that favored the expansion of university programs in all fields on both undergraduate and graduate levels. Widening possibilities for specialized courses in the humanities helped to propel the establishment of graduate programs to provide staff for such courses. Certainly the personal magnetism of Krautheimer and Wittkower and the intelligence of their writing helped to attract a dedicated cadre of research-oriented students, but the presence of these men also served as a link to a tradition of research that could be traced back to the very foundations of architectural history as a discipline. With a century and more of spadework in the field, current work to be done in the 1950s and 1960s must have seemed all too evident and, for that reason, especially seductive.

In the 1970s the traditional definition of useful work seems to have broadened in scope to include more extensive fields and methods. Garden architecture, landscape design, and town planning are seen to have explanations in the social fabric of given times and places. The architecture of fortifications, of popular housing, and of religious orders is each being studied and understood as a genre in its own right, dependent on a multitude of considerations generally regarded as beyond the competence of an art historian. At the same time, the possibility of writing a traditional monograph on an architect, a period, or a style becomes increasingly remote, as the requirements of time abroad and the necessity for laborious archival research become standard even for the most imaginative studies. With the rehabilitation of history in schools of architecture has come a new dedication to issues that deal with purely formal problems, as well as with cultural contexts. These schools themselves have become training grounds for architectural historians in a manner that was completely without precedent earlier in this century. Today the younger students do not speak of a "definitive" publication or of exclusive rights over architects or buildings of historic interest. Rather, it is acknowledged that well-written history will have a point of view and method unique to the writer, who will bring to a topic a multitude of perceptions gleaned from a variety of academic experiences. If the complaints registered against traditional art history—elitism, gentility, isolation of context—could once be registered against most histories of Renaissance and baroque architecture, that is no longer the case. New work has begun to emerge, and in it we may hope to validate the faith of our predecessors in the progress of the discipline.

NOTES

1. See David Watkin, *The Rise of Architectural History* (London, 1980), 8, citing Nikolaus Pevsner in *The Listener* 48 (1952), 715. For timely advice on many other historiographic matters, I wish to thank Henry Millon, dean of the Center for Advanced Study in the Visual Arts, National Gallery of Art, Washington, D.C.

2. The term *baroque* was first used in Jacob Burckhardt, *Der Cicerone* (1855). The term is discussed by O. Kurz, "Barocco: storia di una parola," in *Lettere italiane* 12 (1960). For more general discussions, see *Manierismo, Barocco, Rococo: concetti e termini* (Accademia nazionale dei Lincei 359. Problemi attuali di scienza e di cultura, quaderno 52, 1962). Burckhardt's handbook of 1867 is now available in an English translation edited by Peter Murray (London, 1985).

3. For a discussion of the book, see Peter Murray's introduction to the English translation (London, 1964) and Howard Hibbard's review in *Journal of the Society of Architectural Historians* 25 (1966), 141–143.

4. This book was followed by Gurlitt's *Geschichte des Barockstiles, des Rococo, und des Klassicismus in Belgien, Holland, Frankreich, England* (Stuttgart, 1888), providing for the rest of the Continent a survey whose thoroughness would not be challenged for thirty years.

5. A note in Norton's *Historical Studies of Church-Building of the Middle Ages* refers to Ruskin's *Stones of Venice* and his *St. Mark's Rest* as "the books from which a better acquaintance with the qualities of Venetian art and of Venetian character may be gained than from all others besides. The dry bones of history are changed to a body with a living soul by the inspiration of his genius".[59] Yet Norton's bibliographic citations far outstripped those of Ruskin.

6. See, for example, Norton's citations from Mothes, *Geschichte der Baukunst und Bildhauerei Venedigs* (Leipzig, 1859); Verneilh, *L'Architecture Byzantine en France* (Paris, 1851); and Lorenzi, *Monumenti per servire alla storia del Palazzo Ducale di Venezia,* (Venice, 1868).

7. See Norton's appendix I. Norton had already published part of the Sienese archival campaign in German: C. E. Norton, "Urkunden zur Geschichte des Doms von Siena," *Zahns Jahrbücher* 5 (1873), 66.

8. Compare the details of payments, chronology, and other matters to the account in John White, *Art and Architecture in Italy, 1250–1400* (Baltimore, 1966).

9. See Richard G. Kenworthy, *The Italian Garden Transplanted: Renaissance Revival Landscape Design in America, 1850–1939* [exh. cat., Troy State University] (Troy, Alabama, 1988). This reference was kindly brought to my attention by Phoebe Cutler.

10. Kenworthy 1988.

11. Reported in the *Journal of the American Society of Architectural Historians* 2 (January 1942), 38.

12. The book was the first of three in the series, "College History of Art," edited by John C. Van Dyke, a professor in the history of art at Rutgers College, New Brunswick, New Jersey. Van Dyke wrote the companion history of painting, and his neighbors at Princeton, Allan Marquand and Arthur L. Frothingham, wrote the volume on the history of sculpture.

13. I am using the edition of Hamlin published in New York in 1923. The earlier editions date from January 1896, December 1896 (revised), 1898, 1900, 1902, 1904, 1906, 1907, 1909, September 1909 (revised), 1911, 1915, 1918, 1920, 1922 (revised). This was obviously a popular book.

14. A. D. F. Hamlin, *A Text-Book of the History of Architecture* (New York, 1896; rev. ed. 1923), 285. Again on page 286, Hamlin defines the Italian term *seicento* as referring "to the seventeenth century or Decline."

15. Hamlin 1923, 316.

16. The other volumes of the series, listed as "in preparation" opposite the title page, are: *A History of Sculpture*, by George Henry Chase and Chandler Rathfon Post and *A History of Painting* by Arthur Pope. These men all taught at Harvard. See Lauren Weiss Bricker, "The Writings of Fiske Kimball: A Synthesis of Architectural History and Practice," in this volume.

17. Fiske Kimball and George Harold Edgell, *A History of Architecture* (New York, 1918), xxi. This point of view was in fact the key to the series as Chase conceived it. His "Editor's Introduction" states that "the office of the historian is to trace development, to show how the art of any period grew out of that of earlier times and in turn conditioned that of later days. Too many of the older histories were written to uphold a particular system of aesthetics or to glorify a particular phase of artistic development. . . . The aim of the writers of this series has been to point out the qualities in the works of any period which have appealed most strongly to the creators of those works and to endeavor to emphasize what has enduring value. It is hoped that the resulting 'objectivity' of the books will add materially to their usefulness."

18. Kimball and Edgell 1918, 452–453.

19. It should be noted that Kimball was addressing the architecture of France, Spain, Germany, and England, as well as Italy.

20. The Batsford series included, in addition to Anderson's volume: Andrew N. Prentice, *Renaissance Architecture and Ornament in Spain* (London, 1893); J. A. Gotch, *Architecture of the Renaissance in England* (London, 1894); John Belcher, *Later Renaissance Architecture in England* (London, 1901); and William H. Ward, *The Architecture of the Renaissance in France* (London, 1911).

21. Talbot F. Hamlin, "Some Necessary but Still Unwritten Architectural Histories," *Journal of the American Society of Architectural Historians* 2 (April 1942), 26.

22. William Dinsmoor, "The Literary Remains of Sebastiano Serlio," *Art Bulletin* 24 (1942), 55–91, 115–154.

23. John Coolidge, "Vignola and the Little Domes of St. Peter's," *Marsyas* 2 (1942), 63-123. Coolidge's book on Lowell is entitled *Mill and Mansion: A Study of Architecture and Society in Lowell, Massachusetts, 1820-1865* (New York, 1942).

24. John Coolidge, "The Villa Giulia; A Study of Central Italian Architecture in the Mid-Sixteenth Century," *Art Bulletin* 25 (1943), 177-225; and Coolidge, "Vignola's Character and Achievement," *Journal of the Society of Architectural Historians* 9 (1950), 10-14. For Lotz's views on the later sixteenth century, see note 41.

25. Richard Krautheimer, "The Carolingian Revival of Early Christian Architecture," *Art Bulletin* 24 (1942), 1-38; and Krautheimer, "Introduction to an 'Iconography of Medieval Architecture,'" *Journal of the Warburg and Courtauld Institutes* 5 (1942), 1-33. The essays are reprinted with additional notations in Krautheimer, *Studies in Early Christian, Medieval, and Renaissance Art* (New York, 1969), 115-150, 203-256.

26. Richard Krautheimer, "Alberti and Vitruvius," *Acts of the Twentieth International Congress of the History of Art*, II (Princeton, 1963), 42-52. Reprinted in Krautheimer 1969, 323-332.

27. Richard Krautheimer and Trude Krautheimer Hess, *Lorenzo Ghiberti* (Princeton, 1956).

28. Howard Hibbard's *Carlo Maderno and Roman Architecture 1580-1630* (London, 1971), is dedicated to Krautheimer. In the preface Hibbard acknowledges that "had he not given a fascinating series of lectures on Roman Baroque architecture in 1953, I would never have written this book." Hibbard was a graduate student at Columbia for a year and took Krautheimer's course at the Institute of Fine Arts before moving to Harvard University to complete his doctorate.

29. Krautheimer retired to live in Rome at the Bibliotheca Hertziana after the spring term of 1971.

30. Geoffrey Scott, *The Architecture of Humanism* (London, 1914), quoted from the epilogue of 1924. Scott here goes on to suggest that beauty "is experienced, consciously, as a direct and simple intuition, which has its ground in the subconscious region where our physical memories are stored. . . ." Interestingly, Wittkower often claimed in conversation that a sensitive visitor could *feel* the correspondent proportions in fifteenth-century churches or Palladian villas even before knowing them intellectually. Incidentally, Watkin has mentioned in passing that Heinrich von Geymüller's *Architektur und Religion* (Basel, 1911) argued for a Renaissance "interpretation of beauty as a conscious reflection of God." Watkin 1980, 10. This thesis may well have affected Wittkower in the genesis of his *Architectural Principles*, which sought to demonstrate in Renaissance proportions the attempt to emulate a divinely ordered cosmos.

31. Rudolf Wittkower, "Zur Peterskuppel Michelangelos," *Zeitschrift für Kunstgeschichte* 2 (1933), 348-370. Republished with additions in *Arte antica e moderna* 20 (1962), 390-437, and again as a book, *La cupola di San Pietro de Michelangelo* (Florence, 1964). The argument is taken up again in a lecture of 1970 published in the posthumous collection *Idea and Image: Studies in the Italian Renaissance* (London, 1978), 73-89.

32. Rudolf Wittkower, "Michelangelo's Biblioteca Laurenziana," *Art Bulletin* 16 (1934), 123-218. Reprinted in Wittkower 1978, 11-71.

33. Heinrich Brauer and Rudolf Wittkower, *Die Zeichnungen des Gianlorenzo Bernini* (Leipzig, 1931), and "Carlo Rainaldi and the Roman Architecture of the Full Baroque," *Art Bulletin* 19 (1937), 242-313. The former was republished with a short introduction (New York, 1970), and the latter was reprinted in the posthumous *Studies in the Italian Baroque* (London, 1975), 9-52.

34. In his foreword Wittkower mentions precisely these topics as beyond the scope of the book. The influence of Wittkower's model for the period may be judged in a recent text for Italian baroque architecture that essentially repeats the organization, though adding significant new summaries of material on South Italian regions, especially Sicily, where Wittkower is notably weak. John Varriano, *Italian Baroque and Rococo Architecture* (New York, 1986).

35. "Francesco Borromini: personalità e destino," in *Studi sul Borromini* (Atti del convegno promosso dell'Accademia di San Luca) 1 (1970), 19-48. Reprinted as "Francesco Borromini, His Character and Life," in Wittkower 1975, 153-176.

36. "Introduzione al Guarini," in *Atti del convegno su Guarini e l'internationalità del barocco* (Turin, 1970), 20-32. Reprinted in *Studies in the Italian Baroque* as "Guarini the Man," 178-186.

37. James Ackerman, *The Architecture of Michelangelo* (London, 1961).

38. James Ackerman, *Palladio* (Baltimore, 1966).

39. See note 28.

40. "Maderno, Michelangelo, and Cinquecento Tradition," in *Stil und Ueberlieferung in der Kunst des Abendlandes* (Akten des 21. Internationalen Kongresses für Kunstgeschichte, 1964) 2 (Bonn, 1967), 33-41.

41. Wolfgang Lotz, "Architecture in the Later Sixteenth Century," *College Art Journal* 17 (1958), 129-139 and "Mannerism in Architecture: Changing Aspects," *Acts of the Twentieth International Congress of the History of Art* 2 (Princeton, 1963), 239-246. The American point of view, largely shaped by Lotz's writings, tends to find the term *mannerism* useful to the extent that it lacks specificity, but this is hardly a satisfactory state of affairs. In Lotz's section of the Pelican volume on Renaissance architecture, the term is used just once—in a bibliographic heading at the back of the book. See Ludwig Heydenreich and Wolfgang Lotz, *Architecture in Italy 1400-1600* (Baltimore, 1974).

42. Howard Saalman, "Filippo Brunelleschi: Capital Studies," *Art Bulletin* 40 (1958), 113-137; Saalman, "Michelozzo Studies," *Burlington Magazine* 108 (1966), 242-250; and Saalman, *Filippo Brunelleschi:*

The Cupola of Santa Maria del Fiore (London, 1984).

43. However, see Hibbard, "Borromini e Maderno," in *Studi sul Borromini* I (Rome, 1970), 499–503, where a beginning was made, and his *Michelangelo* (New York, 1974) and *Caravaggio* (New York, 1983).

44. See Richard Pommer, *Eighteenth-Century Architecture in Piedmont:* The Open Structures of Juvarra, Alfieri, and Vittone (New York, 1967), and Henry Millon's still unpublished dissertation on Guarini's Palazzo Carignano (Harvard University, 1964).

45. Henry Millon, "The Architectural Theory of Francesco di Giorgio," *Art Bulletin* 40 (1958), 256–261. Millon had begun this research under the auspices of Wittkower during his first summer session at Harvard.

46. David Coffin, *The Villa D'Este at Tivoli* (Princeton, 1960).

47. See Elisabeth Blair MacDougall, *"Ars Hortulorum*: Sixteenth-Century Garden Iconography and Literary Theory in Italy," in *The Italian Garden*, First Dumbarton Oaks Colloquium on the History of Landscape Architecture, ed. D. Coffin (Washington, D.C., 1972); "*L'Ingegnoso Artifizio*: Sixteenth-Century Garden Fountains in Rome," in *Fons Sapientiae: Renaissance Garden Fountains*, Dumbarton Oaks Colloquium on the History of Landscape Architecture 5, ed. E. MacDougall (Washington, D.C., 1978).

48. For a list of Hager's contributions to Roman baroque architecture, see the bibliography in Allan Braham and Hellmut Hager, *The Drawings by Carlo Fontana in the Royal Library in Windsor Castle* (London, 1978).

NANCY SHATZMAN STEINHARDT
University of Pennsylvania

East Asia:

Architectural History across War Zones and Political Boundaries

The architecture of East Asia has received less scholarly attention in North America than the architecture of almost any other major geographical and cultural region with so large and so richly documented a group of surviving buildings. So many of the North American scholarly contributions have relied heavily on excavation, measuring, or other research conducted in East Asia that it can almost be said that without the East Asian component, little research could have been undertaken on this side of the Pacific. This statement is especially pertinent to the investigation of premodern architecture of East Asia, defined here as construction before the year 1870.[1]

Nineteenth-Century Beginnings

By 1870 there was already an interest in, and a growing awareness of, East Asian architecture among certain circles in North America, notably historians of architecture and missionaries. In 1848, Louisa C. Tuthill included a three-page chapter on Chinese architecture in her *History of Architecture from Earliest Times.*[2] Relying on the word of French writer M. Barron, the author notes the architectural achievements of the so-called "first emperor" and unifier of China, Qin Shi Huangdi of the third century B.C., in particular his construction of the Great Wall, the materials

for which, Tuthill writes, would have been "more than sufficient to build a wall twice round the globe, six feet high and two feet thick."[3] Her information about the First Emperor's building program clearly points to the second to first century B.C. text *Shi ji* (Record of the Grand Historian) of Sima Tan and Sima Qian and to Miao Changyan's late third century A.D. work *Sanfu huangtu* (Illustrated description of the three districts of the metropolitan area) as the ultimate sources, although they probably were unknown to Mrs. Tuthill. Both texts are still important literary works for use in reconstruction of Chinese architecture of the Qin and Han dynasties (c. 256 B.C.–A.D. 220). Besides describing the building projects of the First Emperor, Mrs. Tuthill makes scant references and only general statements about pagodas, gates, and residential architecture. She concludes her chapter with a quotation from Sir William Chambers, who praises the design capability of this race who, "separated from the polished nations of the world, have without any model . . . been able . . . to mature the sciences and invent the arts."[4]

Benson J. Lossing's *History of Fine Arts* of 1840 accords only two paragraphs to Chinese architecture, and none to that of other East Asian traditions.[5] In the brief passage Lossing makes a few sweeping statements, such as: "The ancient and modern architecture of the Chinese are similar, both having been fashioned after the tent; or rather the ancient Chinese first imitated the original tent in their buildings and the modern have improved only in advancing the tent style to that of the pavilion"; or: "The reader can get the best idea of the form of Chinese dwellings from the ornaments on old East India earthen ware, or from the tin boxes in which tea is often kept in groceries." In the second paragraph Lossing tries to explain why Chinese architecture can be so capsulized, stating that it, like other things Chinese, has been unchangeable because rigidly enforced laws "prescribe the style in which palaces or houses of persons of various grades shall be built. Hence the officers of police are the arbiters of taste in this matter."[6]

Other works of the mid-nineteenth century, such as Miss Ludlow's *A General View of the Fine Arts*, include some discussion of non-Western architecture, but none of it is East Asian.[7] More information about East Asian architecture could be found in contemporary European works, even in general books such as Joseph Gwilt's *The Encyclopedia of Architecture*, published in London in 1867. In North America, however, information about East Asian architecture came to writers on architectural history second- or thirdhand, and no American scholar or general writer was intimately involved in East Asian material.

Before the end of the century, however, the situation was greatly changed. With one main exception, there was still no significant interest in East Asian architecture. Yet North Americans were living in China and Japan in greater numbers than early in the nineteenth century, and more important, they were sending reports to journals about what they saw. Christian readers who subscribed to the *Foreign Missionary*, a journal of Presbyterian church missions, for instance, could learn about peoples, places, and occasionally architecture of East Asia during the years the Tuthill, Lossing, and Ludlow works were published. A survey of this periodical in the decade of the 1850s[8] showed several articles with some information about Chinese or Japanese architecture in each year, although not in every issue of any given year. Certain missions, in particular those in

Ningbo and Shanghai, South China, submitted articles with special frequency. Most informative for architectural history were descriptions of native Chinese or Japanese worship in temples or halls and tidbits found in more general travel accounts. The October 1851 issue, for instance, carried an article with an illustration taken from a Chinese painting of "The Judgment Hall at Sung-te [Songde]," the description of which came from the *London Juvenile Missionary Magazine*.[9] The illustration showed one of the Chinese Kings of Hell presiding in a columned hall, a raised platform in the center, and various deities of the afterlife. In the August 1854 issue readers saw a picture entitled "A Japanese Temple."[10] Upon reading they learned that "this picture is a copy of one that was published a year ago in an English missionary magazine. No description accompanied it, nor can we tell our young readers where this temple stands in Japan, nor to what gods it is dedicated. But yet we have thought it worth while to insert this engraving, because it will serve to remind our readers that the people of Japan are destitute of the gospel."[11] The reader was then informed of Commodore Perry's progress, that the illustration was most probably a Buddhist hall, that the religion was one of "absurd mythology, and a considerable number of gods," and that practitioners of the Shinto faith worshipped *kami*.[12] Nevertheless, the illustration is fairly accurate in its placement of images, although deities like a winged horse on the upper wall belie a Western illustrator. Reverend M. S. Culbertson's "A Journey to Hang-chow [Hangzhou]" told readers almost nothing of the city or its architecture except for passing mention of West Lake and one temple.[13] Still, for North American sponsors of the Presbyterian church and its missions, some images of East Asia had become available by the mid-nineteenth century.

Readers of the *American Architect and Building News* were also exposed to East Asian material via firsthand reports and many more illustrations than could be found in the *Foreign Missionary*. The first volume of this periodical contained an excerpt from M. Viollet-le-Duc's then-forthcoming *The Habitations of Man in All Ages* on the residence of the man known to his servants as "fat Fau," together with a house plan, three drawings of the house and its details, one drawing of its structural framework, and two illustrations of the Japanese system of joinery.[14]

By the turn of the century numerous references to East Asian architecture or related issues were carried in *American Architect and Building News*, from paragraph references in the "Notes and Clippings" section to multipart serious articles. From the "Tid-bit" category one could learn of plans for a memorial to Commodore Perry;[15] that in China more wood is designated for coffins than for any other purpose;[16] that in Japan compass points may be indicated on hotel room ceilings so that guests do not mistakenly sleep head-north, the position of a corpse;[17] and that the Russo-Japanese War had broken out.[18] One could also learn that the numbers three and nine are symbolic in China;[19] of the magnitude in export of Chinese wood oil to the United States;[20] of a Thousand-Mat Hall in Japan;[21] that C. T. Yerkes sent W. B. Van Ingen to Japan to remove and rebuild a Japanese room in the United States;[22] that the P'ung-duk Pagoda was "raped" from Seoul by the Japanese because, according to the bandits, the Koreans did not respect it (a similar situation, according to *American Architect and Building News*, to that of the Elgin marbles);[23] or that buildings in Tokyo had been designed by European architects Ende and Benckmann.[24]

More significant, however, was a report of a trip to the Ming tombs initially submitted by H. J. Gallagher to the *Army and Navy Journal*.[25] Writing just ten years after the first notice of such a trip in the scholarly literature of East Asia,[26] Gallagher described the multimile approach to the tombs, the ceremonial gateway (*pailou*), the monumental animal sculpture along the spirit-path, and the earliest of the individual mausoleums, Changling. Gallagher's article concludes with a brief description of his climb up the Great Wall the next day. Three years later Edward T. Foulkes reported on his travels in Japan and India on a Rotch Travelling-Scholarship.[27]

His must be one of the first mentions of the seventeenth-century mausoleum of shogun Ieyasu at Nikko or of sixteenth- to seventeenth-century Nagoya Castle. After a month of travel Foulkes concluded that "aside from the temple architecture, the Japanese have little of interest to offer the student. Their castles are not worth spending much time over and their domestic architecture is beautiful only in its extreme simplicity and suitability to their climate. Their gardens, excepting in few cases where trees, rocks, and lakes were happily combined, were a disappointment to me."[28] Foulkes does, however, assess Japan's wooden architecture as the most interesting in the world, viewing the Japanese masters of timber architecture comparable to the Greeks and the Romans as masters in stonework.[29] These opinions would probably not be shared by today's American students abroad. Still, the architecture of East Asia came to be known in North America in the nineteenth and early twentieth centuries primarily through such imprecise and impressionistic glimpses.

Such was the case even in the contemporary book on Japanese architecture best known to architectural historians in North America, Ralph Adams Cram's *Impressions of Japanese Architecture*, first published in 1905. Cram writes: "Carefully analyzed and faithfully studied, Japanese architecture is seen to be one of the great styles of the world. In no respect is it lacking in those qualities which have made Greek, Medieval, and Early Renaissance architecture immortal: as these differ among themselves, so does the architecture of Japan differ from them, yet with them it remains logical, ethnic, perfect in development."[30] In other words, in spite of his training as an architect, his opportunity to see monuments, book-length detail, and some good photographs, Cram's view of Japanese architecture had progressed beyond that of earlier North American observers only to the point of admitting that it was a tradition in its own right and that looking at it could be justified. How to define the tradition remained the work of others.

The difference between the writing of Cram, Foulkes, Gallagher, Tuthill, Lossing, or any of the other nineteenth- or early twentieth-century North Americans about East Asian architecture and those who formed what may be called "the scholarly tradition" is apparent first in the person and work of Edward S. Morse. He and the successful North American scholars who were to follow would have the ability to read and converse in the language of the country or countries they studied, the privilege of seeing the monuments about which they wrote, and the benefit of good to exceptional colleagues in East Asia. The results of research on East Asian architecture by non–East Asians who lacked even one of these criteria uniformly have been restricted to specific subfields (such as pure translation of texts), extremely limited in scope, written for a popular audience, or have been simply unsuccessful.

Comparison of a passage from Cram and a passage from the writing of Edward S. Morse reveals the distinction between a secondary observer and someone who, if not a Japanologist by training, was well versed in and comfortable with the language, the people, and the culture. Born in Portland, Maine, in 1838 and trained as a mechanical draftsman, Morse became a self-educated zoologist and is credited with the discovery that brachiopods (animals with bivalve shells) are worms, not mollusks. Morse's quest for coastal brachiopods took him to Japan in 1877. Once there, he received the first chair in zoology at Imperial University in Tokyo. His three consecutive years of residency and his later research trips brought five thousand pieces of pottery to the Museum of Fine Arts, Boston. From 1880 to 1914 Edward Morse was director of the Peabody Museum, Salem.

Morse's major contribution to the field of Japanese architecture is his book *Japanese Homes and Their Surroundings* of 1886.[31] The work remains an initial source for the investigation of Japanese vernacular architecture. The drawings in *Japanese Homes and Their Surroundings* were unique in their own time, and today they offer rare detail of the interior and exterior life of Japan, from bathing rooms to private gardens to inns.

American Architect and Building News

was a frequent recipient of Morse's writing. In 1892 he published a four-part series entitled "Terra Cotta Roofing,"[32] certainly the first serious discussion of this subject in the West, and perhaps in Japan as well. The next year he wrote an article on East Asian latrines, again perhaps still the sole Western-language publication on the subject.[33] Edward Morse's major contribution to *American Architect and Building News* dealt with Chinese architecture. In articles entitled "Journal Sketches in China,"[34] the author presented facts and drawings of subjects from coffin design to a palanquin shop, to stoves, to aristocratic housing, farmhouses, infant seats, school interiors, and an examination hall in Shanghai or Guangzhou (Canton). Interspersed among the descriptions and Morse-esque drawings are comments about the success of Catholic as opposed to Protestant missionaries, or a rare example of cleanliness in contrast to the general filth and squalor in cities, or the appeal of Chinese food, or the practice of archery.

Edward S. Morse was not an architectural historian and would never have given himself anything close to that label. He was the kind of writer who could capture the minute details of what he saw, often in an out-of-the-way and seemingly insignificant place, details that might well otherwise have been lost. Whether or not Morse realized, as Cram did, that Japan's architecture, especially its residential architecture, could have an impact on the Western tradition, his manner of presentation marked a turning point in what would become an American scholarly tradition in the twentieth century. Edward Morse died in 1925.

The Scholarly Tradition in the Twentieth Century

Neither the Japanese nor the Chinese fields, broadly defined, would have received noteworthy scholarly attention in America had not a Princeton-trained architect named Alexander Coburn Soper gone to Japan to study in 1935. Born in Chicago in 1903, Soper spent some of his youth on a ranch outside Santa Barbara. Memories of the dry and mountainous California coast resurged when he saw the Chinese city of Datong in 1935.[35] Soper received his master of architecture from Princeton in 1929, and, as he tells the story, the lack of jobs for architects after the stock market crash in 1929 caused him to make a career change, which he says he never regretted.[36]

While at Princeton, Alexander Soper had taken several courses in art history with George Rowley, a Renaissance-trained art historian who taught East Asian material.[37] Soper decided to pursue his interest in the subject matter. During the academic year 1932–1933 he took a year of Chinese studies at Columbia University and then returned to Princeton. Rowley had in the interim been in Beijing, where he had heard about the current Chinese interest in old buildings, and he had brought back to Princeton several volumes of what is still an extremely important periodical on Chinese architecture, *Zhongguo yingzao xueshe huikan* (*Bulletin of the Society for Research in Chinese Architecture*).[38] After passing his exams, Soper went to Japan in the fall of 1935 on a Rockefeller Foundation fellowship. His plan was to spend a year in Japan followed by a year in China and to return with a dissertation on Japanese painting. By 1937, however, a Sino-Japanese War had broken out.

This war was just one in an almost constant succession of military conflicts in East Asia that began at the time of Edward Morse's return from Japan and continue to the present. They have had a profound impact on the possibilities for anyone, of any nationality, to do research in East Asia, and they have given rise to the title of this paper. Beginning with the Sino-Japanese War in 1894, China, Korea, Japan, the Soviet Union, what was Manchuria, and what was to become the Republic of China (Taiwan) were engaged in small-scale border disputes and all-out warfare, culminating in World War II. From the establishment of the People's Republic in 1949 until the mid-1970s, China was closed to Americans for research or for any other purpose. Throughout this period large areas of China were inaccessible even to the Chinese. Japan, early in this century a funnel for information about China, became ve-

hemently anti-Chinese and would remain somewhat so even after World War II, the one period when Japan was, obviously, closed to American research also.

Alexander Soper spent his year in Japan looking at buildings and reading books on architecture, rather than painting. In the spring of 1938 he traveled to China for one month, but the only safe area for him outside of Beijing was the Western Hills. He managed to make a short trip to Datong in northern Shanxi province, repository of more eleventh- to thirteenth-century Chinese architecture than any other single site, but he was not able to get to the fifth- to sixth-century Yungang Caves, source of some of China's earliest *in situ* Buddhist art and architecture, some ten miles west of the city.[39] This was the only time Alexander Soper set foot on Chinese soil. Of the other North Americans—or the other nationals who would come to teach in North America—who were in China before World War II, none actively engaged in research on Chinese buildings, although several books and articles that dealt to some extent with architecture were written by North Americans who lived in China during those years.[40]

Soper returned to the United States in 1938, completed his dissertation, and published it several years later, in 1942, under the same title, *The Evolution of Buddhist Architecture in Japan*.[41] In 1939 Soper began his career as a teacher of East Asian art at Bryn Mawr College, where he remained until he moved to the Institute of Fine Arts at New York University in 1960. In his forty-five years as a teacher, Soper never taught a course solely on Chinese or Japanese architecture and never trained a student in the field. When questioned about this in the fall of 1988, he said that he felt it was useless to train students in material that they had so remote a possibility of seeing.

Now in his mid-eighties, Alexander Soper keeps up with the field, including current literature in Chinese, and his contribution has been monumental; he is the only American whose contribution can be so described. His major works include coauthorship of *The Art and Architecture of China* with Laurence Sickman in 1956 and coauthorship of *The Art and Architecture of Japan* with Robert Paine in 1955.[42] When Soper's section of the second volume was revised in 1977, corrections were made only to two elevations and to the bibliography. The revisions were by a Japanese architectural historian.[43] *The Art and Architecture of China* is currently under revision by a British historian of Chinese art and archeology who is not a specialist in architecture. In addition to the books, Soper wrote a response to Karl Lehmann's "Dome of Heaven" article entitled "The Dome of Heaven in Asia." He also wrote a study of Xiangguo Monastery from the Song dynasty in Kaifeng and "Record of Buddhist Temples of Chang'an," both relying heavily on texts and both published without illustrations, as well as many other articles.[44] Soper has been equally superb as a translator of texts on Buddhist art and Chinese painting.[45]

Although largely self-taught as an "architectural historian" of East Asia, Alexander Soper is the first person to whom the label can be applied. He came to research only after serious study of the modern and classical languages of China and Japan, after coursework at several institutions of higher learning in the history of Western art and to a lesser extent in East Asian art, after experience as a practicing architect, and after residence and travel in East Asia. This combination of skills was unique in the 1930s; among the present group of researchers on the subject it has been amassed only without the architectural license. As an art and architectural historian trained in the 1920s and 1930s, Soper's dissertation and his early articles included much stylistic analysis of buildings, definition of chronology, and extensive documentation and bibliography. A turning point in Soper's presentation of his research came in 1948 with his "Dome of Heaven" article. In this first interpretative paper in the East Asian field by a North American, Soper addressed a problem of concern to art and architectural historians of European material, with examples not just from China, Korea, and Japan, but from the greater Asian continent. After this paper, Soper's work on architecture was both documentary and historical. He reconstructed the history of major monuments through surviving documents, thereby establishing further chronological sequences. His chapters in the Pelican History of Art books provide this sort of documentation and offer capsule historical surveys of China and Japan through their buildings and literature about them. After his move to New York in 1960, Soper applied the rigorous documentary method almost exclusively to nonarchitectural material of East Asia. Without his contributions in those fields, as in architecture, historians of East Asian material could not be doing what they are today.

The China Field since 1960

In the 1960s, as Alexander Soper was turning almost exclusively to Buddhist art and painting, a new potential historian of Chinese architecture and a new book emerged. The historian was Nelson Wu, born and college-educated in China, who, after extensive travel in Asia, had come to Yale and done a Ph.D. in Chinese painting under Leroy Davidson, a scholar of primarily Bronze Age and Buddhist art of China. The book was *Chinese and Indian Architecture*, which has since been reissued and has been translated into numerous languages, including Chinese.[46] In the United States, however, the reception for the book was not what Wu had hoped.[47] Around 1960, when Wu was an assistant professor at Yale, Braziller Press approached him to write a book for the Great Ages of World Architecture series. Wu immediately questioned the publisher's decision to combine China and India in one volume. The press had two concerns. One was an adequate audience for such a "specialized subject," and the other was that Nelson Wu was an unknown among the American scholarly public.

The result of combining two subjects into one short book was a beautifully written but highly speculative fifty-page essay of a kind that had never appeared in the East Asian field. Wu explored the symbolism of Chinese architecture, hypothesizing that most architectural forms, except the garden, conformed to a square-shaped world of rigidly defined boundaries and that the Indian architectural world, by contrast, could be interpreted as a continuum, with its lack of bounded beginning and end points resembling a circle. Architects in the Western world and Asia continue to use Wu's book today, but in the United States in the 1960s it received a negative review, especially of the China sections.[48] The review was no doubt a factor in Yale's denial of Wu's tenure. More unfortunate for the field, a native who had grown up with traditional Chinese architecture in his back courtyard, but who was trained in the United States and literate in English, terminated his scholarly research on Asian architecture, thereafter writing almost exclusively on Chinese painting and literature and producing original literary pieces. Wu moved from Yale to a chair at Washington University, where every two years or so he taught a seminar on Chinese architecture, mostly populated by students from the architecture school. Today he is professor emeritus.

Nine years after the publication of Nelson Wu's book, geographer Paul Wheatley's *Pivot of the Four Quarters* appeared.[49] Wheatley set for himself the difficult task of placing the genesis of the Chinese city and its fundamental spaces, such as the palace complex and ceremonial sectors, into global perspective. In his book he compares, for example, the imperial sectors of mid-second millennium B.C. Anyang, royal capital in China, with equivalent sectors of Copán, Cempola, Teotihuacán, Polonnaruva Yasodharapura, and Afin Oyo. Based on the existence of certain spaces among multiple formative urban systems, Wheatley postulates necessary criteria for the genesis of urbanism. The challenge was that of many global studies—the author's knowledge of one subject matter, in his case China, was far superior to his experience with the cultures used for comparison and his ability to read sources of those cultures. Today a university professor at the University of Chicago, Wheatley also coauthored a book on Japanese urbanism in the 1970s and has written several articles on the Chinese city.[50]

The handful of young scholars researching and writing about Chinese architecture in the United States since the late 1970s have profited from the above-mentioned works, but they are trained, as were their predecessors, in related fields, such as Sinology, art history, or geography. Their more intimate contact with East Asian architecture has come by way of residence and travel in East Asia and by self-education in libraries on both sides of the Pacific Ocean. Drawn into the field during the Cultural Revolution, when travel to China was not possible, these scholars have received strong linguistic training (often in Taiwan or Japan) and are schooled in a post-1970 art historical methodology. They realize the necessity of blending into their work both the rigorous textual study of someone such as Alexander Soper and the desire to take immediate advantage of the newly accessible buildings and sites in China and of the dramatic surge of archaeological information and carefully measured drawings made available by the Chinese, especially in the last fifteen years. Each admits satisfaction at being the first Westerner to gain access to and then publish a formerly restricted monument, yet each is equally aware of the necessity to sit back and assess current scholarship and criticism of Western architecture in search of model studies or new methodology that might be applicable to the East Asian tradition.[51]

Two doctoral dissertations have been produced in the United States on Chinese architecture: one by Robert Thorp, a professor at Washington University, on mortuary art and architecture of the Han dynasty,[52] and one by this author, on the faculty of the University of Pennsylvania, a reconstruction of Khubilai Khan's imperial city.[53] A third investigator of Chinese architecture is Ronald Knapp, a geography professor at the State University of New York, New Paltz, who did his early research on the historical geography of Taiwan. He has written a book about Chinese vernacular architecture, a book about residential architecture in Zhejiang province (the only regional study of Chinese architecture produced in America), and several articles.[54] In Canada the Chinese field is represented by Barry Till, curator of Asian art at the Art Gallery of Greater Victoria.

He has written *In Search of Old Nanking* and many articles, some in collaboration with his Dutch wife, Paula Swart.[55]

In 1984 Wan-go Weng, the Chinese-American director of the China Institute in New York, negotiated the only exhibition of Chinese architectural models ever arranged outside of China or Taiwan. Coauthor of a book on the Palace Museum, Beijing,[56] Weng hoped to generate long-overdue enthusiasm in the United States for Chinese architecture. The book on Chinese architecture that accompanied the exhibition is now used in the few courses on Chinese architecture in U.S. universities.[57]

North American universities where courses on Chinese architecture are or recently have been offered include the University of Pennsylvania, MIT, Washington University, the University of Virginia, the University of Washington, and Cornell.[58] Penn's program has not been continuous, but its ties to Chinese architecture are the oldest in the United States. Its connection with Chinese architecture dates to the 1920s, when Liang Sicheng and Yang Tingbao were students in the School of Architecture and Lin Huiyin was a student in the Fine Arts Department. Liang took his knowledge back to China, and after two decades of research in his homeland returned to the United States in 1949 to teach Chinese architecture at Yale. He stayed in New Haven only a semester, but while in residence worked on an English manuscript, which, had it been published then, would have saved this generation of architectural historians a tremendous amount of work. Liang's friend Wilma Fairbank, a great promoter of Chinese architectural studies in the United States, saw the manuscript through to publication forty years later,[59] and this book is now also used as a text.

Korean and Japanese Fields

Almost no research has been conducted in North America on Korean architecture. To date no book has appeared on the subject, and only a few articles have been written.[60]

Unlike China and Korea, Japan has been open to American researchers for most of this century. Moreover, unlike the situation in the other two countries, once in Japan, Americans have been subject to no more restrictions than natives in their pursuit of research.[61] North Americans have been enamored of things Japanese since the nineteenth century, not because of Edward Morse, but because of a more influential associate of the Museum of Fine Arts, Boston, Ernest F. Fenollosa (1853–1908), and the Japanese Okakura Kakuzo (1862–1913), who traveled to Japan and gathered objects for the museum. One might, therefore, expect Americans to have made a more extensive and advanced contribution to the study of Japanese architecture than to the study of Chinese architecture, but the facts are quite to the contrary.

Between the publication of Morse's book and Alexander Soper's thesis, no book that dealt primarily with Japanese architecture was published in North America or was written by a North American. It is appropriate to mention one U.S. citizen whose contribution to the study of Japanese architecture is legendary, if not historical. Langdon Warner (1881–1955) never wrote a book on Japanese architecture, but he did help Okakura Kakuzo with the translation into English of a Japanese government publication entitled "Japanese Temples and Their Treasures."[62] Warner is better known and loved by Japanese nationals for his alleged letter to President Roosevelt during World War II in which he is said to have pleaded that Kyoto, in particular, be spared in the bombing of Japan. Warner was a member of the America Defense—Harvard Group, formed in 1943 and later merged with a similar group established by the American Council of Learned Societies as the Roberts Commission, whose members set for themselves the task of urging the preservation of cultural relics throughout the Axis territories. The ultimate decision about what to bomb was, of course, made by Secretary of War Stimson, who wrote in his memoirs of 1947 that in spite of the strategic benefits of bombing Kyoto the city was taken off the list of targets because of its cultural significance. A Langdon Warner letter has never been found, yet there are those who say it was certainly written and those who say Warner, himself, denied writing it.[63] To this day the Japanese credit Warner with convincing the United States to spare their monuments, and shrines to him can be seen all over Japan.

Through the 1940s and 1950s it was primarily Alexander Soper who kept the field of Japanese architecture alive for the American scholarly audience. By the late 1950s another figure appeared in the Japanese architectural field. Jonathan Edward Kidder received his Ph.D. from the Institute of Fine Arts, New York University under Alfred Salmony, who, like Leroy Davidson at Yale, conducted research primarily in early Chinese art. Kidder taught briefly at Washington University, but he has spent most of his academic life as a professor at International Christian University in Tokyo, with sabbatical teaching stints at Yale and the University of Oregon. Kidder is essentially a historian of Japanese art, broadly defined. He makes extensive use of archaeological data and the voluminous current scholarship from Japan, and his writings often provide accounts of Japanese culture and history through a study of the art. Kidder wrote a book entitled *Japanese Temples* in 1964 and includes sections on Japanese architecture in almost all of his writings.[64]

In the 1950s and 1960s North Americans wrote four books on Japanese architecture. In 1955 architect Norman Carver wrote *Form and Space of Japanese Architecture*, largely a photographic publication, which was the result of time spent in Japan on a Fulbright fellowship, and Arthur Drexler, curator of architecture and design at the Museum of Modern Art, wrote *The Architecture of Japan*. In the early 1960s John Kirby wrote *From Castle to Tea-house, Japanese Architecture of the Momoyama Period*, and William Alex wrote *Japanese Architecture* for the Braziller Great Ages of World Architecture series.[65] Carver and Drexler were not trained in Japanese studies, and if Kirby and Alex were, neither stayed in the field. The majority of publications about Japanese architecture in North America during this period dealt with contemporary Japanese architecture and Japanese gardens, the former heavily

influenced by the Western tradition and the latter influencing Western architecture.

Interest in Japanese architecture also gave way to the removal of teahouses to the United States, including the teahouse in Fairmount Park, Philadelphia, and the one acquired under the directorship of Fiske Kimball for the Philadelphia Museum of Art.

Like the Chinese field, the Japanese field has produced no monograph on one monument by an American, but there have been several bright spots. One has been large-scale translation projects undertaken by the joint cooperation of American translators and Weatherhill or Kodansha Press in Japan. Two of the three series have included titles in the history of architecture, and two of the three series have been edited by John Rosenfield.[66] These books are used as textbooks in courses on Japanese art and have been important sources of information about Japanese architecture for American students. Other books of exceptional quality in Japanese have been translated into English by North Americans, notably Seike's *The Art of Japanese Joinery* and Nishi and Hozumi's *What Is Japanese Architecture?*[67]

Japanese architecture was also brought to the attention of a United States audience by a recent exhibition. Curator Mino Yutaka of the Art Institute of Chicago negotiated an exhibition of treasures from the Nara monastery Tōdai-ji, and in the catalogue architecture was discussed equally with sculpture and painting.[68]

Finally, in the 1980s authors trained to do primary research in Japanese have published a book on a single subject of Japanese architecture and several articles. Mary Neighbor Parent, who has spent several decades of her adult life in Japan, published *The Roof in Japanese Buddhist Architecture* in 1983.[69] Japanese-born and Harvard-educated William Coaldrake, on the faculty of the Australian National University, has written several articles, especially on the subject of seventeenth- to twentieth-century Japanese architecture and urbanism.[70]

Thus the East Asian field exists without scholarly treatments in English or any other Western language of such major monuments as the Hall of Great Harmony, Altar of Heaven, Summer Palaces, Hōryū-ji, Himeiji Castle, the imperial mausoleums at Nikko (several of which came to the attention of North Americans more than eighty years ago in the *American Architect and Building News*), or any of the less universally well-known East Asian buildings. Still, there is no cause for pessimism about the future study of Chinese, Korean, or Japanese architecture in North America. The buildings are, after all, spectacular, and their existence and now their accessibility will give way ultimately to scholarly interest. The documentation about these buildings, although different from documentation in the Western tradition, is equally rich. There is a vast and untapped potential for restoration of Chinese buildings. Finally, with no major theoretical Chinese or Western works in the field, there is the chance to explore a variety of methodologies. What is necessary is a commitment on the part of universities and libraries to teach and purchase in the East Asian field,[71] maintenance of the standards that turned the study of East Asian architecture from travelers' jottings toward a legitimate scholarly tradition, and continued persistence by researchers, even across new war zones or political boundaries.

NOTES

1. For helpful conversations and correspondence regarding the topic of this paper, I would like to thank John Coolidge, Renata Holod, Annette Juliano, Ronald Knapp, Thomas Lawton and his associates at the Arthur M. Sackler Gallery and the Freer Gallery of Art, John Rosenfield, Alexander Soper, Robert Thorp, Barry Till, and Mary Woods. This paper and its notes include information about the study of East Asian religious, palatial, residential, and urban architecture, but not landscape architecture or Chinese geomancy.

2. Louisa C. Tuthill, *History of Architecture from Earliest Times* (Philadelphia, 1848), 64–66, pl. 4.

3. Tuthill 1848, 65.

4. Tuthill 1848, 66.

5. Benson J. Lossing, *History of Fine Arts* (New York, 1840).

6. Lossing 1840, 98.

7. Miss Ludlow, *A General View of the Fine Arts, Critical and Historical*, with an introduction by D. Huntington, 4th ed. (New York, 1851).

8. *Foreign Missionary* 9, no. 8 (January 1851) through 18, no. 4 (September 1859) are the earliest and latest issues of this decade in which articles relevant to East Asian architecture were published. The January 1851 issue was the earliest one available to me.

9. *Foreign Missionary* 10 (October 1851), 78–79.

10. *Foreign Missionary* 13 (August 1854), 84.

11. *Foreign Missionary* 13 (August 1854), 85.

12. *Foreign Missionary* 13 (August 1854), 85.

13. *Foreign Missionary* 18 (September 1859), 117–120.

14. *American Architect and Building News* (hereafter *AABN*) 1 (26 February 1876), 68–70. I thank Mary Woods for providing me with a copy of this article. Viollet-le-Duc's *The Habitations of Man in All Ages* was published in London and Boston in 1876.

15. *AABN* 71 (12 January 1901), 16.

16. *AABN* 77 (17 May 1902), 88. This fact was taken from the New York Evening Post.

17. *AABN* 76 (14 June 1902), 88.

18. *AABN* 83 (13 February 1904), 50, and 87 (28 January 1905), 26.

19. *AABN* 85 (9 July 1904), 16.

20. *AABN* 84 (16 April 1904), 28.

21. *AABN* 87 (25 March 1905), 100.

22. *AABN* 99 (6 January 1906), 8.

23. *AABN* 92 (10 August 1907), 42.

24. *AABN* 92 (7 September 1907), 74.

25. *AABN* 73 (20 July 1901), 22–23.

26. In *T'oung Pao*, series 1, 2 (1891), 162, G. Schlegel reported in the "Variétés" section on a visit by an M.C.F. Caspari of Hong Kong, earlier printed in *Globus* 17, to the Ming tombs, with a correction to Caspari's statement that the emperor's body was in the above-ground mausoleum. Two years later Camille Imbault-Huart wrote the first scholarly article on the subject, "Les Tombeaux des Ming près de Peking." *T'oung Pao*, series 1, 4 (1893), 391–401.

27. *AABN* 83 (12 March 1904), 83–84.

28. *AABN* 83 (12 March 1904), 83.

29. *AABN* 83 (12 March 1904), 83.

30. Ralph Adams Cram, *Impressions of Japanese Architecture and the Allied Arts* (1905; repr. Rutland, Vt., 1982), 38. A review of Cram's book appears in *AABN* 88 (30 December 1905), 215.

31. The first edition of Edward S. Morse's *Japanese Homes and Their Surroundings* was published by the University Press in 1886. It was reprinted with information about the author's life by Tuttle Press, Rutland, Vt., in 1972, with many subsequent reprintings. *Japanese Homes and Their Surroundings* was reviewed by Henry Van Brunt in a three-part article, *AABN* 19 (2 January 1886, 16 January 1886, 23 January 1886), 3-4, 31-33, 41-42.

32. *AABN* 35 (27 March 1892), 197-200; 36 (2 April 1892), 5-7; 36 (9 April 1892), 24-27; and 36 (23 April 1892), 52-57.

33. *AABN* 39 (18 March 1893), 170-174.

34. Edward Morse's "Journal Sketches in China" appeared in the following issues of *AABN*, volume 76: 12 April 1902, 11-13; 10 May 1902, 34-36; 17 May 1902, 51-53; 24 May 1902, 61-63; 7 June 1902, 75-78; and 14 June 1902, 83-85.

35. Much of the information about Alexander Soper is taken from an interview with Soper in October 1988. The author gratefully acknowledges Professor Soper for his time then and during later phone conversations. A published source on Soper's life and work to 1972 is Penelope Mason Scull, ed., *Writings of Alexander Coburn Soper: A Bibliography up to 1972* (New York, 1973). I thank Annette Juliano for making this source available to me.

36. Soper worked briefly as an architect for the firm of Corbett, Harrison, and MacMurray.

37. George Rowley's *Principles of Chinese Painting* (Princeton, 1947) was a standard textbook in courses on Chinese art at mid-century.

38. Volumes 1 through 7 were produced by the Society for Research in Chinese Architecture between 1930 and 1945. All but the last volume, which was issued in Sichuan, were published in Beijing.

39. This trip probably explains why the Liao-Jin buildings of Datong figure so heavily in the comparative material from China used in Soper's dissertation.

40. These publications include: Sidney Gamble, *Peking, A Social Survey* (New York, 1921); Anne Swann Goodrich, *The Peking Temple of the Eastern Peak* (Nagoya, 1964), based on research of the 1920s and 1930s; and George Kates, *The Years that Were Fat* (Cambridge, Mass., 1952). Kates also wrote "A New Date for the Origins of the Forbidden City," *Harvard Journal of Asiatic Studies* 7 (1942-43), 180-202. Carl Whiting Bishop wrote "An Ancient Chinese Capital: Earthworks at Old Ch'ang-an," *Antiquity* 13 (1938), 68-78.

41. The book was published by Princeton University Press.

42. Both titles are part of the Pelican History of Art series published by Penguin Books, Ltd. (Harmondsworth).

43. David B. Waterhouse, a Canadian, revised the painting and sculpture sections, and Bunji Kobayashi revised the chapters on architecture.

44. Of Alexander Soper's long bibliography, the following articles are most pertinent to East Asian architecture: "The 'Dome of Heaven' in Asia," *Art Bulletin* 29 (December 1947), 225-248; "Correspondence to the Editor: The Chinese Dome," *Architectural Review* 123, no. 732 (1958), 2; "A Bibliography for the Study of Japanese Temple Architecture," *Monumenta Serica* 4, no. 1 (1939), 345-354; "Japanese Evidence for the History of the Architecture and Iconography of Chinese Buddhism," *Monumenta Serica* 4, no. 2 (1940), 638-678; "Hsiang-kuo-ssu, An Imperial Temple of Northern Sung," *Journal of the American Oriental Society* 68 (1948), 19-45; "Two Stelae and a Pagoda on the Central Peak, Mt. Sung," *Archives of the Chinese Art Society of America* 16 (1962), 41-48; and "A Vacation Glimpse of the T'ang Temples of Ch'ang-an: The Ssu-t'a Chi by Tuan Ch'eng-shih," *Artibus Asiae* 23, no. 1 (1960), 15-40.

45. For titles of these see Scull 1973.

46. The publisher was Braziller, and the first printing was in 1963

47. The information about Wu's book was learned in conversations with Nelson Wu in the early 1970s.

48. For the review see Soper, *Artibus Asiae* 26, no. 3/4 (1963), 362-364.

49. Paul Wheatley, *The Pivot of the Four Quarters* (Chicago, 1972).

50. Paul Wheatley and Thomas See, *From Court to Capital: A Tentative Interpretation of the Origins of the Japanese Urban Tradition* (Chicago, 1978). Wheatley's articles include "Archeology and the Chinese City," *World Archeology* 2, no. 2 (1970), 159-185 and "The Ancient Chinese City as a Cosmological Symbol," *Ekistics* 39, no. 232 (March 1975), 147-158.

51. Other North American publications prior to 1980 include: Amos Chang, *The Tao of Architecture* (Princeton, 1956); Wolfram Eberhard (born in Germany but a professor at the University of California, Berkeley, until his retirement), "Temple-Building Activities in Medieval and Modern China: An Experimental Study," *Monumenta Serica* 23 (1964), 264-318; Clay Lancaster (trained in Baroque art), "The Origin and Formation of Chinese Architecture," *Journal of the Society of Architectural Historians* 9, nos. 1 and 2 (1950), 3-10; and G. W. Skinner, ed., *The City in Late Imperial China* (Stanford, 1977).

52. Robert L. Thorp, "Mortuary Art and Architecture of Early Imperial China" (Ph.D. diss., University of Kansas, 1979). Thorp's other publications pertinent to Chinese architecture include: "Burial Practices of Bronze Age China," in *The Great Bronze Age of China: An Exhibition from the People's Republic of China*, ed. Wen Fong (New York, 1980), 51-64; "The Sui Xian Tomb: Re-thinking the Fifth Century," *Artibus Asiae* 43 (1981-1982), 67-110; "Origins of Chinese Architectural Style: The Earliest Plans and Building Types," *Archives of Asian Art* 36 (1983), 22-39; "An Archeological Reconstruction of the Lishan Necropolis," in *The Great Bronze Age of China: A Symposium*, ed. George Kuwayama (Seattle, 1983),

72–83; "The Architectural Heritage of the Bronze Age," in *Traditional Architecture*, ed. Nancy Shatzman Steinhardt (New York, 1984), 60–67; "Architectural Principles in Early Imperial China: Structural Problems and Their Solution," *Art Bulletin* 68 (1986), 360–378; "The Qin and Han Imperial Tombs and the Development of Mortuary Architecture," in *The Quest for Eternity* (Los Angeles, 1987), 17–37; and "Mountain Tombs and Jade Burial Suits: Preparations for Eternity in the Western Han," in *Symposium on the Quest for Eternity* (Los Angeles, 1989).

53. This author's dissertation was "Imperial Architecture under Mongolian Patronage: Khubilai's Imperial City of Daidu" (Harvard, 1981). Other publications by this author relevant to Chinese architecture include *Chinese Traditional Architecture* (New York, 1984); *Chinese Imperial City Planning* (Honolulu, 1990); "The Plan of Khubilai Khan's Imperial City," *Artibus Asiae* 44, no. 2/3 (1983), 137–158; "Why Were Chang'an and Beijing So Different?" *Journal of the Society of Architectural Historians* 45 (1986), 339–357; "Toward the Definition of a Yuan Dynasty Hall," *Journal of the Society of Architectural Historians* 47, no. 1 (1988), 57–73; and "Imperial Architecture along the Mongolian Road to Dadu," *Ars Orientalis* 18 (1989), in press.

54. Ronald Knapp's publications include: *China's Traditional Rural Architecture: A Cultural Geography of the Common House* (Honolulu, 1986); *China's Vernacular Architecture: House Form and Culture* (Honolulu, 1989); "Chinese Walled Cities," *Orientations* 11, no. 11 (1980), 43–49; "Taiwan's Rural Architecture," *Orientations* 12, no. 4 (1981), 38–47; "Chinese Rural Dwellings in Taiwan," *Journal of Cultural Geography* 3 (1982), 1–18; "Chinese Bridges," *Orientations* 14, no. 6 (1984), 36–47; "Bridge over the River Xiao," *Archaeology* 40, no. 1 (January/February 1988), 48–54; and coeditorship of *Chinese Walled Cities: A Collection of Maps from Shina Jōkaku no Gaiyō* (Hong Kong, 1979).

55. Till's publications on East Asian architecture, some coauthored with Paula Swart, include *In Search of Old Nanking* (Hong Kong, 1982); *The Japanese Shinto Shrine at the Art Gallery of Greater Victoria* (Victoria, 1987); "Two Tombs of the Southern Dynasties at Huqiao and Jianshen in Dan-yang County, Jiansu Province," *Chinese Studies in Archeology* 1 (Winter 1979/80), 75–124; "A Chinese General's Tomb, Identification of the 'Ming Tomb'," *Rotunda* 14, no. 1 (1981), 7–11; "Balizhuang Ta, a Forgotten Ming Dynasty Pagoda," *Orientations* 12, no. 7 (1981); "The Eastern Mausoleums of the Qing Dynasty," *Orientations* 13, no. 2 (1982), 26–31; "Qian Ling, a Tang Dynasty Mausoleum," *Orientations* 13, no. 7 (1982); "Ming Tombs in Guilin," *Orientations* 15, no. 11 (1984), 37–41; "The Diamond Seat Pagoda, Indian Architectural Influences in China," *Orientations* 16, no. 2 (1985); "The Imperial Xi Xia Tombs at Yinchuan, Ningxia," *Orientations* 17, no. 11 (1986), 48–54; and "Nurhachi and Abahai: Their Palace and Mausolea," *Arts of Asia* 18, no. 3 (1988), 148–157.

56. Wan-go Weng and Boda Yang, *The Palace Museum, Peking: Treasures of the Forbidden City* (New York, 1982).

57. Steinhardt 1984.

58. There certainly may be others of which the author is not aware. This list was compiled from conversations and correspondence with colleagues.

59. Liang Ssu-ch'eng [Sicheng], *A Pictorial History of Chinese Architecture: A Study of the Development of Its Structural System and the Evolution of Its Types*, ed. Wilma Fairbank (Cambridge, Mass., 1984).

60. A general introduction to Korean architecture by a North American is found in the sections on architecture in Evelyn McCune, *The Arts of Korea: An Illustrated History* (Rutland, Vt., 1962). In the middle of the century Helen Chapin wrote several articles about Korean architecture: "A Little-known Temple in South Korea and Its Treasures: A Preliminary Renaissance," *Artibus Asiae* 11, no. 3 (1948), 189–195; and "A Hitherto Unpublished Great Silla Pagoda," *Artibus Asiae* 12, no. 1/2 (1949), 84–88.

61. Occasionally one needs special permission to enter or photograph a monument.

62. Imperial Japanese Commission to the Panama-Pacific International Exposition, *Japanese Temples and Their Treasures* (Tokyo, 1915).

63. Colonel Henry L. Stimson's memoirs are entitled, *On Active Service in Peace and War* (New York, 1948). On Langdon Warner's involvement in the Roberts Commission, see Theodore Bowie, ed., *Langdon Warner through His Letters* (Bloomington, Ind., 1966), especially 166–170. Alexander Soper relates that Warner wrote the letter and asked others, including Soper, to do the same. John Coolidge says that Warner told him that the letter to Roosevelt was never written.

64. J. Edward Kidder's books with sections on architecture include: *Japan before Buddhism* (London, 1959); *Japanese Temples, Sculpture, Paintings, Gardens, and Architecture* (London, 1964); *Early Japanese Art* (Princeton and London, 1964); *The Birth of Japanese Art* (New York and London, 1965); *Early Buddhist Japan* (London, 1972); *Ancient Japan* (Oxford, 1977); and *The Art of Japan* (English ed., New York, 1985). Kidder's articles relevant to Japanese architecture include: "The Newly Discovered Takamatsuzuka Tomb," *Monumenta Nipponica* 27, no. 3 (1972), 245–251; "Asuka and the Takamatsuzuka Tomb," *Archaeology* 26, no. 1 (1973), 24–31; and "The Fujinoki Tomb and Its Grave Goods," *Monumenta Nipponica* 42, no. 1 (1987), 57–87.

65. These works are: Norman F. Carver, Jr., *Form and Space of Japanese Architecture* (Tokyo, 1955); Arthur Drexler, *The Architecture of Japan* (New York, 1955); John Kirby, *From Castle to Tea-house, Japanese Architecture of the Momoyama Period* (Tokyo and Rutland, Vt., 1962); and William Alex, *Japanese Architecture* (New York, 1963). For a bibliography of more general relevance to Japanese architecture, see Council of Planning Librarians, "Bibliography of Japanese Architecture," Exchange Bibliography No. 539. See also Patricia Amy Thompson, *An Outline History of Japanese Architecture* (Ithaca, N.Y., 1956).

66. The earlier series that includes titles on Japanese architecture, translations of a thirty-volume series of

books on Japanese art by Heibonsha Press of Japan, was published by Weatherhill Press of New York. Its titles relevant to Japanese architecture are: Minoru Ooka, *Temples of Nara and Their Art*, trans. Dennis Lishka (1973); Toshio Fukuyama, *Heian Temples: Byodo-in and Chuson-ji*, trans. Ronald K. Jones (1976); Kiyoshi Hirai, *Feudal Architecture of Japan*, trans. Hiraoki Sato and Jeannine Ciliotta (1973); Naomi Okawa, *Edo Architecture: Katsura and Nikko*, trans. Alan Woodhull and Akito Miyamoto (1975); and Teiji Itoh, *Traditional Domestic Architecture of Japan*, trans. Richard L. Gage (1972). Translations of the Japanese monthly *Nihon no bijutsu*, published by Shibundō Press of Japan, have been published by Kodansha Press (Tokyo, New York, and San Francisco) under the editorship of John Rosenfield as the Japanese Arts Library. This series includes Kakichi Suzuki, *Early Buddhist Architecture in Japan*, trans. Mary N. Parent and Nancy S. Steinhardt (1980); Fumio Hashimoto, *Architecture in the Shoin Style*, trans. H. Mack Horton (1981); and Motoo Hinago, *Japanese Castles*, trans. William H. Coaldrake (1986).

67. Kiyosi Seike, *The Art of Japanese Joinery*, trans. Yuriko Yubuko and Rebecca M. Davis (New York, 1977) and Kazuo Nishi and Kazuo Hozumi, *What Is Japanese Architecture?*, trans. H. Mack Horton (Tokyo, New York, and San Francisco, 1985).

68. See Yutaka Mino, *The Great Eastern Temple: Treasures of Japanese Buddhist Art From Tōdai-ji* (Chicago, 1986).

69. Mary N. Parent's thesis from Tokyo University was on the monastery Hōrin-ji. Six articles on the subject were published in the periodical *Japan Architect* in 1977. Her book is *The Roof in Japanese Buddhist Architecture* (New York and Tokyo, 1983).

70. William H. Coaldrake's articles include: "Edo Architecture and Tokugawa Law," *Monumenta Nipponica* 36, no. 3 (1981), 235–284; "Order and Anarchy: Tokyo from 1868 to the Present," in *Tokyo: Form and Spirit*, ed. Mildred Friedman (Minneapolis and New York, 1986), 63–75; "The Gatehouse of the Shogun's Senior Councillor: Building Design and Status Symbolism in Japanese Architecture of the Late Edo Period," *Journal of the Society of Architectural Historians* 47, no. 4 (1988), 397–410; and "Manufactured Housing—The New Japanese Vernacular," *Japan Architect* 352, 353, 354, 357 (August, September, October 1986, January 1987), 60–67, 60–65, 62–67, 58–62.

71. My computer searches of the holdings of major East Asian libraries on selected topics of Japanese architecture reveal that at least 50 percent of the bibliography found in footnotes of current Japanese literature on the subject is not available at even one United States library. For the Chinese field the number of publications is fewer, and the percentage of books available, based on my nonmathematical survey, seems higher, but about 50 percent of the periodicals currently used by researchers on Chinese architecture in China are not available in the United States.

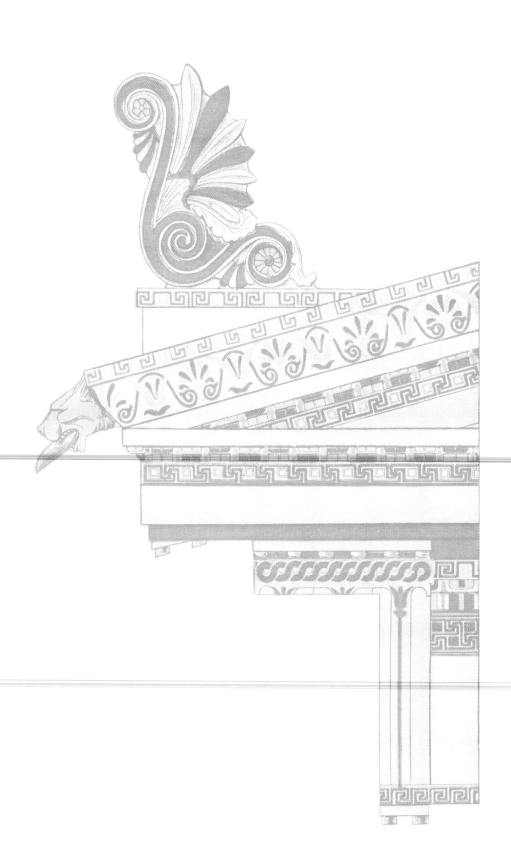

GEORGE KUBLER

Yale University (emeritus)

Architectural Historians before the Fact

An early world history of art and architecture was written by Franz Theodor Kugler in Berlin in 1841. Its pre-Columbian section was illustrated with a few copies of engravings by travelers to America. These were garnered from older engravings, such as those illustrating Kingsborough's eight-volume *Antiquities of Mexico* (London, 1831–1848).

The most useful trail through five centuries of Americanist studies might join two epochs at 1841. This year marked the end of many generations of diminishing information. It also began a new age of humanistic study with Kugler and of archaeological exploration with J. L. Stephens. Both men had predecessors, but both saw more clearly than their preindustrial forebears the aesthetic implications of the works they discussed. Both men's books were exploratory, and both relied on similar philosophical and historical traditions for their conclusions.

For this first period (1492–1841), the principal writings consisted of firsthand accounts of America or speculations without direct knowledge. In the second period (1841–1942), the main works are in anthropological science and in history. The earliest deliberate and conscious history of the art of ancient America was Kugler's in 1841, but the anthropological syntheses did not begin to appear until 1914–1940.

The nineteenth-century enlargement of the visual base of information in America began with Alexander von Humboldt, who was in Mexico in 1803, but was more active as a naturalist than as an art historian. His contemporary, Guillermo Dupaix, was a military officer commissioned by Charles III of Spain to discover and record antiquities on a three-year reconnaissance extending from Mexico to Puebla, Oaxaca, and Guatemala, in ninety stages from place to place.[1] His party included a draftsman, José Luciano Castañeda, who taught drawing and architecture at the Real Academia de San Carlos, and a clerk and two soldiers. Dupaix left all the drawing of places and objects to Castañeda, who sketched quickly in bare outline using many schematic indications. These first sketches were later reworked from memory with detailed shading. While Castañeda sketched, Dupaix dictated his observations and comments to the clerk. Dupaix always saw more than Castañeda, whose final drawings benefited from Dupaix's comments. Being both verbally and visually adept, Dupaix also guided the first sketches, composing the log of the journey himself and noting thoughts and descriptions rewritten, often several times, as commentaries on the finished drawings.

Dupaix was especially alert to examples of the reduction of living forms to their geometrical counterparts. This was in defense of his contention that Amerindian peoples possessed a theoretical base in geometry for their representations of natural forms. Of Mixtec jades at Yanhuitlán in 1806, he says that they are "purely Mexican, found in infinite numbers in the tombs of this ancient Mexican nation . . . of prismatic configuration, in three or four planes . . . needing no cutting instrument, but having 'natural' angles." He went on to say that "the essence of the arts is decided neither by material nor magnitude" (1:105).

Monte Albán reminded him of Pompeii, where he had been at the time of the early excavations before 1760 (1:117), but he noted (1:116) that this "most ancient, original American school" proceeded from theory to practice on geometric plans devised before building began and that, in addition, its artists possessed the ability to portray individuals recognizable as such (1:116). Interesting is his repeated use of "ideal" as signifying the "schematic" or stylized opposite of academic design by rules (2:62, 155).

Confronting Mitla, Dupaix divulges at last the underlying rule of his procedure as a historian of non-European art. He says "the only data and authority to which we need to appeal are the artistic monuments. They in their mute but expressive and meaningful language will perhaps explain to us some of our problems" (1:121). One of these is the function of the "palaces" at Mitla: he prefers, after considering ritual halls or temples, to think of them as tombs (1:139).

Of the mosaics on their walls, he is unable to decide whence the artists took "the *type* of this beautiful thought," or which of them could be earliest (1:138), since complex and simple were mixed among them. At Zaachila, thinking of types and prototypes, he supposes that clay sculptures in relief must have preceded (as prototypes) the same expressions in stone and in metal (1:153).

At Palenque Dupaix faced some of the major monuments of Mesoamerican antiquity. First he had difficulty describing the corbel-vaulted system, but he resolved it by writing of vaults both as planes and in bulk (*bóvedas recta y de vulto*) in angles varying from acute to obtuse (1:202). After

identifying the subject matter of the figural reliefs as rulership and conquest (1:207–208) and analyzing the technique of building the stucco reliefs (1:206), he went on to say that "the style of Palenque being original, it cannot be related with Mexican or Zapotec remains" (1:229), nor are these "indebted to any other known nation on earth" (1:225).

These remarks were his final observations based on twenty years of residence in New Spain (1:232). He concludes by saying that he had labored greatly to find technical terms to describe the arts of design in ancient America, because the works themselves were "original and unprecedented elsewhere in the world" and useful for what he called illustrating "the general history of the fine arts of these ancient and celebrated nations." He also noted that "another ancient and underground world still existed of the heathen era on this continent, and that it could only be known by excavations" (1:188).

Reading Dupaix, however, one cannot today escape the conclusion that this work by him and his draftsman Luciano Castañeda provides us with the earliest approach to a history of ancient American art. It makes use of the concept of the "fine arts" as architecture, sculpture, and painting to cover a broad range of material culture and to discuss craft, meaning, and expression in America as original rather than derivative from any recent Old World tradition.

The next was John Lloyd Stephens (1805–1852).[2] Being apprised of J. G. von Herder's *Philosophy* of 1784[3] before 1822 at Columbia College in New York City, Stephens was prepared to approach another civilization and to see its own quality and worth, when he landed among the Maya peoples late in 1839. Herder's novel aesthetic phenomenology gave aesthetics a place within anthropology, in reaction against a philosophical aesthetics divorced from human conduct. Herder is also regarded as a forerunner of historical relativism, insisting on the "unique quality and innate validity of each civilization." But Herder, unlike Stephens, was obliged for the sake of the unity of mankind to derive China from Egypt and to see America as related to Africa by a remote, common Asiatic origin.

Stephens wrote with delight of discovering "that eye for the picturesque and beautiful . . . which distinguishes the Indians everywhere."[4] Some pages later he took issue with William Robertson's anti-Amerindian *History of America* (1777), denying that anti-Indian conclusion with evidence of his own eyes at Copan that the stelae and buildings were "works of art" more than "remains of unknown peoples," proving that the peoples of ancient America were "not savages" but possessing "architecture, sculpture and painting, all the arts which embellish life."[5]

Frederick Catherwood accompanied Stephens on his first trip to Yucatán in 1839. They each had a role in recording what they saw. Stephens' role was to prepare the objects for "Mr. C." to draw "by scrubbing and cleaning, and erecting the scaffold for the camera lucida" (reducing prism). Catherwood "made the outline of all the drawings on paper divided in regular sections, to preserve the utmost accuracy of proportion." For publication the drawings engraved on wood were eventually discarded as unsatisfactory and reengraved on steel with corrections by Catherwood.[6] Both men expressed dissatisfaction with the published drawings made for Antonio del Rio in 1787 and Guillermo Dupaix, finding them "poorly served" by the "incomplete and incorrect" work of their artists.[7]

At Palenque their judgment—that the palace was a residence of rulers, adorned with their portraits, and having their dwelling in the southeast portion, as well as rooms for "public and state occasions" in the north half—is generally accepted today after a century of contrary opinion.[8] After ten months among the Maya, Stephens looks back: "We began our explorations without any theory to support. He concludes that ancient American monuments "are different from the works of any other known people, of a new order, and entirely and absolutely anomalous. They stand alone."[9]

Stephens and Catherwood returned to Yucatán in 1843 equipped with Daguerre's paraphernalia, although the camera lucida prism continued in use by Catherwood at Uxmal and Kabah.[10] At Ticul Stephens admired a carved pottery vase portraying a Maya personage among glyphs, which he presented as proof that the Indians he saw were of the same race as the ancient builders.[11] In this second book on the Maya Stephens makes much more use of his library preparation among colonial chronicles. He anticipated the methods of ethnohistory in using recent evidence for ancient events among the same people, but he concludes that the "want of tradition, the degeneracy of the people, and the alleged absence of historical accounts" do not deny "the cities as works of the ancestors of the present inhabitants." Stephens' insights and Catherwood's plates worked a major change in the study of American antiquity, as did Kugler's vision in the *Handbuch* for the future of the history of art.

In the next generation came the long career of William Henry Holmes (1846–1933). He began as an artist, turned to geology and American Indians, and ended as curator and first director of the National Gallery of Art. In 1879–1880 he returned to art studies in Munich and Italy, and he continued in Washington during 1882–1885 in "museum work and the study of primitive art in its various branches."[12] He became head curator in the Columbian Museum of Chicago in 1894, after having taken part in the installation of the exhibits of the Smithsonian Institution at the World's Columbian Exposition. This was the most extended exhibition of ancient American art that had been assembled in the hemisphere, with effects soon appearing in architecture and art.[13] Full-sized replicas of Maya buildings were shown from Labna and Uxmal, as well as houses of cliffdwellers and other shelters of Amerindian peoples, all arranged for "comparative study" under the direction of F. W. Putnam in the Anthropological Building as "Man and his Works."[14]

Holmes has been presented as "virtually self-taught in the use of pencil, pen, and brush," against "parental disapproval."[15] Drawn to art, he decided in 1871 to study in Washington with Theodor Kaufmann at his studio (Kaufmann studied with Wilhelm von Kaulbach in Munich before emigrating to America in 1855). Holmes was first encouraged by a fellow student, Mary

Henry, the daughter of the Smithsonian Institution's first secretary, to draw in the collections. There he met many of the illustrators with whom he would soon work on the United States Geological and Geographical Survey of the Territories, drawing paleontological shells for F. B. Meek. Meek tutored Holmes in lithography and employed him as a piecework illustrator, in the company of the young scientists living in the Smithsonian "castle" building.[16]

As to architecture, a major work by Holmes came from his travels to Mexico and Yucatán. In 1884 he and three professional photographers traveled through Mexico on a private railroad car for two months, studying museums, cities, and peoples.[17] In 1894–1895 he was invited to explore Yucatán from the yacht of Allison V. Armour of Chicago. The published results of these travels were two volumes by him entitled *Archaeological Studies among the Ancient Cities of Mexico.*[18] The plans and drawings were by Holmes, including the panoramas of Chichén Itzá, Uxmal, Palenque, Monte Albán, and Teotihuacán. They are both grandiose and specifically exact, like the Grand Canyon drawings. Part 1 of his Mexican publication is mainly about architecture, and part 2 is about sculpture.[19]

His descriptions of pre-Columbian architecture are still sound and his theories interesting, as when he offers a typology of roofing construction, from "beam-span" to single, double, and circular "lean-in" types. His "cuneiform arch" is the corbel vault of Maya building, and it is also a "double lean-to," in his words.[20] Anticipating Spinden's detailed analyses, he described Maya ornament as owing nine-tenths of its forms to "associated thought" in "geometric reductions" of animal shapes representing mythological figures. He estimated that "symbolism and aestheticism" take up three-fourths of the "labor and cost" of Maya architecture, with "symbolism" determining the "location" of work and "aestheticism" determining the "spread."[21] Maya drawing recalled Egypt, by its "lacking perspective" and mixing of sizes.[22] As to the meaning of Maya art, he believed, like Maya scholars

today, that "names, titles or devices of rulers" were the subjects in priestly accounts of rites and ceremonies. Like Stephens, Holmes rejected all analogies with arts elsewhere in the world than America.[23]

Holmes' opinions of Monte Albán anticipate Blanton's computer study of house remains in the 1970s. In part 2 he saw the significance of Monte Albán in southern Mexico as of "an actual city . . . of an agricultural people who utilized the valleys" up to the "very crests of the mountains."[24] Of Teotihuacán in the Valley of Mexico, he thought like René Millon[25] that "the city was largely one of residence" by "a culture differing decidedly from that of Tenochtitlán." Holmes saw an "absence of indications of a warlike spirit . . . though it is next to impossible to think of a great American nation not built up and kept together on a military basis."[26]

As director from 1920 to 1933 of the first National Gallery of Art, Holmes wrote the catalogue of its collections in the north wing of the United States National Museum building (erected in 1910 to house the natural history collection of the country).[27] Holmes' life may be said to anticipate the present-day pattern of one school of Americanist studies: begun in the history of art, continued in anthropology and archaeology, finding support in ethnology, and returning to the art museum after the appearance of Hodge's *Handbook of American Indians* in 1907. Characteristic of this broad tradition is the "lesson" Holmes learned: "that ideas associated with any . . . conventional decorative forms may be as diverse as are the arts, the peoples, and the original elements concerned in its evolution."[28] In brief, Holmes' long life was even more in search of Amerindian art and architecture than of anthropological science.

Finally, last among our precursors, is Alfred Vincent Kidder (1885–1963). Kidder's generation and their students, followers, and critics mark the beginning of the separation of archaeology as history from its earlier consideration as art (as with W. H. Holmes), in the expanding merger of archaeology into environmental and anthropological sciences. At the same time, however, Gordon Willey marked Kidder as "deeply humanist in outlook."[29] He refers to Kidder's "aversion to the idea that human culture, being a fabric of the actions and belief of men, could be understood in accordance with any rigid doctrine or scheme."[30] Many humanists today, caught between history and science, are neither artists nor scientists, but consumers of archaeology in their positions as historians of art.

During Kidder's education at Harvard, he was just such a consumer of archaeology, ingesting chronology, including stratigraphic theory and trade relations, with the Egyptologist G. A. Reisner. He also studied with Franz Boas, as well as with George Chase on Greek vase painting.[31] Kidder "definitely linked archaeology with history" in 1926 as being "to recover and to interpret the story of man's past."[32] These self-imposed limitations were modest, like the man, whose work was attacked by C. Kluckhohn in 1940 and by W. W. Taylor in 1948, when Kidder had been head of the Carnegie Institution's Division of Historical Research for twenty-two years. Kidder had already organized studies in 1929 on a "pan-scientific" front,[33] including physical anthropology, medicine, social anthropology and ethnology, as well as linguistics, archival research, and environmental studies in plant and animal biology and physical sciences. But the division was closed down in 1958, having been an unviable administrative grouping of humanistic studies that comprised history of science, United States history, and history of Greek thought.[34] Kidder's own works and those of his associates in Maya studies are still a monument to his chairmanship of the Division of Historical Research, and they are indispensable to Americanist studies everywhere.

Yet their importance bred discontent among Maya anthropologists and archaeologists who felt excluded by the division's concentration on other studies. Kluckhohn called them "antiquarians" without "methodological and historical development," and Taylor attacked Kidder as failing in "cultural synthesis" and "cultural process," without "historiography or cultural anthropology."[35] Kidder conceded in his final annual report before retiring that the "pan-scientific" program of 1929 was "made to cover too great a range of time and too extensive an area."[36]

Kidder's defenders are many[37] and still growing in number. In R. Wauchope's words, Kidder was "at his best" with "synthesis of cultural history, of broad developmental trends, of general life patterns, of foreign relationships," but not interested enough in "anthropology's concern with specific culture processes and specific cultural dynamics" to "investigate them empirically and in depth himself."[38] Yet in his final report on the activities of the Carnegie Institution in anthropology and archaeology, H.E.D. Pollock observes that in 1902 the committee for anthropology, consisting of W. H. Holmes, Franz Boas, and G. A. Dorsey, could find only one person qualified for research "in middle and South America."[39] Kidder's critics maintained that "this perfect laboratory for research" contributed "little material useful to anthropology." Wauchope answered this charge in a review: "The kindest explanation is that synthesis and interpretation have only recently become possible."[40] But the "science" camp is still divided.

Kidder's other lasting achievements include the excavation of Pecos pueblo in New Mexico (1924) and the archaeological recovery of the early Maya buildings of Kaminaljuyu (1946) in a suburb of Guatemala City. Both works are his lasting memorials. With them new perspectives opened on the history of Amerindian architecture over a thousand years ago. To conclude, the closing of Kidder's Division of Historical Research at the Carnegie Institution of Washington in 1958 marked the beginning of an alienation still persisting between social science and humane scholarship in the ancient American field. Fortunately, humanistic studies continue to expand in universities and research institutes.

On the scale between social sciences and humanities, there is room for both. But at present, the common task remains undone, among anthropology, archaeology, and the history of art and architecture.

NOTES

1. Guillermo Dupaix, *Expediciones acerca de los antiguos monumentos de la Nueva España*, ed. J. Alcina Franch, 2 vols. (Madrid, 1969), 2:103. Supposing natural crystals he was in error, but the point made his principle clear. Further references to Dupaix's *Expediciones* are cited in the text.

2. John Lloyd Stephens, *Incidents of Travel in Central America, Chiapas and Yucatán*, 2 vols. (New York, 1841).

3. Johann Gottfried von Herder, *Outlines of a Philosophy of the History of Man* (1784 [trans. Churchill 1799]; repr. New York, 1966), 161. Herder said in 1784 that "the peaceful peril . . . has scarcely entered the minds of travellers, the workers do not paint forms." See K. E. Gilbert, *A History of Esthetics* (Bloomington, 1953).

4. Stephens 1841, 1:32.

5. Stephens 1841, 1:97, 102, 105. From his previous travels in Egypt, Arabia, Greece, Turkey, and Russia, Stephens concluded on leaving Copán that its sculpture was "excellent, rich in ornament, different from the works of any other people" in its "tone . . . of deep solemnity" (158).

6. Stephens 1841, 1:137, 2:309.

7. Stephens 1841, 2:343, 346.

8. Stephens 1841, 2:313–314, 319–320. For present opinions, see the articles in *Primera Mesa Redonda de Palenque: A Conference on the Art, Iconography, and Dynastic History of Palenque, Chiapas, Mexico*, ed. Merle Greene Robertson (Pebble Beach, Calif., 1974).

9. Stephens 1841, 2:455, 442.

10. John Lloyd Stephens, *Incidents of Travel in Yucatán*, 2 vols. (New York, 1843), 1:iv, 149 illus., 306 illus.

11. Stephens 1843, 1:273–275.

12. The "Brief Biography of William Henry Holmes" in *Ohio Archaeological and Historical Quarterly* 36 (October 1927), 493–511, was probably written by the editor, C. B. Galbreath, in Columbus with the subtitle "Artist, Geologist, Archaeologist, and Art Gallery Director."

13. H. H. Bancroft, "Anthropology and Ethnology," vol. 3 of *The Book of the Fair . . .*, 3 vols. (Chicago, 1895), 629–663. Louis Sullivan and Frank Lloyd Wright both knew the exhibition and used its forms in their own ways.

14. Bancroft 1895, 631–633.

15. C. M. Nelson, "William Henry Holmes: Beginning a Career in Art and Science," *Records of the Columbia Historical Society* 50 (1980), 254.

16. Nelson 1980, 263–264.

17. Mr. and Mrs. Chain, with W. H. Jackson, were the photographers. "Brief Biography," 503. Mr. and Mrs. Chain provided the private car.

18. W. H. Holmes, *Archeological Studies among the Ancient Cities of Mexico*, 2 vols., Publications of the Field Columbian Museum, Anthropological Series (Chicago, 1895–1897). Part 1 (1895) was entitled "Monuments of Yucatán," part 2 (1897) "Monuments of Chiapas, Oaxaca, and the Valley of Mexico." A third part (not published) was to be on "Ceramic Art of Mexico."

19. For part 1 he depended on books by J. L. Stephens, D. Charnay, A. Le Plongeon, A. Maudslay, A. Bandelier, and H. H. Bancroft. On ancient writings he also knew the works of E. Seler, E. H. Thompson, C. Thomas, D. G. Brinton, E. W. Förstemann, P. Schellhas, and P. Valentini.

20. Holmes 1895, 1:48–52.

21. Holmes 1895, 1:52.

22. Holmes 1895, 1:53.

23. Holmes 1895, 1:54–55.

24. Holmes 1897, 2:226.

25. René Millon, *Urbanization at Teotihuacán, Mexico*, 2 vols. (Austin, Tex., 1973), 1:46–47.

26. Holmes 1897, 2:289–290.

27. W. H. Holmes, *Catalogue of Collections* [National Gallery of Art, Smithsonian Institution] (Washington, 1922). The works of art were property of the Congress.

28. W. H. Holmes, "On the Evolution of Ornament—An American Lesson," *American Anthropologist* 3 (April 1890), 137–146. Pàl Kelemen notes Holmes' importance as a writer on art in "Pre-Columbian Art and Art History," *American Antiquity* 11 (1946), 148.

29. Gordon Willey, "Alfred Vincent Kidder," *Biographical Memoirs, National Academy of Sciences* 39 (1964), 308–322.

30. Willey 1964, 308.

31. In "Alfred Vincent Kidder, 1885–1963," *American Antiquity* 31 (1964), 152, R. Wauchope notes Chase's influence on Kidder's analysis of Southwestern ceramics. Richard B. Woodbury, *Alfred Kidder* (New York, 1973), 21.

32. Wauchope 1964, 152.

33. *Carnegie Institution of Washington Year Book* 49 (1949–1950), 192.

34. H.E.D. Pollock et al., "Report: Department of Archaeology," *Carnegie Institution of Washington Year Book* 57 (1957–1958), 435–455. This history of the activities of Carnegie Institution of Washington in anthropology and archaeology covers more than fifty years.

35. Clyde Kluckhohn, "The Conceptual Structure in Middle American Studies," in *The Maya and Their Neighbors: Essays on Middle American Anthropology and Archaeology*, ed. Clarence L. Hay et al. (New York, 1940), 41–51; Walter W. Taylor, Jr., *A Study of Archaeology*, Memoir Series of the American Anthropological Association, no. 69 (Menasha, Wis., 1948), 47–48.

36. A. V. Kidder, "Division of Historical Research,"

Carnegie Institution of Washington Year Book 49 (1949–1950), 192.

37. Willey 1964, 293–322; R. Wauchope, ''Obituary,'' *American Antiquity* 31 (1965), 161–164; Woodbury 1973.

38. Wauchope 1965, 163.

39. Pollock 1957–1958, 435.

40. R. Wauchope, review of ''Study of Classic Maya Sculpture,'' by Proskouriakoff, *American Antiquity* 12 (1951), 161.

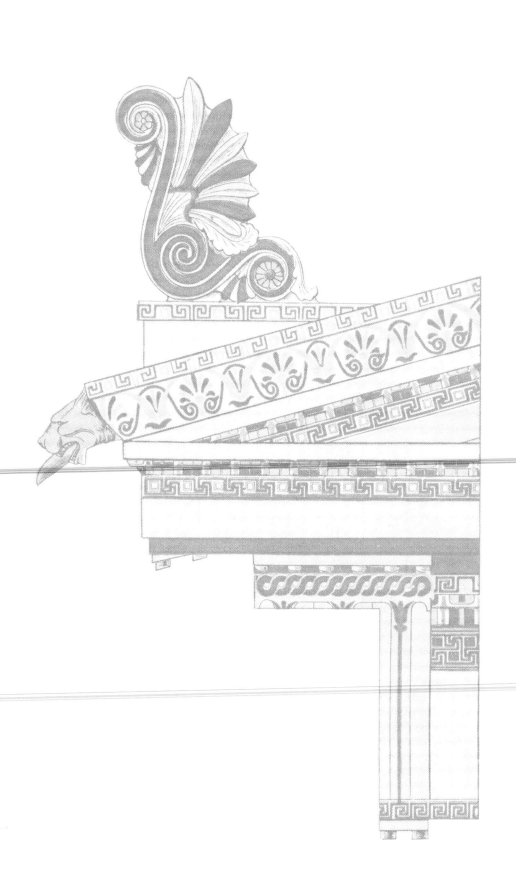

DELL UPTON
University of California, Berkeley

Outside the Academy:

A Century of Vernacular Architecture Studies, 1890–1990

As the Society of Architectural Historians approached its fiftieth anniversary, the scholarly study of vernacular architecture passed its hundredth.[1] Its intellectual foundations are a century older. Ideas and attitudes formed in the eighteenth century shaped the first antiquarian exploration of the American vernacular in the early nineteenth century, as well as the first scholarly analyses in the 1880s and 1890s. In this essay, I want to discuss origins and then to sketch a portrait of the current state of the field, as a way of stressing the continuity of paradigms and methods. Uncharacteristically for a study of the vernacular, I will concentrate on scholarly monuments rather than attempt a thorough survey of the landscape.

There have been two dominant strains in American vernacular architecture scholarship, which I call the historical and the cultural (or more precisely ethnogeographic) traditions. The historical tradition seeks to understand architectural change in detail by relating it to patterns of social structure, economic differentiation, and craft tradition. The cultural tradition searches for large patterns, common values, and shared perceptions through typological, statistical, or geographical analyses of architecture. Architectural historians have learned from both strains and contributed to both.

Nevertheless, vernacular architecture scholarship is distinctive from most other varieties of architectural history both for its interdisciplinary character and for having been conducted largely outside the academy.[2] For much of its history the study of vernacular architecture has been intertwined with visual design, historical commemoration, architectural preservation, and social and artistic theory more than with so-called pure scholarship. Thus while the first analysts of American vernacular architecture—men such as Norman Morrison Isham, Irving Whitall Lyon, and Henry Chapman Mercer—were careful scholars, the impulses and assumptions that motivated their work were not scholarly.

The story begins in the eighteenth century, when a new relativism began to undermine unitary theories of history and culture.[3] At the same time, philosophers argued for an associational aesthetic theory, claiming that visual forms could evoke the qualities of the places or eras that produced them.[4] Associationism linked the picturesque visual mood, which was based on the power of images to evoke emotional responses, with a didactic intellectual mood that asserted the responsibility of the visual arts to convey historical information and public values.[5] These new intellectual attitudes were commonly expressed in a fascination with the *exotic*, meaning nonclassical and non-Western buildings; the *primitive*, based on the assumption that earlier and cruder forms were more innocent, natural, or spontaneous, and therefore truer, than later, refined ones; and later the *native*, since local styles, particularly the Gothic, were thought to embody national character.[6]

While none of these new ideas at first was applied to vernacular buildings, picturesque preferences for the exotic, the primitive, and the nationalistic, as well as didactic inclinations toward the nationalistic and the moralistic, laid the foundations for the first vernacular architecture studies. As developed by Gothic revival and Arts and Crafts theorists, these aesthetic attitudes were blended with the English antiquarian and topographical tradition, a nationalistic expression of the profound moral satisfaction of being English.[7] This dual aesthetic and antiquarian legacy, with its deep moralistic tint, was the inheritance of the first American scholars of vernacular architecture in the late nineteenth century.

If these scholars' intellectual origins lay in England, their attention was drawn to American topics by antiquarian activities closer to home. The antiquarian preservation of American vernacular artifacts dates, perhaps, from the acquisition of "a chair in the antique fashion" by the newly founded Massachusetts Historical Society in 1793.[8] It soon encompassed vernacular architectural relics, such as the window from Newport's seventeenth-century Coddington house acquired by the Rhode Island Historical Society in 1834.[9] By 1850, patriotic antiquarians engineered the preservation of an entire vernacular building, the Hasbrouck house, an eighteenth-century Dutch structure in Newburgh, New York, that had been used briefly as George Washington's military headquarters.[10] The early national period also produced the first topographical antiquarian publications. John Fanning Watson's *Annals of Philadelphia and Pennsylvania in the Olden Time*, published in 1830, was filled with descriptions and images of vernacular buildings and landscapes in the colonial and early national city, drawn from life and memory.[11] In all these instances, the artifacts attracted attention for their historical as-

1. Norman Morrison Isham (1864–1943)

From *Providence Journal*, 2 January 1943. Courtesy of the Rhode Island Historical Society, neg. no. RHi x3 1117

sociations rather than as "vernacular" objects. The effect, however, was to single out ordinary buildings and furnishings as objects of attention and veneration.

Aesthetic antiquarianism, introduced by ecclesiologists, turned from European to American subject matter as early as 1858, when George Snell enlarged Newport's colonial Redwood Library. By the 1870s, colonial revival architects had explicitly embraced American vernacular as well as high-style colonial architecture as a source for contemporary architectural design.[12]

These, then, were the assumptions and preoccupations that shaped the first scholars of American vernacular architecture. The founding document of the historical tradition was Norman Morrison Isham (1864–1943) (fig. 1) and Albert F. Brown's (1862–1909) *Early Rhode Island Houses: An*

Historical and Architectural Study, one of the neglected classics of American architectural history.[13] At first glance, *Early Rhode Island Houses* is a product of the colonial revival, consistent with Isham's long architectural career, which encompassed the restoration of many familiar colonial buildings as well as new designs in a colonial mode.[14] However, Isham's commitment to the colonial ran deeper than simple adherence to current architectural fashion. His work is more properly seen as another, deeper branch of the common antiquarian-picturesque stream that also fed the colonial revival.

Isham acknowledged his debts to both the antiquarian-topographical and colonial revival traditions, and he referred to the houses he studied simply as "colonial" buildings.[15] However, his major writings focused almost exclusively on seventeenth-century New England vernacular houses.[16] For Isham, "the seventeenth century is the mediaeval period in American architecture. Its work is Tudor or late Gothic in character and, simple and rude as it may seem to be, has yet something of the beauty and charm with which Gothic attracts us. It was the native tradition."[17] This statement reflects the early colonial revival partiality to the seventeenth century, but it also echoes the exoticist and primitivist premises of eighteenth-century picturesque theory. At the same time, it links Isham to the Gothic revivalists and their Arts and Crafts successors. Both sounded nationalistic and moralistic themes in their celebration of medieval traditions. From the Gothic revivalists Isham inherited the principle of the direct field inspection and detailed measured drawing of antiquities that had originated among eighteenth-century classicists.[18] The English Arts and Crafts legacy included the emphasis on domestic (rather than ecclesiastical) forms, the equation of seventeenth-century vernacular building with the Gothic, and the belief in the superiority of medieval craft traditions rooted in preindustrial labor systems. Isham dedicated his book on Rhode Island and its successor on Connecticut to the craftsmen of the two colonies, and much of his work was devoted to the evolution of plan types

and structural systems, presented in carefully detailed measured drawings. He gave little attention to decoration and none to style, thus setting himself apart from the predominantly visual interests of other Queen Anne and colonial revival architects. *Early Rhode Island Houses* was the first scholarly work on Euro-American vernacular architecture published in the United States. Only one similar English work, Ralph Nevill's *Old Cottages and Domestic Architecture in South-West Surrey* (1889), antedated it.[19]

Norman Isham's membership in the Walpole Society of collectors, founded in 1914, emphasizes the holistic approach to the colonial material world shared by many early students of vernacular architecture. Isham's principal competitor, for example, was Hartford physician Irving Whitall Lyon (1840–1896), who published a pioneering study of early New England furniture in 1891, then turned to a study of colonial New England houses that was nearly complete when he died.[20] Both of Lyon's books were efforts to codify the classification and naming of artifacts by comparing survivals with documents, particularly with probate inventories; to identify European precedents of American forms; and to catalogue methods and materials of construction. Isham's analogous interest in technology and in English origins, as well as his 1939 glossary of colonial architectural terms (part of a Walpole Society series that sought to establish uniform terminology throughout antiquarian studies of material culture) thus allied him with the late nineteenth-century antique collectors.[21]

The Walpole Society members were wealthy capitalists and aristocrats whose collecting was an expression of their social elitism and desire to be insulated from the vulgar world.[22] Isham's "honored membership" in this society points to another aspect of early vernacular architecture studies: its conservative political and cultural values, strongly tinged with nativism.[23] Most current vernacular architectural historians are openly, even proudly, leftist in their intellectual principles and antielitist attitudes. Not so the founders. Although the first generation found aesthetic inspiration in the Arts and Crafts movement, they did not share its political radicalism. Lyon warned his son, a medical student at Johns Hopkins University, against tainting himself socially by registering to vote in Baltimore, and his letters are full of fear and condescension toward the occupants of the houses he studied.[24] Henry Chapman Mercer (1856–1930), a third pioneer student of the vernacular, turned his attention from Native American archaeology to traditional carpenters' tools and log houses.[25] Mercer applied Gothic Revival techniques of dating by moldings to American vernacular buildings.[26] He attempted to revive Pennsylvania German folk ceramics, apprenticing himself to a traditional practitioner.[27] In short, as his eulogist wrote, he was able to break with "the old prejudice" that only the works "of the so-called 'upper' classes are worthy of investigation."[28] Nevertheless, Mercer's was not a proletarian temperament. According to a long-time friend, he was "a romantic. His taste was formed in the tradition of the Gothic revival, which was, in part, a protest against the ugliness of the industrial age." Mercer "detested the philistines who menaced his world" and hated contemporary popular music, which "smacked of the cabarets of Eastern Europe."[29]

Isham, Lyon, and Mercer, pioneers of American vernacular architecture study, were antiquarians, exoticists, nativists, primitivists, and associationists in the nineteenth-century tradition. All accepted the moral superiority of the old ways and believed that the material world somehow embodied the essence of past life. Mercer saw his work, for instance, as "a new presentation of the history of our country from the point of view of the work of human hands."[30] If they are indistinguishable from their romantic predecessors in these beliefs, however, they are set apart by their more rigorous scholarship. No longer satisfied to interpret ancestors on the basis of assumptions, they sought hard evidence and historical specificity. In common with other turn-of-the-century Americans, they likened their enterprise to the natural scientist's.[31] Lyon's contemporaries noted the correlation between his progressive medical views and his antiquarian studies. Both were based conspicuously on detailed

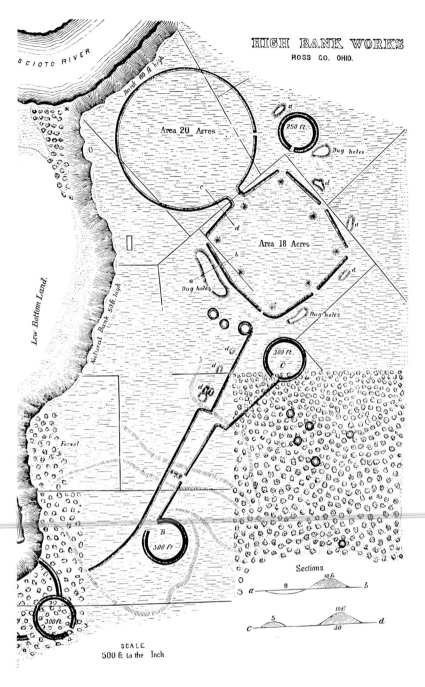

personal research and "very full notes": he "trusted nothing to his memory." In "diagnosing he always wanted to get back to ultimate causes and . . . he worked at the houses the same way."[32] Isham in particular recast the eighteenth-century fondness for fieldwork as an intellectual imperative. He presented his drawings as "veritable historical data. . . . The collection of sci-

2. Plan of the prehistoric earthworks at High Bank, Ohio, from Ephraim Squier and E. H. Davis, *Ancient Monuments of the Mississippi Valley* (1845), as reproduced by Lewis H. Morgan, who labeled it "Ground Plan of the High Bank Pueblo"
From Lewis H. Morgan, *Houses and House-Life of the American Aborigines* (1881; repr. Chicago, 1965), fig. 46

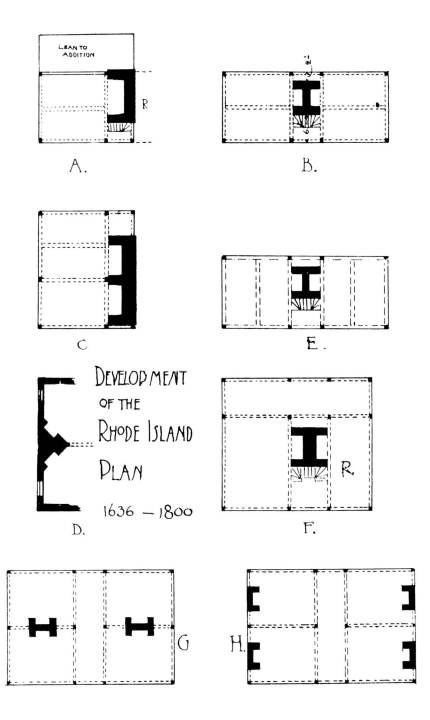

A.

B.

C

DEVELOPMENT
OF THE
RHODE ISLAND
PLAN

1636 — 1800

D.

E.

F.

G

H.

3. "Development of the Rhode Island Plan," illustrating the evolution of colonial Rhode Island house plans, compared with the plans typical of Connecticut (B) and of Salem, Massachusetts (E)
From Norman Morrison Isham and Albert F. Brown, *Early Rhode Island Houses: An Historical and Architectural Study* (Providence, 1895), fig. 1

entific data" through "accurate measured drawings" was a necessary corrective for "the vague descriptions of too many of our town histories."[33]

Isham's historicism set him apart from Lyon, Mercer, and other contemporaries who had raised antiquarianism to such a high technical level. He attempted to link New England's early architecture to its so-

cioeconomic history, interpreting regional architectural differences as evidence of craft training traditions and the regional origins of immigrant craftsmen, but also in terms of political divisions and patterns of emigration within New England.[34] Where antiquarians focused on the appreciation of small details, Isham looked for larger patterns. Where they emphasized the timeless, Isham, a true historian, was always interested in change.[35] His aims were analytical, rather than merely descriptive.

Fourteen years before *Early Rhode Island Houses* appeared, the Smithsonian Institution published the first cultural analysis of vernacular buildings. It was *Houses and House-Life of the American Aborigines*, the last work of Rochester lawyer-anthropologist Lewis Henry Morgan (1818–1881) and the fruit of thirty years' research into Native American culture.[36] It, too, had an antiquarian prehistory in such works as Ephraim Squier and E. H. Davis' *Ancient Monuments of the Mississippi Valley*, a series of measured plans of prehistoric earthworks in the Midwest (fig. 2).[37] Morgan's book, like Isham's, assumed an informative connection between architecture and social life, and it proposed to construct a systematic portrait of Native American traditions. Similarly, both men assumed an evolutionary progression in social life that was manifested in architecture. For Isham, social progress was most clearly depicted through house plans, and both the Rhode Island and Connecticut books contained carefully constructed evolutionary plan charts (fig. 3).[38] For Morgan domestic arrangements in houses reflected cultural evolution and provided evidence of the human journey from savagery through barbarism to civilization, to use his categories (fig. 4).[39]

The difference was that Morgan sought to use architecture to explain Indian social structure, while Isham used his understanding of social and political history to explain architecture. More important, Morgan's was a mentalist model that sought high-level cultural patterns transcending local and historical specifics. He argued that "all the forms of this architecture sprang from a common mind, and exhibit, as a consequence, different stages of

4. "Room in Pueblo of Taos."
In keeping with his interest in
social organization, Morgan
preferred to illustrate architectural spaces in use
From Lewis H. Morgan, *Houses and
House-Life of the American
Aborigines* (1881; repr. Chicago, 1965),
fig. 28

development of the same conceptions, operating upon similar necessities. Their
houses will be seen to form one system of
works, from the Long House of the Iro-
quois to the Joint Tenement houses . . . of
stone in New Mexico, Yucatán, Chiapas,
and Guatemala."[40] The colonialists, on the
other hand, thrived on particularism, em-
piricism, and localism, noting minute distinctions between locales only a few miles
apart and between buildings only a few
years different in date.

The legacy of the original historians of
vernacular architecture has been a long-
lasting one. Isham's work in particular inspired a continuous scholarly tradition.
Between the wars Isham protegés such as
J. Frederick Kelly (1888–1947) of Connecticut and Antoinette Forrester Downing of
Rhode Island produced local architectural
histories whose historicism set them aside
from the antiquarian collections of photographs and measured drawings of colonial
architecture that were produced in great
numbers during those years.[41] Colonial
Williamsburg, restored by the New England architectural firm of Perry, Shaw, and
Hepburn, might be counted with Isham's

legacy as well, given the associationist
connection between architecture and history implied in its motto, "That the present may learn from the past."[42]

More generally, the first generation of
historians set the agenda for contemporary
vernacular architecture study. Methodo-
logically they instilled an abiding interest
in building technology and a fieldwork
ethos. Their predisposition toward the exotic, the primitive, and the domestic, typically expressed in the study of the oldest
buildings of their localities, still pervades
vernacular architecture studies. Their progressive paradigm persists in the many surveys of American architectural history that
notice vernacular building only in their
seventeenth-century chapters. Their most
significant intellectual legacy, however,
was their organizing assumption that architecture is an expression of social practice and their consequent emphasis on spatial type over visual style, use over design.

Lewis Morgan undoubtedly overshadows
Norman Isham in the larger scheme of
nineteenth-century intellectual history.
For vernacular architecture studies, however, his work seems noteworthy primarily

5. "Charcoal burners' hut, South Yorkshire." An example of the primitive stage of English vernacular architecture, supplied to Fiske Kimball by Charles F. Innocent

From Fiske Kimball, *Domestic Architecture of the American Colonies and of the Early Republic* (New York, 1922), fig. 1

6. Whipple house, Ipswich, Massachusetts. Illustrated by Kimball as an example of the advanced development of English vernacular architecture in New England

From Fiske Kimball, *Domestic Architecture of the American Colonies and of the Early Republic* (New York, 1922), fig. 4

in retrospect. The cultural tradition of vernacular architecture studies was only an undercurrent until after World War I. The preconditions for its emergence were the identification of an autonomous vernacular tradition in architecture and the introduction of ethnographic and geographic methods to its study.

Fiske Kimball (1888–1955) satisfied the first of these prerequisites. The scholars of Isham's generation never used the term vernacular architecture, nor did they distinguish their buildings categorically from other kinds of colonial architecture. They saw them as the products of a unitary English tradition, made plain by pioneer circumstances and economic limitations and altered somewhat by transplantation to North America. To Isham, for example, the supplantation of traditional by classical forms in eighteenth-century New England represented an incidental relocation of visual sources rather than an intellectual reorientation. Kimball thought differently. His *Domestic Architecture of the American Colonies and of the Early Republic*, a prescient and generally accurate account of colonial vernacular building, marks a turning point in setting off the vernacular as a separate category of architecture.[43] Kimball interpreted crude nineteenth-century English peasant shelters as shards of a distinctive, older architectural tradition, rather than makeshifts arising from deprivation, as his predecessors had done (fig. 5).[44] By juxtaposing them with more substantial seventeenth-century Anglo-American vernacular buildings, one could read "a general rise in the 'culture stage' of the English yeomanry" (fig. 6).[45]

Kimball was not an anthropologist, however, but an art historian. His point was that the introduction of "the academic spirit and the academic architectural forms" at the beginning of the eighteenth century represented a qualitative intellectual transformation. "It involved a transference of the emphasis from functional considerations to those of pure form."[46] The corollary was that Kimball conceived vernacular architecture—still lacking the name—as a discrete though archaic tradition, one based on function rather than aesthetics and thus existing outside of academic canons. This separate tradition enjoyed a long life after upper-class builders had bypassed it. The log house, for example, was relegated to the pioneer, the wooden chimney and the leaded casement to country districts. Some vernacular practices, wrote Kimball, had survived "to this day in obscure corners of Europe."[47]

For Kimball, colonial vernacular houses were the homes of a social type, the Anglo-American yeoman, rather than relics of noteworthy individual ancestors, as they had been for Isham. Thus, Kimball's *Domestic Architecture* set the stage for subsequent works that conceived vernacular architecture as an anonymous and undifferentiated backdrop, the medium of the common man and woman, against which to set the mutable and distinctive building of the prominent patron and the named architect. The assignment of vernacular building to a timeless and socially homogeneous folk allowed vernacular architectural historians to pick up where Lewis Morgan had left off forty years earlier and interpret it in cultural terms, as an expression of collective mind.

A decade after Kimball wrote, the first cultural models for the study of vernacular architecture were proposed. Unlike scholars in the historical tradition, whose assumptions and methods have remained relatively stable, cultural analysts have encompassed at least three paradigms, introduced in the 1930s, 1940s, and 1960s. The three paradigms were cumulative rather than successive in their influence.

When cultural analyses were reintroduced to American vernacular architectural history in the 1930s, Morgan's cultural evolutionism was no longer the dominant model. Instead, scholars applied historic-geographic, or cultural diffusionist, paradigms derived from European folklife studies and historical geography. Geographer Fred Kniffen's 1935 article, "Louisiana House Types," was the first such study of American vernacular buildings. Kniffen used road-traverse observations (often called "windshield surveys") of the external characteristics of fifteen thousand Louisiana buildings to define and map nine house types in an attempt to develop "an areal expression of *ideas* regarding houses—a groping toward a tangible hold on the geographical expression of culture" (fig. 7).[48] Kniffen's 1965 article, "Folk Housing: Key to Diffusion," traced patterns of population movement and settlement throughout the eastern and central United States by mapping common nineteenth-century building types, partic-

ularly the ubiquitous one that he named the *I house*.[49]

In their use of the historic-geographic method, geographers and folklorists explicitly accepted the vernacular-academic dichotomy that Kimball had suggested.[50] As a mass phenomenon, vernacular buildings could be studied en masse. Although these scholars studied plan type and structural systems as keenly as the historians did, they treated plan and structure as diagnostic of change at the level of entire populations.[51] Regional, rather than class, aesthetic, or craft origins, distinguished vernacular buildings from one another and from academic architecture. Consequently, historic-geographic scholars were as unconcerned as Morgan had been with the fine points of individual buildings that fascinated the historians. And where historians focused on the oldest buildings, geographers and folklorists tended to fasten on those of any date that seemed culturally "early" and static—for example, log building—as opposed to rapidly changing academic or popular architectural forms.[52] In the process, the historic-geographic school tended to meld the entire vernacular landscape into a misleading architectural consensus, overlooking class differentiation and chronological change.

A second form of cultural analysis arose in the late 1940s. It concentrated on the ordinary, an intersecting but much larger set than the traditional. John Kouwenhoven's *Made in America* (1948) depicted ordinary products of the industrial age, including pattern-book houses, as an American folk art that could provide clues to the "characteristic impulses of the new [American] civilization," while Sigfried Giedion's *Mechanization Takes Command*, published in the same year, sought to define "our mode of life" in terms of "the general guiding ideas of an epoch."[53] Giedion labeled his project "anonymous history." The search for a national popular ethos had obvious affinities both with the art historical concept of zeitgeist and with the emerging American studies movement. Kouwenhoven's book in particular has been widely used as an American studies text.

For J. B. Jackson, the ordinary landscape

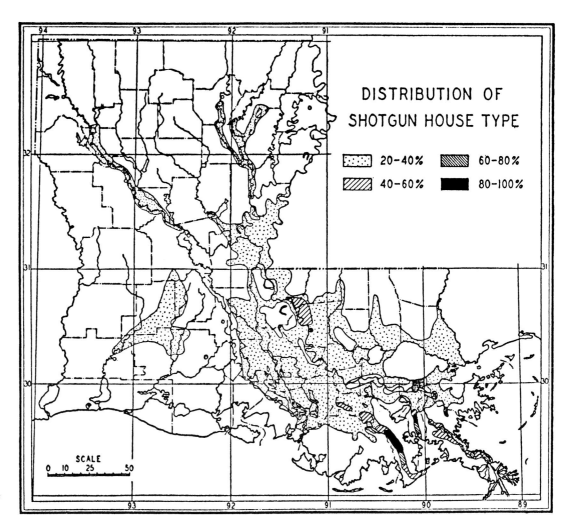

DISTRIBUTION OF SHOTGUN HOUSE TYPE

| 20-40% | 60-80% |
| 40-60% | 80-100% |

SCALE
0 10 25 50

7. "Distribution of shotgun house type"
From Fred B. Kniffen, "Louisiana House Types," *Annals of the Association of American Geographers* 26 (1936), fig. 16

provided the evidence of collective values that Kouwenhoven and Giedion sought in commonplace technology. Beginning in 1951, Jackson's magazine *Landscape* interleaved architects' and geographers' studies with his own commentary on contemporary American mores as depicted in vernacular landscape. Jackson's essays stood outside the bounds of the academy; they owed more to the nineteenth-century belletristic tradition than to any scholarly discipline.[54] Their connection to the cultural tradition lay in Jackson's preference for analyzing the vernacular landscape in terms of the typical, as a representation of normative experience and the collective mind.[55]

Cultural analysis of the vernacular returned to anthropological and mentalist models in the 1960s. Amos Rapoport's *House Form and Culture*, a study that focused primarily on non-Western architecture, was an extended attack on all forms of determinism, arguing for the primacy of culture—socially transmitted concepts and assumptions—in shaping architectural responses to environment, economics, technology, defense, and site.[56] Henry Glassie's *Folk Housing in Middle Virginia*, on the other hand, looked to transformational grammar and sociolinguistics in constructing a geometrical model of the folk design process and of changes in the vernacular formal repertoire. The first part of Glassie's book presented a formal grammar or ideal total system of Virginia folk architecture—its *competence*, in linguistic terminology (fig. 8). In the second part of the book, Glassie turned to what linguists call the *performance* to examine the cultural history of Virginia building. Here he used cultural concepts derived from anthropologist Robert Plant Armstrong and a structuralist model based on the work of Claude Lévi-Strauss to define the psychological odyssey of rural Virginians from an open to a closed outlook (fig. 9).[57]

This historical sketch, brief as it has been, goes a long way toward explaining the current landscape of vernacular architecture studies.[58] There are several subgenres of vernacular architecture studies that are remarkably balkanized by discipline, subject matter, and region, but that can reasonably be located within the historical-cultural dichotomy.

The historical tradition is the more cohesive as well as the more highly developed of the two. It is maintained chiefly by architectural historians, historians, and archaeologists. Historical studies are immensely more sophisticated than in Isham's day, in part as a result of the radical enlargement and revision of the data base since 1970 and in part because the boom in early American social and economic history over the last twenty-five years offers vast new analytical resources. Nevertheless, most historical studies adhere closely to the analysis of individual colonial and early-national-period buildings in rural districts of the East Coast, and often to the very buildings Isham and his contemporaries first studied. Historians maintain their allegiance to fieldwork and detailed graphic recording, their interest in building technology, and their faith in the primacy of form. Recent cautious forays into the nineteenth-century and into the history of women and of consumerism have not significantly altered the traditional picture.[59]

Culturalist scholars have been less single-minded. Current historic-geographic studies of the vernacular focus on the upland and deep South and the Midwest (in which I include the Great Basin).[60] As a legacy of early twentieth-century regionalism, the upland South has attracted folklorists seeking a rich, surviving traditional culture. Geographers, on the other hand, have used the national popular domestic and agricultural building types of the nineteenth century as material for diffusion studies.

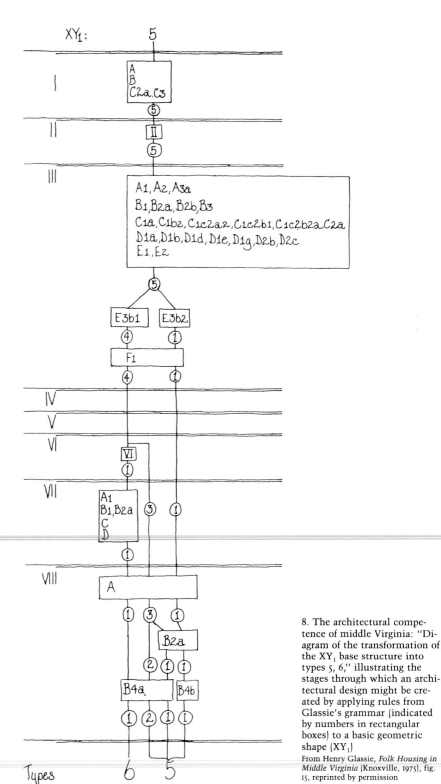

8. The architectural competence of middle Virginia: "Diagram of the transformation of the XY_1 base structure into types 5, 6," illustrating the stages through which an architectural design might be created by applying rules from Glassie's grammar (indicated by numbers in rectangular boxes) to a basic geometric shape (XY_1)
From Henry Glassie, *Folk Housing in Middle Virginia* (Knoxville, 1975), fig. 15, reprinted by permission

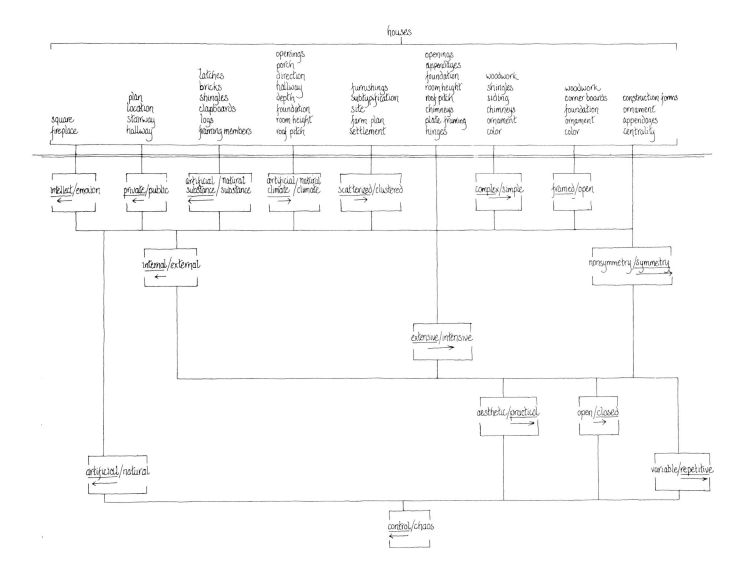

houses

square / fireplace | intellect/emotion
plan, location, stairway, hallway | private/public
latches, bricks, shingles, clapboards, logs, framing members | artificial substance / natural substance | internal/external | artificial/natural
openings, porch, direction, hallway, depth, foundation, room height, roof pitch | artificial climate / natural climate
furnishings, subtypification, site, farm plan, settlement | scatterized/clustered | extensive/intensive | aesthetic/practical | control/chaos
openings, appendages, foundation, room height, roof pitch, chimneys, plate framing, hinges | complex/simple
woodwork, shingles, siding, chimneys, ornament, color | | nonsymmetry/symmetry | open/closed
woodwork, corner boards, foundation, ornament, color | framed/open
construction forms, ornament, appendages, centrality | variable/repetitive

9. The architectural performance of middle Virginia: "The architecture of design." Based on the patterned architectural features listed above the double line, Glassie has diagramed "the paradigmatic structure of the mind of the Middle Virginia architect—a guide to decision making." From Henry Glassie, *Folk Housing in Middle Virginia* (Knoxville, 1975), fig. 76, reprinted by permission

Historic-geographic models have been employed by some students of the commercial strip, who treat it as a case of modern urban economic development.[61] Where they indulge in analysis at all, however, most scholars of the strip and other contemporary popular architecture draw on the second cultural model and treat pop forms as manifestations of the collective mind in the automobile era. Most such studies have been undertaken by historic preservationists and architects in northeastern and West Coast cities. The strip can also be treated within the context of the total urban cultural landscape, as cultural landscape scholars in the Jacksonian mode have done, particularly for midwestern and far western cities. These studies have focused overwhelmingly on twentieth-century urban culture.

The mentalist models of the 1960s and 1970s, though more sophisticated than the other cultural models, have found fewer followers among scholars of American vernacular architecture. Rapoport's cultural determinism is widely cited, but his particular anthropological models are most often applied in studies of Third World and, to a lesser extent, Native American architecture than they are to the ordinary landscape of North America. Similarly, Glassie's work on Middle Virginia has been influential in providing folklorists and archaeologists with a rigorously supported body of assumptions about vernacular design, but no one has undertaken another study that replicates the precise methods of *Folk Housing in Middle Virginia*.

I have not yet defined vernacular architecture. In fact, I have avoided doing so for two reasons. First, I am confident that twenty years of missionary work have made every informed architectural historian aware of the nature and importance of vernacular architecture. Second, the nature of the material is such that the definition is best derived from the history, rather than being offered a priori. Although vernacular architecture has acquired its name only recently, we have seen that the field has a relatively coherent century-old history based on remarkably tenacious themes and assumptions. Some, I think, define the essential and still valuable historical core of vernacular architecture studies, in particular the emphasis on social process and its relation to plan and structure. Other traits, such as the fieldwork ethos, are characteristic more than diagnostic. Still others arise from emotional attachments and historical accident more than from intellectual commitment. All of these are unfortunate, some even pernicious. I include in the former category the widespread inability to look beyond the rural and the domestic, and in the latter the continuing taint of exoticism and primitivism, which has left so much of the vernacular landscape overworked while other aspects are underexamined. Compare, for example, the number of studies of seventeenth-century New England vernacular houses with those of the nineteenth- and twentieth-century New England vernacular.

From these longstanding assumptions and methods two intuitive models of vernacular architecture developed. The newer of the two is a negative model that Fiske Kimball originated. This defines vernacular architecture by what it is not: it is not the academic architectural tradition, and therefore it is a catch-all that includes not only folk houses, but tract houses, hamburger stands, and anything else that does not fit the traditional canon. It embodies the tinge of moralism that we have seen is part of the ancient heritage of vernacular architecture studies, infused recently by the oppositional, ultimately Marxist, intellectual tradition out of which the best recent social history emerges. In this respect, it has honorable roots and legitimate value for its critical, antihierarchical stance.

The second intuitive model is a positive one, and it can be traced back to the founders, Norman Isham and Lewis Morgan. It identifies the vernacular as an architecture that grows directly out of social and cultural process. In Isham's words, this model presumes that vernacular building is produced by "an actual correspondence of a state of mind and a manner of life."[62] Because it emphasizes issues rather than categories, the processual model of vernacular architecture studies is at least as catholic as the opposition model, and could include nearly any building. Consequently, vernacular architectural historians could colonize even the most sacred precincts of the art historian, through studying the socioeconomic foundations of the Renaissance palazzo, for example, or the social impulses underlying Frank Lloyd Wright's prairie houses.[63]

In the next few years, I hope that vernacular architecture studies will transcend the longstanding limitations I have discussed. There are signs that this may happen. Some scholars are rediscovering the founders' holistic emphasis and easing the isolation of vernacular architecture from its furnishings and landscape. Others are beginning not only to look at academic buildings through vernacular eyes, but to take up issues of visual form and aesthetics in the light of ideology, power, and symbolic communication. Vernacular architecture studies, that is, are drawing nearer to cultural theory and to the new art history. In the absence of serious challengers, perhaps vernacular architecture studies can claim the title, the new *architectural* history.

Eventually, Fiske Kimball's line between vernacular and academic architecture will be erased and the vernacular-academic dichotomy will be replaced by a much more complex paradigm that recognizes change and stasis, diversity and conflict, pattern and discontinuity in all varieties of architecture. Kimball's division will have served its purpose when misleading, unitary, hierarchical models of cultural process and architectural value are discredited and replaced by truer, pluralistic ones. Then there will be no vernacular architecture studies, only a larger and more genuine architectural history.

NOTES

1. I am indebted to my research assistant, Tim Stokes, for assistance with this article.

2. This is more true for the historical tradition than for the cultural tradition. Vernacular architecture has had a secure, though secondary, place in geography departments since the 1930s and in folklore since the 1960s.

3. Peter Gay, *The Enlightenment: An Interpretation* (New York, 1969), 2: 319-320, 392-395; Peter Collins, *Changing Ideals in Modern Architecture 1750-1950* (Montreal, 1965), 29-41.

4. Collins 1965, 45, 48, 61-66; George Hersey, *High Victorian Gothic: A Study in Associationism* (Baltimore, 1972), 1-22.

5. Hugh Honour, *Neo-classicism* (Harmondsworth, 1968), 80-87.

6. Collins 1965, 67-69, 100-105.

7. Stuart Piggott, *Ruins in a Landscape: Essays in Antiquarianism* (Edinburgh, 1976), 101-132.

8. Richard H. Saunders, "Collecting American Decorative Arts in New England, Part I: 1793-1876," in *Pilgrim Century Furniture: An Historical Survey*, ed. Robert Trent (New York, n.d.), 14.

9. Charles B. Hosmer, Jr., *Presence of the Past: A History of the Preservation Movement in the United States before Williamsburg* (New York, 1965), 32.

10. Dorothy C. Barck, "The First Historic House Museum: Washington's Newburgh Headquarters, 1750-1850," *Journal of the Society of Architectural Historians* 14 (May 1955), 30-32.

11. John Fanning Watson, *Annals of Philadelphia, and Pennsylvania, in the Olden Time; Being a Collection of Memoirs, Anecdote, and Incidents of the City and Its Inhabitants from the Days of the Pilgrim Founders* (Philadelphia and New York, 1830).

12. Norman Morrison Isham, *In Praise of Antiquaries* (Boston, 1931), 5; Vincent J. Scully, Jr., *The Shingle Style and the Stick Style: Architectural Theory and Design from Downing to the Origins of Wright*, rev. ed. (New Haven, 1971), 19-53; Alan Axelrod, ed., *The Colonial Revival in America* (New York, 1985), 19-21; Richard Guy Wilson, "The Early Work of Charles F. McKim: Country House Commissions," *Winterthur Portfolio* 14 (Autumn 1979), 248-252, 257-259. For additional discussion of this issue, see William B. Rhoads, "The Discovery of America's Architectural Past," and Mary N. Woods, "History in the Early American Architectural Journals," both in this volume. Isham praised Snell's work as "the last decent treatment accorded to a Georgian work—or perhaps the first!" (Isham 1931, 5).

13. Norman Morrison Isham and Albert F. Brown, *Early Rhode Island Houses: An Historical and Architectural Study* (Providence, 1895).

14. Brown spent his brief working life as a draftsman in the Providence architectural offices of Stone, Carpenter, and Wilson, where Isham also began his career. Brown's obituary credits him with all the structural drawings in the Rhode Island and Connecticut books, but they are indistinguishable from those in Isham's later books (Sons of the American Revolution Rhode Island Society, *Memorials of Compatriots Who Died During the Year 1909-1910* [Providence, 1910], 4-5). In any event, I assume Isham to be the intellectual author of the men's coauthored works on Rhode Island and Connecticut houses.

15. Isham acknowledged his antiquarian sources in a 1931 lecture to the Walpole Society. In his eyes, the forerunners of his own generation's work included Snell, for his work on the Redwood Library; the topographical antiquarians John W. Barber, Edwin Whitefield, and Edwin R. Lambert; Richard Upjohn, for his 1869 paper on American colonial architecture; Arthur Little, for his book *Early New England Interiors: Sketches in Salem, Marblehead, Portsmouth and Kittery* (Boston, 1878); A. B. Bibb, for two articles on Virginia architecture in the *American Architect*; and Joseph Everett Chandler, for an 1889 collection of photographs of Chesapeake colonial architecture (Isham 1931, 4-19). I am grateful to Charles Hosmer for calling this essay to my attention.

16. The exceptions were a book on ancient Greek architecture and, in later years, monographs on two Rhode Island churches and an unfinished book on early nineteenth-century Providence architect John Holden Greene (Norman Morrison Isham, *The Homeric Palace* [Providence, 1898]; "Norman M. Isham Dead in Wickford," *Providence Journal*, 2 January 1943, 1, 8).

17. Norman Morrison Isham, *Early American*

Houses: The Seventeenth Century (1928; repr. Watkins Glen, N.Y., 1968), 3.

18. Collins 1965, 72-73. Although the architect John Hubbard Sturgis had made measured drawings of Boston's colonial Hancock house before its demolition in 1863, colonial revival architects before Isham preferred photographs and sketches to measured drawings, in keeping with the visual emphasis of their allegiance to the colonial (Margaret Henderson Floyd, "Measured Drawings of the Hancock House by John Hubbard Sturgis: A Legacy to the Colonial Revival," in *Architecture in Colonial Massachusetts*, ed. Abbott Lowell Cummings [Boston, 1979], 87-111; see Isham 1931, 17, 19).

19. Ralph Nevill, *Old Cottages and Domestic Architecture in South-West Surrey and Notes on the Early History of the Division* (1889; 2d ed. Guildford, 1891).

20. Irving W. Lyon to Molly L. Albree, 6 December 1894; Lyon to Chester B. Albree, 26 December 1894, Lyon papers, 78x99.1-45, Winterthur Museum. Lyon encouraged Isham, but wrote privately that he expected his book to "knock Isham & Brown into pie." This keen sense of competition prompted the Lyon family to decline Isham's offer to complete the book after its author's death (Lyon to Molly L. Albree, 19 January 1896, Lyon papers; Isham 1931, 12-13). The manuscript survives, but it has never been published or studied. Lyon's furniture book was *The Colonial Furniture of New England: A Study of the Domestic Furniture in Use in the Seventeenth and Eighteenth Centuries* (Boston and New York, 1891).

21. Norman M. Isham, *A Glossary of Colonial Architectural Terms* (1939; repr. Watkins Glen, N.Y., 1976).

22. Elizabeth Stillinger, *The Antiquers: The Lives and Careers, the Deals, the Finds, the Collections of the Men and Women Who Were Responsible for the Changing Taste in American Antiques, 1850-1930* (New York, 1980), 167-169.

23. "Norman M. Isham Dead," *Providence Journal*, 8.

24. For example, Lyon was outraged that he was denied admission to Maryland's Whitehall by "the boorish proprietor—a common farmer," and he warned his son, who was conducting field research for him in Europe, to "be careful about seeking entrance into farmers houses & cottages &c.—learn from well-informed natives whether such visits are acceptable, & just how to proceed—as the customs of every country varies, & a foreigner who cannot use idioms & easy expressions is at a disadvantage— so be careful to secure full & free permission to enter, & then use great courtesy & tact so as not to be suspected, or doubted, or maltreated. You know in many countries of Europe it is not allowed, or dangerous, to be seen writing & making notes in public" (Lyon to Irving Phillips Lyon, 9 June 1895, 23 June 1895, Lyon papers).

25. Henry Chapman Mercer, *Ancient Carpenters' Tools, Together with Lumbermen's, Joiners' and Cabinet Makers' Tools in Use in the Eighteenth Century* (1929; 5th ed. Doylestown, Pa., 1975); Henry Chapman Mercer, *The Origin of Log Houses in the United States* (1926; repr. Doylestown, Pa., 1967).

26. Henry Chapman Mercer, *The Dating of Old Houses* (New Hope, Pa., 1923).

27. Helen H. Gemmell, *The Mercer Mile: The Story of Dr. Henry Chapman Mercer and His Concrete Buildings* (Doylestown, Pa., 1972), 7.

28. Rudolph Hommel, quoted in Mercer 1975, x.

29. Joseph E. Sandford, *Henry Chapman Mercer, A Study* (Doylestown, Pa., 1966), 4-5, 8.

30. Gemmell 1972, 23.

31. On scientism, see Robert H. Wiebe, *The Search for Order 1877-1920* (New York, 1967), 115-121; Richard Guy Wilson, "The Great Civilization," in Richard Guy Wilson, Dianne H. Pilgrim, and Richard N. Murray, *The American Renaissance* (New York, 1979), 57-58.

32. Horace S. Fuller, "Irving Whitall Lyon, M.D., of Hartford," in *Proceedings of the Connecticut Medical Society 1896* (Bridgeport, Conn., 1896), 329-330; Isham 1931, 11-12.

33. Isham and Brown 1895, 5-6. For Isham, the use of measured drawings distinguished "the scientific idea" of the Walpole Society from the "old-fashioned" sketches, perspective drawings, and photographs of the colonial revivalists (Isham 1931, 17, 21).

34. Isham and Brown 1895, 11, 13, 15.

35. Isham 1931, 11. Compare, for example, Isham's periodization of early New England vernacular building with Mercer's belief that traditional woodworking tools "*have remained unchanged in construction since Roman times. . . . In these specimens, the past has survived into the present.*" As a result, examples recently made were nevertheless "the master-tools of ancient and extinct peoples" (Mercer, *Ancient Carpenters' Tools*, xi-xii; his italics).

36. Lewis H. Morgan, *Houses and House-Life of the American Aborigines* (1881; repr. Chicago, 1965).

37. Ephraim G. Squier and E. H. Davis, *Ancient Monuments of the Mississippi Valley: Comprising the Results of Extensive Original Surveys and Explorations* (Washington, 1848).

38. Isham and Brown 1895, 16-18; Isham and Brown, *Early Connecticut Houses: An Historical and Architectural Study* (1900; repr. New York, 1965), 6-11.

39. Morgan 1881, 42-45.

40. Morgan 1881, xxiii-xxiv.

41. John Frederick Kelly, *Early Domestic Architecture of Connecticut* (New Haven, 1924); John Frederick Kelly, *Early Connecticut Meetinghouses: Being an Account of the Church Edifices Built Before 1830 . . .* (New York, 1948); Antoinette Forrester Downing, *Early Homes of Rhode Island* (Richmond, Va., 1937). Walpole Society member George Dudley Seymour wrote of Kelly in 1935 that "Isham is very keen about him because Kelly pays attention to structural details rather more than to form [appearance]" (George Dudley Seymour papers, Group no. 442, Topical files, ser. V, box 105, doc. 105/1507, Yale University Manuscripts and Archives).

42. Dell Upton, "New Views of the Virginia Landscape," *Virginia Magazine of History and Biography*

96 (October 1988), 414–419.

43. Fiske Kimball, *Domestic Architecture of the American Colonies and of the Early Republic* (1922; repr. New York, 1966). For more on Kimball, see Lauren Weiss Bricker's article, "The Writings of Fiske Kimball: A Synthesis of Architectural History and Practice," in this volume.

44. In this, Kimball followed architect C. F. Innocent's *The Development of English Building Construction* (Cambridge, England, 1916) and Sidney O. Addy's ethnographic study *The Evolution of the English House* (London, 1898).

45. Kimball 1966, 16, 3.

46. Kimball 1966, 53.

47. Kimball 1966, 50.

48. Fred B. Kniffen, "Louisiana House Types," *Annals of the Association of American Geographers* 26 (December 1936), 179–193 (quote on 192).

49. Fred B. Kniffen, "Folk Housing: Key to Diffusion," *Annals of the Association of American Geographers* 55 (December 1965), 549–577, reprinted in Dell Upton and John Michael Vlach, eds., *Common Places: Readings in American Vernacular Architecture* (Athens, Ga., 1986), 3–26. The I house is named in Kniffen 1936, 185–186.

50. I am not suggesting that geographers and folklorists borrowed the distinction from Kimball, but that, like him, they borrowed from European ethnography.

51. For a pioneering example of the geographical use of structural systems, see Fred B. Kniffen and Henry Glassie, "Building in Wood in the Eastern United States: A Time-Place Perspective," *Geographical Review* 56 (January 1966), 40–66, reprinted in Upton and Vlach 1986, 159–181.

52. For efforts to separate folk from popular and academic material culture, see Henry Glassie, *Pattern in the Material Folk Culture of the Eastern United States* (Philadelphia, 1968), 1–17; for a comparable differentiation of primitive, vernacular, and high-style architecture, see Amos Rapoport, *House Form and Culture* (Englewood Cliffs, N.J., 1969), 1–17.

53. John A. Kouwenhoven, *The Arts in Modern American Civilization*, repr. ed. of *Made in America* (New York, 1967), 13–14 (quote on 14); Sigfried Giedion, *Mechanization Takes Command: A Contribution to Anonymous History* (repr. New York, 1969), 3–4.

54. J. B. Jackson, *The Necessity for Ruins and Other Topics* (Amherst, Mass., 1980), 1–18.

55. See J. B. Jackson, "The Westward-Moving House" (1953), reprinted in *Landscapes: Selected Writings of J. B. Jackson*, ed. Ervin H. Zube (Amherst, Mass., 1970), 10–42; J. B. Jackson, *Discovering the Vernacular Landscape* (New Haven, 1984), 83–89.

56. Rapoport 1969, 46–58.

57. Henry Glassie, *Folk Housing in Middle Virginia: A Structural Analysis of Historic Artifacts* (Knoxville, 1975).

58. This passage is not intended as a survey of current literature. For those, see Dell Upton, "Ordinary Buildings: A Bibliographical Essay on American Vernacular Architecture," *American Studies International* 19 (Winter 1981), 57–75; Upton, "The Power of Things: Recent Studies in American Vernacular Architecture," in *Material Culture: A Research Guide*, ed. Thomas J. Schlereth (Lawrence, Kans., 1985), 57–78; and Upton 1988, 403–470.

59. Upton 1988, 442–444.

60. The Great Basin—usually described as the Mormon cultural region—was settled from the Midwest and is characterized by a similar mixture of British and Scandinavian populations and vernacular building types. See Donald W. Meinig, "The Mormon Culture Region: Strategies and Patterns in the Geography of the American West, 1847–1964," *Annals of the Association of American Geographers* 55 (June 1965), 191–220.

61. Chester Liebs, *Main Street to Miracle Mile: American Roadside Architecture* (Boston, 1985).

62. Isham 1976, 61.

63. I am of course thinking of such works as Richard Goldthwaite's *The Building of Renaissance Florence: An Economic and Social History* (Baltimore, 1980) and Robert C. Twombly's "Saving the Family: Middle Class Attraction to Wright's Prairie Houses," *American Quarterly* 27 (1975), 57–72.

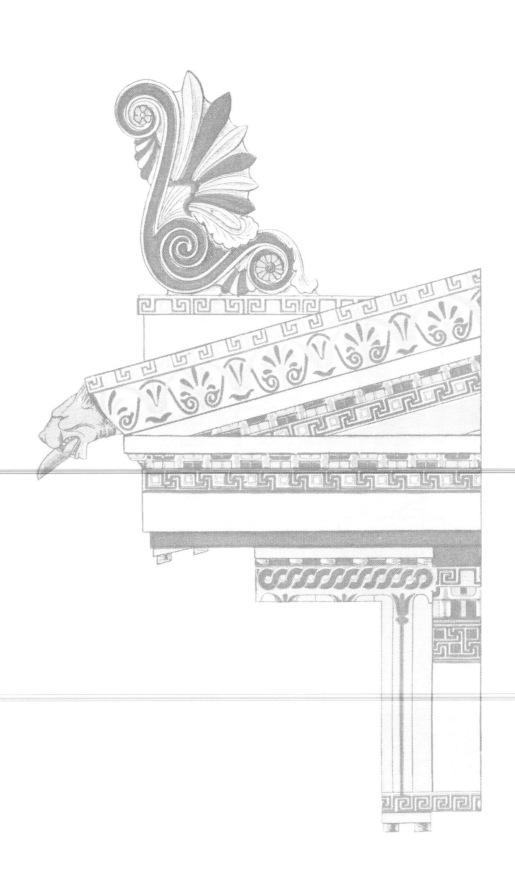

LAUREN WEISS BRICKER

[University of California, Santa Barbara]

The Writings of Fiske Kimball:

A Synthesis of Architectural History and Practice

In 1946, Fiske Kimball's article "Rococo and Romanticism" appeared in the volume *To Doctor R.*, published in honor of the seventieth birthday of the collector Dr. A. S. W. Rosenbach.[1] Kimball's essay was inspired by Nikolaus Pevsner's critical review of Kimball's volume *The Creation of the Rococo* (1943),[2] published anonymously in the *Times Literary Supplement*.[3] Pevsner suggests that Kimball's exphasis on the rococo, as a vocabulary of the eighteenth-century French interior, neglects the related contemporary developments in spatial form and the English picturesque garden, "which held the seeds of English Romanticism."[4] For Pevsner, Kimball's seeming insensitivity to two predilections of German scholarship—spatial form as the dominant stylistic determinant and the notion of a zeitgeist whether labeled "rococo" or "romanticism"—deprives "his thesis of that universal applicability which is the ultimate test of any historian's hypothesis of style."[5]

In response, Kimball suggests that a difference of methodology separates Pevsner's approach from his own: do we "apply the term Rococo to the sum of spontaneous European artistic movements of the earlier 18th century. . . . Or do we apply it as it was originally applied—to the French style created in decoration primarily by Lepautre and Pineau [and] in painting by Watteau?"[6] Kimball's preference for the latter method led him to pursue what he characterized by the early 1940s as his "consciously old-fashioned" study of written and graphic documents to establish "the sequence of events and identify the personalities individually concerned" with the development of the rococo.[7] Kimball had successfully applied this historical method since the publication of *Thomas Jefferson, Architect* (1916).[8] The rational basis of the method was founded on his own Beaux-Arts architectural training. His practice, encompassing independent commissions (principally early in his career), restorations of historic structures and gardens, and the installation of the period rooms of the Pennsylvania Museum (later the Philadelphia Museum of Art) was traditional in imagery and in its dependence on historic precedent.

Kimball was a product of the Boston suburbs, born in West Newton in 1888 and raised in Milton. He and his sister Theodora Kimball Hubbard, who became an authority on American landscape architecture and city planning, were brought up in a household that nurtured the intellectual and aesthetic values associated with the New England landscape.[9] Fiske Kimball lovingly described his father as "an enthusiast of that Nature whose prophets were Emerson and Darwin, . . . who had visited and talked with the great figures of the flowering of New England."[10] Ancestral ties and family property cushioned a fundamentally middle-class upbringing.

Kimball received his professional architectural training at Harvard University (B.A. 1909, M. Arch. 1912). At Harvard, architectural history was emphasized to the point where, according to Kimball, the students "tended to graduate into teaching, writing and editing rather than practice."[11] Kimball credited the architectural history courses taught by the program's founder Herbert Langford Warren with providing "almost the only instruction that gave a broad view of the history of culture,"[12] though his critical assessment was limited to structural expression, "with no real analysis of spatial or plastic form."[13] Under Warren's leadership, Harvard's architecture program cautiously espoused the teaching methods of the Ecole des Beaux-Arts. In American schools of architecture, the symbolic endorsement of the Ecole was an appointment to the faculty of one of its graduates (frequently a French native). At Harvard this did not take place until 1910, when E.J.A. Duquesne, a Prix de Rome winner, joined the faculty; before that time the advanced design work was conducted by the Massachusetts Institute of Technology's Désiré Despradelle.[14]

The architecture students were required to take courses in the philosophy of the fine arts and aesthetics taught by George Santayana. In his volume *The Sense of Beauty* (1896), Santayana attempts to reconcile recent investigations in the psychology of perception with his own interest in the "origin and conditions of [aesthetic judgments]."[15]

Kimball also took classes in the Architecture Department from Denman Waldo Ross, author of *A Theory of Pure Design: Harmony, Balance, Rhythm* (1907).[16] Ross' analysis of works of art based on abstract principles was intended to develop a sensitivity to beauty and the power of the imagination. An avid collector of oriental art and a trustee of the Museum of Fine Arts, Boston, Ross kept selections from his collections on permanent display in the Architecture Department's Robinson Hall. In later years, Kimball found it strange that Ross was not able to see the contemporary movements of cubism and fauvism as a

"vindication of his faith in pure design."[17]

While Kimball was a graduate student he read Charles Langlois and Charles Seignobos' *Introduction to the Study of History* (1899, trans. 1908).[18] Langlois proposed a historical method based on the use of original documents and manuscripts. For Kimball, the book was something of a revelation: "all my intellectual instincts and ambitions were sharpened."[19]

Kimball's study of Thomas Jefferson as an architect (begun c. 1912) provided his first opportunity to apply Langlois' method. The existing literature on Jefferson's architecture generally limited his works to Monticello and the University of Virginia. Controversy over the ownership of Monticello, its current state of preservation, and the applicability of its design to new work made Jefferson's residence the subject of numerous articles in popular and professional architectural periodicals. The historian Herbert B. Adams published a series of Jefferson drawings in his volume, *Thomas Jefferson and the University of Virginia* (1888), a work that coincided with a movement among many universities to adapt Jefferson's education innovations as well as the plan of his campus.[20] In 1913, William Alexander Lambeth and Warren H. Manning published their *Thomas Jefferson as an Architect and a Designer of Landscapes*.[21] Unfortunately, the authors introduced little new graphic and written documentation to support Jefferson's status as an architectural practitioner; as a result, the work was vulnerable to the criticism of the restoration architect-historian Norman M. Isham, whose review of the volume expressed the professional's bias against the dilettante architect.[22]

In contrast with his contemporaries, Kimball's interest in Jefferson had begun with his examination of the published documentation. In particular, he was fascinated by Jefferson's perception of the Virginia Capitol as a project providing "a favorable opportunity of introducing . . . an example of architecture in the classic style of antiquity."[23] By this time, Kimball had been engaged by George H. Chase, editor of the *Harpers' Fine Arts Series* and professor of fine arts, Harvard, to write *A History of Architecture* for the series. Kim-

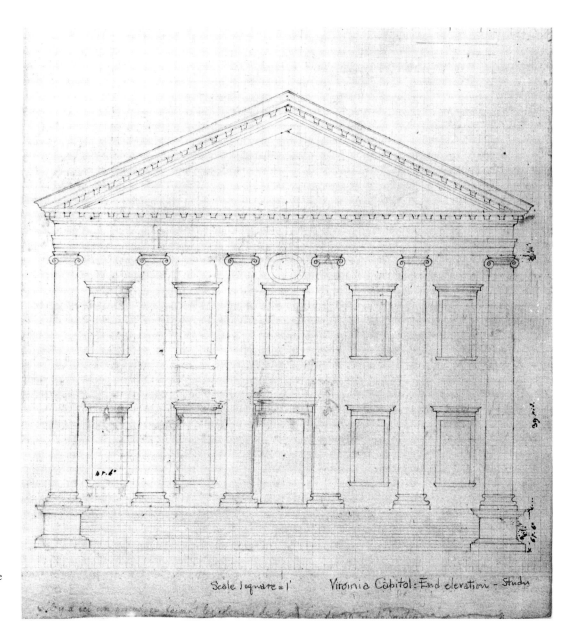

1. Thomas Jefferson, *Virginia Capitol*, Richmond, c. 1785. Preliminary study for entrance elevation

Jefferson Papers, Coolidge Collection, Massachusetts Historical Society, Boston

ball asked his colleague George H. Edgell to write the medieval sections of the volume; their work was published in 1918.[24] During this period Kimball found time to review scholarly and popular works on European and American architecture and history for the *Dial*.[25] These endeavors compelled him to place historic American architecture within the context of contemporary European developments. This attitude led Kimball to conclude that Jefferson's design for the Capitol, modeled on the Roman Maison Carrée, predated the major European works of the neoclassic movement (fig. 1). The support of graphic documentation of the project, coupled with Jefferson's published writings, would enable Kimball to confirm that the authorship of this American work was conceptually innovative rather than derivative of European precedent. This opportunity was presented by his discovery in 1914 of the Thomas Jefferson Coolidge Collection of Jefferson's architectural drawings housed at the Massachusetts Historical Society. By the end of the year, Kimball had produced articles on the Virginia Capitol and Monticello; he also had made final arrangements for the Jefferson monograph.[26]

In these publications, Kimball developed a historical method that merged his "scientific" investigation of the material remains of structures—an approach he and his American peers popularly associated with the field of archaeology—with a dependence on primary documents, as stressed by Langlois, and the study of architectural drawings as primary documents, indicators of architectural intent, and aesthetic objects. Kimball's utilization of historic architectural drawings had limited precedent in American architectural history. More frequently, new measured drawings were used for study and illustrative purposes, and these focused on decorative elements of buildings—doorways, windows, and mantel details. The Jefferson drawings, dating to 1769, proved to be an invaluable resource for knowledge of architectural design and practice from the mid-eighteenth century. Kimball dated the majority of the drawings, based on an examination he and his wife Marie Goebel Kimball made of watermarks and drawing technique. Their analyses employed methods familiar to specialists of the representative arts.[27]

As a trained practitioner Kimball might have shared the professional's skepticism about Jefferson's achievements as an amateur architect. This view was tempered, however, by an early appraisal of architectural literature, which made him aware of the potent influence of architectural writing and the dilettante architect on eighteenth- and early nineteenth-century architectural practice:

[With] the transference of the arts from the realm of tradition to that of reason, we see the amateur and the literary man boldly uttering their criticism, . . . converting some architects to their credos at a stroke while they permanently influence the current of architectural thought.[28]

Kimball was acutely aware of the division between his approach to architectural history and that of his fellow architect-historians. In submitting his article on the

Virginia Capitol to Charles H. Whitaker, editor of the *Journal of the American Institute of Architects*, Kimball noted:

I should be particularly glad if the paper could appear in the Institute journal rather than elsewhere, for I have hoped that by the method employed in it we might encourage more accurate and fundamental studies of our early monuments to replace the loose jumble of tradition and probability which fills too much of the writing on the subject.[29]

During the course of his Jefferson research, Kimball discovered untapped treasures of architectural drawings, correspondence, and other materials related to early American architecture in state and local historical societies and private collections. With the assistance of the first Sachs Fellowship in the Fine Arts offered by Harvard, Kimball was able to spend a year (1916–1917) gathering material for what he projected as a "fundamental history of American architecture during its most interesting and important period, the first half-century of the Republic."[30] Rather than incorporating his findings in a single volume, Kimball published a multipart article on "The Competition for the Federal Buildings" (coauthored with Wells Bennett) in the *Journal of the American Institute of Architects* and several pieces on Benjamin Henry Latrobe, also in professional periodicals (fig. 2). He was commissioned by the Essex Institute of Salem, Massachusetts, to produce a monograph on Samuel McIntire utilizing their collection of his drawings: *Mr. Samuel McIntire, Carver: The Architect of Salem.*[31]

In 1917, Kimball completed the "American Architecture" chapter for the projected *History of Architecture*. Kimball divided the early developments of American architecture between the Colonial and National periods, based on social, cultural, and economic factors rather than the stylistic criteria that many of his contemporaries continued to use. He discussed the question of periodization of American architecture with the medieval art historian, Arthur Kingsley Porter, explaining to Porter that he sought "a division into periods that . . . should be tenable in as large a field as possible. Thus in the case of the fine arts it should be tenable in all the arts."[32] Kim-

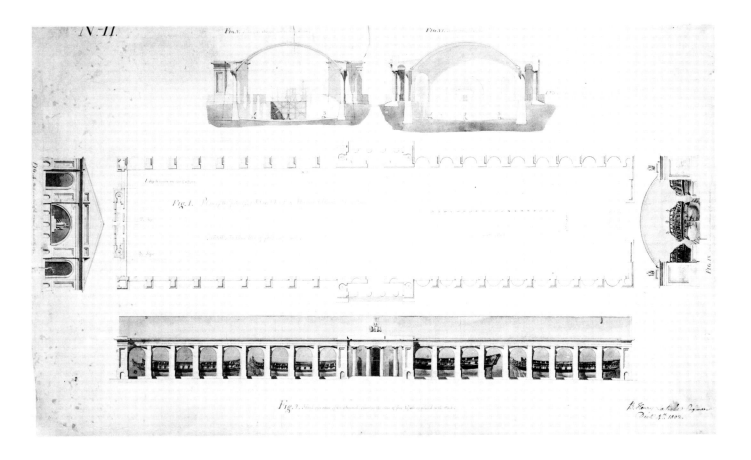

2. Benjamin Henry Latrobe, *Proposed Storage Drydock for the United States Navy*, Washington, 4 December 1802. Preliminary study of exterior elevations, floor plan, and cross sections
Library of Congress, Washington, D.C.

ball applied a consistent approach in his presentation of European architecture in the volume, utilizing the colorless term "post-Renaissance" to cover the period extending from c. 1550 to c. 1750. Elsewhere in the volume, he cautioned the reader to see the historic periods as linked by subtle transitions to epochs rather than rigidly isolated by their distinguishing features. In a letter to Porter (May 1918), Kimball credits his presentation of the early Renaissance, involving "neither a sharp interruption of the developments of the Middle Ages nor a negation of originality or modernity" to the writings of the European historians Hans Tietze and Carl Neumann.[33]

Throughout this fertile literary period, Kimball was establishing himself as an educator, administrator, and architect. He held an academic post at the University of Illinois in 1912–1913, when he met and married Marie Goebel. This was followed by a stint at the University of Michigan, first in the School of Architecture and later in the

Department of Fine Arts.[34] In 1919, Kimball was appointed professor of art and architecture and head of the new McIntire School of Fine Arts at the University of Virginia. The program marked the realization of Jefferson's 1814 proposal for a department of fine arts, embracing civil architecture, garden design, painting, sculpture, and the theory of music, with the ensemble of buildings framing the Lawn intended to function "as specimens for the architectural lecturer."[35]

The McIntire School was one component of the campus development endorsed by university president Edwin A. Alderman.[36] Alderman's program entailed an energetic building campaign for which Kimball supervised the construction of the Memorial Gymnasium (1920–1923) and the McIntire Amphitheater (1920–1921), among other buildings (figs. 3, 4).[37] Each project presented Kimball and his small staff with the challenge of adapting new works to the established Jeffersonian vocabulary. Siting

3. Fiske Kimball, John Kevan Peebles, Walter D. Blair, R. E. Lee Taylor, W. A. Lambeth, Architectural Commission, *Memorial Gymnasium*, University of Virginia, Charlottesville, 1921–1923
Prints Collection, Special Collections Department, University Archives, University of Virginia Library

4. Fiske Kimball, *Paul Goodloe McIntyre Amphitheatre*, University of Virginia, Charlottesville, 1919–1921
Presentation drawing by S. J. Makielski. From *Corks & Curls* 34 (1921), 212.

often proved the greater challenge, since new structures needed to fit into the formal, axial plan and also respond to shifts of grade characteristic of local topography.

Kimball was made Samuel F. B. Morse Professor of the Literature of the Arts of Design at New York University in 1923.[38] The position had been established in 1832, but had remained dormant since the late nineteenth century.[39] It was revived under

5. *Room from Haverhill,*
Massachusetts, c. 1805. Parlor,
American Wing, Metropolitan
Museum of Art, photographed
October 1924
Metropolitan Museum of Art, Rogers
Fund, 1912 (12.121)

6. Ogden Codman, Jr.,
Codman Residence, New
York, 1915
Philadelphia Museum of Art Archives

the joint patronage of the Altman Foundation, headed by Col. Michael Friedsam, and the Art-in-Trades Club, an organization of design professionals led by W. S. Coffin of the furniture department store W. & J. Sloane & Co. Under Kimball's leadership, the newly conceived department encompassed three programs: professional instruction for the decorator; a combined college and art school series of courses taught in collaboration with the National Academy of Design; and a program in the history and criticism of fine and applied arts taught by scholars at the Metropolitan Museum of Art and the university's Washington Square campus.[40] The synthetic character of the department is revealed in the publication, *The House Beautiful Furnishing Annual, 1926,* to which Kimball and other instructors contributed articles and illustrative materials.[41] Kimball provided the introduction and assistance in gathering the images, which reflected contemporary interpretations of traditional architecture and furniture design, for example, the room from the Eagle House, Haverhill, Massachusetts, installed in the newly opened American Wing at the Metropolitan Museum, and a dining room designed by Ogden Codman (figs. 5, 6).

In 1924, Kimball was made university architect at New York University, with McKim, Mead, and White as consulting architects.[42] Among their responsibilities was to establish guidelines for the future development of the University Heights campus on Fordham Heights, the Bronx. The architects proposed an amplification of the original campus plan and buildings (1894–c. 1901) designed by McKim, Mead, and White (fig. 7). A central domed library would preside between the original three-part ensemble to the west with a similar arrangement to the east. To the north, the architects projected a new graduate school, distinguished by a tower that Kimball suggested would incorporate elements of the tower and colonnade from McKim, Mead, and White's Madison Square Garden, New York City, then facing imminent demolition (1887–1891; demolished 1925). While reflective of contemporary practice, Kimball's proposal was an act of preservation.

7. McKim, Mead and White Architects; Fiske Kimball, University Architect, *View of Campus, New York University*, 1924. Project for University Heights campus extension, Bronx, New York
Courtesy of the New-York Historical Society, New York City

At the time Kimball was chairman of the American Institute of Architects' Committee on Historic Monuments and Scenic Beauties. In this capacity, he penned a resolution to salvage the tower. Ultimately the only portion of the building that Kimball was able to retain was Augustus Saint-Gaudens' free-standing sculpture of Diana, which had surmounted the structure; it was given to the Pennsylvania Museum in 1933.[43]

The work of McKim, Mead, and White evidently had an impact on Kimball's own practice in New York (and previously in Charlottesville). Kimball discussed their larger role in American architecture in his critical writing of the 1920s, which included the 1928 volume *American Architecture*.[44] He presented the view that the late nineteenth- and early twentieth-century work of the firm furthered the tradition of a "classic unity of form" established by Jefferson and other figures of the Republican-Federal period. As David Brownlee has

recently noted in his study of Fairmount Parkway and the Philadelphia Museum of Art building, Kimball utilized the language of the critic Roger Fry in equating the classical designs of McKim, Mead, and White with contemporary works by Cézanne as a shared rejection of previous "realistic movements" in favor of "a purely abstract art of form and color."[45]

Throughout the 1920s, Kimball continued to pursue his examination of historic American architecture. His *Domestic Architecture of the American Colonies and of the Early Republic* appeared in 1922.[46] Since the late nineteenth century, the field of American architectural history had been dominated by local and regional studies of residential architecture. Despite the great value of many of these works, especially those publications intended as source material for new design, Kimball believed that "the general development of domestic architecture had not yet been adequately handled."[47] In *Domestic Architecture* he

8. *The Puritans*, from one of the *Chronicles of America Photoplays*, c. 1923. English wigwams

Beginning in the late 1910s and especially throughout the 1920s, publications on American history included studies of achievements in the fine and applied arts. Among these scholarly efforts was the *Dictionary of American Biography* (DAB), initiated by the American Council of Learned Societies in 1922 and published between 1928 and 1936, with later supplements.[50] Historian Allan Nevins commented on the timing of the enterprise:

Probably not until recent years have we had in America either the collections of material brought to the surface by numerous biographers, genealogists, historians, historical societies, publications of State and national archives—or the expert scholarship which is necessary to lift such work to the requisite standard.[51]

The DAB included entries on architects and planners of the recent and distant past. Allen Johnson, the original editor of the DAB, asked Kimball to furnish a list of architects to be included.[52] Kimball's contributions to the series included the biographies of Pierre Charles L'Enfant, Benjamin Henry Latrobe, and Bertram Grosvenor Goodhue.

During this period, publications on architecture, city planning, and the decorative arts were included in multivolume histories of America. Yale University Press, under the leadership of George Parmly Day, was particularly active in its attempts to visualize American history. In addition to the *Chronicles of America* (1918–1921), edited by Allen Johnson and Allan Nevins, and the *Pageant of America* (1926), edited by Ralph H. Gabriel, Yale established the Chronicles of America Picture Corporation in c. 1921.[53] This commercial venture was intended to develop "educational photoplays" based on the press' published series. To this end, Kimball was engaged as "advisor of the Colonial sets" (1923–1924). He was sufficiently impressed with the authenticity of the sets that he reproduced a scene from "The Puritans" as an illustration of English wigwams in his *American Architecture* (fig. 8).

had an opportunity to present the ideas and methodology formulated in the Jefferson volume to a much wider audience. As the architectural historian Donald Millar noted in his review of the work, Kimball's study was a "summary of all available information, structural and documentary" on the subject.[48] Kimball sought to retain, through language and imagery, the aesthetic appeal of his subject for the architectural practitioner. Reviews of the book attest to its attraction for the architect and historian. The reviewer for the professional periodical *Architecture* noted, "Professor Kimball, himself a trained architect, set out to write first a book of value to the professional; and he has succeeded in making it one that every architect should be grateful for."[49] As one would anticipate of the trained architect, Kimball kept the presence of architectural elements preeminent in his assessment of the "evolution" of particular styles. However, his formal observations were set in the context of current research on the social, economic, and cultural factors of the period. As a result, the book also enjoyed popularity among American cultural historians.

The visualization of America's past was certainly one factor stimulating John D. Rockefeller, Jr., to undertake the restoration of Colonial Williamsburg beginning in 1927 (fig. 9). According to W.A.R. Goodwin, rector of Bruton Parish, Williamsburg, Rockefeller saw the project as a means of presenting "a picture which, while not absolutely a reproduction, will be representative of the past . . . [and will] create a center which will foster the spirit of patriotism."[54] Kimball was appointed to the Advisory Committee of Architects for the restoration in 1928. His scholarly knowledge of historic American architecture, coupled with his own experience as a restoration architect (which had begun with the restoration of Monticello in the early 1920s) established him as a leading figure in the field of historic preservation.

In a letter to Laurence Vail Coleman of the American Association of Museums (June 1933), Kimball rehearsed his views on preservation:

In a precious building the dominant thought, no doubt, should be preservation—*and the greatest conservatism should be exercised as to changing anything, even if this is believed to be changing it back the way it is supposedly formerly to have been. I think there should be general agreement that at least any work which preserves the classical tradition, even down to the Confederate War should be undisturbed.*[55]

To a considerable extent, Kimball's attitude toward the restoration of Colonial Williamsburg had been influenced by his experience with the restoration of the Fairmount Park houses in Philadelphia. Kimball's appointment as director of the Pennsylvania Museum in 1925[56] included as his residence Lemon Hill (1798), a country house located in Fairmount Park (fig. 10). The house was one of several eighteenth- and early nineteenth-century park houses such as Mount Pleasant (1761), many of which remained on their original sites. In 1926, Kimball inaugurated a program to restore, furnish, and landscape a selection of houses that would be open to the public;[57] he called the project the "Chain of Colonial Houses," borrowing a concept from the writer-collector Wallace Nutting.[58]

Kimball's program for the restoration of the park houses was an important episode in the "historic house movement" in America. Founded in the tradition of the late nineteenth-century European outdoor museum, the movement merged an inter-est in the preservation of historic houses (and other building types) with a desire to provide sympathetic settings for mobile works of art. The development of the American practice of preserving historic

9. *Governor's Palace Garden*, Colonial Williamsburg. View of tulip beds looking southeast

Photograph courtesy of the Colonial Williamsburg Foundation, Williamsburg, Virginia

10. *Lemon Hill*, Fairmount Park, Philadelphia, 1798; restored by Fiske Kimball, 1925. View of north exterior elevation

Philadelphia Museum of Art Archives

residences and furnishing them with objects of the period was documented by Laurence Vail Coleman in *Historic House Museums* (1933).[59]

In contrast with other historic houses that survived in isolation from their contemporary settings, the Fairmount Park houses were located within a single homogenous environment whose significance had been recognized since the nineteenth century. The park's historic importance was a factor in its promotion by the Fairmount Park commissioners as the site for the Centennial exhibition of 1876. The houses had also been the subject of painters and graphic artists since the early nineteenth century.[60]

In the 1920s, there was a renewed interest in the park houses and the concept of Fairmount Park as a museum environment. Administrators of museums of natural science, history, and the fine arts sought an environment for combining the dual activities of education and outdoor recreation.[61] Their solution was the "outdoor museum," in all its interpretations. Among the many applications of the concept was a district in which historic structures would be preserved as aesthetic and historic documents of civilization.[62] Repeatedly, in publications addressed to a professional and a popular museum-going audience, this "outdoor museum" concept was credited to museums of nineteenth-century northern Europe, particularly Scandinavia. Skansen, founded by Artur Hazelius, was the most frequently cited source for the phenomenon.[63] At its location in Stockholm, historic and reconstructed buildings representing the building traditions of Sweden were collected. Costumed guides greeted the museum's visitors as they experienced structures dating from the medieval period through the eighteenth century. In American publications of the 1910s, Skansen was described as a "living illustration of the culture-history of Sweden"[64] that "perpetuates the houses of by-gone days with all they contained."[65]

The restoration of the park houses constituted one phase of Kimball's program at the Pennsylvania Museum (fig. 11).[66] His principal task was to fill the classical shell of the new museum building, designed by Borie, Trumbauer, and Zantzinger. Kimball's scheme was based on European precedent; he proposed to install the Kaiser-Friedrich Museum of Berlin above the Victoria and Albert Museum of London (figs. 12, 13).[67]

The first floor was designed to house the study collections, with works grouped by

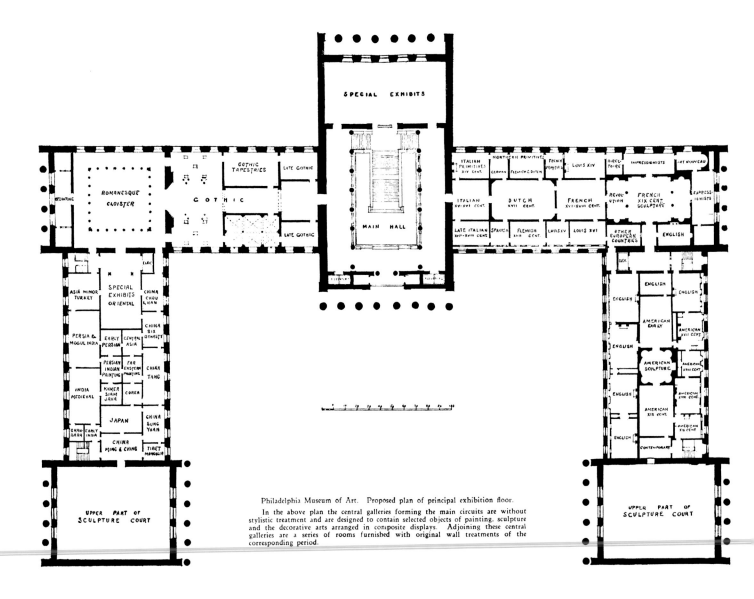

Philadelphia Museum of Art. Proposed plan of principal exhibition floor.

In the above plan the central galleries forming the main circuits are without stylistic treatment and are designed to contain selected objects of painting, sculpture and the decorative arts arranged in composite displays. Adjoining these central galleries are a series of rooms furnished with original wall treatments of the corresponding period.

material and technique to present an "encyclopedic view" of world art. This installation continued a tradition established at Memorial Hall, parent to the present Philadelphia Museum of Art, which drew its inspiration from the Victoria and Albert model. In the 1920s the compelling reason for the inclusion of the study collections was the demand to improve the quality of American industrial design and applied arts and the view that the art museum could play a vital role in that effort.[68]

On the second or principal floor, Kimball projected a series of galleries flanked by period rooms, where works of painting, sculpture, and the decorative arts of consistent time and location would be arranged according to evolutionary se-

quence. Period ensembles of European, American, and Far Eastern furniture and architectural elements had been installed in Memorial Hall and other American museums.[69] However, Kimball credited the idea of the "culture-history" museum of northern Europe of the late nineteenth century as inspiring the division of the museum into historic periods, and he attributed the idea of the composite installation to Wilhelm von Bode of the Kaiser-Friedrich Museum.[70]

In order to complete the principal floor scheme, Kimball and his staff waged a remarkable campaign from 1927 to about 1931 to acquire historic interiors of independent artistic merit that were suitable as sympathetic backgrounds for the displays. The

12. Fiske Kimball, *Pennsylvania (now Philadelphia) Museum of Art*, Philadelphia, c. 1927. First-floor plan
Philadelphia Museum of Art

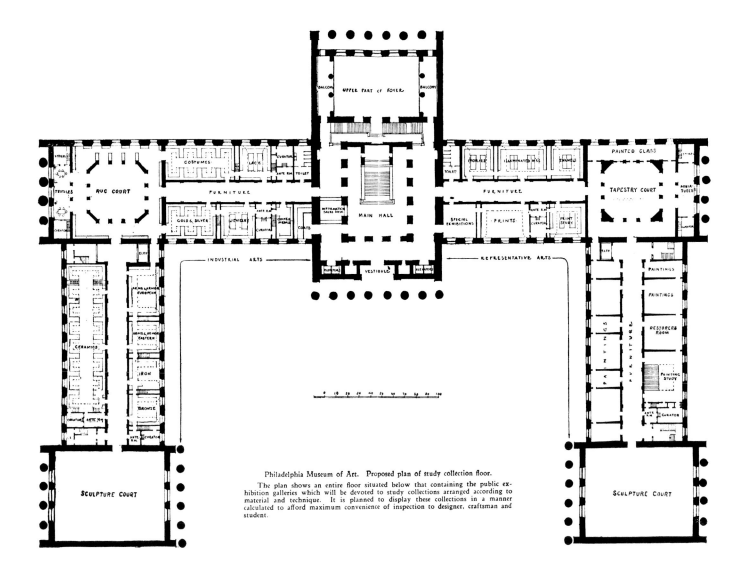

Philadelphia Museum of Art. Proposed plan of study collection floor.

The plan shows an entire floor situated below that containing the public exhibition galleries which will be devoted to study collections arranged according to material and technique. It is planned to display these collections in a manner calculated to afford maximum convenience of inspection to designer, craftsman and student.

13. Fiske Kimball, *Pennsylvania (now Philadelphia) Museum of Art*, Philadelphia, c. 1927. Second-floor plan
Philadelphia Museum of Art

rooms representing the periods of Louis XV and Louis XVI were taken from the Château de Draveil, built in 1723 by Marin de la Haye and decorated in 1730, and the Hotel Letellier, designed by Louis Letellier, c. 1728 (fig. 14).[71] In his search for French interiors Kimball consulted American expatriates Ogden Codman, architect, and William M. Odom, interior designer and head of the Paris ateliers of the New York School of Fine and Applied Arts.[72] He also worked closely with André Carlhian and other Paris dealers in French decoration. In the process of assessing the aesthetic character of available interiors and substantiating their authenticity and original appearance, Kimball became fascinated with the rococo. He claimed an early sympathy

for the Style Louis XVI and doubtless his interest was piqued by Jefferson's favorable response to contemporary French architecture of the late eighteenth century (in fact, during the course of his travels, Kimball asked Carlhian to take him to the Hotel de Tessé, a favorite of Jefferson's; its Grand Salon was soon purchased by an American, and in 1943 it was given to the Metropolitan Museum).[73]

Ironically, as Kimball's best-known study, *Domestic Architecture of the American Colonies and of the Early Republic*, was being published, the author found his "intellectual instincts" increasingly drawn to European architecture. In 1923 he told Codman, "I want to devote my time more and more to the European background, the

14. *Room from the Château de Draveil*, Philadelphia Museum of Art, c. 1723
Philadelphia Museum of Art, given by Mrs. Alexander Hamilton Rice

art of Italy, France and England from the time of Palladio onward."[74] His publications on European architecture center on discrete "problems."[75] They include a piece on the Italian baroque sources of the seventeenth- and early eighteenth-century work of Sir Christopher Wren;[76] a defense of the eighteenth-century dilettante architect Lord Burlington (Richard Boyle) based on a study of his drawings (a methodology obviously patterned on Kimball's Jefferson research);[77] and an article on the fifteenth-century Italian architect Luciano Laurana as a founder of the "high Renaissance" in the representational arts as well as architecture, in which Kimball attributed to him two of three famous anonymous works entitled "View of an Ideal City" (Walters Art Gallery, Baltimore and Galleria Nazionale delle Marche, Palazzo Ducale, Urbino) on the basis of their aesthetic affinity with his architecture.[78]

By the early 1930s, the architecture of the eighteenth-century French interior was the focus of Kimball's scholarly attention. The appeal of the subject was, in part, its "problematic" treatment (in Kimball's view) by German scholars. Specifically, Kimball suggested that Schmarsow and Brinckmann, among others, defined the rococo according to the plastic and spatial characteristics of the German rococo.[79] In contrast, Kimball suggested that the style first emerged in France; based on this assumption, he proceeded to delve into the historic records, notably architectural drawings, to ascertain the creators and their decisive works. As in his previous publications, Kimball typically sought to concentrate on the leading individuals associated with a particular movement or trend; he shared this approach with the art historian Lionello Venturi, who described the pursuit with the motto "Cherchez l'homme."[80]

Kimball's francophilia (which he acknowledged) was an aesthetic predilection he shared with other American designers and collectors at this time; these would include Codman; Odom; Walter Gay, the popular painter of interiors;[81] the Misses Hewitt, who left their collection of drawings of French architecture and furniture to the Cooper Union; George Hoentschl; Pierpont Morgan; and others.[82] Similarly, Kimball's installation of the French period rooms was part of the tradition where American architects incorporated imported historic interiors or emulated such models in the design of new structures.[83]

The results of Kimball's French research appeared in a series of scholarly articles, culminating in his *The Creation of the Rococo*.[84] He systematically documented the emergence of a style, from a late seventeenth-century fusion of surface ornament with the architectural frame, found in the work of Pierre Lepautre, to the full-fledged rococo or *genre pittoresque*, where a taste for the asymmetry of naturalistic exotic forms implied a separation between the interior shell and the building's structural system.

Kimball credited the mid-eighteenth-century turn to classicism, represented by the work of A. J. Gabriel among others, to a taste for English neo-Palladianism. Though ordinarily no champion of English architecture and design, Kimball had argued earlier for British influence on continental architecture and landscape.[85]

For Kimball, by far the most significant instance of English influence was the phenomenon of the picturesque garden. He saw the English landscape garden style as the romantic movement's contribution to a tradition that championed artistic creation over academic imitation. He believed the garden also provided a verdant setting for a broadened concept of history. In an article in the *Gazette des Beaux-Arts*, Kimball characterized the presence of the classical temple in the eighteenth- and early nineteenth-century garden as one phase of "Romantic Classicism."[86] His interpretation of the term differed somewhat from its usage by Sigfried Giedion in his volume *Spätbarocker und romantische Klassismus* (1922).[87] Kimball saw neoclas-

sical works as part of an international phenomenon, rather than the inheritance from a single nation. He viewed these as allusions to a distant past motivated by historical associations rather than, in Giedion's terms, the reaffirmation of the "tectonic" principles of classicism, expressed in the language of discrete prismatic volumes.

The concept of artistic creation also formed the critical basis for Kimball's assessment of contemporary work in the 1930s and 1940s; he described it as a state where "fused in living breathing form, the work must be deeply felt in the soul of the artist, the outcome of a true creative act, a new birth."[88] The breadth of the concept led him to endorse the work of Frank Lloyd Wright as free of the "academicism" of the "International Style,"[89] as the architecture of John Russell Pope remained unsullied by hackneyed interpretations of classical forms.[90]

When present, the quality of "artistic creation" in Kimball's own practice was defined in somewhat different terms. His restoration projects beginning in the 1910s and occasional new works from the 1920s, many of which were realized in collaboration with the Philadelphia architect Erling H. Pedersen, embody the characteristic modest approach of a preservation-restoration architect. According to Kimball, the qualities of such a specialist are quite different from those of an architect: "not imagination, but historical knowledge, not originality, by self-abnegation [sic]." The ongoing installation of the Pennsylvania Museum's interiors, which by the 1930s was carried out with the assistance of the Works Progress Administration, kept Kimball's hand in the practice of architecture. In contrast, the residence Kimball designed for Marie and himself presents a highly personal artistic expression (fig. 15).[91] Shack Mountain (or more poetically, Tusculum or Bellevue, Charlottesville, 1935–1937) also functions as something of a demonstration of the inherent synthesis of architectural history and practice in Kimball's works.

Shack Mountain is a romantic garden pavilion set on a 110-acre tract just west of the University of Virginia. Beyond the classical portico, a pair of octagonal bays recal-

15. Fiske Kimball, *Shack Mountain*, Charlottesville, 1935–1937. View of entrance looking east
Photograph by Daniel Grogan

16. Fiske Kimball, *Shack Mountain*, Charlottesville, 1935–1937. Interior view looking from the living room to the dining room
Photograph by Daniel Grogan

ling Farmington (a house Jefferson remodeled for George Divers, 1802) accommodate the living and dining rooms (fig. 16). Polygonal spatial transitions separate the spaces, recalling elements of Pavilion IX at the university, Jefferson's project for the Governor's House in Richmond, and other unrealized structures. In plan and mechanical core the house is thoroughly modern: all the principal living spaces are on a single story and the shell of the building—brick veneer on wood-frame—encloses a sophisticated system of climate control (imperative for Marie's health).

The multiple Jeffersonian references at Shack Mountain and the personal interpretation of the concept of the temple in the garden refer to Kimball's early advocacy of historic, graphic, and literary material as sources for new design. It is indicative of Kimball's opposition to European functionalism as an aesthetic vocabulary that he adapted the architectural language of the local building tradition to a thoroughly contemporary "machine for living."

This private retreat merely hints at the attitudes and accomplishments of Kimball's public life. Yet it reveals the highly personal association he felt with Jefferson's built environment. In addition, Shack Mountain attests to the livability of the past, which Kimball publicly endorsed through his publications and educational projects at the Philadelphia Museum, in the restoration of Colonial Williamsburg, and in many other programs with national significance.

NOTES

1. Fiske Kimball, "Rococo and Romanticism," in *To Doctor R.: Essays Here Collected and Published in Honor of the Seventieth Birthday of Dr. A. S. W. Rosenbach, July 22, 1946* (Philadelphia, 1946), 120–123.

2. Fiske Kimball, *The Creation of the Rococo* (1943; repr. New York, 1964).

3. [Nikolaus Pevsner], "Rococo to Romanticism," *Times Literary Supplement* (23 March 1946), 133–134.

4. Pevsner 1946, 134.

5. Pevsner 1946, 134.

6. Kimball 1946, 120.

7. Fiske Kimball, "The Creation of the Rococo," *Journal of the Warburg and Courtauld Institutes* 4 (1940–1941), 120; Kimball 1943, 7.

8. Fiske Kimball, *Thomas Jefferson, Architect* (1916; repr. New York, 1968).

9. Among Theodora Kimball Hubbard's publications are the following: *City Planning: A Comprehensive Analysis of the Subject Arranged for the Classification of Books . . . and other . . . Material*, ed. with James Sturgis Pray (Cambridge, Mass., 1913); *Landscape Architecture: A Comprehensive Classification Scheme*, ed. with Henry Vincent Hubbard (Cambridge, Mass., 1920); *Frederick Law Olmsted, Landscape Architect, 1822–1903 (Forty Years of Landscape Architecture: Being the Professional Papers of Frederick Law Olmsted, Senior)*, ed. with Frederick Law Olmsted, Jr. (New York, 1922; repr. 1928). Theodora Kimball Hubbard was librarian of the School of Landscape Architecture at Harvard University from 1911–1924 and served as special consultant until her death in 1935. See her obituaries: *New York Times* (9 November 1935); June R. Donnelly, "Theodora Kimball Hubbard 1887–1935," *Boston Evening Transcript* (14 November 1935).

10. Fiske Kimball, "Architecture at the Turn of the Century," unpublished manuscript, Fiske Kimball Papers, Philadephia Museum of Art Archives (hereafter FKP), series 17, ssa, folder 34.

11. Kimball, "Architecture at the Turn of the Century."

12. Fiske Kimball, "Art History and Cultural History," *College Art Journal* 2 (January 1943), 34. For biographical information about Warren, see R. Cliptston Sturgis, "Herbert Langford Warren," *Journal of the American Institute of Architects* 5 (1917), 352–353; John Taylor Boyd, Jr., "Professor H. Langford Warren," *Architectural Record* 42 (December 1917), 588–591; Fiske Kimball, "Introduction," in Herbert Langford Warren, *The Foundations of Classic Architecture*, ed. Fiske Kimball (New York, 1919), ix; and more recently, Anthony Alofsin, "Toward a History of Teaching Architectural History: An Introduction to Herbert Langford Warren," *Journal of Architectural Education* 37 (Fall 1983), 2–7.

13. Kimball, "Architecture at the Turn of the Century."

14. Regarding the role of French instructors in Harvard's architecture program, see Fiske Kimball to H. Langford Warren, 28 September 1912, FKP, series 7, ssb, "Correspondence with Warren." For information on Despradelle, see Frank A. Bourne, "On the Work of the Late Désiré Despradelle," *Architectural Record* 34 (August 1913), 185–189; and Francis S. Swales, "Master Draftsmen XI: Désiré Despradelle 1862–1912," *Pencil Points* 11 (May 1925), 58–70.

15. George Santayana, *The Sense of Beauty: Being the Outlines of Aesthetic Theory* (1896; repr. New York, 1955), 5–6.

16. Denman W. Ross, *A Theory of Pure Design: Harmony, Balance, Rhythm* (Boston and New York, 1907).

17. Fiske Kimball, "Harvard in Transition," unpublished manuscript, FKP, series 17, ssa, folder 35.

18. Charles V. Langlois and Charles Seignobos, *Introduction to the Study of History*, trans. G. G. Berry (New York, 1908; first published in 1897).

19. Kimball, "Harvard in Transition."

20. Herbert B. Adams, *Thomas Jefferson and the University of Virginia*, U.S. Bureau of Education, Circular of Information No. 2 (Washington, D.C., 1888).

21. William Alexander Lambeth and Warren H. Manning, *Thomas Jefferson as an Architect and a Designer of Landscapes* (Boston and New York, 1913).

22. Norman Morrison Isham, "Jefferson's Place in Our Architectural History," *Journal of the American Institute of Architects* 2 (May 1914), 230–235. A similar professional skepticism of Jefferson's architectural accomplishments colored the writings of Montgomery Schuyler, "History of Old Colonial Architecture," *Architectural Record* 4 (January 1895), 348–351; Russell Sturgis, ed., *Dictionary of Architecture and Building* 3 (New York, 1902), 907–908; Glenn Brown, "Letters from Thomas Jefferson and William Thornton, Architecture, Relating to the University of Virginia," *Journal of the American Institute of Architects* 1 (January 1913), 21.

23. From Thomas Jefferson's *Memoirs* (1821) excerpted in vol. 1 of *The Writings of Thomas Jefferson*, ed. Andrew A. Lipscomb and Albert E. Bergh (Washington, 1903–1904), 70.

24. Fiske Kimball and George H. Edgell, *A History of Architecture* (New York and London, 1918).

25. From 1913 to 1917 Kimball published more than fifteen book reviews in the *Dial*. Under the editorship of W. R. Brown, the journal allowed young writers like Kimball and others to review works that would appeal to a professional and popular audience. See Lauren Weiss Bricker, "The Contributions of Fiske Kimball and Talbot Hamlin to the Study of American Architecture," Ph.D. diss., University of California, Santa Barbara, forthcoming.

26. Fiske Kimball, "Thomas Jefferson as Architect: Monticello and Shadwell," *The Architectural Quarterly of Harvard University* 2 (June 1914), 89–137. Kimball presented a paper entitled "Thomas Jefferson and the Origins of the Classical Revival in America," at the General Meeting of the Archaeological Institute of America in conjunction with the American Philological Association and American Anthropological Association, Philadelphia and Haverford, Pennsylvania, 28–31 December, 1914; a popular version of the paper appeared in *Art and Archaeology* 1 (May 1915), 219–227. The final version, which was also his doctoral dissertation (University of Michigan, 1915) appeared as "Thomas Jefferson and the First Monument of the Classical Revival in America," *Journal of the American Institute of Architects* 3 (September–November 1915), 371–381, 421–433, 473–491. Kimball had decided to pursue a graduate degree in the fine arts while he was teaching at the University of Michigan.

27. For an assessment of American architectural drawings see David Gebhard, "Drawings and Intent in American Architecture," in David Gebhard and Deborah Nevins, *200 Years of American Architectural Drawing* [exh. cat., Whitney Museum of American Art] (New York, 1977), 24–27, 294. Gene Waddell has recently questioned Kimball's dependence on watermarks for the dating of the drawings; see Gene Waddell, "The First Monticello," *Journal of the Society of Architectural Historians*, 46 (March 1987), 27.

28. Fiske Kimball, "Development of Architectural Thought," unpublished manuscript and notes, c. 1912–1914, Fiske Kimball Papers, Fogg Art Museum, Harvard University (hereafter FK Fogg), box 36.

29. Fiske Kimball to Charles H. Whitaker, 5 June 1915, FKP, series 7, ssb, "AIA Journal."

30. Fiske Kimball to George Chase, 5 April 1916, and attached "Memorandum of Manuscript Material for Research toward a History of American Architecture Especially the Period 1776–1825," "Modified Plan of Work," "General Proposals for Work on the Sachs Research Fellowship," FKP, series 7, ssb, "Harvard University."

31. Fiske Kimball and Wells Bennett, "The Competition for the Federal Buildings, 1792–1793," *Journal of the American Institute of Architects* 7 (1919), 8–12, 98–102, 202–210, 355–361, 521–528 and 8 (March 1920), 117–124; Kimball, "Benjamin Henry Latrobe and the Beginnings of Architecture and Engineering Practice in America," *Michigan Technic* 30 (December 1917), 218–223; Kimball, "Latrobe's Designs for the Cathedral of Baltimore," *Architectural Record* 42 (December 1917), 540–550 and 43 (January 1918), 37–45; Kimball, "The Bank of Pennsylvania 1799, An Unknown Masterpiece of American Classicism," *Architectural Record* 44 (August 1918), 132–139. Regarding the McIntire volume, see George Francis Dow (Secretary of the Essex Institute) to Fiske Kimball, 20 June 1917, FKP, series 3, ssa, folder 1; and Fiske Kimball, *Mr. Samuel McIntire, Carver, The Architect of Salem* (Portland, Maine, 1940).

32. Fiske Kimball to Arthur Kingsley Porter, 26 September 1917, FK Fogg, box 11, folder 1.

33. Fiske Kimball, "Renaissance Architecture," in Kimball and Edgell 1918, 344; Kimball to Porter, 7 May 1918, FKP, series 7, ssd, "M-P"; Hans Tietze, *Die Methode der Kunstgeschichte: ein Versuch* (New

York, 1973, repr. of 1913 edition), 90–93; Carl Neumann, *Byzantinische Kultur und Renaissancekultur* (Berlin and Stuttgart, 1903), 42.

34. Fiske Kimball to Emil Lorch, 30 August 1913, FKP, series 7, ssd, "University of Michigan 1913–1919." On the history of the School of Architecture at Illinois, see Kimball, "The University of Illinois: The Department of Architecture—Development, Conditions, Ideals," *Illinois Alumni Quarterly* 7 (April 1913), 87–96.

35. Fiske Kimball, "The School of Architecture at the University of Virginia," *University of Virginia Journal of Engineering* 1 (February 1921), 2; "New Courses to be Offered by the University this Fall," *University of Virginia Alumni News* 8 (August 1919), 13.

36. A number of the new programs and the structures to house them were underwritten by Paul Goodloe McIntire; see John S. Patton, "Paul Goodloe McIntire, '79, Founder of the School of Fine Arts," *University of Virginia Alumni News* 7 (April 1919), 182–183.

37. Fiske Kimball, "The Amphitheatre at the University of Virginia," *Architectural Review* n.s. 11 (9 November 1920), 141–144, 147; Kimball, "The New Gymnasium for the University of Virginia," *Architecture* 47 (February 1923), 49–52 (reprinted from "The New Gymnasium," *Corks and Curls* 35 [1922], 242–244). See also Bricker, "The Contributions of Fiske Kimball and Talbot Hamlin."

38. Theodore Francis Jones, *New York University: 1832–1932* (New York and London, 1933), 207.

39. Jones 1933, 207.

40. Fiske Kimball (?), "Fine Arts," 23 April 1924, E. E. Brown Papers, box 13, folder 6, New York University Archives. See also Course Catalogues (1923–1924) in Metropolitan Museum of Art Archives.

41. *House Beautiful Furnishing Annual, 1926* (Boston, 1925). See also correspondence between Fiske Kimball and Eleanor White, managing editor of the *House Beautiful Furnishing Annual, 1926*, FKP, series 16, ssa, "Wh., 1920–1942."

42. See FKP, series 16, ssa, "New York University—Move to NYU 1923–1925, 1920–1942."

43. For discussion of the acquisition of Madison Square Garden fragments by NYU, see Fiske Kimball to E. E. Brown, 11 July 1924 and 13 January 1925, E. E. Brown Papers, box 43, folder 2, New York University Archives. As precedent for his proposals, Kimball cited Donn Barber's successful reuse of McKim, Mead, and White fragments in his design of the *Hartford Times* Building; see "The Hartford Times Building," *American Architect* 118 (4 August 1920), 140–141 and plates.

44. Fiske Kimball, *American Architecture* (Indianapolis and New York, 1928, repr. New York, 1970).

45. Fiske Kimball, "What Is Modern Architecture?" *Nation* 119 (30 July 1924), 129; see also Kimball 1928, 160; David Brownlee, *Building the City Beautiful: The Benjamin Franklin Parkway and the Philadelphia Museum of Art* [exh. cat., Philadelphia Museum of Art] (Philadelphia, 1989).

46. Fiske Kimball, *Domestic Architecture of the American Colonies and of the Early Republic* (1922; repr. New York, 1966).

47. Fiske Kimball to Henry W. Kent, 10 October 1919, FKP, series 6, ssa, folder 3, "Correspondence with Metropolitan Museum of Art."

48. Donald Millar, review of *Domestic Architecture of the American Colonies and of the Early Republic*, in *Architectural Record* 53 (January 1923), 86.

49. Review of *Domestic Architecture of the American Colonies and of the Early Republic*, in *Architecture* 47 (February 1923), 64.

50. [Allen Johnson], "Introduction," and [Dumas Malone], "A Brief Account of the Enterprise," *Dictionary of American Biography*, vol. 10 (New York, 1936), vii–xvi; v–vi.

51. Allan Nevins, "A Great Undertaking," *Saturday Review of Literature* 5 (12 January 1929), 581.

52. Allen Johnson to Fiske Kimball, 9 February 1926, FKP, series 16, ssa, "*Dictionary of American Biography*, Correspondence, 1920–1942."

53. *Chronicles of America*, ed. Allen Johnson and Allan Nevins (New Haven, 1918–1951); *Pageant of America*, ed. Ralph H. Gabriel (New Haven, 1926). Gay Walker, *The Works of Carl P. Rollins* (New Haven, 1982); Hawthorne Daniel, "American History in Moving Pictures," *Moving Pictures of America in the Making* (n.d.), 545; "The American Spirit in Architecture, Vol. 13 of the *Pageant of America*," *Architectural Record* 60 (September 1926), 284.

54. "Williamsburg Restoration Report on the Meeting of the Advisory Committee of Architects Invited to Williamsburg to Confer upon the Various Policies Touching the Restoration," 25–26 November 1928, 5, FKP, series 9, ssb.

55. Fiske Kimball to Laurence Vail Coleman, 16 June 1933, FKP, series 16, ssa, "American Association of Museums, Correspondence, 1920–1942."

56. Fiske Kimball, "Pennsylvania Museum of Art Acceptance and Successes of First Years, 1925–1926," in "The Art Racket," unpublished manuscript, FKP, series 6, ssc; Fiske Kimball to John D. McIlhenny, 12 June 1925, FKP, series 16, ssa, "Philadelphia Move, 1924–1925."

57. Fiske Kimball, "Philadelphia's 'Colonial Chain,'" *Art and Archaeology* 21 (April 1926), 198–203.

58. While Nutting used the concept of a "chain of houses" as a means of thematically linking a geographically dispersed group of structures, Kimball's "chain" could be appreciated readily by a tour through Fairmount Park. [Wallace Nutting], *The Wallace Nutting Colonial Chain of Picture Houses*, (n.p., 1915).

59. Laurence Vail Coleman, *Historic House Museums* (Washington, D.C., 1933).

60. For comments on the historic importance of Fairmount Park, see Commissioners of Fairmount Park, *Annual Report* (Philadelphia, 1878), 5. For early views

of Fairmount Park houses, see Edwin Wolf, *Philadelphia, Portrait of an American City: A Bicentennial History*, 1st ed. (Harrisburg, Pa. 1975).

61. For a selection of publications on the park as a museum environment, see Hermon C. Bumpus, "Relations of Museums to the Out-of-Doors," *Publications of the American Association of Museums*, n.s. 1 (1926), 7–14, and the discussion, 14–15; Chauncey J. Hamlin, "The Educational Value of Museums in National Parks," *Playground* 18 (July 1924), 243–244.

62. "Open-Air Museums," *School and Society* 30 (16 November 1929), 669–670.

63. See Edward P. Alexander, "Artur Hazelius and Skansen: The Open Air Museum," in *Museum Masters: Their Museums and Their Influence*, ed. Edward P. Alexander (Nashville, Tenn., 1983), 241–275; Naboth Hedin, "Sweden's Open Air Museum," *Art and Archaeology* 29 (May 1930), 225–231.

64. "Skansen and the Outdoor Museums of Europe," *Proceedings of the American Association of Museums* 8 (May 1914), 144.

65. Lucy M. Salmon, "The Historical Museum," *Educational Review* 41 (February 1911), 153.

66. Documentation of Kimball's views on museum design and his concept for the Pennsylvania Museum in particular is to be found in the following: "Museum Values," *Magazine of Art* 19 (September 1928), 480–482; "The Museum of the Future," *Creative Art* 4 (April 1929) and supplement, xxxvi–xlv; "The Modern Museum of Art" and "Planning the Art Museum," in *Architectural Record* 66 (December 1929), 559–580 and 582–590; "Le Programme Modern des Musées en Amerique" in *Musées, Cahiers de la République des Lettres, des Sciences et des Arts* 13 (1931), 45–59; "Schemes of Museum Arrangement and Installation in Recent American Museums," n.d., FKP, series 14, folder 14; grant application from the Pennsylvania Museum of Art to General Education Board, 22 April 1927, General Education Board Collection, series 2, folder 3350, Rockefeller Archive Center, Pocantico Hills, North Tarrytown, New York.

67. Kimball, "The Museum of the Future," xli.

68. For a selection of views, see Charles R. Richards, *Industrial Art and the Museum* (New York, 1927) and *The Industrial Museum* (New York, 1925); John Cotton Dana, "The Use of Museums," *Nation* 115 (11 October 1922), 374–376; Richard F. Bach, "American Industrial Art at the Metropolitan Museum," *Architectural Record* 55 (December 1929), 304–306; Gladys Potter Williams, "The Art Museum's Educational Service to Industrial Arts," *School Life* 15 (December 1929), 74–75, 79; and more recently, Edgar Kaufmann, Jr., "Industrial Design in American Museums," *Magazine of Art* 42 (May 1949), 179–183.

69. Kimball, "Modern Museum of Art," 565.

70. Edward P. Alexander, "Wilhelm Bode and Berlin's Museum Island: The Museum of World Art," in Alexander 1983, 205–238.

71. Fiske Kimball, "A Louis XVI Room: The Gift of Mrs. Alexander Hamilton Rice," *The Pennsylvania Museum Bulletin* 28 (November 1932), 3–13; [Room from Hotel de Draveil], *Pennsylvania Museum Bulletin* 32 (May 1937), 28; Kimball, "Château de Draveil," unpublished typescript, Fiske Kimball Records (hereafter FKR), Objects, series 4, "Château de Draveil," Philadelphia Museum of Art Archives.

72. Kimball's extensive correspondence with William M. Odom and Ogden Codman is housed in FKP and FKR; additional correspondence with Codman can be found in FK Fogg. See also William M. Odom, *A History of Italian Furniture from the 14th to the Early 19th Centuries*, 2d ed., 2 vols. (New York, 1966, repr. of 1916 ed.) and "The Influence of William Odom on American Taste," *House and Garden* 90 (October 1946), 88–93, 162; Ogden Codman, *The Decoration of Houses* (New York, 1897); and Pauline C. Metcalf, "Ogden Codman, Jr., Architect, Decorator: Elegance without Excess" (masters thesis, Columbia University, 1978).

73. Fiske Kimball, "Spoils of Europe," in "The Art Racket."

74. Fiske Kimball to Ogden Codman, 31 January 1923, FKP, series 7, ssd, "General Correspondence—C., 1919–1923."

75. In a letter to André Carlhian (29 November 1954), Kimball describes himself as a " 'student of problems,' " FKP, series 16, ssa, "Carlhian."

76. Fiske Kimball, "Wren: Some of His Sources," *Architectural Review* (London) 42 (March 1924), 90–96.

77. Fiske Kimball, "Burlington Architectus—Part 1," *Journal of the Royal Institute of British Architects* 3d ser., 34 (15 October 1927), 675–693; "Burlington Architectus—Part 2," *Journal of the Royal Institute of British Architects* 3d ser., 35 (12 November 1927), 14–16.

78. Fiske Kimball, "Luciano Laurana and the 'High Renaissance,' " *Art Bulletin* 10 (December 1927), 125–151.

79. See Kimball 1943, 5–7.

80. See Lionello Venturi to Fiske Kimball, 13 May 1941, and Kimball to Venturi, 27 May 1941, FK Fogg, box 26, folder 2b. Their shared views led to a collaborative authorship of *Great Painting in America* (New York, 1948).

81. *Walter Gay: A Retrospective* [exh. cat., Grey Art Gallery and Study Center] (New York, 1980).

82. Fiske Kimball, "French Art—XVI–XVIII Centuries," *Parnassus* 4 (November 1932), 22. Kimball gives an extensive list of American collectors of French objects.

83. One of the finest examples of twentieth-century emulation of French eighteenth-century interior design is the Rice Room, Philadelphia Museum of Art, executed by Carlhian of Paris, Inc.; for a similar surface treatment, see "Renderings of Interiors Made in the Office of Carlhian, of Paris, Decorators," *American Architect* 127 (26 August 1925), 183–184.

84. See Mary Kane, *A Bibliography of the Works of Fiske Kimball*, ed. Frederick Doveton Nichols (Charlottesville, 1959). For a succinct assessment of *The Creation of the Rococo*, see Erwin Panofsky to the American Council of Learned Societies (16 Septem-

ber 1942), FKP, series 6, ssa, folder 6.

85. Fiske Kimball, "Les Influences Anglaises dans la Formation du Style Louis XVI," *Gazette des Beaux-Arts* s6 5 (January, April 1931), 29–44; 231–255.

86. Fiske Kimball, "Romantic Classicism in Architecture," *Gazette des Beaux-Arts* s6 27 (February 1944), 95–112. The impetus for this article may have been a lecture series on "Aspects of Romanticism in XIX Century America," held in conjunction with the exhibition *The Greek Revival in the United States.* Kimball's lecture, "Romantic Classicism in Architecture" (9 January 1944) was the first in the series. *The Greek Revival in the United States* [exh. cat., Metropolitan Museum of Art] (New York, 1944), Talbot Faulkner Hamlin Papers, Collection of Talbot Fancher Hamlin.

87. Sigfried Giedion, *Spätbarocker und romantischer Klassismus* (Munich, 1922).

88. Fiske Kimball, "Artistic Creation," *The Pennsylvania Museum Bulletin* 29 (February 1934), 39.

89. Fiske Kimball, "Builder and Poet—Frank Lloyd Wright," *Architectural Record* 71 (June 1932), 379–390.

90. Fiske Kimball, "John Russell Pope, 1874–1937," *American Architect and Architecture* 151 (October 1937), 87.

91. Preliminary sketches and documents for Shack Mountain are found in FKP, series 8, ssb, number 3—Shack Mountain." The working drawings for the house are located in the Marie G. Kimball Collection, Manuscript Division, University of Virginia Library.

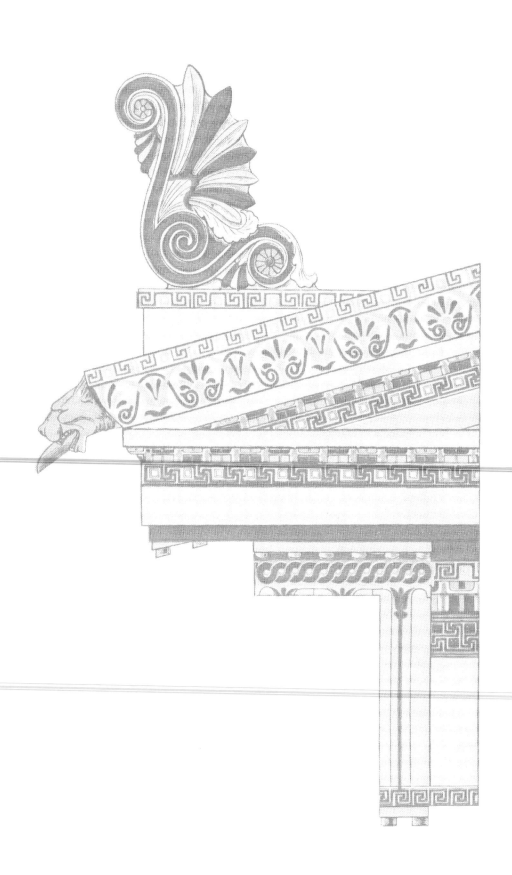

ROBERT WOJTOWICZ

[University of Pennsylvania]

Lewis Mumford:

The Architectural Critic as Historian

Lewis Mumford was not an architectural historian, but an architectural critic whose contributions to history were primarily the product of a methodology known as the "usable past." This phrase was coined by his colleague Van Wyck Brooks in a 1918 article concerning the contemporary malaise in American literary criticism. According to Brooks, "the spiritual past has no objective reality; it yields only what we are able to look for in it."[1] Mumford first applied this dictum to American architecture in his book *Sticks and Stones*, published in 1924, and he refined this approach to history in his 1931 book *The Brown Decades*.[2] In these two pioneering works, he established a pantheon of nineteenth-century American architectural geniuses that has greatly influenced later scholarship in this field. Mumford's subsequent writings on the history of cities and the history of technology continued to ransack the "usable past" for solutions to the overwhelming problems of the Machine Age and the life-threatening Atomic Age that followed. Moreover, Mumford recognized the importance of the "usable past" to the contemporary scene at a time when the modern movement in architecture rejected all ties to history. Although he was a participant in the creation of the International style, he was among the first to recognize its limitations as a historical term.

Mumford (fig. 1), who was born in 1895, had no formal training in art history, and his extensive knowledge in this and other fields was largely self-taught. He dropped out of the City College of New York for health reasons after two years of study. Although he later took courses at Columbia University, New York University, the New School for Social Research, and again at City College, he never completed his undergraduate degree. Mumford was an intellectual rebel during his college years, rejecting what he viewed as the overspecialization within the academic establishment in favor of a synthetic approach to knowledge. This distrust of academia persisted throughout his career, even after his appointments to the faculties of Dartmouth College (1929–1935), Stanford University (1942–1944), and the University of Pennsylvania (1951–1956 and 1959–1961). Putting his unsatisfactory college experience behind him, Mumford initially set out on a career in journalism, establishing himself as a leading writer and cultural critic by his early thirties. A self-defined "generalist" with a broad knowledge of other disciplines—including literature, philosophy, economics, sociology, religion, and political science—Mumford brought a fresh, often iconoclastic approach to art history at a time when the field was dominated by formalist methods. In his critical view, art and architecture were integral components of a nation's living cultural heritage, rather than isolated aesthetic elements from a dead past.

The key figure in Mumford's early intellectual development was the Scottish biologist, statistician, town planner, and occasional art critic Sir Patrick Geddes. Geddes' wide-ranging interests issued from a central organic theory of life that was based upon his studies in evolution. This theory, which rejected artificial barriers between branches of knowledge, was particularly attractive to Mumford when he was floundering in college and unable to make a career decision. Although the two men corresponded for fifteen years until Geddes' death in 1932, they met only twice, and it was primarily the Scotsman's writings in science and town planning that influenced Mumford.[3] In his own writings, Mumford developed and adapted many of his mentor's organic theories and terms concerning architecture and city planning, including the importance of regional surveys, the strangulation and death of the modern city through overdevelopment, the rejuvenation of historic city centers through "conservative surgery," and the role of utopian ideas in the shaping of the built environment.

Geddes' influence was most apparent in Mumford's first book, *The Story of Utopias*, published in 1922.[4] Heeding Geddes' call for diagnosis before treatment, Mumford viewed his exploration of the "usable past" in this and subsequent books as the foundation from which present concerns could be analyzed. His survey of utopian thought ranged from Plato to H. G. Wells, and it concluded with a vision of regionally based communities that he saw as achievable with cooperative planning in the twentieth century. Mumford wrote in the final chapter, "The inhabitants of our eutopias will have a familiarity with their local environment and its resources, and a sense of historic continuity, which those who dwell within the paper world of Megalopolis and who touch their environment mainly through the newspaper and the printed book, have completely lost."[5] In the book Mumford also addressed the increasing fragmentation of scientific knowledge and its separation from the arts. Con-

1. Lewis Mumford
Courtesy of Monmouth College

sequently, he saw the alienation of the architect and artist from mainstream society as a particular concern in the twentieth century. "The result has been that work which should have been done by artists of great capacity has been done by people of minor or degraded ability," Mumford wrote. "Anonymous jerrybuilders have erected the greater number of our houses, absurd engineers have laid out our towns with no thought for anything but sewers and paving contracts."[6] Mumford would explore further many of these themes concerning the technological and social ills of Western civilization during the 1930s in the "Renewal of Life" series.

Following his early success with *The Story of Utopias*, Mumford turned his attention to the study of American culture. One of his most significant and enduring contributions to architectural history during this period was the creation of a pantheon of American architectural geniuses. Prompted by Brooks and other literary colleagues, Mumford's inquiry into the "usable past" of American architecture eventually led him to the rediscovery of Henry Hobson Richardson, Louis Sullivan, John and Washington Roebling, and Frederick Law Olmsted. These figures had not been entirely forgotten, but they largely had fallen into disfavor in the early decades of the twentieth century. Mumford regarded their work as a brief, creative efflorescence in the closing decades of the century. They were seen as leaders in the development of "the new organic architecture," with its "new forms of expression," uniquely suited to its age and region.[7] Most important, Mumford saw this group as the first to make a decisive break with the European tradition.

As a native-born New Yorker, Mumford was intimately acquainted from his youth with the most celebrated works of Olmsted and the Roeblings, namely Central Park and the Brooklyn Bridge. He related in his autobiography how the monotony of his childhood on New York's Upper West Side was relieved in part by walks with his grandfather through Central Park and, during his adolescence, by physical exercise and romantic encounters at the 95th Street tennis courts.[8] The Brooklyn Bridge was perhaps an even more profound influence on Mumford in his technically oriented youth. In another section of his autobiography he noted that during his teens, the bridge was the scene of a great epiphany in which the confluence of sky, water, and city revealed to him his future calling.[9] After his move to Brooklyn Heights not far from Washington Roebling's former home, the bridge became so deeply embedded in Mumford's psyche that in 1927 he wrote a play about the span.[10]

Mumford's contacts with Richardson and Sullivan occurred later in his life, but they made a firm impression on his more developed interest in architecture. While stationed by the navy in Cambridge, Massachusetts, during World War I, Mumford attended radio classes in Richardson's Austin Hall on the Harvard University campus.[11] This experience aroused his interest in the architect's other buildings in the Boston area. His first contact with Sullivan occurred through the architect's *Autobiography of an Idea*, which appeared in 1924, and the unpublished manuscript for *Kindergarten Chats*, lent to him by Charles Harris Whitaker, editor of the *Journal of the American Institute of Architects*.[12] (Whitaker was, incidentally, the most instrumental in steering the young journalist toward architectural criticism.) Mumford

did not, however, encounter Sullivan's work directly until the mid-1920s when he made his first visit to Chicago. During the same trip Mumford became acquainted firsthand with the architecture of Frank Lloyd Wright.

Before the publication of *Sticks and Stones* in 1924, many scholars viewed American architectural history as a minor chapter in the larger history of western European architecture. In his book, Mumford sought to regain this vital aspect of the nation's cultural heritage from the "usable past." He also strove to establish a direct creative line between the architects of the late nineteenth century and his more progressive contemporaries. In *Sticks and Stones* he analyzed the past in terms of the broad social movements and ideas that lay behind stylistic developments. For example, Mumford saw in the New England village the last vestiges of medieval order, and he urged architects and city planners to use this tradition for more than stylistic models. "If we wish to tie up with our colonial tradition," he wrote, "we must recover more than architectural forms: we must recover the interests, the standards, the institutions that gave to the villages and buildings of early times their appropriate shapes."[13] In the text, Mumford made special note of the accomplishments of Richardson in architecture and the Roeblings in engineering, and this marked the genesis of his architectural pantheon.

Seven years separated the publication of *The Brown Decades* in 1931 from *Sticks and Stones*. At this point in his career, Mumford was equally involved in American literary criticism, and he belonged to a circle of writers and critics instrumental in legitimizing American cultural studies as a scholarly discipline. This group, which included Van Wyck Brooks, Waldo Frank, and Paul Rosenfeld, rejected the traditional academic view that American culture was merely an offshoot of that of western Europe. In their investigations into the "usable past," they sought to rehabilitate and elevate the achievements of nineteenth-century writers and artists to a place of preeminence in American intellectual history.

Mumford's next book, published in 1926,

was an investigation of nineteenth-century American literature, metaphorically titled *The Golden Day*. It continued a line of inquiry initiated three years earlier by D. H. Lawrence in *Studies in Classic American Literature*, which Mumford acknowledged as a source.[14] In it he created the literary pantheon of Nathaniel Hawthorne, Herman Melville, Henry David Thoreau, Ralph Waldo Emerson, and Walt Whitman, and this group became a chief reference point for all of his later writings in a variety of fields. Mumford's architectural criticism was deeply rooted in his literary criticism, and this was a natural outcome of his synthetic approach to American culture. His research for *The Golden Day* caused him to consider the creation of a complementary pantheon in America's visual arts during the same period, which eventually coalesced in *The Brown Decades*. In addition to *The Golden Day*, Mumford wrote a critically acclaimed revisionist biography of Herman Melville in 1929 and served as an editor of *The American Caravan: A Yearbook of American Literature.*

Mumford, however, kept in touch with the architectural scene through the numerous articles and book reviews that he produced as a critic for the professional and mainstream journals. Of particular importance was his discussion of some of the pantheon's members in the context of the Chicago school in a 1927 article, "New York *vs.* Chicago in Architecture." He argued that their work was the source for modern architecture in both America and Europe. "The Americans who look to-day at the work of Gropius and Mendelssohn and Taut in Germany, of Oudt [sic] in Holland, of Garnier and Le Corbusier and Mallet-Stevens in France, do not perhaps realize that the inspiration of this work came largely from America, and in particular from Chicago," he wrote.[15]

The dearth of substantial scholarship in American architectural history was only beginning to be rectified in the mid-1920s, and in his book reviews Mumford criticized the newly published surveys by other authors in an effort to reconstruct the achievements of the late nineteenth century. This period was most neglected by

scholars of the time, but it interested him the most. Of Talbot Hamlin's *The American Spirit in Architecture*, Mumford wrote in a 1926 review: "He for the first time gives something like their public due to Richardson, Halsey Wood, Louis Sullivan, and Frank Lloyd Wright, a continuous succession of American architects whose buildings expressed the first originality in design, apart from plan and purely functional elements, that had appeared in American architecture."[16] Mumford's criticism of Henry-Russell Hitchcock's 1929 book, *Modern Architecture: Romanticism and Reintegration* was more pointed in that he fundamentally disagreed with the two stylistic categories that the author had delineated. "In feeling [of modernism], there was far more of the New Pioneer in John Root's Monadnock Building than there was in the subsequent work of Wright and Sullivan," Mumford wrote in a 1930 review, "and one suspects that terms like the New Traditionalist and the New Pioneer describe stable aspects of the modern spirit, rather than schools of thought that follow in succession."[17] Despite his reservations about Hitchcock's analysis of the contemporary scene, and particularly his treatment of Frank Lloyd Wright, Mumford admired the breadth and soundness of his scholarship. Furthermore, Mumford's "Towards Modern Architecture" chapter in *The Brown Decades* was formulated partly in response to Hitchcock's chapter "The New Tradition in America" in *Modern Architecture.*

Mumford's review of Suzanne La Follette's *Art in America* the same year praised her overall analysis of American architectural history, but it faulted her for missing Richardson's importance. In the same review, he launched a direct attack on Fiske Kimball, the doyen of American architectural history, and his generally conservative views: "[La Follette] upsets Mr. Fiske Kimball's perverse interpretation of the progress of modern architecture and demolishes his silly attempt to supplant the virile modern design initiated by Sullivan and Mr. Frank Lloyd Wright by the feeble classicism of his favorite Fifth Avenue apartment house."[18]

In this last review Mumford echoed the

feelings of Wright himself on the factionalized state of contemporary architectural scholarship. The architect, of course, had a particularly vital stake in this stylistic debate, since his work in America had been largely obscured during the 1920s. "Fiske Kimball has just sent me a copy of his new book," the architect wrote Mumford in a 1928 letter. "A well written brief for the 'Classic' bracketing McKim, Meade [*sic*] and White's thought in Architecture with Lewis [*sic*] Sullivan's God save the mark! And this is 'history'. It would be hard to beat that for grave robbing, I say."[19] Mumford simultaneously viewed Wright as a living link to the past achievements of the Chicago school and as the most vital force on the contemporary scene. Moreover, as a disciple of Geddes, Mumford was particularly drawn to Wright's organic theory of architecture, not only because it meshed so closely with that of his mentor, but because it rejected purely mechanical aesthetics in favor of the American landscape and its regional culture and values. Mumford, however, carried the theory of the organic further than Wright, using it to describe a system of living in which man was in harmony with nature, the machine, and, most important, himself.

As an architectural historian, Mumford was not the first to recognize the achievements of the Chicago school, since such diverse writers as Montgomery Schuyler, Hitchcock, and Kimball had treated their work as a distinct phase in American architecture. As an architectural critic, however, Mumford was the most fervent supporter of the Chicago school during the 1920s, and in his articles and book reviews his overriding goal was to establish a lineage that extended from their work down to the present. The transplanted Richardson was viewed as the progenitor of modern form, and he was followed by Sullivan, the expositor of its rules. When the 1893 Columbian Exposition interrupted this period of original expression, it was left to Frank Lloyd Wright to carry it into the twentieth century. Mumford sometimes included Bertram Grosvenor Goodhue in this tradition, as well as Wright's former employee, Barry Byrne.[20]

In Mumford's parallel analyses of the histories of landscape architecture and engineering, Olmsted and the Roeblings occupied the same leadership positions in their fields as Richardson did in architecture. Central Park and the Brooklyn Bridge were seen as the direct ancestors of the garden city and the machine, respectively, a dialectic fundamental to Mumford's later studies of technology and culture. Olmsted's direct design successors were Charles Eliot, Jr., the driving force behind Boston's metropolitan park system, and Henry Wright, site planner of Radburn, New Jersey. Not coincidentally, Henry Wright and Mumford were both prominent members of the Regional Planning Association of America. While Mumford found no direct successors to the Roeblings, the Brooklyn Bridge represented the positive technical advances of which the Machine Age was capable. Ultimately, by awakening his contemporaries to this tradition in architecture, landscape architecture, and engineering, Mumford hoped to spark a period of creativity equal to that of the late nineteenth century, especially at a time when European innovations threatened to dominate the scene.

The publication in 1931 of *The Brown Decades* was the culmination of more than a decade of Mumford's critical observations. At a time when colonial studies predominated, the book broke new ground in late nineteenth-century American architecture. It also covered American literature and painting in separate chapters, using the color metaphor of the title to delineate unifying themes in the arts. Thus earth tones link the buildings of Richardson, the paintings of Albert Pinkham Ryder, and the verse of Whitman. In his chapters on architecture and the American landscape, Mumford examined the work of Sullivan and Olmsted, while expanding upon his previous analyses of Richardson and the Roeblings. The early commissions of McKim, Mead, and White and the works of John Wellborn Root and Frank Lloyd Wright were discussed in some detail as well. While Mumford's analyses of Richardson and Root loosely paralleled those of Hitchcock in *Modern Architecture*, the two diverged sharply in their assessments of Sullivan and Wright. Hitchcock placed

2. The Monadnock Building, Chicago, by John Wellborn Root
From Lewis Mumford, *The Brown Decades* (New York, 1931), pl. opposite p. 136

3. The Schlesinger and Mayer Store, Chicago, by Louis Henry Sullivan
From Lewis Mumford, *The Brown Decades* (New York, 1931), pl. opposite p. 164

these figures at the end of the "New Tradition" in America, but Mumford saw them as vital links between the nineteenth century and the younger generation of American architects. In contrast to *Sticks and Stones, The Brown Decades* was illustrated by photographic plates, including Root's Monadnock Building (fig. 2) and Sullivan's Schlesinger and Mayer Store (fig. 3). Mumford chose these images carefully for their iconic effect.

The book made a profound impact in the field of architectural history. Frank Lloyd Wright wrote to Mumford in 1931, calling the book "a useful work in your splendid style." He added, however, that he "didn't agree in toto but admire and respect [it]."[21] Hitchcock had an even more favorable response. "[*The Brown Decades*] seems to me the finest thing ever written on American architecture and indeed one of the finest things written on the architecture of the last fifty years," he wrote to Mumford in 1931, "for few fine things have I fear been written on American architecture."[22] Hitchcock added, "You convert me positively to Sullivan. You see him justly, I

have not."[23] While Mumford substantially changed Hitchcock's perspective on Sullivan, the younger historian resisted the older critic's analysis of Wright. Hitchcock concluded his letter, however, in an oddly prophetic manner: "When the discipline begins to bind, and the imitators of L[e] C[orbusier] to flourish doubtless I will return with gusto to Wright but now I am for reintegration, socialization, international style, to the founding of which the American Brown Decades surely led the way."[24] Hitchcock did, of course, "return" to Wright and reevaluate his work in his 1942 monograph, *In the Nature of Materials*. As for the "international style," which appears in Hitchcock's letter in the lower case, this phrase would take on new meaning the following spring when the Museum of Modern Art's "Modern Architecture: International Exhibition" opened.

Mumford's use of the pantheon in *The Brown Decades* was part of his highly individualistic critical methodology, culled from a variety of sources. The seminal influence of Giorgio Vasari can be seen in the glorification of the individual artist in short biographical sketches in *The Brown Decades*, a format ultimately derived from the *Lives of the Most Eminent Architects, Painters, and Sculptors*.[25] Furthermore, Mumford's elevation of the artist to the status of cultural hero was taken from his reading of Thomas Carlyle. Jakob Burckhardt was another nineteenth-century cultural historian who exerted considerable influence on Mumford, and his views of the development of the individual in Renaissance Italy found their analogous expression in Mumford's views of the emergence of the distinctly American individual in nineteenth-century society. During the 1920s, Mumford was particularly intrigued by the theories of the Italian philosopher Benedetto Croce; however, he accelerated the philosopher's belief that genius is established by consensus over a substantial period. Thus, in Mumford's view, architects who lived a generation or two immediately preceding the present could qualify for membership in the pantheon. Mumford underscored this point in the opening sentence of *The Brown Decades:* "The commonest axiom of history is that every generation revolts against its fathers and makes friends with its grandfathers."[26]

The creation of the pantheon itself lies within the tradition of art criticism as well. In a review of Walter Pach's *Ananias, or the False Artist*, Mumford discussed his views on the designation of such groups: "The standard is not, of course, 'absolute' in the sense that it is registered in heaven for all time; but it varies in slow movements and cycles. El Greco may drop out for a while or Raphael may be over-valued; but in the end a steady process of canonization goes on."[27] Mumford mixed hagiography with historiography in his writings, using the names of the revered group's members as a kind of litany that gained in authority through repetition and over time.

Not everyone agreed with Mumford's methodology and purpose in calling attention to individual genius in *The Brown Decades*. Writing in the second volume of the fledgling *Journal of the Society of Architectural Historians* in 1942, Robert Anderson argued that the glorification of the creative individual ignored the substantial achievements of the rank and file during this period. "Great men do not create out of a void," Anderson wrote, paraphrasing Mumford's analysis of Richardson. "They merely fuse and synthesize the product of the labor of their fellow men. If they be geniuses, they are the geniuses of the finishing room, the masters of the final stage of a vast and complicated production-assembly line."[28] Mumford, however, intended that *The Brown Decades* be viewed as an exploratory series of critical essays. He believed that he had laid the groundwork for future scholarship in the architecture of the late nineteenth century in general and for biographical studies of the pantheon's members in particular. When Hugh Morrison's biography of Sullivan and Hitchcock's biography of Richardson appeared in the mid-1930s, Mumford felt justified in writing in his review: "These two biographies bear witness to the fact that the day of pleading for a usable past is now over."[29] Gradually, the historical gaps were filled in during the next decade. Sigfried Giedion's *Space, Time and Architecture* of 1941 contained an extended discussion of the Chicago school. When Carl Condit's definitive survey, *The Rise of the Skyscraper*, appeared in 1952, he gratefully acknowledged Mumford's contributions. "Perhaps the first to . . . [rediscover the Chicago school] . . . was Lewis Mumford, whose sensitive and discerning chapter on the school in *The Brown Decades* . . . awakened interest on the part of those prepared to appreciate it," Condit wrote.[30]

Mumford eventually codified the writings and achievements of the members of his architectural pantheon in the collection of essays that he published as *Roots of Contemporary American Architecture* in 1952.[31] At the same time, he connected them in spirit to a select group of his contemporaries. From the "usable past" he exhumed the writings of Horatio Greenough and Joseph Warren Yost and placed them beside texts by such nineteenth-century architects, philosophers, and journalists as Sullivan, Thoreau, and Mariana Griswold Van Rensselaer. To this group Mumford added some of his own writings and the writings of his associates in the Regional Planning Association of America, including Clarence Stein, Benton Mac-

Kaye, and Catherine Bauer. Mumford anointed this particular group as heir to the American tradition, which he defined as "a mode of thinking and feeling, of planning and organizing and building, that Americans became conscious of only after they had established their political independence, had thrown off their colonial ways, and had begun to create a new mold for their life."[32] Their contributions on planning were in turn balanced by the writings of more widely known architectural historians and critics, such as Giedion, Hitchcock, and Philip Johnson. Out of this disparate group of texts, Mumford forged a critical and synthetic view of the origins and development of American architecture that was part documentary in its sources and part mythological in its proposed genealogy. Despite its historical idiosyncrasies, *Roots of Contemporary American Architecture* became a popular textbook that did much to establish a distinctly American basis in the past for the modern movement. At the same time, it refuted the antihistorical polemics of the newly transplanted Europeans. In the preface to the 1959 edition, Mumford attacked this view of the past as disposable:

The notion that modern architecture emerged from a long foreground in our American past doubtless comes as a surprise to many laymen whose historical perspective scarcely spans more than a decade; and this would apply to many architectural students coming out of professional schools where courses in architectural history were ruthlessly wiped out, in the revolt against academic clichés, instead of being re-thought and re-cast so as to establish the living continuity between past, present, and the emerging future.[33]

Between the publication of *The Brown Decades* in 1931 and *Roots of Contemporary American Architecture* in 1952, Mumford completed his colossal, four-volume "Renewal of Life" series.[34] As his title suggests, it was a comprehensive philosophical treatise that argued for a profound reorientation of modern life in all of its aspects. In researching this enormous undertaking, Mumford attempted to plumb the "usable past" of the whole of Western civilization to support his thesis. Of particular relevance to architectural history

are the first two volumes, *Technics and Civilization* of 1934 and *The Culture of Cities*, published in 1938. *Technics and Civilization* was Mumford's response to both the machine aesthetics of the modern movement in architecture and the mechanical consumption promoted by American industrial designers and manufacturers during the Depression. In the book, he analyzed the dialectic of the organic and the technic, whose synthesis he saw as vital to man's future survival. Mumford argued in the conclusion to this broad survey of technology that only a dramatic shift in man's subservient attitude toward the machine could improve his quality of life. Moreover, in addition to rejecting what he viewed as the teleological doctrine of mechanical progress, Mumford called for a reorganization of the capitalist system that supported it.

The publication of *The Culture of Cities* in 1938 established Mumford as a leading authority on urban history and planning. Borrowing heavily from Geddes, Mumford chronicled the birth, life, and decay of Western cities from the idyllic unity of the Middle Ages to the postindustrial disintegration of the twentieth century. He concluded that the life of American cities was quickly being drained by overpopulation, real estate speculation, and congestion along transportation arteries. In his view, small regional cities offered the most viable solution, with their economies closely tied to the local land and culture. This was essentially an updated version of Ebenezer Howard's garden city model, of which Mumford was the chief American proponent during this period.

Mumford projected his analysis of the history of urbanism further into the past in his 1961 book *The City in History*.[35] Making use of newly available data in prehistoric and Near Eastern archaeology, the book's analysis began with the Paleolithic cave. Mumford hypothesized that it was the container—a label that he applied to a whole range of primitive objects, from jars to houses—rather than the oft-cited tool that propelled man's progress at this early stage of his development. Furthermore, he argued that the first real urban centers emerged when organized religion and politics, represented by the two poles of priesthood and kingship, joined forces to consolidate scattered, rural populations. Following his discussion of classical civilizations, *The City in History* joined the narrative of *The Culture of Cities* during the medieval period. Mumford viewed this high point in Western civilization as the result of an organic synthesis that was achieved through Christianity's emphasis on the individual's inner transformation. Mumford's analysis of the twentieth century in the latter book, however, was far bleaker in its outlook on such contemporary problems as suburban sprawl, highway congestion, government and business bureaucracies, and, not least, the threat of nuclear annihilation.

The two-volume *Myth of the Machine*, published in 1967 and 1970, was the last of Mumford's big works.[36] What began as an amplification of *Technics and Civilization* concluded as Mumford's damning indictment of modern science and the American government, which he saw as modern counterparts to the ancient priesthood and kingship, respectively. Volume 1, *Technics and Human Development*, continued Mumford's analysis in *The City in History* along technological and psychological lines, introducing the concept of the human-powered megamachine in ancient civilizations. *The Pentagon of Power*, volume 2 of *The Myth of the Machine*, traced the history of science from the fifteenth century to the present. He argued in this book that the profession has repeatedly abetted the political establishment in its destructive path, a path that ultimately led to the development of the atomic bomb.

The balance of Mumford's writings on architecture and city planning are found in the numerous articles and book reviews that he wrote both for architectural journals and for general-interest periodicals from the 1920s through the 1960s. Mumford's most important forum as an architectural critic was "The Sky Line," a column he wrote for more than thirty years for the *New Yorker* magazine. Encouraged by the *New Yorker*'s founding editor, Harold Ross, Mumford transformed the column into a controversial, national forum that was oriented primarily to the edu-

cated layman. Mumford's sociological views and organic philosophy set him apart from his contemporaries, and he deliberately estranged himself from most academic and professional circles. Instead, he forged a close bond with the ordinary citizen, using a straightforward, often humorous, analytical style that stressed common-sense solutions to architectural problems. Mumford was an astute observer of the architectural scene from this unique vantage point, wielding enormous influence in the writing and definition of contemporary history as it unfolded in the United States.

To assess just one example of Mumford's participation in this historiographic process, it is useful to analyze his role in creating and then debunking the cult of the International style. Along with Henry-Russell Hitchcock and Philip Johnson, Mumford was a key participant in the Museum of Modern Art's 1932 "Modern Architecture: International Exhibition." His chief contribution was an essay on housing, which he wrote in collaboration with Catherine Bauer. The essay avoided aesthetic issues and instead concentrated on the social requirements of new communities, including improved construction standards, the exclusion of nonfunctional features, and comprehensive site planning. "The modern house is a biological institution," Mumford wrote, evoking a characteristically Geddesian concept. "It is a shelter devoted primarily to the functions of reproduction, nutrition and recreation."[37] By taking a combination sociological-functional approach, moreover, Mumford avoided having to compromise his material in order to achieve stylistic unity between the foreign and domestic camps. Photographs and plans of the new European *siedlungen*, such as Ernst May's Frankfurt Römerstadt development, were shown for the first time along with such progressive American suburbs as Clarence Stein and Henry Wright's Radburn.

In his criticism of the contemporary scene, Mumford eschewed labels and strove to isolate elements vital to a new humane architecture, regardless of the stylistic allegiance of the designer. He continued to recognize the plurality of American architecture during his involvement with the exhibition, and while he did not subscribe to the conservative views of Fiske Kimball, he also did not accept Hitchcock and Johnson's more radical ideas wholesale. Consequently, he was often thrust into the position of apologist for Americans who refused to follow stylistic instructions. It is not surprising, then, that during the planning of the show, Mumford acted as a mediator between Hitchcock and Johnson and Frank Lloyd Wright, that is, between the chief protagonists of International style and of romantic individualism, respectively. Wright objected to the inclusion of the foreign-born Richard Neutra and William Lescaze in the American section and to Raymond Hood as a wholly inappropriate choice despite his nationality. "Neutra is the eclectic 'up to date', copying the living," the architect wrote to Mumford in January of 1932. "Hood is the eclectic copying the dead, is now the improved eclectic, copying the living. I do not propose to 'take the road' in fellowship with eclecticism in any form!"[38] Wright threatened to pull out of the show, but Mumford managed within a few days to convince him to remain in the exhibition. "I have conceded capitulation to the New York show not because I believe it is more than internationalist propaganda but because I took your judgement as to the reaction of withdrawal," Wright remarked in a letter to Mumford on 1 February.[39]

Mumford's review of the exhibition in the *New Yorker*, while generally favorable, was almost subversive to the goals of the International style in its ultimate conclusions. He called the show "a great triumph" for Frank Lloyd Wright and suggested that his European counterparts showed signs of learning from the revitalized American master.[40] Furthermore, as a confirmed regionalist, Mumford was uneasy with the implications of the term. He suggested in the column that the International style label be dropped:

In discussing the forms of architecture which integrate both the practical and the ideal elements in modern civilization, I prefer Mr. Wright's term "organic," to the more current adjectives, "modern" or "international"; and this organic architecture is not merely a mat-ter of using new materials and techniques or of conceiving new forms for their effective employment; it is a matter of relating air, sunlight, space, gardens, outlook, social intercourse, economic activity, in such a fashion as to form a concrete whole.[41]

After the exhibition, Mumford persisted in his pluralistic conception of the new architecture, and in his writings he avoided endorsing the stylistic clichés of the International style. He was interested in all currents of contemporary architecture, and the diversity of subject matter covered in his "Sky Line" column and in other articles ranged from the lowly New York lunch counter to the United Nations complex. Although historians such as Hugh Morrison began to question the direction of the International style as early as 1940, a controversial "Sky Line" that Mumford wrote in 1947 about the Bay Region style spurred the first major reassessment of the 1932 show.[42] In this piece, Mumford heartily endorsed the spread of this West Coast movement, since design revolved around a mode of living rather than a set of aesthetic principles. As Mumford concluded, "The change that is now going on in both Europe and America means only that modern architecture is past its adolescent period, with its quixotic purities, its awkward self-consciousness, its assertive dogmatism."[43] Mumford's definition of the Bay Region style was broad enough to admit both the work of Bernard Maybeck in the first quarter of the twentieth century and the work of William Wurster a generation later.

The resulting brouhaha in the architectural community was so great that the Museum of Modern Art organized a symposium to reassess the importance of the International style the following spring, almost sixteen years after the exhibition's opening. Although the title of the symposium posed the seemingly simple question, "What Is Happening to Modern Architecture?", no definitive answers were reached by the diverse panel, which included Mumford, Hitchcock, Johnson, MoMA Director Alfred Barr, Walter Gropius, Marcel Breuer, Eero Saarinen, and Ralph Walker, among others. Mumford held fast to his views about the California-based movement and its potential adaptation in other regions of the United States. "What is the Bay Region Style?" he asked at the symposium's conclusion. "Nothing but an example of a form of modern architecture which came into existence with our growth and which is so native that people, when they ask for a building, do not ask for it in any style. . . . To me that is a sample of internationalism, not a sample of localism and limited effort."[44]

Although the symposium did not succeed in reaching a consensus on the state of modern architecture, it did initiate a period of revisionism about the International style that has continued to the present. Barr was one of the first scholars to reconsider his views on the subject. As he wrote to Mumford in a defensive tone after the symposium, "You speak of my 1932 formula. . . . It is not my formula at all but one arrived at by Hitchcock and Johnson, principally Hitchcock who, although he now seems rather evasive about it, was teacher and theorist for both Johnson and myself. I was, however, chiefly responsible for applying the phrase International Style to architecture which Hitchcock in his earlier book called the work of the New Pioneers."[45] Hitchcock reevaluated his own opinions on the matter in a 1951 article for the *Architectural Record*, in which he concluded that the "International style" could be dropped as a descriptive term. "Perhaps it has become convenient now to use the phrase chiefly to condemn the literal and unimaginative application of the design clichés of 25 years ago," he wrote; "if that is really the case, the term had better be forgotten. . . . The living architecture of the twentieth century may well be called merely 'modern.' "[46]

Mumford's own opinion of the International style became increasingly negative as his overall view of the failure of modern architecture to learn from the past and to effect social change solidified during the 1950s. "The notion that modern architecture had not existed in America until the so-called 'International Style' was transported here was almost too silly to be worth refutation . . . ," he wrote in the 1959 preface to *Roots of Contemporary American Architecture*. "This made no sense as

history either in Europe or America."[47] Mumford last addressed the subject of the International style at a 1982 symposium on the fiftieth anniversary of the exhibition held at Harvard University. To the bewilderment of many of those in attendance, Mumford chose to discuss atomic rather than architectural matters. "We are in the deepest crisis mankind has known," Mumford said in this, one of his last public appearances, "and what's left to us may not be worth salvaging. . . . Maybe it's too late; maybe it isn't."[48] This pessimistic summary of the condition of modern man was not a spontaneous outburst by an octogenarian, but a conclusion drawn from his own writings on the destructive proclivities of modern technology, architecture, and urbanism, writings that he felt were increasingly ignored in his own time.

As Mumford advanced in years, he turned to more autobiographical works. He began to come to terms with his own place in history and with the absorption of his writings into the "usable past" for others to mine. With the publication of *Architecture as a Home for Man* on the occasion of his eightieth birthday in 1975, Mumford was hailed as the successor to Montgomery Schuyler in the field of American architectural criticism.[49] This collection of essays from the *Architectural Record*, however, is just a sampling of the voluminous writings that form Mumford's enduring contribution to the field of American architectural history. During his lengthy career, Mumford continually challenged his colleagues to expand their view of architecture and planning to include more than formal criteria. "Art historians, like archaeologists and anthropologists, have too sedulously confined their attention to individual structures or fragments of structures," he wrote in the *Journal of the Society of Architectural Historians*, "so that it is still true that the Stones of Venice are better known, so to say, than Venice itself."[50] A pioneer in the rediscovery of American forms from the past, Mumford was also a critic who invested architectural history with a complexity of meanings and uses for his contemporaries to ponder in the present.

NOTES

1. Van Wyck Brooks, "On Creating a Usable Past," *Dial* 64 (11 April 1918), 338.

2. Lewis Mumford, *Sticks and Stones: A Study of American Architecture and Civilization* (New York, 1924) and *The Brown Decades: A Study of the Arts in America, 1865–1895* (New York, 1931).

3. Of particular importance to Mumford's intellectual development were Geddes' books: *City Development: A Study of Parks, Gardens, and Culture-Institutes, A Report to the Carnegie Dunfermline Trust* (Edinburgh, Westminster, and Birmingham, 1904), *Evolution*, coauthored with J. Arthur Thomson (New York and London, 1911), and *Cities in Evolution* (London, 1915). Geddes' letters to Mumford are located at the Lewis Mumford Papers, Van Pelt Library, University of Pennsylvania, Philadelphia, while the majority of Mumford's letters to Geddes are deposited at the National Library of Scotland, Edinburgh.

4. Mumford, *The Story of Utopias* (New York, 1922).

5. Mumford 1922, 305. In the book, Mumford defines "eutopia" as "the good place" (267).

6. Mumford 1922, 289–290.

7. Mumford 1931, 165, 166.

8. Mumford, *Sketches from Life: The Autobiography of Lewis Mumford, The Early Years* (New York, 1982), 16–18, 95–97, 103–104.

9. Mumford 1982, 129–130.

10. Mumford, "The Builders of the Bridge," in *Findings and Keepings: Analects for an Autobiography* (New York and London, 1975), 213–312.

11. Mumford 1982, 202.

12. Mumford 1931, 256.

13. Mumford 1924, 30–31.

14. Mumford, *The Golden Day: A Study in American Experience and Culture* (New York, 1926), 92.

15. Mumford, "New York *vs.* Chicago in Architecture," *Architecture* 56 (November 1927), 243.

16. Mumford, "The Pageant of American Architecture," *Journal of the American Institute of Architects* 14 (September 1926), 410.

17. Mumford, "Modern Architecture," *New Republic* 62 (19 March 1930), 131.

18. Mumford, "Art in America," *New Republic* 62 (5 March 1930), 77.

19. Frank Lloyd Wright to Lewis Mumford, 30 April 1928, fiche no. M003A07, copyright 1986, Frank Lloyd Wright Foundation.

20. Mumford, September 1926, 410 and "The Barclay-Vesey Building," *New Republic* 51 (6 July 1927) 176–177.

21. Frank Lloyd Wright to Lewis Mumford, 9 December 1931, fiche no. M025E04, copyright 1986, Frank Lloyd Wright Foundation.

22. Henry-Russell Hitchcock, Jr., to Lewis Mumford, 5 November [1931?], Lewis Mumford Papers, Van Pelt Library, University of Pennsylvania, folder no. 2215.

23. Hitchcock [1931?].

24. Hitchcock [1931?].

25. It is interesting to note that in Mumford's autobiography he recalled that he had read Vasari's *Le Vite* as a young man and that, consequently, he chose Leonardo da Vinci as one of his early "heroes" (Mumford 1982, 449).

26. Mumford 1931, 3.

27. Mumford, "On Judging Art," *New Republic* 58 (20 March 1929), 130.

28. Robert L. Anderson, "The Brown Decades Revisited," *Journal of the [American] Society of Architectural Historians* 2 (July 1942), 23. Here Anderson is paraphrasing Mumford's line in *The Brown Decades*: "In back of it stands a colossal man, Henry Hobson Richardson, an architect who almost single-handed created out of a confusion which was actually worse than a mere void the beginnings of a new architecture." Mumford 1931, 114.

29. Mumford, "Giants of Modern Architecture," *New Republic* 86 (26 February 1936), 87.

30. Carl W. Condit, *The Rise of the Skyscraper* (Chicago, 1952), 9.

31. Mumford, ed., *Roots of Contemporary American Architecture: A Series of Thirty-Seven Essays Dating from the Mid-Nineteenth Century to the Present* (New York, 1952).

32. Mumford 1952, 4.

33. Mumford, ed., *Roots of Contemporary American Architecture: A Series of Thirty-Seven Essays Dating from the Mid-Nineteenth Century to the Present*, 2d rev. ed. (New York, 1959), viii.

34. The four volumes of Mumford's "The Renewal of Life" series are, in order: *Technics and Civilization* (New York, 1934), *The Culture of Cities* (New York, 1938), *The Condition of Man* (New York, 1944), and *The Conduct of Life* (New York, 1951).

35. Mumford, *The City in History: Its Origins, Its Transformations, and Its Prospects* (New York, 1961).

36. Mumford, *The Myth of the Machine, I: Technics and Human Development* (New York, 1967) and *The Myth of the Machine, II: The Pentagon of Power* (New York, 1970).

37. Mumford, "Housing," *Modern Architecture: International Exhibition* [exh. cat., Museum of Modern Art] (New York, 1932), 183.

38. Frank Lloyd Wright to Lewis Mumford, 19 January 1932, fiche no. M027D05, copyright 1986, Frank Lloyd Wright Foundation.

39. Frank Lloyd Wright to Lewis Mumford, 1 February 1932, fiche no. M028B08, copyright 1986, Frank Lloyd Wright Foundation.

40. Mumford, "The Sky Line: Organic Architecture," *New Yorker* 8 (27 February 1932), 45.

41. Mumford, 27 February 1932, 46.

42. See Hugh Morrison, "After the International

Style—What?" *Architectural Forum* 72 (May 1940), 345–347.

43. Mumford, "The Sky Line: Status Quo," *New Yorker* 23 (11 October 1947), 110.

44. Mumford, quoted in "What Is Happening to Modern Architecture?" *Museum of Modern Art Bulletin* 15 (Spring 1948), 18.

45. Alfred H. Barr to Lewis Mumford, 27 February 1948, Lewis Mumford Papers, Van Pelt Library, University of Pennsylvania, folder no. 3461. Also published with some variations in the text in *Museum of Modern Art Bulletin* 15 (Spring 1948), 21.

46. Henry-Russell Hitchcock, "The International Style Twenty Years After," *Architectural Record* 110 (August 1951), 97.

47. Mumford 1959, viii.

48. Mumford, quoted in Andrea Oppenheimer Dean, "International Style: A Lively Dissection Fifty Years Later," *Journal of the American Institute of Architects* n.s. 71 (June 1982), 9.

49. Mumford, *Architecture as a Home for Man: Essays for Architectural Record*, ed. Jeanne M. Davern (New York, 1975), ix–x.

50. Mumford, review of *The Ideal City: In Its Architectural Evolution*, by Helen Rosenau, *Journal of the Society of Architectural Historians* 19 (March 1960), 38.

HELEN SEARING
Smith College

Henry-Russell Hitchcock:

The Architectural Historian as Critic and Connoisseur

Aconsideration of the place of Henry-Russell Hitchcock (1903–1987) in the architectural history profession can best begin with a rather lengthy excerpt from the *Harvard Class Notes*.[1] In this passage Hitchcock sums up with characteristic self-awareness his own view of his role, and he also points to the formative influence of Harvard, which, as I hope to demonstrate in this paper, was critical. Hitchcock wrote in 1949:

The pattern of my life was evidently fully formed within some five years of finishing college—writing, teaching, travelling, preparing exhibitions and lecturing. Balanced between activities related to the architecture of the past, which are historical and scholarly, and activities concerning current architectural issues, which are critical and even controversial; equally balanced between a preoccupation with American achievements in their own autochthonous right and with the relations—in the past often the debt—of America to the outside world, I may credit (or blame) my Harvard training for a certain cultural agnosticism which seems to more partisan associates an insidious form of the once-famed Harvard "indifference. . . ." Yet the enthusiasms of the critic should help to give warmth and present relevance to the discriminations of the historian; while the professional impartiality of the scholar can temper the hasty partisanship of the writer on current issues. Above all for a teacher, an informed interest in the present and a perpetual awareness of the past . . . help

to bridge the gap between theoretical and practical approaches. . . . If this is to be a liberal and neither a conservative nor a radical, I am not ashamed.

Hitchcock continued:

Doubtless the small collection of pictures with which I live, with its modern French, English and American paintings, some abstract and some neoromantic, and its English water colors and early American family portraits, most clearly epitomizes this liberal attitude. . . . I find no reason why a Feke, and several Ruskins should not hang in the same room with a . . . [Edward] Burra and a [Eugene] Berman [which are] linked by many threads of a common Western European and American pattern which is, for all its diversities, continuous and humane, rarely absolute or exclusive.

"Rarely absolute or exclusive"—these words as well describe the sage himself. Within his own field Hitchcock was an inclusivist who was able to recognize the virtues of apparently antithetical modes of artistic expression. In his first book, *Modern Architecture: Romanticism and Reintegration*,[2] he demonstrated his affectionate comprehension and positive evaluation of works belonging to the New Tradition—under which he grouped figures such as H. P. Berlage and Peter Behrens, as well as Eliel Saarinen and Michel de Klerk—no less than of works representative of the

New Pioneers (as he then called the avant-garde), a term that embraced Le Corbusier, J.J.P. Oud, Walter Gropius, and Ludwig Mies van der Rohe. He could write with comparable authority on German Renaissance architecture and Latin American architecture since 1945, evaluate with comparable equanimity the oeuvre of Henry Hobson Richardson and Skidmore Owings and Merrill,[3] and apply himself with comparable energy to a specific problem, such as the influence of the Beaux-Arts on Frank Lloyd Wright,[4] and a vast commission, like the Pelican volume.[5]

This inclusiveness also fostered an encyclopedic range of interests beyond architectural history. Hitchcock was a polymath whose grasp of abstruse subjects like the monetary system of the Aztecs and the layout of little villages in Turkey consistently astonished friends and listeners.[6] Mark Twain would have recognized in him the "cool confidence of a Christian holding four aces" (though as will become clear, "Christian" is more appropriately rendered as "Harvard man"). He could assess the virtues of various translations of Marcel Proust and the claims of film journals and movie magazines, as well as write manuals for Pratt and Whitney aircraft[7] and be instrumental in bringing *Four Saints in Three Acts* to the American stage.[8]

It is necessary to insist on this inclusivity of both taste and interest, for too often Hitchcock has been seen one-sidedly as an architectural historian concerned only with formal issues on the one hand[9] and an exclusive champion of a particular brand of orthodox modernism on the other. The first misapprehension—that Hitchcock viewed architecture purely from a formalist stance—is given the lie by his intellectual curiosity about so many different fields. He was in no way ignorant of the diverse social, cultural, and scientific contexts in which architecture is embedded, but the method by which he wove these strands together was more subtle than that of numerous present-day authors who exalt the context at the expense of the work of architecture itself.

The other misapprehension arises from his association with the 1932 Museum of

Modern Art exhibition, "Modern Architecture: International Exhibition" and his coauthorship with Philip Johnson in the same year of *The International Style*. While he later acknowledged that these were "definitive and controversial acts of participation in the dialectic of architectural development in this century," he soon recognized that modern architecture was anything but monolithic while warning the reader of

the subjectivity of the critic writing of events he knew at first hand. Concerning them, the later opinions have no more real historical validity than those the critic held and published nearer the time when the events occurred.[10]

In any case, Hitchcock always viewed architecture from the standpoint of historian as well as critic, rejecting as illusory the *tabula rasa* desired by many apologists for modern architecture. Indeed, as early as 1929 he had complained that

the literature of the architecture of the present seems disproportionately profuse beside that of the architecture of the past. Thus the illusion is reinforced that the present is a period distinct from and opposed to the past. Historical

Henry-Russell Hitchcock, c. 1950, with terra-cotta portrait bust by Frances Rich
Photograph: Smith College Archives, Northampton, Massachusetts; bust: Wesleyan University, Middletown, Connecticut

criticism should however be able to show that as regards architecture the present is the last realized point in the dialectic of history, and that even the most advanced contemporary forms constitute no rootless phenomenon but the last phase in a long line of development.[11]

These are hardly the words of an unreconstructed modernist.

Background and Education

Any call for a revolutionary break with the past would have been uncongenial to Hitchcock's upbringing. He could trace his lineage back to the *Mayflower*, and he grew up in Plymouth surrounded by family treasures from the colonial period. These were augmented when, during the depression, his physician father accepted works of eighteenth- and early nineteenth-century art and crafts from other New Englanders in lieu of fees. This background also accounts for his "preoccupation with American achievements in their own autochthonous right."

On the other hand, his interest in European culture and his appetite for contemporary artistic manifestations were stimulated at Harvard. He completed his undergraduate studies in three years and passed the final year waiting to graduate magna cum laude with the class of 1924 by attending architecture school. However, he tells us that he "found work in architectural history under [Arthur] Kingsley Porter more satisfying and soon gave up the idea of becoming an architect."[12]

Teaching in the graduate program at Harvard, besides Porter, were Edward Waldo Forbes (1873–1969), director of the Fogg Museum from 1909 to 1944,[13] and the legendary *Kunstfreund* Paul J. Sachs (1878–1965).[14] Virgil Thomson, Harvard 1922, a close friend of Hitchcock, has written of the influence of Forbes and Sachs in orienting their students "toward the modern."[15] A generation of museum directors whom they trained—including Alfred Barr of the Museum of Modern Art, A. E. "Chick" Austin, Jr., of the Wadsworth Atheneum, James Rorimer of the Metropolitan Museum of Art, Agnes Rindge Claflin of the Vassar College Art Gallery,

and Jere Abbott of the Smith College Museum of Art (whom Hitchcock would follow as director in 1949)—dedicated themselves to introducing the American public to artistic innovation at the same time that they fostered an informed sympathy for the great works of art of the past.[16]

Forbes and Sachs were committed to the appreciation of the art of many times and places. Both were known for the catholicity of their tastes, and both were avid collectors whose possessions eventually would enrich immeasurably the holdings of the Fogg Art Museum. Their students learned to emphasize two facets of art scholarship: a thorough knowledge of the materials of art, and connoisseurship. In 1924 Forbes initiated a famous course in which students were taught to work in such Italian Renaissance techniques as tempera and fresco; one observer remembered that his office was filled with jars of pigment and other art materials. This gave the art historian a firsthand knowledge of the metier. Hitchcock from his very earliest researches was fascinated by the material and technical aspects of architecture, and this tendency no doubt was fostered, if not engendered, by his studies at the Fogg.

Essential as well was connoisseurship, the close scrutiny of the most minute visual features of a work of art to ascertain authenticity and authorship. At Harvard, this acquired ability was considered an essential tool of art history.[17] Admittedly, such an emphasis has been more common among scholars focusing on painting, drawing, or sculpture than architecture, but Hitchcock made this an integral part of his approach to architectural history. In any case, he was an art historian specializing in the analysis of works of architecture, not a member of a separate discipline with its own distinct methodology.[18]

In Hitchcock's stress on the visual he surely was inspired also by Kingsley Porter, who insisted on experiencing works of architecture at first hand and who recognized the indispensability of illustrations to one's arguments. On his trips to examine medieval architecture, Porter was accompanied by two photographers whose function was to document consistently in that medium his conclusions; indeed, he traveled with a portable darkroom so that the negatives could be developed immediately at the site.[19]

First Writings

"The Decline of Architecture," which marked Hitchcock's debut as an author, appeared in 1927, the year he received the master of arts degree from Harvard. However, it was probably written slightly later than an essay based on his master's thesis, "Banded Arches before the Year 1000," which was published in 1928 in *Art Studies*.[20] Both essays shed light on his future priorities while demonstrating the range of his interests.

If the earliest period to which Hitchcock would devote extensive examination is represented by his last book, *German Renaissance Architecture*, his earliest written article took him back to the first millenium. Although not indicative of the subjects he would subsequently pursue, "Banded Arches" was prophetic with regard to his approach, for it demonstrated Hitchcock's concern with technique and materials no less than form. He noted there that

parallel to the history of forms in architecture between the beginning of the Christian era and the Romanesque period, runs a history of the structural and decorative use of materials equal to it in importance; indeed for brick and incrustation, since they are in this architecture characteristic, of special and even greater importance.[21]

Based on studies with his admired professor, Kingsley Porter, "Banded Arches" is curiously inconclusive and lackluster. Can one speculate that the examples he cited were known to him chiefly from illustrations? Only two photographs in the article are unattributed.[22] In view of his later practice of grounding his architectural analysis in dedicated examination of the built work, this detachment from the actual monument inevitably would have caused him some discomfort. Further, the works he dealt with were often in fragmentary state and anonymous as to architect. Hitchcock's preference for dealing with complete artifacts that can be attributed to

an individual designer probably discouraged him from pursuing archaeological topics; henceforth he would not study pre-Renaissance architecture except as it influenced work done after the fifteenth century.

In contrast to "Banded Arches," the tone of "The Decline of Architecture"[23] is impassioned rather than dutiful, and the approach critical rather than historical. Yet the two articles share traits beyond a convoluted syntax. In "Banded Arches," Hitchcock cited Oswald Spengler, whose monumental work[24] inspired the title of the first published essay, and both articles demonstrate the author's intention to grapple with the interrelation of structure, materials, and aesthetic form. Hitchcock's mannered prose contains topical references to "Mr. Loew's palaces, Mr. Scott's cathedral on the Mersey [Gilbert Giles Scott's Liverpool Anglican Cathedral, 1903–1960] and Mr. Cram's on the Hudson [Ralph Adams Cram's Cathedral of St. John the Divine in New York City, 1915–1941],"[25] as well as to Erich Mendelsohn and Le Corbusier. He challenges the view, which he ascribes to the surrealists but might more accurately be ascribed to such unredeemed functionalists as Hannes Meyer, that contemporary architecture is only building science, or that

the intelligence may not function artistically but only technically and that the introduction of the aesthetic intelligence into building makes today no monuments of modern architecture but merely bad machines.

Rather, Hitchcock argued that "the architect makes on ordered aesthetic grounds and not on accidental economic grounds, those free choices which are the elements of the architectural problem." In other words, while recognizing the impingement on architectural design of materialistic factors, Hitchcock insists on the priority of the imaginative vision of the architect in the realization of architecture, which he characterizes as "that one great branch of our civilization whose past monuments have been as symbols and for themselves almost its greatest glory."

These words appeared in the first issue of the "little magazine," *Hound & Horn*, founded by Lincoln Kirstein when he was a Harvard undergraduate. According to its historian, Leonard Greenbaum, the contents of *Hound & Horn* reflected three themes: the individual as person and artist; the necessity of the artist choosing techniques that would enhance his work; and the need to find a point of reference from which to make value judgments. In his study, Greenbaum singled out Hitchcock's article for particular mention, calling it "in this first issue the most precise expression of the role of the individual as artist,"[26] but one could add that it is no less telling an illustration of the two other themes.

In these first two articles Hitchcock had not yet integrated his activities as critic and historian, but later, in a second essay written in French in 1928 for *Cahiers d'Art*, these would be fused.[27] The title, "L'architecture contemporaine en Angleterre," is somewhat misleading, for Hitchcock begins his essay with a consideration of the Crystal Palace, which he praises highly, but notes regretfully that since that time in England "the technique of building always lacked the spirit of adventure." Again, his particular focus is on materials and technology, and critical judgment is based on the "quality of execution and of detail."

Of the contemporary works Hitchcock cites, only two receive his approbation: the Underground Stations in London (1924–1927), by Charles Holden of Adams, Holden, and Pearson, which "show radical ideas, most particularly those from Berlin," and the houses at the estate village of Silver End, near Braintree, Essex (1926–1928), designed by Thomas S. Tait for the Crittall Metal Windows Company. Nevertheless, the latter,

for a critic . . . should appear somewhat inferior to the best French, Dutch and German buildings, constructed by those who have discovered during the last decade "un nouvel analogue du beau. . . ." For the historian, the importance of [Tait's houses] is considerable because they verify that which Gropius wrote in the preface to the second edition of Internationale Architektur, *when he said that since its first appearance, the style, of which he remains one of the masters, has steadily received the support of the entire Occident.*

Hitchcock noted that because of their very imperfections, Tait's houses had a national character, and—in a conclusion perhaps surprising for one of the future authors of *The International Style*—he found this to be a strength "too often lacking in the work of European architects who have converted to the new aesthetic . . . without thinking of their country or of local condition."

For the same publisher—*Cahiers d'Art*—the gifted linguist penned monographs on J.J.P. Oud and Frank Lloyd Wright, the latter the first—and perhaps still the only—book in French on the work of the famous American.[28]

The earliest phase of Hitchcock's published oeuvre culminated in 1929 with the appearance of *Modern Architecture: Romanticism and Reintegration*. This comprehensive monograph is an astonishing achievement for someone who had not yet completed his twenty-seventh year, and it may be considered a surrogate for the doctoral dissertation that he never wrote. In this authoritative work, Hitchcock broke new ground in the study of contemporary architecture no less than he summed up with extraordinary breadth both the strengths and the shortcomings of nineteenth-century architecture.[29]

Hitchcock as Curator

Shortly after completing his first book, Hitchcock took on another role within the discipline of art history, that of guest curator. No doubt this activity was fueled by his training in connoisseurship, and exhibitions would become as essential to his practice of architectural history as publications.

The first architectural exhibition that Hitchcock was involved in was the notorious "International Exhibition: Modern Architecture," organized with Alfred Barr and Philip Johnson for the recently founded Museum of Modern Art.[30] This was followed by "Early Modern Architecture: Chicago" (1933), also arranged in collaboration with Philip Johnson for the same institution. The year 1934 brought "Early Museum Architecture," assembled for the Wadsworth Atheneum, at that time directed by Hitchcock's friend A. E. "Chick" Austin, Jr., and the following year saw the first exhibition ever devoted to surveying the building history of an American city—in this case, Springfield, Massachusetts—held to inaugurate the new Museum of Fine Arts in that city.

In 1936, Hitchcock mounted the Henry Hobson Richardson show for MoMA. In the preface to the accompanying book he explained that

book and exhibition are by no means merely alternative methods of presenting Richardson's work. They are intended to complement one another. In an exhibition it is possible to have a few photos enlarged to a great scale and to display many original drawings. For there exist a considerable number of drawings in Richardson's own hand. In the book the illustrations are necessarily much smaller and they can hardly do justice to such drawings. But it is possible to round out the story of Richardson's development and background with more graphic material than can be shown in an exhibition.[31]

Note the emphasis in this passage on the visual material. The archival research that Hitchcock did for the book and exhibition was almost exclusively concerned with drawings and photos, relying as he did on Mariana Griswold Van Rensselaer's monograph for biographical information.[32] A voracious reader of published texts, Hitchcock allotted the time he spent among original documents to examining illustrative material.

The Architecture of H. H. Richardson and His Times—dedicated, incidentally, to Kingsley Porter, who had died in 1933—and *The International Style* testify to the fact that many of Hitchcock's most memorable books have been catalogues for, or grew out of, exhibitions. They were followed by *Modern Architecture in England* (1937); *In the Nature of Materials* (1942), which complemented the exhibition "Frank Lloyd Wright" (1940), both for MoMA; and *Rhode Island Architecture* (1939), written in connection with an exhibition held at the Rhode Island School of Design. After the war were exhibitions and books such as *Painting toward Architecture* (1948) and—for the Museum of Modern Art—*Built in*

USA: Post War Architecture (1952), *Latin American Architecture since 1945* (1955), and *Gaudí* (1957).

Hitchcock and the Writing of Architectural History

While Hitchcock was fairly consistent in his approach to architectural history, his critical judgments were subject to change, whether they concerned recent or older buildings. His view of 1928 that, except for the Crystal Palace, English architecture was greatly wanting and that the Gothic revival made "architecture a branch of archaeology rather than of building" received total reassessment in 1954, when *Early Victorian Architecture* appeared.[33] This book was responsible for a major revision of the way buildings from the Victorian period in the United States as well as in England were evaluated and opened many eyes to the glories of mid-nineteenth century English and American architecture.

In the introduction, Hitchcock enunciated his aims and method:

to sort out the architectural remains of the Victorian Age into their principal categories in order that relative aesthetic quality and historical significance within those categories may become more recognizable. Such a sorting out must in the first place be chronological . . . but within that main chronological category there are typological and stylistic subcategories that require distinct recognition also.[34]

Still, he noted in *German Rococo: The Zimmerman Brothers* of 1968 that

the written history of styles, including their definition and their morphology . . . is generally less useful than study of the work of particular artists considered, if not timelessly, at least in their own particular contexts. Such very great architects as Michelangelo and Frank Lloyd Wright fit awkwardly into stylistic pigeon-holes and those who concentrate their attention on problems of style usually find these men difficult to handle. Without necessarily going so far as to omit such figures entirely—as Gombrich did Ingres from his general history of European painting—some historians are tempted to distort their achievements on *Procrustean beds of* a priori *categories and distinctions.*[35]

The refusal to view architecture according to *a priori* categories distinguished Hitchcock from many of his continental predecessors and contemporaries in the field. He explained in *Rococo Architecture in Southern Germany* that his method was "not inductive, from supposed principles to more or less perfect examples, but deductive."[36] This is not to say that he eschewed stylistic categories altogether; furthermore, when necessary, he invented his own—"Byzantinoid Italian Romanesque" must surely be his very own neologism. He also displayed a penchant for turning proper names into adjectives: the words Shavian, Puginian, Durandesque, Schinkelesque, Voysey-like, Soanic, and Ledolcian pepper the text of *Architecture: Nineteenth and Twentieth Centuries.*

Despite his reliance on descriptive stylistic terms, Hitchcock's method went far beyond formalism. He was always aware of the factors—historical, social, economic, political, technological, and ideological—that can deform and transform the intentions of the designer. His books are studded with references to military and dynastic events, business conditions, patronage issues. But he was wary of going too far beyond the monument itself; in *German Renaissance Architecture* he wrote:

Economic historians try to explain the rise and fall of great cities and individual fortunes by the hows and whys of inflation; architectural history can only record the results.[37]

Sir John Summerson has eloquently described Hitchcock's method.

As an historian he had his own perfectly consistent style and method. Each building had to be seen [emphasis added], *then turned over and over in his mind till its elements fell into an order significantly related to the historical context. He let nothing slip. Irresistibly, one thinks of him as a finely tuned mechanism, "processing" material and delivering a closely-woven historical fabric, perfect in its way.*[38]

But finally, the starting point was the building, and that was also the final goal—elucidating its creation and interpreting its meaning. And that attitude was rooted in Hitchcock's training in connoisseurship.

An example of this attitude may be cited from *German Renaissance Architecture*, though there are numerous other examples from publications throughout his career. Discussing the Englischer Bau at Schloss Heidelberg, he writes:

No authorship for the design of the Englischer Bau has been, nor probably can be, firmly established. Certain circumstances associated with the Anglo-Palatine marriage of 1613 support, as does the traditional name, the probability that the designer was English and specifically Inigo Jones, whose well-known later architectural productions it certainly brings to mind.[39]

He goes on to argue on the basis of similarities with the earlier designs for masques and the later buildings that Jones is probably the author, although the executant may have been Salamon de Caus, whose own realization at Heidelberg, the Elisabethentor,

has a touch of fantasy in the vine-carved semi-rustic columns and their capitals not unlike that of various details in Jones' drawings for masques . . . and the scrolled broken pediments in particular can be closely matched in a masque project dated 1610/11. Thus it is not extravagant to surmise that some sort of drawings for the Englischer Bau were prepared during the early months of 1613 by Jones in London—or later, actually in Heidelberg—for the new wing and possibly for the gate.[40]

For all his brilliance, Hitchcock of course was not infallible, as he would have been the first to point out. A foolish consistency was never his hobgoblin, nor was every word that flowed from his pen or fell from his lips solid gold. Sometimes there are astonishing condemnations without further comment. In the Richardson book, for example, he speaks of "Ruskin, the fascist"[41]—a reference that leaves this author thoroughly puzzled. On occasion he blithely mixed denunciation with description[42] and offered value judgments on the basis of vague words like "fine" or "sound," one of his favorite adjectives, although the precise denotation or even connotation of the word escapes definition. Thus he writes of the Dutchman, J.J.P. Oud: "In any period he would have been a very great architect, in our own he is of all great architects the most sound."[43]

Yet more characteristically Hitchcock was precise, judicious, and appreciative in his descriptions, especially of the works of those who fell outside the modern mainstream. Compare his treatment of Casa Milá by Antonio Gaudì with Nikolaus Pevsner's description of the same building. Hitchcock wrote:

As regards the masonry, it is really wrong to speak of detailing, for the very fabric of the structure, not just its edges and its trimmings as on the Casa Batlló, has been completely moulded to the architect's plastic will. Whether or not it be correct to consider the Casa Milá an example of the Art Nouveau—and technically it is not—La Pedrera remains one of the greatest masterpieces of the curvilinear mode of 1900, rivalled in quality only by the finest of [Louis] Sullivan's skyscrapers which it does not, of course, resemble visually at all.[44]

Pevsner wrote:

Surprising is the fact that the same uncompromising style [called in the previous sentence "this intransigent brand of Art Nouveau"] was accepted for blocks of flats. Who would be ready to live in rooms of such curvy shapes, under roofs like the backs of dinosaurs, behind walls bending and bulging so precariously and on balconies whose ironwork might stab at you any moment? Who but an out-and-out aesthete or a compatriot of Gaudí and Picasso?[45]

In the first edition of the book—*Pioneers of Modern Design*—Pevsner had relegated Gaudí to a footnote. In Sigfried Giedion's *Space, Time and Architecture*,[46] there are no references at all to the Catalan genius, whereas Hitchcock had singled him out for discussion already in 1929.[47] Again and again, Hitchcock's truly encyclopedic vision of architecture astonishes.

John Jacobus had called the Pelican volume a cross between a Sears, Roebuck catalogue and Thomas Wolfe,[48] and that is a pithy epithet for a book stuffed with names of architects and monuments that often receive only a sentence or two of commentary. Yet to the daunting task of supplying a *summa architecturalis* of the nineteenth and twentieth centuries, Hitchcock brought an eye that was not only remarkably discerning but equally disinterested,

concerned to expose the reader to as much architecture of the period as possible, the unusual and the idiosyncratic as well as the representative. Furthermore, there are peerless chapters in the Pelican book, such as "Building with Iron and Glass, 1790–1855," "The Development of the Detached House in England and America from 1800 to 1900," and "The Rise of Commercial Architecture in England and America," that not only are readable but offer wonderfully synthetic interpretations. Hitchcock was especially good when dealing with specific building types, a particularly useful tack for clarifying directions in architecture.

The table of contents of *Early Victorian Architecture in Britain* shows the subtlety of Hitchcock's method of dealing with a vast quantity of diverse material. Individual buildings and architects are not subordinated to a strict organization that bleeds out originality or imposes a straitjacket on specific solutions. Chapter headings include "The 1830s," "Pugin as a Church Architect," "Barry as an Architect of 'Palaces,'" "Royal and State Patronage," "Corporate Architecture," "Housing in the Mid-Century," and "Early Railway Stations and Other Iron Construction."

Hitchcock was not very interested in architectural theory. He noted in the Pelican volume that "were this a history of architectural thought rather than of architecture—that is, of what was actually built in the 19th and 20th centuries—Viollet-le-Duc would play a much larger part."[49]

Precisely that lack of theoretical content led at least one reviewer to excoriate *Netherlandish Scrolled Gables of the 16th and Early 17th Centuries*, which appeared in 1978 and to my eyes is one of Hitchcock's weakest performances. E.R.M. Taverne complained of Hitchcock's "foredoomed attempt to typify Netherlandish architecture solely on the basis of gable details" and faults his "negative attitude towards the extensive literature on architectural theory produced in northern Europe in the 16th and 17th centuries."[50]

But he was certainly not ignorant of it. He was already familiar in 1929 with the writings of the Abbé Laugier, before Louis Hautecoeur called attention to the Jesuit and his "primitive hut." Nor did Hitchcock's lack of interest in theory per se mean that he was not concerned with ideas; in the quotations already given one can see that an interest in ideas is paramount. But it was the manifestation and embodiment of ideas in built form that attracted and held his attention.

Hitchcock's insistence on seeing the monuments saved him from miscalculations made by more hasty and less circumspect architectural historians. Indeed his motto as expressed in *Modern Architecture: Romanticism and Reintegration*, was *Si monumenta requiris, circumspice*.[51] He would never have suggested, as did Vincent Scully, that Fallingwater represented Frank Lloyd Wright's capitulation to the International style. It is indeed telling to compare each man's analysis of the Kaufmann house at Bear Run, Pennsylvania, 1936. Hitchcock wrote in 1942:

There are no projects leading up to the Kaufmann house unless it be the "House on the Mesa." It seems to have sprung as suddenly from the brow of Wright as did the River Forest Golf Club, with the difference that the world was now prepared . . . to receive with loud acclaim a building that seemed to epitomize the aspirations not of Wright alone, but of all modern architects. After the twenties, in which the direction of the European leaders and the direction of Wright seemed sharply opposed, despite all the coincidences which we now recognize, as new countries came to achievement in modern architecture equalling that of France and Holland and Germany in the previous decade, architecture could be seen to be advancing on a deeper and broader, if less "international" front. And the Kaufmann house was one of the first and most striking demonstrations that a new cycle of world architecture had opened.[52]

Compare this with Scully's assessment, based, when it appeared in 1954, entirely on illustrative material.

It is a plan which has been more than touched by the gentle, open rhythms of Mies' designs of the twenties. Again one feels De Stijl. . . . The influence of another International Style architect can also be felt in the Kaufmann house. The clean planes, the dark window voids, and most of all, the spatial play of curved against rectangular planes . . . most decisively recall Le Corbusier's Villa Savoie, and other of Le Corbusier's published designs.[53]

Not surprisingly, Edgar Kaufmann, Jr., who knew the house intimately, protested in a letter to the editor that "no two houses were ever less alike in concept, effect, intent or detail than Fallingwater and the Villa Savoie,"[54] a judgment with which anyone who has seen both houses in actuality has to agree.

Most important, Hitchcock had a genuine affection for buildings, a quality all too rare among architectural historians. For him, they were friends, and indeed his experience of them was usually tied to his many friendships with an international cadre of artists and intellectuals, students and peers. John Coolidge pointed out at the symposium that generated these essays that the astounding range of architecture Hitchcock wrote about could in part be traced to his travels to visit friends, and an earlier tribute acknowledges the same point by its title, "Architectura et Amicitia."[55] His extensive research on German Renaissance architecture was prompted not only by the desire to correct "the injustice of the continued rejection of German Renaissance architecture on grounds of taste by many scholars—German and foreign both,"[56] but by his close friendship with the German-born Robert Schmitt.

Hitchcock's enduring contribution to our discipline, beyond the information and insight that he added to our knowledge of architecture, which will continue to be the source and starting point for so many of us as we pursue our own investigations, is his consistent commitment to understanding and appreciating the work of architecture on its own terms. In fact, as I wrote in a short piece in the now-defunct *Skyline* regarding Hitchcock's formidable forays into literary, musical, and theatrical criticism, "he was always conscious of the distinguishing features of the metier he was discussing and never confused one means of expression with another."[57] At a time when *Baukunstgeschichte* seems in danger of becoming a *Geschichte ohne Baukunst*, reduced to a mere branch of philosophy, linguistics, or literary criticism or skewered on the sabers of economic determinism, Hitchcock's understanding that the architectural historian should begin and end his researches with built form remains an important insight. Deriving intellectual sustenance no less than sensual pleasure from the act of seeing, Hitchcock grounded his critical and historical sensibilities in the physical substance of the work of architecture, an approach that remains enduringly viable, if not indispensable, to the architectural historian in America.

NOTES

1. I am grateful to Professor Thomas McCormick of Wheaton College for calling my attention to this source and to Rodney Armstrong, librarian of the Boston Athenuem, for supplying photocopies of the *Harvard Class Notes*. I thank William Kornegay and David and Sally Austin for sharing reminiscences of Hitchcock with me. The papers of Henry-Russell Hitchcock, which have been given to the Archives of American Art, are to be available by early 1990.

2. Henry-Russell Hitchcock, *Modern Architecture: Romanticism and Reintegration* (1929; reprint, New York, 1972).

3. Hitchcock, *German Renaissance Architecture* (Princeton, 1981). Hitchcock, *Latin American Architecture since 1945* (New York, 1955). Hitchcock, *The Architecture of H. H. Richardson and His Times* (1936; rev. ed. Hamden, Conn. 1961). Hitchcock, "Introduction," *Architecture of Skidmore, Owings & Merrill, 1950–1962* (New York and London, 1963), 7–13.

4. "Frank Lloyd Wright and the 'Academic Tradition' of the Early Eighteen-Nineties," *Journal of the Warburg and Courtauld Institutes* 7 (1944), 46–63. This is a superb short article which for the first time demonstrates that in the 1890s, "Wright was then almost certainly the ablest academic designer in Chicago." It was reprinted in *Nineteenth and Twentieth Century Architecture*, Garland Library of the History of Art, Vol. 11 (New York, 1976), together with two other essays by Hitchcock. Two of the reprinted articles are by S. Fiske Kimball, but none of the other architectural historians represented, including John Summerson, C.L.V. Meeks, Reyner Banham, and William Jordy, have more than one article therein.

5. Henry-Russell Hitchcock, *Architecture: Nineteenth and Twentieth Centuries* (Harmondsworth, Middlesex, 1958). This surely is a definitive work on the subject and has been translated into many languages and reprinted in English numerous times.

6. According to Bernard Lubetkin, who toured Europe with Hitchcock in 1937 and is quoted in Gavin Stamp, "Henry-Russell Hitchcock," *AA Files* 16 (Autumn 1987), 4. This obituary contains several inaccuracies.

7. Hitchcock, "Marcel Proust 1927," *Hound & Horn* 1 (March 1928), 254–260. Hitchcock, "Movie Magazines," *Hound & Horn* 2 (September 1928), 95–98. The aircraft manuals were Hitchcock's form of service to his country during World War II. He was able to explain the intricate construction of aircraft engines for those who were to service them.

8. Hitchcock first heard Virgil Thomson play the score in 1927, when they were both in Paris. Gertrude Stein wrote the book, and Hitchcock encouraged the production, which premiered at the Wadsworth Atheneum, directed by Hitchcock's good friend, A. E. "Chick" Austin, Jr., in 1934. See Eugene Gaddis, ed., *Avery Memorial, Wadsworth Atheneum: First Modern Museum* [exh. cat., Wadsworth Atheneum], (Hartford, 1982).

9. In the obituary by Andrea Oppenheimer Dean published in *Architecture* 76 (April 1987), 28, Richard Guy Wilson is quoted as saying that "unlike Mumford, Hitchcock . . . focused on formal, esthetic aspects of building." The author of the obituary recognized, however, that in later years he "remained aloof from stylistic controversies, which partly explains why historians and practitioners of conflicting convictions claim him as mentor and his work as inspiration." William Jordy in his thoughtful obituary "Henry-Russell Hitchcock, 1903–1987" in the *New Criterion* 5 (April 1987), 81, writes that "Hitchcock's emphasis was formalistic." He goes on to note perspicaciously, however, that "the criticism is somewhat unfair, insofar as his visual analysis was not merely descriptive but addressed itself to what was of consequence *architecturally*. Moreover, acute biographical, social, and cultural commentary is copious (if allusive) in his writing. Even so, it is the act of perceptive looking that prevails."

10. Hitchcock 1958, 380.

11. Hitchcock 1929, xv–xvi.

12. *Harvard Class Notes*, 1949. Hitchcock, like Alfred Barr (who was subsequently granted an honorary doctorate), did not receive the Ph.D. from Harvard. From one source I heard that by avoiding the courses in Spanish art taught by Chandler Post, he alienated the powerful professor. John Coolidge has suggested, more plausibly, that the subject he became most involved with—contemporary architecture—was not considered suitable as a subject for a dissertation. A transcript of his years in the Graduate School of Arts and Sciences, provided me by Neil Levine, shows that he received two As, two A minuses, one B plus, and one B: not bad in the days before grade inflation.

13. See *Edward Waldo Forbes: Yankee Visionary* [exh. cat., Fogg Art Museum] (Cambridge, Mass., 1971).

14. Paul Sachs, who became professor of fine arts in 1927, had no graduate training, but as a Harvard undergraduate (A.B. 1900) he had become enamored of works of art and began to collect prints, photographs, and art books. See *Memorial Exhibition: Works of Art from the Collection of Paul J. Sachs* [exh. cat., Fogg Art Museum] (Cambridge, Mass., 1965).

15. Virgil Thomson, *Virgil Thomson* (New York, 1966), 214. In her obituary, "Paul Joseph Sachs (1879–1965)," Agnes Mongan pointed out "how extraordinary it was in a conservative university for a college course to be given which included, as Professor Sachs' French painting course did, those hotly disputed 'modern painters,' Cézanne, Degas, Manet, Gauguin and Van Gogh." *Art Journal* 25 (Fall 1965), 52.

16. To this list should be added Agnes Mongan, who herself would direct the Fogg Art Museum from 1969 to 1971. See Diane De Grazia Bohlen, "Agnes Mongan (b. 1905): Connoisseur of Old Master Drawings," in *Women as Interpreters of the Visual Arts, 1820–*

1979, ed. Claire Richter Sherman with Adele M. Holcomb (Westport, Conn., 1981), 414.

17. Bernard Berenson had established the tradition of connoisseurship at Harvard. "The connoisseur bases his or her studies on the work of art itself rather than on the documents or traditions surrounding it [and] attempts to attribute a work to an individual, a period, or a school by its stylistic characteristics. [Berenson] awoke . . . a sense of the need to come in contact with the original work of art." Bohlen 1981, 416.

18. Hitchcock wrote about painting, in, for example, *Painting Toward Architecture* (New York, 1948) and in the *Wadsworth Atheneum Bulletin* (articles signed JRS were collaborations with Austin, both Hitchcock and Austin being juniors; see Gaddis 1982, 66).

As director of the Smith College Museum of Art from 1949 to 1955, Hitchcock purchased works by Joseph Wright of Derby, Paul Gauguin, Richard Parks Bonington, and William Morris Hunt. Fiske Kimball may have been the only other American architectural historian who was distinguished as a museum director and made major acquisitions of works of art (see Lauren Weiss Bricker, "The Writings of Fiske Kimball: A Synthesis of Architectural History and Practice," in this volume).

19. For further information about Arthur Kingsley Porter, see Linda Seidel, "The Scholar and the Studio: A. Kingsley Porter and the Study of Medieval Architecture before the War," in this volume.

20. *Art Studies* was founded in 1923 by members of the departments of art history at Princeton and Harvard as a supplement to the journal of the Archaeological Institute of America and was supported by funds from the Arthur Sachs Foundation. The most active among its editors were A. Kingsley Porter and Charles Rufus Morey.

21. *Art Studies* 6 (1928), 175–191.

22. Yet apparently he visited Europe in preparation for graduate study. His Harvard transcript indicates that at graduation Harvard awarded him a "prize fellowship for travel and study in Europe." I had hoped to be able to assign the two unattributed photographs to his mentor, but a perusal of the Arthur Kingsley Porter archive at Smith College, which contains duplicates of the photographs held by the Fogg Museum, did not provide conclusive evidence for this hypothesis.

23. *Hound & Horn* 1 (September 1927), 28–35.

24. Oswald Spengler, *Der Untergang des Abendlandes* (Munich, 1922). The English translation, published by Knopf as *The Decline of the West*, appeared in two volumes between 1926 and 1928, so it is probable that Hitchcock initially read the work in the original language.

25. The judgment on Cram's work is consistently negative. Hitchcock seemed to have a particular aversion to the noted Gothic revivalist (whose ideology is discussed by Peter Fergusson in "The Middle Ages: Ralph Adams Cram and Kenneth Conant," in this volume), perhaps because of the somewhat undemocratic and racist elements that underlay Cram's principles. Very much a liberal democrat and a believer in equal rights, Hitchcock took every opportunity to taunt the elitist Anglo-Saxon Protestant. For example, in a response to Rudolph Schindler, who wrote to protest being excluded from the 1932 show at the Museum of Modern Art, Hitchcock replied, "I regret that I have not pleased you and your friends, but think, pray, how little I have pleased Mr. R. A. Cram." Quoted in Thomas S. Hines, *Richard Neutra and the Search for Modern Architecture* (New York, 1982), 105. At this time Hitchcock was uncharacteristically smug and full of himself; in the same letter, he made a claim that goes against the body of his practice of examining buildings at first hand: "I am little likely to be influenced by your apparent contention that the critic is helpless entirely to mention buildings he has only seen photographs of." He adds insult to injury by adding, "I hope of course to see your work in California—although frankly it would be Neutra's which would draw me there."

26. Leonard Greenbaum, *The Hound & Horn: The History of a Literary Quarterly* (The Hague, 1966), 29.

27. Henry-Russel [*sic*] Hitchcock, "L'Architecture contemporaine en Angleterre," *Cahiers d' Art* 3 (1928), 443–446. Hitchcock's French prose is much more straightforward than his English texts, or perhaps the editor of *Cahiers d'Art*, Christian Zervos, was less indulgent than Hitchcock's friends and mentors, acting in the same capacity, had been.

28. Later Wright himself would invite Hitchcock to write the first comprehensive monograph on the founder of the Prairie School—*In the Nature of Materials 1887–1941: The Buildings of Frank Lloyd Wright* (New York, 1942). Grant Manson's Harvard doctoral dissertation of 1940 on Wright's "first golden years" was not yet available in published form; the chief source for Hitchcock, beyond the publications of Wright himself, were articles in journals and material from Taliesin.

29. For a recent appreciation of this book, see Vincent J. Scully, Jr., "Henry-Russell Hitchcock and the New Tradition," in *In Search of Modern Architecture: A Tribute to Henry-Russell Hitchcock*, ed. Helen Searing (Cambridge, Mass., 1982), 10–13.

30. The February 1982 issue of *Progressive Architecture* is devoted to a study of this exhibition.

31. Hitchcock 1936, xi.

32. Mariana Van Rensselaer, *Henry Hobson Richardson and His Works* (Boston, 1888). In the context of this symposium it is not without interest that Hitchcock called her "an admirable architectural critic, intelligent, sensitive and discerning. . . . Her name should not be forgotten nor her work. For she was one of America's few distinguished architectural critics" (Hitchcock 1936, viii).

33. Hitchcock, *Early Victorian Architecture in Britain* (New Haven, 1954).

34. Hitchcock 1954, x–xi.

35. Hitchcock, *German Rococo: The Zimmerman Brothers* (London, 1968), 8.

36. Hitchcock, *Rococo Architecture in Southern Germany* (London, 1968), 12–13.

37. Hitchcock 1981, xxxi.

38. "Obituary: Henry-Russell Hitchcock," *Architectural Review* 181 (May 1987), 4.

39. Hitchcock 1981, 318.

40. Hitchcock 1981, 319.

41. Hitchcock 1936, 301.

42. Of Richardson's Worcester High School he wrote, "A worse adjustment of roof and cornice hardly comes to mind. The tarred brick patterns . . . are worse than 'poor and flat,' as such makeshift polychromy always is" (Hitchcock 1936, 89). The captions for the illustrations in *The International Style: Architecture Since 1922* (New York, 1932; republished as *The International Style* with a new foreword and appendix by Hitchcock, New York, 1966) sound very much as if Hitchcock devised them. Here are a few examples: of the Filling Station by Clauss & Daub, "White band unduly heavy. Good lettering" (113); of Breuninger Department Store by Eisenlohr and Pfenning, "the design is disciplined but lacks individual distinction" (130); of the Bauhaus, "the projection of the roof cap is unfortunate, especially over the entrance at left" (141).

43. *Modern Architecture: International Exhibition* [exh. cat., Museum of Modern Art] (New York, 1932), 97.

44. Hitchcock 1958, 305.

45. Nikolaus Pevsner, *Pioneers of Modern Design, from William Morris to Walter Gropius* (Harmondsworth, Middlesex, 1960), 116.

46. Sigfried Giedion, *Space, Time and Architecture: The Growth of a New Tradition* (1941; 3d ed., enlarged, Cambridge, Mass., 1959). The point here is simply that Pevsner and Giedion were writing polemical surveys of modern architecture that are teleologically determined to end up in the orthodox modern movement. Hitchcock had no such intention.

47. Hitchcock 1929, 88–90. Atypically, in this book he had misidentified the iron-reinforced pitted stonework as "poured concrete"!

48. Jacobus made this observation in a lecture in his course on modern architecture given at the University of California at Berkeley in 1960.

49. Hitchcock 1968, 197. Nor does he deal at all with the important theories of Gottfried Semper, but only cites a few of his buildings in passing.

50. E.R.M. Taverne, review of *Netherlandish Scrolled Gables of the 16th and Early 17th Centuries*, in *Architectura: Zeitschrift für Geschichte der Baukunst* 11 (1981), 192–194.

51. Hitchcock 1929, 240.

52. Hitchcock 1942, 91–92.

53. Vincent Scully, "Wright vs. the International Style," *Art News* 53 (March 1954), 65. In my own observation, the planes are not "clean" at all, but thick and rounded, and the "metal details" have a thick, handcrafted, nonindustrial appearance.

54. "The Wright–International Style Controversy," *Art News* 53 (September 1954), 48. Elizabeth Gordon, at that time editor of *House Beautiful* magazine, also wrote in to complain that Scully "judges architecture in terms of photographs almost exclusively."

55. Helen Searing, "Architectura et Amicitia," in Searing 1982, 3–9. In that essay, I quote the architect Oscar Stonorov, who observed that Hitchcock's "long journeys and European friendships are happily connected with architecture" (8).

56. Hitchcock 1981, xxx.

57. Helen Searing, "Henry-Russell Hitchcock: Formative Years," in *Skyline: The Architecture and Design Review* (December 1982), 11.

EDUARD F. SEKLER
Harvard University

Sigfried Giedion at Harvard University

Sigfried Giedion was appointed the Charles Eliot Norton Professor of Poetry at Harvard University for the academic year 1938–1939, thus becoming the twelfth incumbent of a chair named in honor of the first professor of fine arts the university ever had. In order to understand the full significance of this appointment, one has to realize that the Norton Chair, according to the terms of its endowment, was created with the specific purpose of bringing to the university "men of high distinction and preferably of international reputation." Even if one disregards all practical benefits that went with the appointment, it is clear that for Giedion it represented a powerful boost to his career in the one area where he had been least successful. For despite his numerous publications and successes in other areas of cultural life, at the age of fifty he had yet to find acknowledgment and acceptance in the academic world of his native country, Switzerland.

How Giedion, an architectural historian, could be appointed to a chair of poetry is explained by the Norton Chair's terms of endowment, which stipulated poetry to be interpreted "in the broadest sense, including, together with Verse, all poetic expression in Language, Music or the Fine Arts, under which term Architecture may be included."[1] In 1937 the president of the university, James Bryant Conant, and the dean of the Faculty of Arts and Sciences, George Birkhoff, felt "that if there could be chosen someone representative of architecture this year, it would be decidedly desirable."[2] In keeping with this sentiment the dean of the Graduate School of Design, Joseph Hudnut, was invited to become a member of the selection committee for the Norton professorship.

The process that eventually led to Sigfried Giedion's Charles Eliot Norton lectures and to their published version, *Space, Time and Architecture*, had begun as far back as the spring of 1923, when Giedion went to Weimar to see the first Bauhaus exhibition and on that occasion met Walter Gropius. Years of continuous contact through work for the Congrès Internationaux d'Architecture Moderne (CIAM) followed, and a close friendship developed between the two men.[3] Gropius learned to appreciate Giedion's unique qualities as supporter of the modern movement in architecture just as much as Le Corbusier did. In 1927 Le Corbusier wrote to Giedion, "Let me make you a compliment: you are very intelligent in your considerations about architecture. You know how to extract the essence of things, the vital lines, the root causes."[4] Walter Gropius later remembered Giedion's first visit to the Bauhaus; he wrote that in contrast to most other art historians of the period "who were disconcerted by rather than interested in this first attempt to display the manifold advances of the Bauhaus in the area of design, . . . Giedion was one of the few who understood immediately."[5]

It was not surprising, therefore, that Gropius, soon after his arrival at Harvard University, turned to Giedion for advice about possible candidates "from our circle" who might be suggested for teaching positions in various places in the United States.[6] Giedion in turn made it clear that he was interested in visiting the United States, and in this connection he mentioned an invitation to go to Moholy-Nagy's New Bauhaus in Chicago: "Moholy's proposal has touched me in an extraordinary manner and I have felt it a good fortune, to know there is somewhere a friend who uses his full influence on one's behalf."[7] Giedion may well have intended a subtle hint for Gropius in this statement and, if so, it had the desired effect.

In 1937 Gropius informed Giedion confidentially that Dean Hudnut of the Graduate School of Design, in his capacity as a member of the Norton Committee, had succeeded in having Giedion elected as the first choice for next year's incumbent; in second place Thomas Mann, the great writer, had been proposed. Gropius underlined the importance of this prestigious appointment, which would bring Giedion a lot of publicity and the opportunity to disseminate his ideas far afield. "Since by my coming," Gropius wrote, "and by the presence of Hudnut the entire question of architecture has become topical here in all heads, I thought, nobody could better enlarge the breach and give really fundamental explanations for our movement than you."[8] On a more practical note, Gropius concluded with the advice to Giedion to send a personal letter of thanks to Hudnut, because "he was the one who on my suggestion managed the whole thing even though he knew your work only a little."[9]

The members of the committee other than Dean Hudnut were the art historian Chandler Rathfon Post, the professor of English literature John Livingston Lowes, Dr. Frederick Keppel of the Carnegie Corporation, and Paul Joseph Sachs, the associate director of the Fogg Art Museum, who acted as chairman. It is safe to assume that none of these people knew anything about Giedion other than what could be gleaned from the documentation that Gropius had hastily assembled for Dean Hudnut's presentation to the committee.

Chandler Post was a specialist in the field of Spanish art, and Paul Sachs was a discriminating collector whose taste in architecture is well exemplified by the Fogg Art Museum, which was constructed while he was its associate director. Its most striking architectural feature is a glass-covered courtyard, the elevations of which are direct copies of the Loggia di San Biagio in Montepulciano—hardly something Giedion would have approved. It must have been perfectly clear to Gropius that in the atmosphere of the Fogg Art Museum and the faculty of art historians then at Harvard, Giedion's role would be that of an unorthodox intruder.

Paul Sachs sent Giedion's invitation as a cable and followed it up with a long letter in which he explained that the essential terms of the professorship included the obligation to deliver publicly "not less than six lectures upon poetry" and to make the manuscript of these lectures available for publication by the university.[10] Giedion ended up giving twelve lectures instead of six, and in each he ran over the allotted time span of one hour. Paul Sachs also enumerated for Giedion some of his predecessors, who had included Thomas Stearns Eliot, Robert Frost, and in the field of art history Laurence Binyon, who lectured on "The Spirit of Man in Asian Art," Arthur Mayger Hind, whose topic was "Rembrandt," and Johnny Roosval, whose lecture series was entitled "The Poetry of Chiaroscuro." Giedion's reaction to these topics, found in a letter to Gropius, is typical for his attitude toward traditional academic art history: "When I read the titles of the previous 'lectures,' they were attractive topics of conversation at parties; things that perhaps have already been said frequently and, therefore, more easily possess the kind of social polish that pleases."[11]

Between Giedion's appointment at the beginning of 1938 and the first lecture, which took place in the large lecture hall of the Fogg Art Museum on 15 November, with Dean Hudnut providing the introduction, Gropius and Giedion exchanged an extensive correspondence. It is instructive for what it tells about the working of Giedion's mind and about the expectations Gropius had; it is also amusing when it deals with the fears both Gropius and Giedion harbored about the latter's defective English. Gropius even went so far as to dispense practical advice in the matter of the proper preparation and delivery of lectures in English.

The exchange of statements about this topic was brought about by some errors Giedion had made in his telegram of acceptance. These prompted Dean Hudnut to talk to Gropius about the matter and to request that he should strongly suggest to Giedion the careful preparation of the lectures in good English. Gropius did this diplomatically but in no uncertain terms and wrote on 14 January 1938: "I therefore advise you for the sake of making your pioneering work effective here, to be sure to do everything, in order to prepare yourself also as far as language is concerned. . . . You have time . . . the whole winter and summer to put your matters in order and to prepare your lectures in English.

"I personally have had the experience that a well-considered lecture technique in English renders the people half gained over to begin with. My lectures that, incidentally, I read off, I try therefore to read aloud to myself ahead of time in order to find the correct intonation."[12]

Gropius reiterated his admonitions and suggestions in several letters, and Giedion accepted his suggestions and tried to reassure him. He promised, "it is self-evident that I shall attack English grammar and its complicated to and at and by, and that I shall prepare the lectures in collaboration with Englishmen."[13] But he also admitted, "I specifically find the English intonation terribly difficult because it is so hard to grasp the sound of the words with certainty."[14]

In order to arrive with a manuscript in good English and to improve his own English diction, Giedion went to the trouble of hiring a young Englishman, Royston Bottomley (who later changed his name to Millmore), to work with him as what he called "his amanuensis," a mixture of translator, editor, and language teacher.[15]

He described him to Gropius as a "sensible, modern type who is not familiar with the topic and therefore acts as correcting vox populi."[16]

When one reads both the explicit statements and what is written between the lines in the Giedion-Gropius correspondence, one realizes what a tremendous significance these lectures assumed in the minds of both men. Gropius explained to Giedion that he had learned from Moholy-Nagy about the kind of research Giedion was doing in preparation for his next book and that this information had caused him to promote Giedion's invitation: "As the European who can portray best and in the most scientific manner the entire functional processes of the period in order to derive from them the new architecture."[17] After he had read Giedion's first preliminary outline for the lecture series, Gropius expressed the feeling that such a series would be

inestimable for our entire movement. . . . I see more and more, how much the interconnection is missing and I am happy that the president of Harvard is convinced of this necessity. Thus your contribution will deal with something very topical. In our area synthesis is particularly necessary. A very good English term for it is now coming into use: integrating. I try myself, through innumerable lectures and articles . . . to act in this sense and, where I can, to fight the false aesthetic attitude that has very strong roots here. Because people believe that if someone is artistically gifted, then he must be trained in art history from A–Z. Up to now this is also the firm conviction here at Harvard, and I attempt to set them straight about this.[18]

In reading the letters Gropius addressed to Giedion during this period it becomes obvious that a tremendous psychological pressure on the lecturer was building up. Gropius never failed to include some statements about the importance he attached to Giedion's expected contribution, as when he explicitly wrote, "I expect great things of you and the angle of direction that you indicate in your letter, I can only subscribe to one hundred percent."[19]

The "angle of direction" of Giedion's lectures becomes clear from a number of long letters in which he kept Gropius informed about the way he approached and defined the topic of his lectures. He stressed that he was fully aware of his responsibility, and he was more worried about the question of presentation than anything else. He had no doubts about his goal and his method, and he felt assured that he had collected enough unpublished material during the past years, but he did not like the idea that he would have to stick to his manuscript in the lectures rather than to "develop things freely according to the . . . prevailing atmosphere."[20]

In order to assure a convincing visual presentation of his lectures, Giedion went to the trouble of bringing some five hundred large glass slides across the Atlantic. He assured Gropius that the visual material was collected from remote corners with considerable energy and for the most part would be new even for "those who know all pictures." During the summer of 1938 Giedion had traveled to Belgium and Holland in order to reexamine his impressions, talk to Victor Horta and Henri Van de Velde, and collect material on town planning. He stressed that he only wanted to deal with things he had seen personally and expressed his hope that the forthcoming stay in the United States would enable him to fill a number of gaps in his experience and his knowledge of American historical buildings. Gropius had sent him a copy of Lewis Mumford's *The Culture of Cities* along with words of high praise, and Giedion agreed that Mumford possessed "an entirely astonishing lexicographic knowledge," but added that from his own point of view he was "against condensing too much knowledge into one book."[21]

What Giedion wished to achieve was a combination of extreme selectivity with research in depth and stress on the great historic connections or relationships, including those to the present. "My angle of direction is this: every building should be treated in such a manner that, even without pointing it out, the image of our own period appears by its side."[22] "I want to simplify things," he wrote, "as far as I am capable, and for once to try actually to obtain a total overview. In this manner the students should get the awareness and above all the reassurance that they truly

stand in a tradition and that it is their task, now finally, to arrive at . . . a synthesis. . . . The overcoming of specialization and the preparation for a universalism, that solves even individual problems with consideration of the whole, surely is the altogether essential point concerning us today. I.e., culture or disintegration."[23]

If the desire to achieve a great synthesis was one key motif in Giedion's thinking, the other was the equally strong and closely related desire to create a new kind of *Zeitgeschichte* (history of one's own time), a discipline designed to help one's own period to achieve a consciousness of itself. With this in mind he wrote to Moholy-Nagy about the desire to found an "Institute of Contemporary History and Research."[24]

Giedion arrived at Harvard University in October 1938. He lived at Dunster House among students and was assigned an office in the Fogg Art Museum. As he had requested in his letters, he was given assistance—both with the preparation and delivery of his lectures and with getting them ready for publication. A young graduate student of fine arts who had been asked to assist in making sure the lectures would be clearly presented in good English and accompanied by the correct sequence of slides abandoned his task after the first term because it proved too difficult for him. Not surprisingly, the lectures were not well understood by some members of the audience and attendance dropped somewhat after the first presentations. Others, however, felt that the lectures were eye-openers in more than one sense: through their method of approach, which was something entirely new at Harvard University, and through their convincing visual presentation. Their message, however, only truly came across after they had appeared in book form, having been subjected to the close scrutiny of two sympathetic editors.

Designed by Herbert Bayer, the book was produced lavishly, somewhat against the will of the publisher, Harvard University Press. Concerned with costs, the press had become increasingly discontent with the quantity of changes and corrections Giedion kept making. On 18 May 1941, Gropius finally was able to congratulate Giedion on the appearance in print of *Space, Time and Architecture.* He felt the book was the best statement ever written about the modern movement and predicted that it would not be forgotten. Giedion, in his opinion, had fulfilled what Gropius had had in mind when he proposed him for the Norton professorship, and he suggested that Giedion did not fully comprehend how important his book was for the fight Gropius was leading. "People absolutely did not understand you after your lectures," Gropius concluded, "but now they slowly gain respect; there is a lot of talk about your book and this with respect even in the camp of the enemy."[25]

Many American reviews of the book were full of glowing praise, but Giedion's admired teacher Wölfflin wrote in a letter from Zurich, dated 15 June 1942:

This past fall you sent me your great work on architecture. . . . Consequently the moment had come on my side to say something about it, even if only in a private letter. But I don't get far beyond a simple saying of thank you. I was unable, in the proper sense, to master the material. It is not only the foreign language, that gives me trouble, but also the difference of the generations. You represent the present and I belong to a past period and can only look from afar into the land of the future. That you nevertheless persist in [feeling] an inner connection and speak of a discipleship, has given me great pleasure. The more in old age one is inclined to see only the deficiencies in one's own achievements, the more pleasant it is, still now and then to receive a hand-shake from the realms of the young. All the best, Yours, H. Wölfflin.[26]

In retrospect, it is clear that for Giedion his stay at Harvard University and, connected with it, his intensive exposure to the United States, was a turning point in his life and career. He sensed this himself when he wrote to Dean Hudnut during his homeward journey on board the *Conte di Savoia:* "It seems to me completely out of scale to 'thank you.' You know how the whole atmosphere gave me the necessary joy and 'elan' to carry through the book. I take with me one new 'Erlebnis' which I did not know before: to work in a country with large dimensions. I know that we are

able to influence only a small circle; nevertheless the feeling of having dimensions in the background, you can't calculate, gave me a completely new sensation."[27] In a similar vein Giedion wrote to Paul Sachs: "The sojourn in America was of great fruitfulness for my work. Only now, I believe, is it possible for me to have full insight in my own area."[28]

Not surprisingly, soon after his return to Switzerland, Giedion expressed the wish to visit the States again,[29] this time probably also with an eye to the political situation in Europe that powerfully affected even neutral Switzerland. Immediately after the annexation of Austria he had expressed misgivings when on 21 March 1938 he wrote: "Today everybody here has the feeling that he may experience surprises from one day to the other, and that with the state of mind on the other side [in Germany] it would be possible, without further ado, to wake up some day and to learn that the motorized batteries of Goering have already passed Zurich."[30]

An invitation to deliver the Trowbridge lectures at Yale University surely came as a most welcome opportunity for another trip across the Atlantic. Giedion at that time must have seriously considered an extended stay, for he applied for a quota immigration visa at the U.S. Consulate General in Zurich, using the Czech quota at the advice of the consul; having been born in Prague he was entitled to do so. In September he already wrote to Dean Meeks at Yale from an American address, the Guthrie estate at Locust Valley, Long Island, where he also spent the summer of 1942. He did not return to Zurich until December 1945. During the early 1940s he lectured and traveled widely in the United States, partly in connection with the research for his next book, titled *Mechanization Takes Command.*

In 1943 Giedion had contacts with the newly founded Society of Architectural Historians. He exchanged letters with Turpin Bannister and contributed an article, "On C.I.A.M.'s Unwritten Catalogue," to the January–April 1943 issue of the society's journal. It was a defense of José Luis Sert's *Can Our Cities Survive?* against a critical review Carl Feiss had published in the previous issue. To Roger Hale Newton, secretary of the New York chapter of the SAH, Giedion in January 1944 sent a list of topics suggested for discussion at a planned congress.[31]

At Harvard, despite the case for the study of history Giedion had made in his Norton lectures, architectural history was slowly pushed out of the architectural curriculum. In 1938–1939 three courses in architectural history were still required for a bachelor's degree in architecture; in 1939–1940 the requirement was reduced to two courses; and finally, from 1943–1944 through 1949–1950 no courses in architectural history were required for the degree, though such courses could be taken as electives offered by the Fine Arts Department.

Walter Gropius retired in July 1952, and after the appointment in January 1953 of José Luis Sert as the new dean and chairman of the Architecture Department, the teaching of architectural history was completely reorganized, and Sert did not fail in this connection to avail himself of the advice of his old friend Giedion. Giedion, who had also taught at the Massachusetts Institute of Technology in the meantime, was then chiefly preoccupied with his work about the beginnings of art and architecture (*The Eternal Present*, 1962 and 1964), but he managed to accept appointments as a visiting professor for one term or parts of a term from the mid-1950s through the early 1960s. He lectured on ancient and on modern architecture, and in 1961 gave the first Gropius lecture on "Constancy, Change and Architecture." He also conducted joint seminars with the author, who had been appointed visiting professor in 1955. Four terms of architectural history were now mandatory, as Giedion and the author had recommended in a joint memorandum, and history walked, in Giedion's words, "beside the student as a friendly guide, liberating but not inhibiting his spatial imagination."[32]

The story of Giedion and Harvard University, of course, does not conclude with his last teaching there in the early 1960s. Teaching always reaches only a comparatively small group of people, though in a most powerful and at times unforgettable

Sigfried Giedion (right) and Eduard Sekler during a seminar held at the Harvard University Graduate School of Design, fall 1960
Photograph by Ueli Roth

manner. More important for Giedion's effect on the understanding and teaching of architectural history was the impact of the many editions and translations of *Space, Time and Architecture*. One indicator of the book's success is the number of copies sold. The sales figures also indicate something about the waxing and waning of its impact. Of a total of 114,000 sold copies, more than half—almost 65,000—were sold between 1941 and 1962. By 1972 an average of 2,000 copies was sold yearly; ten years later the figure had dropped to 1,500, and in the late 1980s it fell to between 700 and 800.[33]

A questionnaire about preferred reading handed out by the author in a seminar at Harvard's Graduate School of Design from the early 1960s to the present indicates a similar decline. While *Space, Time and Architecture* was frequently mentioned in the 1960s and still appeared through the 1970s, it practically disappeared from the lists after 1980.

If, in conclusion, one asks what Giedion's relevance for the American historiography of architecture is, it seems to me the answer will be somewhat along the following lines. Through his insistence on space as an analytical and critical category, he materially assisted in making American architectural historians aware of that vast body of interpretative literature that resulted not only from the work of his famous master Wölfflin, but also from that of many other German-speaking scholars, such as Schmarsow, Riegl, Brinckmann, and Frankl. These contributions to scholarship are well known today, but were not so half a century ago.

If the great synthesis Giedion was trying to achieve in his work can no longer convince us today, this is because, in his belief in the possibility of such a synthesis, he stood at the end of a tradition: that of the great art historical system-builders who believed they could create an all embracing *Kunstwissenschaft*. Giedion made his most enduring contribution, however, where he stood not at the end of a line but at the beginning of a new tradition. He shares with Hitchcock and Mumford the distinction of having opened up for research entire new areas in the nineteenth and, above all, in the twentieth centuries. Industrial archaeology, today a well-established field, owes him a debt of gratitude, and in the German-speaking countries *Mechanization Takes Command* (in its German version) recently has made him an admired pioneer of the ecological approach to architecture championed by the so-called "Greens."[34] In addition, the revival of interest in the city as a work of art and in the conservation of its historic centers was clearly anticipated in Giedion's writings about the core of the city.

He was much concerned about the dichotomy between feeling and thinking. Though his own feeling, the impassioned partisanship for the modern movement, may at times have flawed his way of thinking, it also fed his extraordinary creative sensitivity and led him into exciting areas where he was among the first to tread. For this he deserves to be remembered with gratitude.

NOTES

All quoted documents are either in the Giedion Archive (abbreviated GA) of the Eidgenössische Technische Hochschule Zürich or in the Harvard University Archives (abbreviated HA). I am grateful to Professor Werner Oechslin, head of the Institute for History and Theory of Architecture, Zurich, and to Harley Pierce Holden, curator of the Harvard University Archives, for making the Giedion material in their collections available and granting permission to publish the excerpts I selected. For their valuable assistance I am also grateful to Wolfgang Böhm, Jos Bosman, Sokratis Georgiadis, Professors John Coolidge, Sidney Freedberg, and Bernard Lemann, and to my wife, Mary Patricia May Sekler. All translations are by the author.

1. Paul Sachs to Sigfried Giedion, 12 January 1938, GA.

2. Dean Birkhoff to Dean Hudnut, 9 November 1937, HA.

3. Adolf Max Vogt, "Sigfried Giedion and Walter Gropius," in 3. Internationales Bauhaus-Kolloquium, July 1983, GA.

4. "Laissez moi vous faire un compliment: vous êtes très intelligens [sic] dans vos considerations sur l'architecture. Vous savez extraire l'essence des choses, les lignes vitales, les causes matrices." Charles-Edouard Jeanneret to Giedion, 2 April 1927, GA.

5. Walter Gropius, quoted in Hommage à Giedion, Profile seiner Persönlichkeit, ed. Paul Hofer (Basel and Stuttgart, 1971), 118.

6. Gropius to Giedion, 24 June 1937, copy in GA. In the same letter Gropius inquires whether Giedion knowns where Hans Wittwer lives, "whose work I liked so extremely (dessen Arbeit mir so ausserordentlich gefiel)."

7. Giedion to Gropius, 25 October 1937, GA. "Moholy's Antrag hat mich ausserordentlich gerührt und ich habe es als Glück empfunden, irgendwo einen Freund zu wissen, der sich für einen voll einsetzt."

8. Gropius to Giedion, 23 December 1937, GA. In this letter Gropius typed everything, including proper names, lowercase. "da durch mein kommen und hudnut's hiersein die ganze frage der architektur in allen köpfen hier aktuell geworden ist dachte ich es könne keiner besser die bresche erweitern und wirklich fundamentale erläuterungen für unsere bewegung geben als du."

9. Gropius to Giedion, 23 December 1937. "denn er hat die ganze geschichte auf meinen vorschlag hingeschmissen obwohl er dein werk nur wenig kannte."

10. Sachs to Giedion, 12 January 1938.

11. Giedion to Gropius, 21 January 1938, transcript in GA. "Wenn ich die Titel der vorausgegangenen "lectures" lese, so waren das zügige gesellschaftliche Gesprächsstoffe; Dinge, die vielleicht oft schon gesagt wurden und darum leichter jenen gesellschaftlichen Schliff in sich tragen, der gefällt."

12. Gropius to Giedion, 14 January 1938, GA. "Deshalb rate ich Dir, um Deine Pionierarbeit hier wirksam zu machen, doch alles zu tun, um Dich auch sprachlich gut vorzubereiten. . . .

Ich habe persönlich die Erfahrung gemacht, dass eine wohlüberlegte Vortragstechnik in Englisch die Leute . . . schon halb gewonnen macht. Ich versuche mir deshalb meine Vorträge, die ich im übrigen ablese, vorher laut vorzulesen, um die richtige Intonation zu finden."

13. Giedion to Gropius, 21 January 1938. "Dass ich mich auf Englische Grammatik und ihre verzwickten to und at und by stürze und die Vorträge gemeinsam mit Engländern vorbereiten werde, ist selbstverständlich."

14. Giedion to Gropius, 21 March 1938, GA. "Ich finde gerade die Englische Intonation fürchterlich schwer, da die Worte so schwer lautlich sicher anzupacken sind."

15. Royston Millmore, "Working with Sigfried Giedion," Building Design (London), 15 March 1974, 22–24, and 22 March 1974, 14–15. I am grateful to Mr. Millmore for having provided copies of this essay together with additional information in several letters.

16. Giedion to Gropius, 21 March 1938. "Es ist ein sensibler, moderner Typ, der das Thema nicht kennt und daher als korrigierende Vox Populi auftritt."

17. Gropius to Giedion, 14 January 1938. "Als denjenigen Europäer, der am besten und wissenschaftlichsten die gesamten Funktionsvorgänge der Zeit darzustellen vermag, um von da aus die neue Architektur abzuleiten."

18. Gropius to Giedion, 11 February 1938, GA. "Unschätzbar für unsere ganze Bewegung. . . . Ich sehe immer mehr, wie sehr es an einem Zusammenhang fehlt und bin glücklich, dass der Harvard President [sic] von dieser Notwendigkeit überzeugt ist. So wird also Dein Beitrag in eine sehr aktuelle Kerbe fallen. . . . [The reference here is to President Conant's creation of the "University Professorships," which were nondepartmental and meant to bring about crossdisciplinary syntheses.] Auf unserem Gebiet ist die Zusammenfassung besonders notwendig. Eine sehr gute englische Bezeichnung hierfür kommt jetzt auf: integrating. . . . Ich selbst versuche auch, durch zahllose Vorträge und Artikel . . . in diesem Sinne zu wirken und, wo ich kann, gegen die falsche ästhetische Einstellung, die hier sehr eingewurzelt ist, zu kämpfen. Die Leute glauben nämlich, wenn jemand künstlerisch begabt ist, dann muss er von A–Z in Kunstgeschichte trainiert werden. Das ist auch bisher in Harvard eingefleischt und ich versuche, ihnen hier diesen Star zu stechen."

19. Gropius to Giedion, 1 June 1938, GA. "Ich erwarte von Dir grosse Dinge, und den Richtwinkel, den Du in Deinem Briefe gibst, kann ich nur hundertprozentig unterschreiben."

20. Giedion to Gropius, 18 January 1938, GA. "Die Dinge entsprechend der jeweiligen Atmosphäre frei zu entwickeln."

21. Giedion to Gropius, 14 May 1938, GA. "Ein ganz

erstaunliches lexikographes Wissen. . . . bin ich dagegen allzuviel Wissen in ein Buch zu kondensieren."

22. Giedion to Gropius, 14 May 1938. "Mein Richtwinkel ist: Jeder Bau soll so behandelt werden, dass auch ohne Hinweis das Bild unserer eigenen Zeit daneben steht."

23. Giedion to Gropius, 21 March 1938. "Ich will die Dinge so weit vereinfachen, als ich es fertig bringe und tatsächlich einmal versuchen, einen Gesamtüberblick zu gewinnen. Es soll dadurch den Studenten das Bewusstsein und vor allem die Sicherheit gegeben werden, dass sie wirklich in einer Tradition stehen und es ihre Aufgabe ist, nun endlich . . . eine Synthese zu geben. . . . Überwindung des Spezialistentums und die Vorarbeit für einen Universalismus, der auch Einzelprobleme . . . unter Hinblick auf das Ganze löst, ist ja überhaupt der Kernpunkt, um den es heute geht. D.h. Kultur oder Zersplitterung."

24. Giedion to László Moholy-Nagy, 20 November 1940, GA.

25. Gropius to Giedion, 18 May 1941, GA. "Die Leute verstanden Dich absolut nicht nach Deinen 'Lectures' aber nun gewinnen sie langsam Respekt; es wird viel über Dein Buch gesprochen und auch im Feindeslager mit Achtung." The title of Giedion's book may well have been inspired by Samuel Alexander's volume, *Space, Time, and Deity: The Gifford Lectures of Glasgow, 1916–1918* (London, 1920), which stood at eye height on a shelf opposite the entrance to the stacks of Harvard's Widener Library and was hard to overlook by anybody who entered the stacks as often as Giedion did.

26. H. Wölfflin to Giedion, 15 June 1942, GA. "Sie haben mir vorigen Herbst Ihr grosses Architekturwerk zugehen lassen. . . . somit war der Moment gekommen, meinerseits etwas dazu zu sagen, wenn auch nur in einem privaten Brief. Aber ich komme nicht weit über eine simple Danksagung hinaus. Im eigentlichen Sinne des Stoffes Herr zu werden, ist mir nicht gelungen. Es ist nicht allein die fremde Sprache, die mir Schwierigkeiten macht, sondern der Unterschied der Generationen. Sie repräsentieren die Gegenwart und ich gehöre einer vergangenen Zeit an und kann nur von Ferne in das Land der Zukunft hinüber blicken. Dass Sie trotzdem an einem inneren Zusammenhang festhalten und von einer Schülerschaft sprechen, hat mir grosse Freude gemacht. Je mehr man im Alter geneigt ist, nur das

Fehlende in der eigenen Leistung zu sehen, umso wohltuender ist es, noch hie und da einen Händedruck aus den Reichen der Jungen zu empfangen. Alles Gute, Der Ihrige, H. Wölfflin."

27. Giedion to Hudnut, 5 April 1940, HA.

28. Giedion to Paul Sachs, 6 December 1940, GA. "Der Aufenthalt in Amerika war für meine eigene Arbeit von grosser Fruchtbarkeit. Erst jetzt, glaube ich, ist es mir möglich, vollen Einblick in mein eigenes Gebiet zu haben."

29. Giedion to Gropius, 30 July 1940, GA. "Ich möchte wieder hinüber. (I want [to come] across again]."

30. Giedion to Gropius, 21 March 1938. "Jeder hat heute hier das Gefühl, dass er von einem Tag zum anderen Überraschungen erleben kann und dass es bei dem Geisteszustand drüben ohne weiteres möglich wäre, eines Tages aufzuwachen und zu vernehmen, dass die motorisierten Batterien Göhrings bereits Zürich passiert haben."

31. Giedion to Roger Hale Newton, 16 January 1944, GA. The topics were:

"1) Interrelated research: this means to ascertain

2) the most important problems which have to be solved in our scholarly field

3) The kind of collaboration with architects (urgent historical problems)

4) The kind of collaboration with public institutions

5) The way to publish historical articles in American Architectural Magazines

6) The fight against the dictatorship of the American Advertising man, dooming every effort of the editors

7) To go ahead for interesting the press

8) Finally: to create an American public (by all means of radio, press, magazines) which . . . not [sic] longer believe [sic] 'history is bunk.' "

32. Sigfried Giedion, "History and the Architect," in *Architecture You and Me: The Diary of a Development* (Cambridge, Mass., 1958), 119.

33. I am grateful to Peg Fulton of Harvard University Press for providing this information.

34. This fact was kindly pointed out to me by Jos Bosman, ETH Zurich.

SUZANNE STEPHENS
Barnard College

Architecture Criticism in a Historical Context:

The Case of Herbert Croly

In looking back at architecture criticism published in newspapers and magazines, we may often wonder about its ultimate value. Frequently, this form of criticism is misdirected or off-target. Newspaper and magazine critics usually lack the advantage of a perspective given to those who write books. Because critics writing for an ephemeral medium must offer their opinions before they have fully adjusted to or understood the new work, they may overlook some redeeming features or miss some real drawbacks in the scheme. Their values and assumptions may not allow a flexible enough critical stance to judge the merits of a new work of architecture.

There are other reasons that one person's reaction to an architect's latest endeavor can be skewed. In 1903, the much-respected architectural historian and critic Russell Sturgis found Frank Lloyd Wright's Larkin Building "so ungainly, so awkward in grouping, so clumsy in its parts and in its main mass" that he wondered, "How did the designers work when men knew how to design?"[1] As was clear in Sturgis' essay, he was assessing the building on the basis of photographs instead of an actual visit. This, in addition to his own difficulty in adjusting to Frank Lloyd Wright's aesthetic, resulted in a critique that was in time only a historical curiosity.

Then, too, the general appreciation of a work may change dramatically over time.

In 1931 Lewis Mumford wrote of the Chrysler Building, "Heaven help the person who critically looks at this building without the help of distance and heavy mists. The ornamental treatment of the facade is a series of restless mistakes."[2] Today the Chrysler Building is considered one of the significant icons of the city, a monument to a period when skyscraper design was literally at its peak. Mumford considered the Daily News building to be a particularly strong work of architecture, and he was exceedingly enthusiastic about the Hunter College facility built on Park Avenue.[3] Yet neither building today occupies the pantheon of distinguished works of architecture in New York.

On top of the problem of changing perceptions, critics in newspapers and magazines often lack the freedom and space to develop and expand ideas. Much of the content has to be simplified for a broad audience, and in a number of journals and papers there is a pressure to entertain their audiences as well as provide information. The magazine for the general audience most often places more emphasis on the persona of the architect than on the work itself.

Many cases can be cited of critics who were able to identify the important new work of architecture and address the qualities it embodied that were of lasting significance, just as many examples can be shown of judgments that did not survive. Yet there is some benefit to reading criticism published in magazines and newspapers—other than to satisfy our curiosity about the way architecture is perceived at a particular moment. Criticism in magazines and newspapers does generate a climate of debate where certain values are verbalized, principles are articulated, and tentative evaluations (right or wrong) are made.

In addition, a critic may develop a certain approach to thinking about a building or an urban ensemble that spurs others to begin looking at and evaluating architecture in a similar manner. It is the general orientation, not the particular assessment, that counts in this case. Herbert Croly (1869–1930), whose architectural writing appeared primarily in the *Architectural Record* at the beginning of the twentieth century, is interesting to study for this reason.

Croly's approach to evaluating buildings and the urban landscape appears to anticipate, albeit faintly, the recent architectural criticism based on a theoretical analysis of buildings now referred to as "typology," "signification," and "contextualism." Such terms imply a more sophisticated level of conceptual understanding of architecture than that which characterized Croly's own writing. His primary inclination was to evaluate buildings and urban ensembles according to their aesthetic merits using traditional principles of composition, such as proportion, rhythm, and balance in line, mass, and texture.

At the same time his writings showed an interest in the building as the user or observer experienced it, particularly with regard to its intended function. Croly addressed the work of architecture as a symbol—cultural, civic, or residential—and introduced questions about how the architecture expressed larger, less palpable purposes. This sociological and psychological component in his criticism could be seen in articles discussing how a building type established the right setting for its intended use or expressed its particular place in society.

Croly looked at the building as a physical object in the city as well and analyzed its place within the larger urban context.

Again he judged it both as a formal object and as a symbolic one. He did not invent these reference points, nor was he the only one to reveal an interest in type, context, and cultural expression. But these three approaches showed up more frequently and more predominantly in his writing than in that of his contemporaries.

Herbert Croly did not write criticism that paved the way for the new modern architecture. He did not isolate the creative experiments, the new technologies, and the architects of his time whose contributions would weigh heavily in the history of twentieth-century architecture and urbanism. He was not as comfortable with the traditional vocabulary of aesthetic criticism as was Russell Sturgis. Nor did he write about the work at hand from the more explicitly architectural orientation of Montgomery Schuyler, who, like Croly, was not trained as an architect. Croly wrote architecture criticism consistently from the perspective of the layperson. But because of strong sociological and philosophical convictions the young man had acquired at home and at Harvard College, his commentary attempted to place the works in an intellectual framework rather than simply present a series of personal impressions.[4]

The architects Croly wrote about most often included traditionally and classically minded ones such as Charles Platt, John Russell Pope, Howard van Doren Shaw, Trowbridge and Livingston, and Herts and Tallent. As for the coverage of the architectural vanguard forming in the Midwest in the early twentieth century, Croly focused on the work of the Prairie School architects, such as George Maher or Richard Schmidt, rather than on their mentor Frank Lloyd Wright. He did not especially admire the work of the younger generation, however, for it seemed to him to sacrifice proportion and propriety to the desire for new ideas. Nevertheless, Croly agreed the efforts were "sincere" and the technical competence high.[5]

Although Croly gave much attention to houses, his essays on cities, particularly a handful written at the beginning of the century on New York, have commanded more recent attention.[6] They show a particular sensitivity to and astuteness about the inherent problems in the forming of a capital of culture and commerce. Yet even these articles were to be eclipsed by Croly's second career.

As historian David Levy demonstrated so well in his book *Herbert Croly of The New Republic*, Croly is remembered today not as an architectural critic, but as a social commentator, political philosopher, and founding editor of an influential political magazine. In fact, Croly's professional reputation as a political commentator was so entrenched at the time of his death in 1930 that Walter Lippmann, one of the eminent political writers associated with the *New Republic*, described Croly as "the first important political philosopher that appeared in America in the twentieth century."[7]

Croly's much-acclaimed book of political and social commentary, *The Promise of American Life*, appeared in 1909 when he was forty years old. In *Promise*, Croly called for a different kind of government than that encouraged by the Jeffersonian decentralization of the nineteenth century. The economic and political pressures of the twentieth century clearly indicated to Croly that the laissez-faire attitude of the self-interested citizen was no longer a viable role model for American democracy. Instead, he argued that Alexander Hamilton's form of a centralized government was now needed. But unlike Hamilton, who thought the government should be ruled by a wealthy, educated aristocracy, Croly prescribed a responsible government ruled by committed public representatives. Yet Croly and others contended the democratic ethos too often rewarded mediocrity and conformity, which resulted in a leavening of capabilities in leadership. A new leadership was called for.

What type of "constructive individual," as Croly described him in *Promise*, could face new challenges of industrial growth, the urbanization of cities, development of labor, and evolution of the corporation? *The Promise of American Life* advocated a democracy run by highly educated reform-minded leaders (which at that time could be found mostly in certain upper-middle- and upper-class—one could argue "aristo-cratic"—enclaves along the East Coast).[8] Surprisingly, the model for the ideal leader, as the concluding chapter in *Promise* reveals, was the architect. Croly explained later that he had actually been inspired by reading Robert Grant's novel, *Unleavened Bread*, about an unsuccessful architect, which Croly had reviewed for the *Architectural Record* in 1905.[9] In the novel, as Croly pointed out, the architect's mercenary wife represented the "mid-century American point of view of immediate practical achievement at any cost." This, continued Croly, "is the tradition which is the worst enemy of American architecture in American life—the tradition which resents exclusive technical standards and refuses to trust the men who by their thorough training have earned the right authoritatively to represent such standards."

Croly's architect, as described in *The Promise of American Life*, is "independent and authoritative." His work will "grow in distinction and individuality; and as good or better examples of it become more numerous it will attract and hold an increasing body of approving opinion. The designer will in this way have gradually created his own special public. He will be molding and informing the architectural taste and preference of his admirers."[10]

Charles Platt (fig. 1) is probably the architect Croly had in mind when he wrote this chapter in *Promise* on "Constructive Individualism," as Keith Morgan argues in his biography, *Charles Platt: The Artist as Architect*. Platt had been a good friend of Croly's since his days at Harvard and had designed a house for him in Cornish, New Hampshire, in 1897. He had the attributes Croly called for, Morgan maintains, and he eventually built a public support based on "the consistent quality of his work, not on public visibility or polemics."[11]

Critics, Croly felt, should follow a similar line of action, whereby they sought truth and attempted to become the "voice of the specific intellectual interest."[12] According to one of the writers at the *New Republic*, Bruce Bliven, Croly followed his own advice: "He wrote for the superior few, whether in politics, journalism or the learned professions. He thought of this intellectual aristocracy as influencing the

1. Charles A. Platt, Entrance, Russell A. Alger, Jr., house, "The Moorings," Grosse Pointe Farms, Michigan, 1908–1910

From Keith N. Morgan, *Charles A. Platt: The Artist as Architect* (Cambridge, Mass., 1985), fig. 72. Photograph by Richard Cheek

trend of American life to an extent out of all proportion to its very limited numbers."[13]

Before Croly completed *The Promise of American Life*, he had written more than forty-five attributed articles and two books on architecture, urban design, and planning as an editor with the *Architectural Record*, *Real Estate Record*, and *Builder's Guide*, as well as other publications. *Real Estate Record* had been started by Clinton Sweet and Croly's father, David Croly, a well-known newspaperman with a strong reformist orientation. In fact, the senior Croly had served as the managing editor of the *New York World* from 1863 to 1872 during the time Montgomery Schuyler was working there. Herbert Croly's mother, Jane Cunningham Croly, was a journalist as well—the best known female journalist of her time, although she wrote on house-hold notes under the name of Jenny June.[14]

When his father died in 1889, Herbert Croly began to work for *Real Estate Record* and *Builder's Guide* and left Harvard without receiving a degree. He then became an editor and writer for its new sister publication, the *Architectural Record*, which Sweet founded in 1891. Sweet was convinced that an architectural magazine with a literary orientation could appeal to the general public as well as to the architecture profession, largely because of the public interest in architecture being stirred at the time by the plans for the World's Columbian Exposition in Chicago.[15]

Harry Desmond, another *Real Estate Record* and *Builder's Guide* staff member, was designated the first editor of the *Architectural Record*, and later Desmond would be a coauthor of Croly's first book, *Stately Homes in America from Colonial*

Times to the Present Day, published in 1903.

Young Croly did go back to Harvard in 1892, but he returned to the *Architectural Record* in 1900—still without a degree— and stayed there full-time until 1906. After 1906 Croly remained on the staff, but apparently part-time, for he was already busy writing his first political book. *The Promise of American Life* would soon be followed by *Marcus Alonzo Hanna: His Life and Work* in 1912 and *Progressive Democracy* in 1914.

Even when Croly became editor of the *New Republic* in 1914, he continued to contribute articles to the *Architectural Record*. Yet Croly's articles on architecture did not make the same impression as his social and political commentary and the theory of a democratic "new nationalism" he described in *Promise*. Later historians have not been kind: Charles Forcey wrote in 1961, "Neither of [Croly's] two rather prosaic books on architecture, nor his writings for the *Architectural Record* gave much promise of the trenchant political critic to come."[16] Croly's biographer David Levy, and before him Christopher Lasch, had referred to these years of Croly's pre-political life as "the blank years."[17]

Croly's emphasis on the role of the creative individual in guiding a democracy has been discussed by Thomas Bender in *New York Intellect: A History of Intellectual Life in New York City, From 1750 to the Beginnings of Our Own Time*, and more recently in an essay on architectural journalism.[18] Bender argues that Croly's commitment to the role of intellectual thought in American politics and culture played a part in placing architecture criticism in the larger world of ideas at that time. This is an interesting argument, but it does not explain why Croly, the architecture critic, was overlooked so blatantly by his peers in the memorial issue on his work published by the *New Republic* after his death in 1930.

Bender acknowledges there was a curious split between the two Crolys: one the architecture critic and editor writing for a professional audience, the other the political commentator and editor writing for the enlightened public. Judging from the essays on Croly written by his colleagues at

the time of his death, we can see that Croly's affinity for architecture was simply not important except to Croly's longtime friend Charles Platt, who tried to reconcile Croly's architectural values with his political beliefs. "In the domain of sociology he was a progressive, as we all know. He followed the same principle in his attitude toward art, but he was also a reasoned traditionalist, persuaded both by instinct and by study that our evolution needs to be steadied by careful consideration of precedent."[19]

In his own testimonial essay, Edmund Wilson mentioned that Croly "was sometimes accused of a lack of esthetic appreciation and though he believed himself deaf to music and incapable of enjoying poetry, [he had also] something of the sensibility of the artist." Wilson writes in almost a tone of surprise (understandable if he knew little about Croly's previous life as an architectural journalist), that "his imagination was easily touched and he responded to atmospheres and scenes as sensitively as anyone I have ever known."[20]

It seems strange that a critic of Croly's major political accomplishments would not have provided more hints of his earlier talents. Was he a brilliant architecture critic as well as a brilliant political philosopher and simply not recognized as such, even by the professional audience? To a large degree Croly was not given his due, since many of his own articles written while he was on the staff of the *Architectural Record* were signed under the pseudonym Arthur C. David. Others, including a book, *Houses for Town or Country*, published in 1907, were signed William Herbert. Croly's biographer David Levy has made a strong case for Croly having written all of these pseudonymous articles by comparing the essays to his signed work according to subject, style, frequency of certain phrases and words, and parallel sentence construction.[21] Since Croly's style was often somewhat ponderous and syntactically idiosyncratic, Levy's argument seems particularly plausible. The consistency of Croly's criteria for evaluating works of architecture in his signed and pseudonymous pieces further strengthens Levy's case. But the actual reason for the pseudonym—even when the different articles are categorized according to subject matter—is unclear.[22]

One pattern seems evident: when Croly was talking about newly developing building types or urban forms, such as hotels, apartment buildings, or department stores, he would typically use the pen name Arthur C. David or A. C. David. The pseudonym seems to be taken from his father's first name, and perhaps it was combined with the initials of the French social philosopher Auguste Comte, whose positivist philosophical convictions had so influenced the father's and the son's own empirically and sociologically oriented thinking. Comte argued that knowledge was gained through the senses and through the study of science, particularly the science of human relations or sociology.[23] Similarly, there is a strong tendency in Croly's criticism to judge buildings as physical phenomena that are appreciated by understanding the pattern of human activities taking place in and around them.

While Croly's aesthetic criteria were not as developed as Russell Sturgis' or his sense of structure not as informed as Montgomery Schuyler's, like Sturgis and even Schuyler, Croly did rely very much on traditional classical aesthetic standards of evaluation, which served as a framework for criticizing buildings. Proportion, line, mass, and other compositional attributes formed his guidelines to a visual analysis that showed the young critic's increasing confidence as he attained more experience and practice on the job at the *Architectural Record*. Again, like Sturgis and Schuyler, Croly voiced the belief that materials must be expressed honestly. He argued that pure functionalism and efficiency had a place—albeit primarily in factories and office buildings. Function, Croly felt, should be revealed as long as it did not disturb compositional unity.[24]

Croly constantly emphasized the need to work with historical examples and maintain the sense of tradition in architecture. He felt that architecture could not depend totally on new and innovative responses. In 1904, Croly wrote:

American architectural practice has pretty well decided that the safest and most fruitful kind

2. Henry Janeway Hardenbergh, Waldorf-Astoria Hotel, Thirty-fourth Street and Fifth Avenue, New York, 1895
From *The Unofficial Palace of New York: A Tribute to the Waldorf-Astoria*, ed. Frank Crowninshield (New York, 1939). © Hotel Waldorf-Astoria Corporation, New York

of work which the good American architect can do is that of continuing in this country the great European architectural tradition. . . . After the architects have become accustomed to designing, and the public have become accustomed to seeing, good architectural forms, it will be time enough to demand that these forms be modified, with a special view to giving them a higher degree of individual, local and national propriety.[25]

But more interesting than Croly's valuing tradition was his evaluation of buildings as they were experienced—as a hotel visitor, as a theatergoer, and as an apartment dweller. To Croly the experience was still based primarily on visual sensation. Criticism in subsequent decades evolved a more conceptual as well as a kinesthetic analysis based on the critic's experience of moving through the building or around it. In this latter instance, the critic has more than eyes, and the building has to appeal on more levels than mood or impression:

3. Trowbridge and Livingston,
St. Regis Hotel, Fifth Avenue
and Fifty-fifth Street, New
York, 1904
From a postcard

type in order to evaluate it. The success of the scheme was often judged according to the way the formal characteristics of a hotel, for example, differed from an office building, or a theater from an apartment house.

To be sure, Montgomery Schuyler wrote a number of articles on skyscrapers that evaluated the tall building as a distinct type defined by specific formal, structural, and urbanistic considerations. This included the way the skeletal structure was enclosed by a cladding or skin (such as terra cotta) that allowed the steel frame to be revealed, or the tower was massed according to a tripartite division. In other words, the criteria were explicitly architectural. Herbert Croly's discussions, on the other hand, focused on the way the design expressed the intended use to the observer or lay person.

For example, in 1905 Croly criticized three new large hotels for the *Architectural Record*—the Belvedere in Baltimore, designed by Parker and Thomas, the Willard Hotel in Washington, D.C., by Henry J. Hardenbergh, and the Bellevue Stratford in Philadelphia, by B. W. and W. D. Hewitt. Croly argued that Manhattan's own Waldorf-Astoria at 34th Street and Fifth Avenue, also designed by Henry J. Hardenbergh, one part of which opened in 1893, the other in 1897, represented the first major step in the design of a hotel as a special building type (fig. 2). The hotel-skyscraper should not resemble an office building, he argued. The Waldorf achieved a domestic image with its "warmer, more attractive materials" and dormer windows in the mansard roof. To arrive at the requisite residential scale, formal characteristics, such as strong horizontal lines, were needed to counteract the strong vertical thrust of the tower.[26]

In an article on the St. Regis Hotel, designed by Trowbridge and Livingston, Croly extolled the St. Regis' residential character (fig. 3). This character was imparted most visibly to the tall tower by the balcony that doubled as cornice, as well as by the mansard-style roof.[27]

A critique of the theaters built in rapid succession in New York at the turn of the century underscored the necessity for judg-

the viewer is "reading" the building or the urban milieu as a text. He is as conceptually attuned as he is sensitive.

If we look at some of the architecture Croly wrote about and the architectural issues he addressed, we find the reason why certain buildings or urban ensembles were appreciated for qualities other than originality or use of innovative techniques and materials. Croly, it would seem, analyzed the defining characteristics of a building's

ing them from the point of view of the theatergoer. Croly argued that theaters need not necessarily be "vulgar." But he maintained the public should be put in a "gay, exhilarated, if irresponsible" state of mind at the various performances. He argued that "a theater is the last place in the world for the display of ineffective refinement or for any modest reticence of treatment. It is a showroom and a playroom and should be boldly and frankly treated as such."[28]

Of the New Amsterdam Theater (fig. 4, 5) by Herts and Tallent of 1903, one of the more extreme theater designs of its day, Croly said:

Its most dubious aspect consists precisely in the absence of bold and effective color treatment. The color scheme of the auditorium is mother of pearl, violet, and green, which . . . is a harmonious combination, but it is too neutral and delicate in tone for the large surfaces, the long distances, and the necessary showiness of a theater.[29]

However, the architects had kept "propriety, consistency and carefulness of design," which Croly deemed more salutary for American architecture than "originality." Croly considered the Lyceum, also executed by Herts and Tallent, "more conventional," but "a much more energetic piece of architecture. . . . The facade is dominated by an order, which, if anything, counts rather too much than too little."

After he had left the staff of the magazine, Croly wrote frequently for the *Architectural Record* about the large mansion for the very affluent. While housing millionaires does not appear to be serious stuff for someone who was writing political and social commentary elsewhere, he did, however, address these homes as part of a sociocultural milieu. In 1915, for example, Croly wrote about the Duncan house in

4. Herts and Tallent, New Amsterdam Theater Auditorium, 214 West Forty-second Street, New York, 1903–1906
Courtesy of the New-York Historical Society

5. Herts and Tallent, New Amsterdam Theater, 214 West Forty-second Street, New York, 1903–1906
Courtesy of the New-York Historical Society

Newport, Rhode Island, designed by John Russell Pope. He complimented houses built at this time for not being as ostentatious and lavish as the houses of a previous era: "The reaction against building palaces has won a complete triumph, and the good American, no matter how wealthy he may be, is now content to live in a comparatively modest and unpretentious house."[30]

The Duncan house was spacious but still unpretentious, according to Croly, for it looked back to English manor houses for its source in creating a "picturesque and charming" cottage. The late twentieth-century homeowner might think the Duncan house more akin to a college at Princeton University than to a single family home, but Croly's means of approaching the subject, on the level of shifts in tastes of a subculture, was, nevertheless, quite informative.

While it seems anomalous today that mansions and large houses for affluent Americans should be a specialty of someone who became the editor of a leading progressive political journal, it should be underscored that Croly's progressivism came out of the East Coast genteel tradition. His was not a grassroots populist political ideology. On the contrary, he felt affluence and intellectual thought were not antithetical and could be harnessed for a "democratic nationalism," as he frequently put it.

The affluent, Croly observed, were viewed as heroes to the American public; if informed and enlightened, the newly rich could contribute much to the Republic. Architecture was fulfilling a symbolic purpose. The houses should express a sense of achievement and refinement, as well as Croly's favorite attribute, "propriety." Many well-meaning affluent people needed aesthetic guidance in matters of architecture. Rich men had a desire for excellence, but they just lacked taste and discrimination.[31] Croly favored traditional forms adapted to particular site conditions and current needs for residential design.

In addition to seeing a work of architecture as part of an evolution of type—a form that developed from the building's program, physical structure, and role as a cultural symbol—Croly looked at buildings as part of an urban whole, a visual ensemble. For example, he felt strong cornices were important to unify buildings as an urban group. Windows of the tower shafts should be closely spaced to dramatize the tall building's vertical lines, and corners should be emphasized. Croly also maintained that urban structures should relate to their surroundings through scale, massing, materials, and style.[32] This emphasis on the relationship between old and new buildings and their effect on the character of the surrounding milieu was premonitory, in a sense, of what is often called "contextualism" today.[33] The term in its most popular usage generally means designing a building or group of buildings so their height, scale, mass, line, proportion, and materials fits into the surrounding urban fabric.

It should be pointed out that Croly reacted to contextual issues from the point of view of the pedestrian, that is, someone who sees and experiences the buildings from the street and primarily as facades. Today an urban designer might examine the context in terms of the overall morphology of the city and its figure-ground relations. As Croly observed, many of the new retail buildings then cropping up on Fifth Avenue between Twenty-fifth and Fiftieth Streets had no relation to the surrounding context.[34] Looking at the skyscraper form from the vantage point of the pedestrian prompted Croly to argue that tall buildings, such as Daniel Burnham's Flatiron Building of 1903, could be appreciated best from sites such as the one on Broadway and Fifth at Twenty-third Street. Because the site deviated from the New York City grid, the tower could be seen in the round. On other blockfronts, Croly pointed out, one can only see the skyscraper rising up as "an ugly slice" of building, since its blank sides were its most visible element.[35] (As the blocks were filled in with other towers, however, those blank sides disappeared, again proving that the most difficult thing about criticizing according to the context is that the context changes so rapidly.)

In the early part of the century many New Yorkers, architects included, were worried, as they are now, about overdevelopment. Along with his professional colleagues Croly advocated a height limit and a uniform cornice line for urban development in New York. Yet Croly was not a proponent of the "City Beautiful" movement. "The ugly actual cities of today make a livelier appeal to the imagination than does an ideal city, which in sacrificing its ugliness on the altar of civic art, sacrifices also its proper character and inherent vitality," he wrote in 1904.[36]

In the 1920s, after New York had gone through a radical transformation in its growth, Croly wrote a few essays on its skyline for the *Architectural Record.* He had already been at the *New Republic* for a number of years, and New York had been much altered by the zoning regulation of 1916 that encouraged set-back towers and steeplelike tops. The jagged skyline, with its individual spires and crowns, was impressive. Croly called the skyscrapers "monstrosities," but admired their sheer size and the dazzling ensemble created by their jagged silhouettes.[37] Nevertheless, the design for Raymond Hood's American Radiator Building of 1924 (fig. 6) was "a bit crude," even if it illustrated a potential to "glow, flame and glisten."[38]

During this period a number of Croly's editorials focused on issues that would appear more in tune with his social and political interests at the *New Republic.* These essays, published as usual in the *Architectural Record*, advocated reforms in low-rent housing, traffic congestion, and other urban problems.[39] In "Reclamation of a Business Slum," he applauded the fact that the breweries and factories north of Grand Central had disappeared when the train lines were covered. But Croly had hoped cultural facilities would be built immediately north of the station, instead of the apartment buildings of "stupendous dullness" that were constructed there instead.[40]

From the early days of his career as an architectural journalist, Croly had indicated his ability to dissect the social, economic, and cultural character of the urban milieu. For example, in one of his most cited articles, "New York as the American Metropolis," written in 1903, Croly pointed out that the industrial reorganization of the United States was causing the population to reverse its move from the city to the country and from the East to the West. Westerners, it seemed, were now often returning to the East, especially New York, even if they came just for a stop-off. They returned not only for business reasons, but for social advantages too. Croly wondered whether New York could become more of a metropolis in its fullest sense, not just a playground for the rich businessman and his wife. While Croly seemed optimistic that New York was becoming a metropolis, he maintained that the leadership in social and intellectual areas in New York was still more a promise than an achievement: "The people of the U.S. . . . are becoming thoroughly nationalized politically and industrially, but in social and intellectual matters the merely individual and local spirit remains dominant."[41] Business was doing well, he said in the same article, but qualified the statement: "New York has not yet become such a center, partly because American social life is largely still in an invertebrate and amorphous condition."

In due time "the invertebrate and amorphous condition" of New York gave way to a specific urban entity as the cultural, intellectual, and business center of the nation as Croly had thought possible. New types of cultural and commercial institutions, including apartment houses, office buildings, and museums, evolved from their more primordial conditions. Croly had already charted that growth.

Croly's impressionistic and mild-mannered way of addressing these changes by an analysis of type, context, and cultural expression received less emphasis by some, but not all, critics when modern principles of a universal, functional expression seized the imagination of the American architectural community in the 1930s.

When one compares Herbert Croly's architecture criticism to his criticism written for the *New Republic* on political and social issues, it is easy to see why the latter is held in higher regard. At the *New Republic* Croly's style assumed a stronger, authoritative manner, a passion (albeit controlled by reason), and a directness. In

6. Raymond Hood, American Radiator Building, 40 West Fortieth Street, 1924
From *Contemporary American Architects: Raymond M. Hood* (New York and London, 1931)

his essay for the *New Republic* in 1916 on "Unregenerate Democracy," for example, he began:

When the history of President Wilson's administration comes to be written he will be credited with certain sound achievements, certain unnecessary shortcomings, and certain serious mistakes; but a candid commentator, no matter how friendly, can hardly avoid the admission of one conspicuous and egregious failure. Mr. Wilson has failed in his much advertised and cherished attempt to resurrect the Democratic party as an indispensable organ of American government.[42]

Regardless of Croly's sociological interest in how buildings were experienced by their users, he never adopted the exhortatory tone one hears so clearly in the *New Republic*. In "A School for Social Research," which he wrote for the *New Republic* in 1918, he says:

Our American social and political units were created when the specialist expert was unimportant. Conditions have made him not only important but indispensable. Yet our social and political units still omit to recognize his positive political functions and in order to operate he has to be imposed upon the people by state orders of philanthropic pressure.[43]

Judging from his essays in the *New Republic*, it is quite understandable for his colleagues to consider Croly the political and social commentator more interesting than Croly the architecture critic. If Croly had adopted a new architecture as a means for social change to the degree that he argued for political action, he would have made more of an impression in architectural critical history. But the reasons for his not turning his attention toward the architecture developing in Germany, France, and Holland during and after World War I—an architecture consciously integrated with political and social planning—might have had to do with the timing: much of the most inventive town planning and housing schemes began to appear as a solution to the devastation of the war and were not known to Americans until the early and middle 1920s. Croly was already in his fifties and beginning to be disenchanted with his dreams of changing the world (and especially the United States) through social policy. Nevertheless, in the 1920s he frequently commissioned a young writer, Lewis Mumford, to address the subjects of architecture and urbanism in the pages of the *New Republic.*

Although he did not forge a strong tie between architecture and politics, Croly was able to bring a certain approach to the discussion of architecture that we can still benefit from today. He criticized architecture from the point of view of the citizen—the sensitive and civilized man in the street. Architecture was first of all a testament to the level of a country's culture, to its aspirations, and the buildings were to address this general issue. But buildings also had to speak to their own particular users and observers. Here again Croly's criticism consistently placed a subtle emphasis on this value. Finally the building had its own history, its own evolution from the various determinants of form such as use and function, materials and structure, style and aesthetics. Thus one building type should then be judged differently from another type. All told, a building (or an urban ensemble) was an artifact that could be read on several different levels. From this point of view architecture was a text, not just another pretty building.

NOTES

Much of the research for this article was made possible by a grant from the National Endowment for the Arts and by the Brunner Grant of the New York Chapter of the American Institute of Architects. The grants were bestowed for two works in progress, the NEA grant for a book on the history of architecture criticism in magazines and newspapers since 1850 and the Brunner for an annotated anthology of architecture criticism published in American magazines and newspapers from the late nineteenth century to the present.

1. Russell Sturgis, "The Larkin Building in Buffalo," *Architectural Record* 23 (April 1908), 310–321. For Wright's response see Jack Quinan, *Frank Lloyd Wright's Larkin Building: Myth and Fact* (New York and Cambridge, Mass., 1987), 113–116.

2. Lewis Mumford, "Notes on Modern Architecture," *New Republic* 66 (18 March 1931), 119.

3. "Notes on Modern Architecture," 119–122. Mumford says of the Daily News Building, "In many ways this is one of the best skyscrapers that has been erected since the Shelton." For comments on Hunter College, see also Lewis Mumford, "The Sky-Line: Skyscraper School," *New Yorker* 16 (16 November 1940), 84–86. See also Robert Wojtowicz, "Lewis Mumford: The Architectural Critic as Historian," in this volume.

4. For a fascinating and thorough discussion of Herbert Croly's background, see David W. Levy, *Herbert Croly of The New Republic: The Life and Thought of an American Progressive* (Princeton, 1985), 43–71.

5. Croly wrote about Maher's Patten house in Evanston: "The total sacrifice of scale to massiveness of effect, which the building exhibits, remains unappeasably disagreeable. It reminds one of the figure of a man whose arms and legs are swollen so that no matter how old his muscles are, or how vigorous the whole effect of his strong body, that effect is spoiled by the disproportion of certain salient parts." Arthur C. David, "The Architecture of Ideas," *Architectural Record* 15 (April 1904), 361–384.

6. Robert A. M. Stern, Gregory Gilmartin, John Montague Massengale, *New York 1900: Metropolitan Architecture and Urbanism 1890–1915* (New York, 1983), 11, 17, 18, 31, 32. Thomas Bender, *New York Intellect: A History of Intellectual Life in New York City, From 1750 to the Beginnings of Our Own Time* (New York, 1987), 224.

7. Walter Lippmann, "Notes for a Biography," *New Republic* 63 (16 July 1930), 250–252.

8. As John Chamberlain later wrote in 1939 in the *New Republic,* Croly's book *The Promise of American Life* showed that Croly was "an aristocrat in his passionate hope . . . that democrats could be taught to put their political trust in the hands of exceptional men. . . . He was not an equalitarian. And, quite naturally, he detested the Jeffersonian tradition in politics. . . . Croly wanted a central government equipped to run the United States as a unit with power to move in a coordinated way on all fronts at once." See John Chamberlain, "Croly and the American Future," *New Republic* 101 (8 November 1939), 33–35.

9. Herbert Croly, "My Aim in The Promise of American Life: Why I Wrote My Latest Book," *World's Work* 20 (June 1910), 13,086. See also Herbert Croly, "The Architect in Recent Fiction," *Architectural Record* 17 (February 1905), 137–139.

10. Herbert Croly, *The Promise of American Life* (1909; 2d ed., Cambridge, Mass., 1965), 445.

11. Keith N. Morgan, *Charles A. Platt, The Artist as Architect* (New York and Cambridge, Mass., 1985), 77.

12. Croly 1965, 452.

13. Bruce Bliven, "Herbert Croly and Journalism," *New Republic* 63 (16 July 1930), 258–260.

14. See Levy 1985, 18–27, for more on this pioneering female journalist.

15. For an account of Clinton Sweet's intentions for the *Architectural Record*, see Thomas S. Holden and Frederic H. Glade, Jr., "The House that Dodge Built, the Story of a Business Service Organization" (unpublished company history, 1954), 32.

16. Charles Forcey, *The Crossroads of Liberalism: Croly, Weyl, Lippmann and the Progressive Era, 1900–1925 (New York, 1961)*, 11.

17. Levy, 1985, 72–95; Christopher Lasch, "Herbert Croly's America," *New York Review of Books* 4 (1 July 1965), 18–19.

18. Bender 1987, 222–227; "The Rise and Fall of Architectural Journalism," *Design Book Review* 15 (Fall 1988), 47–49.

19. Charles A. Platt, "Herbert Croly and Architecture," *New Republic* 63 (16 July 1930), 257.

20. Edmund Wilson, "H.C.," *New Republic* 63 (16 July 1930), 266–268.

21. Levy 1985, 85.

22. While it has been a practice for trade magazines to give an author a pseudonym when too many articles by the same person appear in one issue, this apportionment to various authors does not follow any systematic rules with regard to Croly. For example, in the *Architectural Record* 18 (July 1905), there are two essays signed by Croly, "An American Country Estate," 1–7, and "The Use of Terra-Cotta in the United States," 86–94, and none by David. In *Architectural Record* 19 (February 1906), there are two signed by David, "Some Houses by Mr. Howard Shaw," 105–122, and "An Architectural Oasis," 135–144, and none by Croly.

23. Auguste Comte, *The Positive Philosophy Freely Translated and Condensed by Harriet Martineau* (New York, 1856), 25–38; Levy 1985, 29–36.

24. For an example, see the article signed William Herbert attributed to Croly, "An American Architecture," *Architectural Record* 23 (February 1908), 111–122.

25. Herbert Croly, "The Architectural Work of Charles A. Platt," *Architectural Record* 15 (March 1904), 181–244.

26. A. C. David, "Three New Hotels," *Architectural Record* 17 (April 1905), 167–188.

27. Arthur C. David, "The St. Regis—The Best Type of Metropolitan Hotel," *Architectural Record* 15 (June 1904), 552–623.

28. A. C. David, "The New Theatres of New York," *Architectural Record* 15 (January 1904), 39–54.

29. "New Theatres," 50.

30. Herbert Croly, "The Stuart Duncan Residence at Newport," *Architectural Record* 38 (September 1915), 289–309.

31. Herbert Croly, "Rich Men and Their Houses," *Architectural Record* 12 (May 1902), 27–32.

32. A. C. David, "The New Architecture: The First American Type of Real Value," *Architectural Record* 28 (December 1910), 389–403.

33. The actual term stems from Colin Rowe's theories and teaching methods about urban design developed (and given the name "contextualism") at Cornell University in the 1960s. Rowe's contextualism is indeed more conceptual than current usage of the term would indicate: it is about urban design as an empirical process with "visual and spatial values" that recognizes the "exigencies and irregularities" of the site. This form of contextualism attempts to create a link between the traditional city where open spaces were carved out of the solid mass, versus the modern one where isolated buildings stood free in open space.

34. A. C. David, "The New Fifth Avenue," *Architectural Record* 22 (July 1907), 1–14.

35. "New Fifth," 13–14.

36. Herbert Croly, "What Is Civic Art," *Architectural Record* 16 (July 1904), 47–52.

37. Herbert Croly, "A New Dimension in Architectural Effects," *Architectural Record* 57 (January 1925), 93–94.

38. "New Dimension," 93.

39. Herbert Croly, "Architects and State Aid to Housing," *Architectural Record* 59 (March 1926), 293–294.

40. Herbert Croly, "The Reclamation of a Business Slum," *Architectural Record* 54 (December 1923), 587–588.

41. Herbert Croly, "New York as the American Metropolis," *Architectural Record* 13 (March 1903), 193–206.

42. Herbert Croly, "Unregenerate Democracy," *New Republic* 16 (5 February 1916), 17–19.

43. Herbert Croly, "A School of Social Research," *New Republic* 15 (8 June 1918), 167–171.

PETER KAUFMAN
Stony Brook, New York

PAULA GABBARD
Columbia University

Appendix

American Doctoral Dissertations in Architectural and Planning History, 1898–1972

This appendix lists 370 doctoral dissertations completed at 42 American universities up to 1972 in the fields of architectural and planning history, culled primarily from the pages of *Comprehensive Dissertation Index, 1861–1972* (Ann Arbor, Mich., 1973), the most comprehensive reference work of its type. Known to most American academics along with its companion tool *Dissertation Abstracts International* as the definitive source of information on American doctoral dissertations, *CDI*, as it is colloquially known, lists dissertations first by general subject area and then by keyword in the title of each dissertation, creating the *raison d'être* for this bibliography. There is no way to find all of the dissertations in architectural and planning history without plowing through hundreds of pages and literally thousands of keyword listings, precisely the task from which this bibliography grew. Coverage is presumed complete only through 1971, judging from the drop in the number of dissertations listed for the following year, probably because a number of dissertations completed in 1972 were completed too late for inclusion in *CDI, 1861–1972*. Warren F. Keuhl's *Dissertations in History*, volumes 1 and 2 (Lexington, Ky., 1965 and 1972) and volume 3 (Santa Barbara, Calif., 1985) were also consulted, but yielded only a handful of additional entries not found, inexplicably, in *CDI*.

To read the chronological sequence of this bibliography is to review the development of architectural history in America from "Culture" to "Kultur" to "Kulcha"—the first bearing Arnoldian overtones from the Victorian era, the second implying that special art historical aura of *Kunstgeschichte*, which affected American architectural history in the mid-twentieth century, and the third calling attention to vernacular interests that accent the present. The steady mushroom growth of the discipline of architectural history over the past century is telltale in two simple facts that can be drawn from this list: first, of all the dissertations listed, fully two-thirds were completed after 1960; and, second, more dissertations were completed in the single year 1971 than before 1940! Many bibliographic landmarks appear in these lists to demarcate the shifts in academic taste and ideology.

Kenneth Conant's 1925 Harvard doctoral dissertation, "The Early Architectural History of the Cathedral of Santiago de Compostela," might well stand as representative of the archaeological bearings of most early doctoral dissertations in the field of architectural history. Of the mere three dozen completed before 1940, more than two-thirds focused on the then-sacred legacy of ancient and medieval architecture, primarily temples and cathedrals. Such dissertations as Lucy T. Shoe's "Profiles of

Greek Architectural Mouldings" (Bryn Mawr, 1935) mixed the positivist worlds of archaeological analysis and Beaux-Arts architectural ideology in memorable fashion. Nevertheless, some surprises appear right at the beginning of this list. For example, George Edgell's "The Development of the Architectural Background in the Painting of the Umbrian Renaissance" (Harvard, 1913) displayed, unexpectedly early, an interest in iconographic, art historical analysis as an avenue to architectural and even urban history; Frederick Sterns' "The Archaeology of Eastern Nebraska, with Special Reference to the Culture of the Rectangular Earth Lodges" (Harvard, 1915) demonstrates that an interest in vernacular architecture was present from early on; and Fiske Kimball's "Thomas Jefferson and the First Monument of the Classical Revival in America" (University of Michigan, 1915) represents a landmark in the development of American architectural history by the father of American scholarship on neoclassicism, who was himself something of a monument.

Vincent Scully's 1949 Yale dissertation, modestly titled "The Cottage Style," serves as a milestone in the development of architectural history in America, signaling the influence of art history, or *Kunstgeschichte* as it is called in German, in the mid-twentieth century. Later rewritten, expanded, and published as *The Shingle Style* (New Haven, 1955), it quickly established a national reputation for its author. Scully emerged as the most brilliant and celebrated member of a Yale contingent of art historians *cum* architectural historians who took upon themselves the task of interpreting modern architecture to, and through, America in the mid-twentieth century. Beginning with Carroll L. V. Meeks, this group included William Pierson, William Jordy, John Jacobus, and H. Allen Brooks (who earned a master's degree at Yale in 1955)—in addition to Robert Branner and Anthony N. B. Garvan, two other Yale-trained art historians of that era who did not write on modern architecture. A list of works by these men would demarcate that special marriage between art historical method and modern architectural

ideology which distinguished mid-twentieth century American architectural history. Art history was also strong at New York University, which quickly rose to second place (after Harvard) in the production of doctoral dissertations after 1950 on the strength of its Institute of Fine Arts faculty, mostly German emigré art historians who fathered dissertations mainly in the fields of ancient, Renaissance, and baroque. James Ackerman's 1952 dissertation on the Vatican Cortile del Belvedere was a harbinger of this development.

In the 1960s the stream of American doctoral dissertation writing broadened to embrace a wider spectrum of ideas, methods, and topics. Perhaps the signal event of this decade was the appearance in 1962 of Barbara Miller Lane's Harvard dissertation, "Architecture and Politics in Germany, 1918–1945," the first American doctoral dissertation on European modern architecture! Planning history also emerged in this decade, with more than ten dissertations to its credit, as a multidisciplinary subspecialty involving history, planning, and architecture. William Murtagh's 1963 dissertation on eighteenth-century Moravian architecture and town planning (University of Pennsylvania) stands out as a model study of vernacular architecture and culture, one of very few in this list, and Stephen Jacobs' 1966 Princeton dissertation on the history of historic preservation, completed in the same year as the National Historic Preservation Act, predicted the later influence of this profession on the practice of architectural history in America.

Statistical analysis of this bibliography confirms much conventional wisdom about American higher education: that most dissertations are produced by northeastern, primarily Ivy League, schools and that Harvard is preeminent in this hegemony. Indeed, of the 370 dissertations listed in this bibliography, 245 (66 percent) were produced at just seven schools. Harvard is in first place in this list with 68 dissertations to its credit, far ahead of its closest rival, New York University, which can be credited with 41 through 1971; in third place are clustered Columbia (35), Yale (31), and Princeton (29), while in last place are Johns Hopkins (23) and the University of Pennsylvania (18), among the most productive schools. Only a handful of other schools can be credited with more than ten dissertations apiece. Chronologically, Harvard has been the consistent leader in the production of dissertations, while Johns Hopkins owes its high ranking to its early productivity before 1955. Somewhat surprising is the absence of production at some major and prestigious centers of learning such as Massachusetts Institute of Technology, University of California at Los Angeles, Cornell, Stanford, University of Illinois, and University of California at Berkeley, each of which produced only a few dissertations through 1971.

Some notes on authorship and coverage are in order: Peter Kaufman wrote the introduction and carried out almost all of the selection, assisted by Paula Gabbard, who ferreted out many dissertations that had been overlooked inadvertently. Almost all of the entries were found in the Archaeology and Fine Arts sections of *CDI*, with lesser numbers derived from History, Regional Planning, Anthropology, and Folklore. The authors are confident that coverage represents better than 90 percent, but two major caveats should be mentioned. First, the listing format of *CDI*, merely by title, gives no indication of subject content; hence, some dissertations may have escaped the search net by dint of their titles. For example, the dissertation title "Frederick Clarke Withers" gives no indication of its relevance to architectural history. Second, some dissertations have undoubtedly been omitted as borderline cases. The following parameters governed

the choice of such entries. Studies of whole stylistic phases of the decorative arts were included, as were studies in garden and landscape history—very few in both cases. On the other hand, studies of church furniture and decorative programs found in frescoes, mosaics, stained glass, mural painting, and sculptural programs were left out as more properly the domain of iconographic, art historical investigation. Dissertations in the field of archaeology were included only if they concentrated on specific buildings, building types, cities, or city types; thus, most gravesite studies and reports limited to site excavations were excluded. Dissertations in city and regional planning were included only if they addressed a historical dimension of their subject matter—often indicated by the words "antecedents" or "origins" in their title. Thus, most case studies in the field of planning were excluded, as were dissertations focused on design itself and on its philosophical and aesthetic dimensions.

Finally, there are two number sequences that follow some of the listed citations. The first sequence cites where the dissertation is abstracted: DAI (*Dissertation Abstracts International*), volume number, part number, and page number. The second sequence is the UM (University Microfilms) order number that can be used to acquire the dissertation from University Microfilms International (UMI). Only those dissertations that can be purchased through UMI have UM numbers. Anyone interested in ordering the remaining dissertations will need to write directly to the degree-granting institution.

ARCHITECTURAL HISTORY

1898

1. VAN BURKALOW, JAMES TURLEY, JR.
Buildings of Nebu-Kadnezzar
University of Pennsylvania

1912

2. MURRAY, STEUBEN BUTLER
Hellenistic Architecture in Syria
Princeton University

1913

3. EDGELL, GEORGE HAROLD
The Development of the Architectural Background in the Painting of the Umbrian Renaissance
Harvard University

1915

4. KIMBALL, SIDNEY FISKE
Thomas Jefferson and the First Monument of the Classical Revival in America
University of Michigan

5. STERNS, FREDERICK HENDERSON
The Archaeology of Eastern Nebraska, with Special Reference to the Culture of the Rectangular Earth Lodges
Harvard University

6. WARD, CLARENCE
Mediaeval Church Vaulting
Princeton University

1925

7. CLAUSING, ROTH
The Roman Colonnade: The Theories of Its Origin
Columbia University

8. CONANT, KENNETH JOHN
The Early Architectural History of the Cathedral of Santiago de Compostela
Harvard University

9. DAY, JOHN
Chapters in the History of the Piraeus
Johns Hopkins University

10. GREENMAN, EMERSON FRANK
The Earthwork Inclosures of Michigan
University of Michigan

11. HUNT, EDWARD FRANCIS
The Architecture of Mont-St.-Michel (1208–1228)
Catholic University

12. WILDES, ADELE MADELEINE
Coordinations in Ancient Greek and Roman Temple Plans
Johns Hopkins University

1930

13. DAVIS, PHILLIP HALDANE
Some Eleusinian Building Inscriptions of the Fourth Century before Christ
Princeton University

1931

14. BRONEER, OSCAR THEODORE
The Odeum at Corinth
University of California, Berkeley

1934

15. BRADBURY, RONALD
The Romantic Theories of Architecture of the Nineteenth Century in Germany, England, and France (Together with a Brief Survey of the Vitruvian School)
Columbia University

16. FREEMAN, SARAH E.
The Excavation of a Roman Temple at Corinth
Johns Hopkins University

1935

17. HERSHEY, CARL K.
Origins and Development of the Salamantine Lanterns
Harvard University

18. SHOE, LUCY T.
Profiles of Greek Architectural Mouldings
Bryn Mawr College

1936

19. JOCHEM, FREDERICK L.
The "Libri Dello Spedal" of the Florentine Foundling Hospital: Sources for the History of Building in the Fifteenth Century in Italy
University of Wisconsin

20. SMITH, ROBERT C., JR.
The Architecture of Joao Frederico Ludovice and Some of His Contemporaries at Lisbon, 1700–1750
Harvard University

21. WALLACE, WILLIAM P.
The History of Eretria to 198 B.C.
Johns Hopkins University

22. WEINBERG, SAUL S.
The Prehistoric House of the Mainland of Greece
Johns Hopkins University

1937

23. WOOD, LYNN H.
The Evolution of Systems of Defense in Palestine
University of Chicago

1938

23a. BROWN, FRANK E.
Pagan Religious Architecture of Dura Europus
Yale University

24. CAEMMERER, H. PAUL
The Influence of Classical Art on the Architecture of the United States
American University

25. MILLS, EDWARD L.
The Cathedral of Barcelona and Related Gothic Churches in France and Spain
Harvard University

26. ROOS, FRANK J., JR.
An Investigation of the Sources of Early Architectural Design in Ohio
Ohio State University

27. SUNDERLAND, ELIZABETH R.
The History and Architecture of the Church of St. Fortunatus at Charlieu in Burgundy
Radcliffe College

1939

28. ALEXANDER, JOHN A.
Potidaea
Johns Hopkins University

29. CASKEY, JOHN L.
House VI F, Building of the Sixth Settlement at Troy
University of Cincinnati

30. EMERY, RUTH
Augustus Welby Pugin and the Gothic Revival
Cornell University

31. MENDELL, ELIZABETH L.
Romanesque Churches of Saintonge
Yale University

32. RICHMOND, WILLIAM D.
Juan Martinez Montanes
Harvard University

33. SCRANTON, ROBERT L.
The Chronology of Greek Walls
University of Chicago

34. SEELE, KEITH C.
The Tomb of Canefer at Thebes
University of Chicago

35. TAYLOR, OTIS E.
Architecture of Northwest Persia Under the Il Khan Mongols
University of Chicago

1940

36. CRAFT, JOHN RICHARD
The Civic Water Supply of Ancient Greece
Johns Hopkins University

37. KUBLER, GEORGE A.
The Religious Architecture of New Mexico
Yale University

38. MCDONALD, WILLIAM A.
The Political Meeting Places of the Greeks
Johns Hopkins University

1941

39. BROWN, DONALD FREDERICK
Architectura Numismatica: I. The Temples of Rome
New York University

40. MANSON, GRANT CARPENTER
The Work of Frank Lloyd Wright before 1910
Harvard University

41. STODDARD, WHITNEY SNOW
Chartres: The Making of a Cathedral Portal
Harvard University

1942

42. ELFORD, ALVA DORIS
Architectural Terracottas in the Greek Archaic Period
Bryn Mawr College
DAI 8, pt. 2, 11. UM 00–01086

43. FORMAN, HENRY CHANDLEE
Jamestown and St. Mary's: Buried Cities of Romance
University of Pennsylvania

44. GROSSBERG, HERBERT ELKAN
The Influence of the Pantheon and Its Relation to Domed Buildings in the History of Architecture
Johns Hopkins University

45. PARSONS, ARTHUR WELLESLEY
Klepsydra and the Paved Court of the Pythion
Johns Hopkins University

46. TRELL, BLUMA L.
Architectura Numismatica: Part II. Temples in Asia Minor
New York University

47. WEATHERHEAD, ARTHUR C.
The History of Collegiate Education in Architecture in the United States
Columbia University

48. WEISMAN, WINSTON ROBERT
The Architectural Significance of Rockefeller Center
Ohio State University

49. WELLER, ALLEN S.
Francesco di Giorgio
University of Chicago

50. YAVIS, CONSTANTINE GEORGE
Greek Altars
Johns Hopkins University

1943

51. RAE, EDWIN CARTER
Gothic Architecture in Ireland
Harvard University

1944

52. SOPER, ALEXANDER COBURN III
The Evolution of Buddhist Architecture in Japan
Princeton University

1945

53. BANNISTER, TURPIN CHAMBERS
Iron and Architecture: A Study in Building and Invention from Ancient Times to 1700
Harvard University

54. HAYES, MARIAN
Life and Architecture in the Connecticut Valley
Radcliffe College

55. SCHAEFER, HERWIN
The Origins of the Two Tower Facade in Romanesque Architecture
Harvard University

1946

56. CAZEL, ANNARIE P.
Greek Propylaea
Johns Hopkins University

57. REITLER, PAUL D.
Form and Function in Some Prehistoric Ceremonial Structures in the Southwest
Harvard University

58. SUNDERLAND, ALICE L.
The Early Romanesque Church of Saint Benignus of Dijon
Radcliffe College

1947

59. ARATOWSKY, BERNARD
Ancient Salamis
Johns Hopkins University

60. SMITH, MYRON B.
The Vault in Persian Architecture: A Provisional Classification with Notes on Construction
Johns Hopkins University

1948

60a. COOLIDGE, JOHN PHILLIPS
Studies on Vignola
New York University

61. GARVAN, ANTHONY N. B.
The Origin of Colonial Architecture and Town Planning in Connecticut: A Study in American Social History
Yale University

62. MEEKS, CARROLL L. V.
The Architectural Development of the American Railroad Station
Harvard University

63. ROUSSEVE, FERDINAND L.
The Romanesque Abbey Church of Saint Martial at Limoges, 1017–1167
Harvard University

1949

64. HILBERRY, HARRY H.
La Charité-Sur-Loire Priory Church: A Reconstruction Study
Harvard University

65. KOUWENHOVEN, JOHN A.
Made in America: The Arts in Modern Civilization
Columbia University

66. NEWMAN, RICHARD K., JR.
Yankee Gothic: Medieval Architectural Forms in the Protestant Church Building of Nineteenth-Century New England
Yale University

67. PIERSON, WILLIAM HARVEY, JR.
Industrial Architecture in the Berkshires
Yale University
DAI 32, pt. 10-A, 5689. UM 72-09553

68. SCULLY, VINCENT J., JR.
The Cottage Style (An Organic Development in Later Nineteenth-Century Wooden Domestic Architecture in the Eastern United States)
Yale University

69. THOMAS, HYLTON A.
The Drawings of Giovanni Battista Piranesi
Harvard University

70. WILBER, DONALD NEWTON
The Architecture of Islamic Iran: The Il Khanid Period
Princeton University
DAI 15, pt. 6, 1042. UM 00-11059

1950

71. CREESE, WALTER L.
American Architecture from 1918 to 1933, with Special Emphasis on European Influence
Harvard University

72. ECKELS, CLAIRE W.
Baltimore's Earliest Architects
Johns Hopkins University

73. FADUM, RALPH E.
Observations and Analysis of Building Settlements in Boston
Harvard University

74. GOWANS, ALAN WILBERT
A History of Church Architecture in New France
Princeton University
DAI 16, pt. 5, 940. UM 00-10910

75. HARTT, FREDERICK
Giulio Romano and the Palazzo del Te
New York University

76. LOVE, PAUL
Patterned Brickwork in the American Colonies
Columbia University
DAI 10, pt. 4, 18. UM 00–01873

77. MCDONOUGH, JAMES VERNON
William Jay—Regency Architect in Georgia and South Carolina
Princeton University
DAI 14, pt. 4, 554. UM 00–10959

78. RAUBITSCHEK, ISABELLE KELLY
Ionicizing Doric Architecture: A Stylistic Study of Greek Doric Architecture of the Sixth and Fifth Centuries B.C
Columbia University
DAI 10, pt. 4, 13. UM 00–01891

79. TATUM, GEORGE BISHOP
Andrew Jackson Downing: Arbiter of American Taste, 1815–1852
Princeton University
DAI 15, pt. 4, 555. UM 00–11042

1951

80. CHAPMAN, EDMUND H.
The Development of the City of Cleveland, Ohio, to 1860
New York University

81. CUMMINGS, ABBOTT L.
An Investigation of the Sources, Stylistic Evolution, and Influence of Asher Benjamin's Builders' Guides
Ohio State University

82. GOTTLIEB, CARLA
The Restoration of the Nereid Monument at Xanthos
Columbia University
DAI 12, pt. 2, 174. UM 00–03432

83. MCLANATHAN, RICHARD B. K.
Charles Bulfinch and the Maine State House: A Study in the Development of American Architecture
Harvard University

84. NIEDERER, FRANCIS J.
The Roman Diaconiae: A Study of the Use of Ancient Building by the Christian Church Prior to 806 A.D.
New York University

85. SHAFFER, ROBERT B.
Charles Eliot Norton and Architecture
Harvard University

86. SOWERS, OSSA RAYMOND
Mediaeval Monastic Planning: Its Origins in the Christian East and Later Development in Western Europe
Columbia University
DAI 12, pt. 1, 3. UM 00–0311

87. TORBERT, DONALD R.
Minneapolis—Architecture and Architects, 1848–1908: A Study of Style Trends in Architecture in a Midwestern City, Together with a Catalogue of Representative Building
University of Minnesota

1952

88. ACKERMAN, JAMES S.
The Cortile del Belvedere (1503–1585)
New York University

89. BUNTING, BAINBRIDGE
The Architectural History of the Back Bay Region in Boston
Harvard University

90. GODFREY, WILLIAM S., JR.
Digging a Tower and Laying a Ghost: The Archaeology and Controversial History of the Newport Tower
Harvard University

91. HALSE, ALBERT O.
A History of the Developments in Architectural Drafting Techniques
New York University
DAI 12, pt. 6, 788. UM 00–04153

92. NORTON, PAUL FOOTE
Latrobe, Jefferson, and the National Capitol
Princeton University
DAI 15, pt. 4, 554. UM 00–10986

93. RICHARDSON, LAWRENCE, JR.
Pompeii: The Casa dei Dioscuri and Its Painters
Yale University

1953

94. BRANNER, ROBERT J.
The Construction of the Chevet of Bourges Cathedral and Its Place in Gothic Architecture
Yale University

95. BUTLER, ALEXANDER R.
McKim's Renaissance: A Study in the History of the American Architectural Profession
Johns Hopkins University

96. EARLY, JAMES
Romantic Thought and Architecture in the United States
Harvard University

97. LEWIS, STANLEY T.
The New York Theatre: Its Background and Architectural Development: 1750–1853
Ohio State University
DAI 20, pt. 1, 261. UM 59–02310

98. ROSENTHAL, EARL E.
The Cathedral of Granada: A Study in the Spanish Renaissance
New York University

1954

99. COFFIN, DAVID ROBBINS
Pirro Ligorio and the Villa D'Este
Princeton University
DAI 14, pt. 12, 2312. UM 00–09402

100. DEZURKO, EDWARD R.
Functionalist Trends in Writings Pertaining to Architecture with Special Emphasis on the Period c. 1700–1850
New York University

101. HALL, LOUISE
Artificer to Architect in America
Radcliffe College

102. NICHOLS, J. B.
A Historical Study of Southern Baptist Church Architecture
Southwestern Baptist Theological Seminary

103. OMOTO, SADAYOSHI
Some Aspects of the So-Called "Queen Anne" Revival Style of Architecture
Ohio State University
DAI 20, pt. 8, 3255. UM 60–00098

104. SPINK, WALTER M.
Rock-Cut Monuments of the Andhra Period: Their Style and Chronology
Harvard University

1955

105. CONNALLY, ERNEST A.
The Ecclesiastical and Military Architecture of the Spanish Province of Texas
Harvard University

106. DOW, HELEN J.
The Rose-Window: Its Origin and Significance
Bryn Mawr College

107. NOFFSINGER, JAMES P.
The Influence of the Ecole des Beaux-Arts on the Architects of the United States
Catholic University

108. WUNDER, RICHARD P.
Giovanni Paolo Pannini
Harvard University

1956

109. ANDREWS, WAYNE
Architecture, Ambition, and Americans
Columbia University

110. DONNELLY, MARIAN CARD
New England Meeting Houses in the Seventeenth Century
Yale University

111. HANSON, JOHN ARTHUR
Roman Theater-Temples
Princeton University
DAI 18, pt. 1, 208. UM 00–23828

112. HAZELHURST, FRANKLIN HAMILTON
Jacques Boyceau, Sieur de la Barauderie: The Origins of the French Formal Garden
Princeton University
DAI 17, pt. 3, 593. UM 00–20120

113. HUPER, MARIE SOPHIE
The Architectural Monuments of the Hypnerotomachia Poliphili
University of Iowa
DAI 16, pt. 10, 1878. UM 00–18540

114. JACOBUS, JOHN MAXWELL, JR.
The Architecture of Viollet-le-Duc
Yale University

115. LUDDEN, FRANKLIN MONROE
The Early Gothic Portals of Senlis and Mantes
Harvard University

116. MACDONALD, WILLIAM LLOYD, JR.
The Hippodrome at Constantinople
Harvard University

117. MYER, PRUDENCE ROYCE
Pre-Islamic Religious Monuments of Bihar and Bengal: A Study in the Evolution of Architectural Forms
Radcliffe College

1957

118. BROOKS, H. ALLEN, JR.
The Prairie School: The American Spirit in Midwest Residential Architecture, 1893–1916
Northwestern University
DAI 17, pt. 12, 2969. UM 00–23485

119. CHISOLM, LAWRENCE WASHINGTON
The Lotus and the Arch
Yale University

120. FALES, DE COURSEY, JR.
The Arena-Bath Area at Curium in Cyprus: A Study of Roman and Early Christian Architecture
Harvard University

121. FILIPIAK, MARY ANGELINA
The Plans of the Poor Clares' Convents in Central Italy: From the Thirteenth through the Fifteenth Century
University of Michigan
DAI 18, pt. 5, 1759. UM 58–01400

121a. GEBHARD, DAVID
William Gray Purcell and George Grant Elmslie and the Early Progressive Movement in American Architecture from 1900 to 1920
University of Minnesota
DAI 20, pt. 6, 2218. UM 59–06052

122. GRAYBILL, SAMUEL HUIET, JR.
Bruce Price, American Architect, 1845–1903
Yale University
DAI 31, pt. 12-A, 6493. UM 71–16123

123. KIRKER, HAROLD C.
California Architecture in the Nineteenth Century: A Social History
University of California

124. LOWRY, BATES
Palais du Louvre, 1528-1624: The Development of a Sixteenth-Century Architectural Complex
University of Chicago

125. OLPP, WILLIAM HENRY
The Church Architecture of Roussillon during the Romanesque Period
New York University
DAI 18, pt. 6, 2105. UM 00-24701

126. STOKSTAD, MARILYN JANE
The Portico de la Gloria of the Cathedral of Santiago de Compostela
University of Michigan
DAI 19, pt. 1, 113. UM 58-01467

127. WINTER, FREDERICK ELLIOTT
Fortifications
University of Toronto (Canada)

128. WINTER, ROBERT WHITE
The Organic Principle in American Architectural Theory
Johns Hopkins University

1958

129. HIBBARD, BENJAMIN HOWARD
The Architecture of the Palazzo Borghese
Harvard University

130. HOAG, JOHN DOUGLASS
Rodrigo Gil de Hontanon: His Work and Writings
Yale University

131. KRAMER, ELLEN W.
The Domestic Architecture of Detlef Lienau: A Conservative Victorian
New York University
DAI 22, pt. 3, 841. UM 61-02634

132. LERSKI, HANNA
The British Antecedents of Thomas Jefferson's Architecture
Johns Hopkins University

133. PATTON, GLENN NEIL
Francisco Antonio Guerrero y Torres and the Baroque Architecture of Mexico City in the Eighteenth Century
University of Michigan
DAI 19, pt. 6, 1335. UM 58-07777

134. WATSON, DAVID S.
The Domestic Revival in English Architecture
University of Chicago

1959

135. BUSH-BROWN, ALBERT
Image of a University: A Study of Architecture as an Expression of Education at Colleges and Universities in the United States between 1800-1900
Princeton University
DAI 20, pt. 6, 2218. UM 59-05164

136. HUEMER, FRANCES
A Study of Roman Architectural Decoration of the Seventeenth Century
New York University
DAI 27, pt. 6-A, 1731. UM 66-09697

137. PEISCH, MARK L.
The Chicago School and Walter Burley Griffin, 1893-1914: Growth and Dissemination of an Architectural Movement and a Representative Figure
Columbia University
DAI 20, pt. 10, 4070. UM 60-01159

138. RUBIN, WILLIAM STANLEY
The Church of Notre-Dame-de-Toute-Grace at Assy
Columbia University
DAI 20, pt. 3, 983. UM 59-03128

139. SMITH, WEBSTER
Studies on Buontalenti's Villas
New York University
DAI 20, pt. 6, 2219. UM 59-02457

1960

140. ANDERSEN, STANLEY PETER
American Ikon: Response to the Skyscraper, 1875-1934
University of Minnesota
DAI 21, pt. 4, 841. UM 60-03499

141. BULLARD, WILLIAM ROTCH, JR.
Pit House Architecture in the Southwestern United States prior to A.D. 900, with Description of the Excavations at Cerro, Colorado, near Quemado, West-Central New Mexico, and a Review and Critique of Southwestern Chronology
Harvard University

142. LEWINE, MILTON JOSEPH
The Roman Church Interior, 1527-1580
Columbia University
DAI 24, pt. 2, 688. UM 63-03688

143. LOZINSKI, JEAN SMITH
The Cathedral of Saint Pierre in Poitiers: An Architectural History through the First Gothic Building Campaign
Yale University

144. NEUERBURG, NORMAN
The Architecture of Fountains and Nymphaea in Ancient Italy
New York University
DAI 21, pt. 8, 2240 UM 60-05288

145. SAALMAN, HOWARD
The Church of Santa Trinita in Florence
New York University
DAI 27, pt. 5-A, 1303. UM 66-09760

146. SPIEGEL, EILEEN
The English Farm House: A Study of Architectural Theory and Design
Columbia University
DAI 21, pt. 4, 843. UM 60-03143

147. STEINBERG, LEO
San Carlo alle Quattro Fontane, A Study in Multiple Form and Architectural Symbolism
New York University
DAI 22, pt. 3, 843. UM 60-05296

1961

148. ALEXANDER, ROBERT LESTER
The Art and Architecture of Maximilian Godefroy
New York University
DAI 22, pt. 2, 530. UM 61-02641

149. BOHAN, PETER JOHN
James and Decimus Burton: Architectural Trends in England Exemplified by Their Work, 1790-1860
Yale University
DAI 30, pt. 3-A, 1089. UM 69-14691

150. CARROTT, RICHARD G.
The Egyptian Revival: Its Sources, Monuments, and Meaning (1808-1858)
Yale University
DAI 28, pt. 4-A, 1356. UM 67-11356

151. KOSTOF, SPIRO KONSTANTIN
The Orthodox Baptistery of Ravenna: A Study in Early Christian Art and Architecture
Yale University

152. POMMER, RICHARD BEHR
Some Eighteenth-Century Piedmontese Interiors by Juvarra, Alfieri, and Vittone
New York University
DAI 26, pt. 10, 5970. UM 65-13025

153. SMITH, NORRIS KELLY
A Study of the Architectural Imagery of Frank Lloyd Wright
Columbia University
DAI 22, pt. 2, 532. UM 61-02668

154. STILLMAN, SAMUEL DAMIE
The Genesis of the Adam Style
Columbia University
DAI 22, pt. 4, 1122. UM 61-03907

1962

155. COLLIER, MARGARET
The Sagrario of Lorenzo Rodriguez: Origins of the Eighteenth-Century Architectural Style in Mexico
Yale University

156. GARNSEY, CLARKE HENDERSON
Early Nineteenth-Century Residences in Central Cuba: The Trinitarian Style
Western Reserve University

157. LANE, BARBARA MILLER
Architecture and Politics in Germany, 1918-1945
Radcliffe College

158. LEWIS, DUDLEY ARNOLD
Evaluations of American Architecture by European Critics, 1875-1900
University of Wisconsin
DAI 23, pt. 6, 2084. UM 63-00602

159. NYBERG, DOROTHEA FREDRIKA
Michel de Fremin, "Memoires Critiques d'Architecture," A Clue to the Architectural Taste of Eighteenth-Century France
New York University
DAI 23, pt. 6, 2085. UM 62-05379

160. QUERA, LEON NEAL
Persistent Principles in Japanese Architecture
Ohio State University
DAI 23, pt. 5, 1655. UM 63-00078

161. SHELLY, LONNIE R.
The Technical Supervision of Masonry Construction in Medieval England
University of North Carolina at Chapel Hill

162. THOMPSON, DONALD ENRIQUE
Architecture and Settlement Patterns in the Casma Valley, Peru
Harvard University

1963

163. COOLEDGE, HAROLD NORMAN, JR.
Samuel Sloan (1815-1884), Architect
University of Pennsylvania
DAI 25, pt. 1, 394. UM 64-07370

164. DENNIS, JAMES MUNN
Karl Bitter (1867-1915), Architectural Sculptor
University of Wisconsin
DAI 24, pt. 1, 244. UM 63-05741

165. EVENSON, NORMA DORIS
Chandigarh—A Study of the City and Its Monuments
Yale University

166. LANDY, JACOB
The Architecture of Minard Lafever, in Relation to the New York Scene from 1825 to 1855
New York University
DAI 27, pt. 3-A, 716. UM 66-05627

167. MCCREDIE, JAMES ROBERT
Fortified Military Camps in Attica
Harvard University

168. MURTAGH, WILLIAM JOHN
Moravian Architecture and City Planning: A Study of Eighteenth-Century Moravian Settlements in the American Colonies with Particular Emphasis on Bethlehem, Pennsylvania
University of Pennsylvania
DAI 24, pt. 6, 2413. UM 63-07072

169. MYERS, EUGENE RUSSELL
The Development of Mid-Twentieth-Century American Metal-and-Glass Architecture in the Curtain Wall Style
University of Pittsburgh
DAI 25, pt. 11, 6519. UM 65-05167

170. OVERBECK, JOHN CLARENCE, II
A Study of Early Helladic Architecture
University of Cincinnati
DAI 24, pt. 12, 5350 UM 64-04654

171. OVERBY, OSMUND R.
The Architecture of College Hill, 1770-1900: Residential Development in the Area of the Original Town of Providence, Rhode Island
Yale University
DAI 25, pt. 2, 1135. UM 64-07144

172. POLZER, JOSEPH
Circus Pavements
New York University
DAI 27, pt. 3-A, 717. UM 64-06494

173. RAVENAL, CAROL MYERS
The Modest Architectural Mode: An Analysis of Five Domestic Dwellings in Providence, Rhode Island, circa 1780-1812
Harvard University

174. STREICHLER, JERRY
The Consultant Industrial Designer in American Industry from 1927-1960
New York University
DAI 24, pt. 6, 2413. UM 63-06683

1964

175. CROOK, DAVID H.
Louis Sullivan, the World's Columbian Exposition, and American Life
Harvard University

176. EDWARDS, SUZANNE CLARKE
Two Critical Aspects of Fourth-Century Architecture at Milan: The Single Nave Cruciform Basilica and the Palace Church
University of Michigan
DAI 25, pt. 6, 3526. UM 64-12587

177. FRAZER, ALFRED KNOX
Four Late Antique Rotundas: Aspects of Fourth-Century Architectural Style in Rome
New York University
DAI 26, pt. 6, 3268. UM 64-10025

178. HERSEY, GEORGE LEONARD
Eclecticism and Associationism in High Victorian Gothic Architecture and Pre-Raphaelite Painting
Yale University

179. JACOBSEN, THOMAS WARREN
Prehistoric Euboia
University of Pennsylvania
DAI 26, pt. 3, 1609. UM 65-05773

180. LUDWIG, ALLAN IRA
Carved Stone-Markers in New England: 1650-1815
Yale University

181. MILLON, HENRY ARMAND
Guarino Guarini and the Palazzo Carignano in Turin
Harvard University

182. PACKER, JAMES E.
The Insulae of Imperial Ostia
University of California at Berkeley

183. SCHNORRENBERG, JOHN MARTIN
Early Anglican Architecture, 1558-1662: Its Theological Implications and Its Relation to the Continental Background
Princeton University
DAI 25, pt. 11, 6519. UM 65-04942

184. WIEBENSON, DORA LOUISE
Stuart and Revett's Antiquities of Athens: The Influence of Archaeological Publications on the Neoclassical Concept of Hellenism
New York University
DAI 27, pt. 11-A, 3800. UM 65-01680

1965

185. AYALA, NINA
Roman Rococo Architecture From Clement XI to Benedict XIV (1700-1758)
Columbia University
DAI 27, pt. 1-A, 151. UM 65-13919

186. BAIGELL, MATTHEW ELI
John Haviland
University of Pennsylvania
DAI 26, pt. 6, 3232. UM 65-13307

187. BERGER, ROBERT WILLIAM
The Architecture of Antoine Le Pautre
Harvard University

188. CHEILIK, MICHAEL
Opus Albarium: A Chronology of Roman Stucco Reliefs in Italy
Johns Hopkins University
DAI 29, pt. 8-A, 2627. UM 69-02419

189. COPE, MAURICE ERWIN
The Venetian Chapel of the Sacrament in the Sixteenth Century: A Study in the Iconography of the Early Counter-Reformation
University of Chicago

190. KARLOWICZ, TITUS MARION
The Architecture of the World's Columbian Exposition
Northwestern University
DAI 26, pt. 12, 7250. UM 66-02721

191. KRINSKY, CAROL HERSELLE
Cesare Cesariano and the Como Vitruvius Edition of 1521
New York University
DAI 27, pt. 11-A, 3789. UM 67-04827

192. MERRILL, DAVID OLIVER
Isaac Damon and the Architecture of the Federal Period in New England
Yale University
DAI 26, pt. 4, 2124. UM 65-09700

193. PATTON, HELEN FRANCES
Public School Architecture in Racine, Wisconsin, and Vicinity from the Time of Settlement to 1900
University of Wisconsin
DAI 26, pt. 5, 3234. UM 65-10648

194. ROGERS, MILLARD BUXTON
A Study of the Makara and Kirttimukha with Some Parallels in Romanesque Architectural Ornament of France and Spain
University of Chicago

195. SANDERSON, WARREN
The Early Medieval Crypts of Saint Maximin at Trier
New York University
DAI 28, pt. 6-A, 2155. UM 66-09555

196. SCOUFOPOULOS, NIKI
Mycenaean Citadels on Mainland Greece
Yale University
DAI 26, pt. 12, 7274. UM 66-01100

197. WALTON, PAUL HENRY
The Drawings of John Ruskin
Harvard University

1966

198. BEGLEY, WAYNE EDISON
The Chronology of Mahayana Buddhist Architecture and Painting at Ajanta
University of Pennsylvania
DAI 27, pt. 11-A, 3788. UM 67-03050

199. CARTER, RAND
The Architecture of English Theatres: 1760-1860
Princeton University
DAI 27, pt. 7-A, 2105. UM 66-13298

200. JACOBS, STEPHEN WILLIAM
Architectural Preservation: American Development and Antecedents Abroad
Princeton University
DAI 27, pt. 9-A, 2962. UM 66-13320

201. JOHNSTON, KENNETH GORDON
The Organic Principle in Industrial America: A Study of the Architectural and Social Philosophy of Frank Lloyd Wright
University of Minnesota
DAI 28, pt. 9-A, 3606. UM 68-01599

202. JONES, GEORGE HENRY GABRIEL
The Italian Villa Style in American Architecture 1840-1865
Harvard University

203. KITAO, TIMOTHY KAORI
Bernini's Church Architecture
Harvard University

204. MARSEGLIA, EUGENE
The Architecture of Santa Maria della Steccata in Parma
Johns Hopkins University
DAI 27, pt. 10-A, 3381. UM 66-12500

205. MILLER, NAOMI
French Renaissance Fountains
New York University
DAI 29, pt. 1-A, 194. UM 68-10118

206. NORRE, ANASTASIA DEMETRIADES
Studies in the History of the Parthenon
University of California at Los Angeles
DAI 27, pt. 6-A, 1743. UM 66-11915

207. O'GORMAN, JAMES FRANCIS
The Architecture of the Monastic Library in North and Central Italy from Michelozzo to Michelangelo
Harvard University

208. PORTE, ILANA D'ANCONA
The Art and Architecture of Palestine under Herod the Great: A Survey of Major Sites
Harvard University

209. SCHWIEBERT, ERNEST GEORGE, JR.
The Primitive Roots of Architecture (Books 1-5)
Princeton University
DAI 28, pt. 10-A, 4068. UM 67-03126

210. SHEAR, THEODORE LESLIE, JR.
Studies in the Early Projects of the Periklean Building Program
Princeton University
DAI 28, pt. 1-A, 169. UM 67-05750

211. SHEON, AARON
Monticelli and the Rococo Revival
Princeton University
DAI 27, pt. 8-A, 2464. UM 66-13352

212. TURAK, THEODORE
William Le Baron Jenney: A Nineteenth-Century Architect
University of Michigan
DAI 28, pt. 2-A, 562. UM 67-01816

213. VASTOKAS, JOAN MARIE
Architecture of the Northwest Coast Indians of America
Columbia University
DAI 28, pt. 2-A, 563. UM 67-00844

1967

214. BARNES, CARL FRANKLIN, JR.
The Architecture of Soissons Cathedral: Sources and Influences in the Twelfth and Thirteenth Centuries
Columbia University
DAI 28, pt. 5-A, 1740. UM 67-14021

215. BOOKIDIS, NANCY
A Study of the Use and Geographical Distribution of Architectural Sculpture in the Archaic Period (Greece, East Greece and Magna Graecia)
Bryn Mawr College
DAI 28, pt. 11-A, 4561. UM 68-04690

216. BOYD, STERLING MEHAFFY
The Adam Style in America, 1770-1820
Princeton University
DAI 28, pt. 2-A, 558. UM 67-09591

217. BRENTANO, CARROLL WINSLOW
The Church of S. Maria della Consolazione in Rome
University of California at Berkeley
DAI 28, pt. 10-A, 4064. UM 68-00036

218. FERGUSSON, PETER JOHN
English Twelfth-Century Cistercian Church Architecture
Harvard University

219. GEMMETT, ROBERT JAMES
William Beckford and the Picturesque: A Study of Fonthill
Syracuse University
DAI 28, pt. 5-A, 1740. UM 67-12062

220. GLASS, STEPHEN LLOYD
Palaestra and Gymnasium in Greek Architecture
University of Pennsylvania
DAI 29, pt. 1-A, 204. UM 68-09201

221. HALL, MARCIA BROWN
Art of the Counter-Maniera in Florence: The Renovation of S. Maria Novella and S. Croce, 1565-1576
Harvard University

222. KATZ, MARTIN BARRY
Leon Battista Alberti: Art as Moral History
Syracuse University
DAI 28, pt. 12-A, 4970. UM 68-07772

223. KLEINBAUER, WALTER EUGENE
The Aisled Tetraconch
Princeton University
DAI 28, pt. 11-A, 4554. UM 68-02492

224. LEWIS, CHARLES DOUGLAS, JR.
The Late Baroque Churches of Venice
Yale University
DAI 28, pt. 7-A, 2610. UM 67-17666

225. MEYER, CHARLES EDWARD
The Staircase of the Episcopal Palace at Würzburg
University of Michigan
DAI 28, pt. 9-A, 3582. UM 67-15657

226. PERRY, REGENIA ALFREDA
The Life and Works of Charles Frederick Schweinfurth, Cleveland Architect, 1856-1919
Case Western Reserve University
DAI 28, pt. 10-A, 4067. UM 67-15552

227. TRACHTENBERG, MARVIN LAWRENCE
The Campanile of Florence Cathedral
New York University
DAI 29, pt. 1-A, 195. UM 68-10098

228. WESTFALL, CARROLL WILLIAM
The Two Ideal Cities of the Early Renaissance: Republican and Ducal Thought in Quattrocento Architectural Treatises
Columbia University
DAI 28, pt. 6-A, 2156. UM 67-10618

1968

229. ANDERSON, STANFORD OWEN
Peter Behrens and the New Architecture of Germany, 1900-1917
Columbia University
DAI 31, pt. 5-A, 2277. UM 70-18782

230. BERNSTEIN, GERALD STEVEN
In Pursuit of the Exotic: Islamic Forms in Nineteenth-Century American Architecture
University of Pennsylvania
DAI 29, pt. 10-A, 3543. UM 69-05609

231. BOYLE, BERNARD MICHAEL
Studies in Ostian Architecture
Yale University
DAI 29, pt. 2-A, 524. UM 68-11160

232. CHAPPELL, SALLY ANDERSON
Barry Byrne: Architecture and Writings
Northwestern University
DAI 29, pt. 10-A, 3543. UM 69-06902

233. DEHONEY, MARTYVONNE
A Resource Guide to Art and Architecture in New Jersey from Pre-Columbian Times to the Civil War
Columbia University
DAI 30, pt. 1-A, 231. UM 69-10537

234. FIELDS, RONALD MILBURN
Four Concepts of an Organic Principle: Horatio Greenough, Henry David Thoreau, Walt Whitman, and Louis Sullivan
Ohio University
DAI 29, pt. 11-A, 3929. UM 69-0509

235. FRANCISCONO, MARCEL
The Founding of the Bauhaus in Weimar: Its Artistic Background and First Conception
New York University
DAI 30, pt. 11-A, 4889. UM 70-07402

236. GLASS, DOROTHY FINN
Studies on Cosmatesque Pavements
Johns Hopkins University
DAI 32, pt. 2-A, 855. UM 71-21042

237. GOLOMBEK, LISA BETH VOLOW
The Timurid Shrine at Gazur Gah: An Iconographical Interpretation of Architecture
University of Michigan
DAI 29, pt. 3-A, 843. UM 68-13314

238. HANDLER, SUSAN
The Architecture of Alexandria in Egypt as Depicted on the Alexandrian Bronze Coinage of the Roman Imperial Period
Bryn Mawr College

239. HYMAN, ISABELLE
Fifteenth-Century Florentine Studies: The Palazzo Medici; and a Ledger for the Church of San Lorenzo
New York University
DAI 30, pt. 11-A, 4889. UM 70-07406

240. IBRAHIM, LEILA
Roman and Early Christian Floor Mosaics from Corinthian Kenchreai
University of Chicago

241. LABRANCHE, CAROL LUSE
Roma Nobilis: The Public Architecture of Rome, 330-476
Northwestern University
DAI 29, pt. 8-A, 2619. UM 69-01876

242. LICHT, MARJORIE EDITH
A Festaiuolo Pattern Book in the Sir John Soane Museum
New York University
DAI 30, pt. 2-A, 634. UM 69-11823

243. PREZIOSI, DONALD ANTHONY
Minoan Palace Planning and Its Origins
Harvard University

244. SERENYI, PETER
Le Corbusier's Art and Thought: 1918-1935
Washington University
DAI 29, pt. 6-A, 1833. UM 68-17204

245. SEVERENS, KENNETH WARREN
The Cathedral at Sens and Its Influence in the Twelfth Century
Johns Hopkins University
DAI 31, pt. 8-A, 4064. UM 71-02950

246. SHEAR, IONE MYLONAS
Mycenaean Domestic Architecture
Bryn Mawr College
DAI 29, pt. 8-A, 2627. UM 69-00731

247. SMITH, MOLLY TEASDALE
The "Ciborium" in Christian Architecture at Rome, 300-600 A.D.
New York University
DAI 29, pt. 11-A, 3931. UM 69-07997

248. STRIKER, CECIL LEOPOLD
The Myrelaion (Bodrum Camii) in Istanbul
New York University
DAI 30, pt. 11-A, 4893. UM 70-07397

249. TWOMBLY, ROBERT CHARLES
The Life and Ideas of Frank Lloyd Wright
University of Wisconsin
DAI 29, pt. 8-A, 2660. UM 68-14031

250. VOGEL, LISE
Studies on the Column of Antoninus Pius
Harvard University

251. WAGGONER, NANCY MANN
The Alexander Mint at Babylon
Columbia University
DAI 29, pt. 8-A, 2628. UM 69-00435

252. WALDBAUM, JANE COHN
The Use of Iron in the Eastern Mediterranean: 1200-900 B.C.
Harvard University

253. WEIL, MARK STEINBERG
The History and Decoration of the Ponte S. Angelo
Columbia University
DAI 30, pt. 2-A, 637. UM 69-09227

254. WILKINSON, CATHERINE
The Hospital of Cardinal Tavera in Toledo: A Documentary and Stylistic Study of Spanish Architecture in the Mid-Sixteenth Century
Yale University
DAI 30, pt. 5-A, 1935. UM 69-13517

255. YAKAR, JAK
The Religious Architecture and Art of Early Anatolia
Brandeis University
DAI 29, pt. 11-A, 3937. UM 69-02070

1969

256. ANDERSON, PHILIP JAMES
The Simple Builders: The Shakers, Their Villages and Architecture
Saint Louis University
DAI 30, pt. 8-A, 3385. UM 70-01840

257. BAUMANN, CHARLES HENRY
The Influence of Angus Snead MacDonald and the Snead Bookstack on Library Architecture
University of Illinois at Urbana-Champaign
DAI 30, pt. 7-A, 2920. UM 70-00787

258. CRAWFORD, JOHN STEPHENS
Roman Commercial Buildings of Asia Minor and Their Relation to Urban Complexes
Harvard University

259. CROUCH, DORA POLK
Palmyra
University of California at Los Angeles
DAI 31, pt. 2-A, 698. UM 70-14268

260. CUTLER, JOHN BAKER
Girard College Architectural Competition, 1832-1848
Yale University
DAI 30, pt. 9-A, 3878. UM 70-02719

261. HEARN, MILLARD FILLMORE, JR.
The Architectural History of Romsey Abbey
Indiana University
DAI 30, pt. 9-A, 3872. UM 69-17761

262. HOLDEN, WHEATON ARNOLD
Robert Swain Peabody of Peabody and Stearns in Boston: The Early Years (1870-1886)
Boston University
DAI 30, pt. 5-A, 1934. UM 69-18776

263. JONES, CHRISTOPHER
The Twin-Pyramid Group Pattern: A Classic Maya Architectural Assemblage at Tikal, Guatemala
University of Pennsylvania
DAI 30, pt. 6-B, 2514. UM 69-21375

264. KOEPER, HOWARD FREDERICK
The Gothic Skyscraper: A History of the Woolworth Building and Its Antecedents
Harvard University

265. MAGIDSOHN, BRUCE ALAN
The Arts and Architecture of Coventry Cathedral: Their Goals and Their Function
Ohio University
DAI 30, pt. 6-A, 2436. UM 69-19868

266. MITTENBUEHLER, ROBERT LOGAN
Aesthetic Currents in German Baroque Architecture
Syracuse University
DAI 31, pt. 1-A, 319. UM 70-10370

267. OLIVER-SMITH, PHILIP EDWARD
Architectural Elements on Greek Vases before 400 B.C.
New York University
DAI 30, pt. 7-A, 2921. UM 69-21269

268. PUNDT, HERMANN GUSTAV JOHANNES
The Environmental Planning of Karl Friedrich Schinkel and His Transformation of Central Berlin
Harvard University

269. RECKMEYER, WILLIAM GEORGE
The Didactic Function of a Work of Architecture as an Art in the Twentieth Century
Ohio University
DAI 30, pt. 6-A, 2438. UM 69-19873

270. SPRAGUE, PAUL EDWARD
The Architectural Ornament of Louis Sullivan and His Chief Draftsmen
Princeton University
DAI 30, pt. 3-A, 1091. UM 69-14436

271. TARR, GARY
The Architecture of the Early Western Chalukyas
University of California at Los Angeles
DAI 31, pt. 3-A, 1165. UM 70-15948

1970

272. BATES, ULKU ULKUSAL
The Anatolian Mausoleum of the Twelfth, Thirteenth, and Fourteenth Centuries
University of Michigan
DAI 32, pt. 1-A, 330. UM 71-15088

273. CARPENTER, JAMES ROBERT
The Propylon in Greek and Hellenistic Architecture
University of Pennsylvania
DAI 32, pt. 1-A, 344. UM 71-19208

274. DEMERS, EDMUND RAOUL
The Origin and Development of the Fountain, both as an Artifact and Image, as Shown in Three Works of the Spanish Renaissance
Ohio University
DAI 31, pt. 5-A, 2278. UM 70-20099

275. FIENGA, DORIS DIANA
The Antiquarie Prospectiche Romane Composte per Prospectivo Melanese Depictore: A Document for the Study of the Relationship Between Bramante and Leonardo da Vinci
University of California at Los Angeles
DAI 31, pt. 7-A, 3443. UM 71-00616

276. FRANK, SUZANNE SHULOF
Michel de Klerk (1884-1923): An Architect of the Amsterdam School
Columbia University
DAI 31, pt. 4-A, 1707. UM 70-18802

277. GOELDNER, PAUL KENNETH
Temples of Justice: Nineteenth-Century County Courthouses in the Midwest and Texas
Columbia University
DAI 31, pt. 9-A, 4649. UM 71-06179

278. HEISNER, BEVERLY FAYE
Giovanni Antonia Viscardi's Mariahilfkirche at Freystadt: An Analysis of its Forms, Sources, and Significance
University of Michigan
DAI 31, pt. 8-A, 4060. UM 71-04630

279. JOHNSON, EUGENE JOSEPH III
S. Andrea in Mantua
New York University
DAI 32, pt. 7-A, 3889. UM 72-03153

280. LOTEN, HERBERT STANLEY
The Maya Architecture of Tikal, Guatemala: A Preliminary Seriation of Vaulted Building Plans
University of Pennsylvania
DAI 31, pt. 6-A, 2809. UM 70-25686

281. MACDOUGALL, ELISABETH BLAIR
The Villa Mattei and the Development of the Roman Garden Style
Harvard University

282. MAHAN, JOSEPH BUFORD, JR.
Identification of the Tsoyaha Waeno, Builders of Temple Mounds
University of North Carolina at Chapel Hill
DAI 31, pt. 5-A, 2289. UM 70-21213

283. MATHEWS, THOMAS FRANCIS
The Early Churches of Constantinople: Architecture and Liturgy
New York University
DAI 31, pt. 4-A, 1708. UM 70-19017

284. MILLER, STEPHEN GAYLORD
The Prytaneion: Its Function and Architectural Form
Princeton University
DAI 31, pt. 12-A, 6500. UM 71-14397

285. RAMAGE, ANDREW
Studies in Lydian Domestic and Commercial Architecture at Sardis
Harvard University

286. REIFF, DANIEL DRAKE
Architecture in Washington, 1791-1861
Harvard University

287. SHAW, JOSEPH WINTERBOTHAM
Minoan Building Materials and Their Uses
University of Pennsylvania
DAI 31, pt. 6-A, 2824. UM 70-25731

288. TAYLOR, ROBERT RATCLIFFE
The Word in Stone: The Role of Architecture in the National Socialist Ideology
Stanford University
DAI 31, pt. 8-A, 4104. UM 71-02840

289. TOLLES, BRYANT FRANKLIN, JR.
College Architecture in Northern New England before 1860: A Social and Cultural History
Boston University
DAI 31, pt. 5-A, 2326. UM 70-22390

290. VAN ZANTEN, DAVID THEODORE
The Architectural Polychromy of the 1830s
Harvard University

291. VARRIANO, JOHN LOUIS, JR.
The Roman Ecclesiastical Architecture of Martino Longhi the Younger
University of Michigan
DAI 31, pt. 9-A, 4652. UM 71-04758

292. WALL, DONALD RALPH
Paolo Soleri Documenta
Catholic University of America
DAI 31, pt. 7-A, 3446. UM 70-22734

293. WEINER, SHELIA LEIMAN
Ajanta and Its Origins
Harvard University

1971

294. ANDRES, GLENN MERLE
The Villa Medici in Rome
Princeton University
DAI 32, pt. 3-A, 1411. UM 71-23339

295. ARNTZEN, ETTA MAE
A Study of "Principii di Architettura Civile" by Francesco Milizia
Columbia University

296. BARSCH, VIRGINIA MARTHA
The Church of St. Trophime, Arles: Architectural and Iconographical Problems
Northwestern University
DAI 32, pt. 7-A, 3888. UM 71-30738

297. BERNIER, RONALD MILTON
The Nepalese Pagoda: Origins and Style
Cornell University
DAI 32, pt. 8-A, 4505. UM 72-08835

298. BETTS, RICHARD JOHNSON
The Architectural Theories of Francesco di Giorgio
Princeton University
DAI 32, pt. 8-A, 4505. UM 72-02688

299. BLIZNAKOV, MILKA T.
The Search for a Style: Modern Architecture in the USSR, 1917-1932
Columbia University

300. CASTELNUOVO-TEDESCO, LISBETH
The Brancacci Chapel in Florence
University of California at Los Angeles
DAI 32, pt. 2-A, 854. UM 71-21317

301. CROCKER, LESLIE FRANK
Domestic Architecture of the Middle South, 1795-1865
University of Missouri at Columbia
DAI 32, pt. 5-A, 2574. UM 71-30639

302. DENNY, WALTER BELL
The Ceramics of the Mosque of Rustem Pasha and the Environment of Change
Harvard University

303. DREWER, LOIS JEAN
The Carved Wood Beams of the Church of Justinian, Monastery of St. Catherine, Mount Sinai
University of Michigan
DAI 33, pt. 5-A, 2259. UM 72-29041

304. FABBRI, NANCY RASH
Eleventh- and Twelfth-Century Figurative Mosaic Floors in South Italy
Bryn Mawr College
DAI 32, pt. 11-A, 6312. UM 72-11196

305. FLYNN, ELISABETH LOUISE
Gideon Shryock, 1802-1880: Greek Revival Architect in Kentucky
Northwestern University
DAI 32, pt. 6-A, 3179. UM 71-30800

306. FRIARY, DONALD RICHARD
The Architecture of the Anglican Church in the Northern American Colonies: A Study of Religious, Social, and Cultural Expression
University of Pennsylvania
DAI 32, pt. 4-A, 2026. UM 71-26010

307. GERSON, PAULA L.
The West Facade of St. Denis: An Iconographic Study
Columbia University

308. GIBBS, DALE L.
The "Forms" of Alienation: Architectural Theory in an Age of Change
University of Pennsylvania
DAI 32, pt. 4-A, 2005. UM 71-26013

309. JAHN, RAYMOND HOYT
Patterns of Change in the Architecture of Gaul from the Late Fourth to the Ninth Century
University of Missouri at Columbia
DAI 32, pt. 6-A, 3189. UM 71-30661

310. KALMAN, HAROLD DAVID
The Architecture of George Dance the Younger
Princeton University
DAI 32, pt. 11-A, 6313. UM 72-13744

311. KELSO, WILLIAM MARTIN
Captain Jones Wormslow: A Historical, Archaeological, and Architectural Study of an Eighteenth-Century Plantation Site near Savannah, Georgia
Emory University
DAI 32, pt. 7-A, 3900. UM 72-03035

312. LIZON, PETER
The Palace of the Soviets: Change in Direction of Soviet Architecture
University of Pennsylvania
DAI 32, pt. 12-A, 6863. UM 72-17387

313. MCCORMICK, THOMAS JULIAN
Charles-Louis Clérisseau and the Roman Revival
Princeton University
DAI 32, pt. 3-A, 1415. UM 71-23374

314. MACDOUGALL, ROBERT DUNCAN
Domestic Architecture among the Kandyan, Sinhalese
Cornell University
DAI 32, pt. 6-B, 3128. UM 71-29259

315. MICHELS, EILEEN MANNING
A Developmental Study of the Drawings Published in American Architect *and in* Inland Architect *through 1895*
University of Minnesota
DAI 32, pt. 10-A, 5688. UM 71-22274

316. MILLER, STELLA GROBEL
Hellenistic Macedonian Architecture: Its Style and Painted Ornamentation
Bryn Mawr College
DAI 32, pt. 10-A, 5695. UM 72-12678

317. MORGAN, WILLIAM DAVIS
The Architecture of Henry Vaughan
University of Delaware
DAI 32, pt. 11-A, 6313. UM 72-14472

318. MULLEN, ROBERT JAMES
Mexico: Sixteenth-Century Dominican Churches and Conventos in Oaxaca
University of Maryland
DAI 32, pt. 9-A, 5128. UM 72-10081

319. OTTO, CHRISTIAN FRIEDRICH
Balthasar Neumann's Major Church Interiors
Columbia University
DAI 32, pt. 6-A, 3179. UM 72-01374

320. RICHARDSON, DOUGLAS SCOTT
Gothic Revival Architecture in Ireland
Yale University

321. SCHNEIDER, DONALD DAVID
The Works and Doctrine of Jacques Ignace Hittorff (1792-1867): Structural Innovation and Formal Expression in French Architecture, 1810-1867
Princeton University
DAI 32, pt. 4-A, 2007. UM 71-23382

322. SEARING, HELEN E.
Housing in Holland and the Amsterdam School
Yale University
DAI 32, pt. 12-A, 6864. UM 72-17171

323. SIMUTIS, LEONARD JOSEPH
Frederick Law Olmsted's Later Years: Landscape Architecture and the Spirit of Place
University of Minnesota
DAI 33, pt. 3-A, 1130. UM 72-05620

324. SMITH, JACK GRAHAM
The Casino of Pius IV in the Vatican Gardens
Princeton University
DAI 32, pt. 11-A, 6313. UM 72-13758

325. TURNER, PAUL VENABLE
The Education of Le Corbusier: A Study of the Development of Le Corbusier's Thought, 1900-1920
Harvard University

326. WIEDENHOEFT, RONALD V.
Workers' Housing in Berlin in the 1920s: A Contribution to the History of Modern Architecture
Columbia University

327. ZIELINSKI, ANN S.
The Cloister of San Pedro in Soria
Syracuse University
DAI 32, pt. 10-A, 5690. UM 72-06648

1972

328. BRYAN, JOHN MORRILL
Boston's Granite Architecture, c. 1810-1860
Boston University
DAI 33, pt. 4-A, 1612. UM 72-25249

329. GESELL, GERALDINE CORNELIA
The Archaeological Evidence for the Minoan House Cult and its Survival in Iron Age Crete
University of North Carolina at Chapel Hill
DAI 33, pt. 4-A, 1626. UM 72-24792

330. HENDERSON, NATALIE ROSENBERG
The Meanings of Le Sueur's Decorative Ensembles for the Hotel Lambert
University of California at Berkeley

331. KOWSKY, FRANCIS RUDY
Frederick Clarke Withers, 1828-1901
Johns Hopkins University

332. LADD, FREDERICK JAMES
The Revival Style Alterations at Corsham Court, 1749-1849
Ohio State University
DAI 33, pt. 2-A, 6760. UM 72-20978

333. LIEBERMAN, RALPH ERIC
The Church of Santa Maria dei Miracoli in Venice
New York University
DAI 33, pt. 6-A, 2837. UM 72-31100

334. MORGAN, WILLIAM TOWNER
The Politics of Business in the Career of an American Architect: Cass Gilbert, 1878-1905
University of Minnesota
DAI 33, pt. 5-A, 2265. UM 72-27860

335. PRESTON, LESLIE ELIZABETH
House F: A Building of the Late Bronze Age at Ayia Irini on Keos
University of Cincinnati
DAI 33, pt. 6-A, 2843. UM 72-31748

336. ROSENFELD, MYRA NAN
The Hotel de Cluny and the Sources of the French Renaissance Palace: 1350-1500
Harvard University

337. TOBRINER, STEPHEN OSCAR
The Architecture and Urbanism of Noto: An Eighteenth-Century Sicilian City
Harvard University

338. WEBSTER, DAVID LEE
The Fortifications of Becan, Campeche, Mexico
University of Minnesota
DAI 33, pt. 1-B, 29. UM 72-20158

UNIVERSITY INDEX

Smith, Webster, 139
Steinberg, Leo, 147
Streichler, Jerry, 174
Striker, Cecil Leopold, 248
Trachtenberg, Marvin Lawrence, 227
Trell, Bluma L., 46
Wiebenson, Dora Louise, 184

North Carolina at Chapel Hill, University of
Gesell, Geraldine Cornelia, 329
Mahan, Joseph Buford, Jr., 282
Shelly, Lonnie R., 161

Northwestern University
Barsch, Virginia Martha, 296
Brooks, Hallen, Jr., 118
Chappell, Sally Anderson, 232
Flynn, Elisabeth Louise, 305
Karlowicz, Titus Marion, 190
Labranche, Carol Luse, 241

Ohio State University
Cummings, Abbott L., 81
Demers, Edmund Raoul, 274
Fields, Ronald Milburn, 234
Ladd, Frederick James, 332
Lewis, Stanley T., 97
Magidsohn, Bruce Alan, 265
Omoto, Sadayoshi, 103
Quera, Leon Neal, 160
Reckmeyer, William George, 269
Roos, Frank J., Jr., 26
Weisman, Winston Robert, 48

Pennsylvania, University of
Baigell, Matthew Eli, 186
Begley, Wayne Edison, 198
Bernstein, Gerald Steven, 230
Carpenter, James Robert, 273
Cooledge, Harold Norman, Jr., 163
Forman, Henry Chandlee, 43
Friary, Donald Richard, 306
Gibbs, Dale L., 308
Glass, Stephen Lloyd, 220
Jacobsen, Thomas Warren, 179
Jones, Christopher, 263
Lizon, Peter, 312
Loten, Herbert Stanley, 280
Murtagh, William John, 168
Shaw, Joseph Winterbotham, 287
Van Burkalow, James Turley, Jr., 1

Pittsburgh, University of
Myers, Eugene Russell, 169

Princeton University
Andres, Glenn Merle, 294
Betts, Richard Johnson, 298
Boyd, Sterling Mehaffy, 216
Bush-Brown, Albert, 135
Carter, Rand, 199
Coffin, David Robbins, 99
Davis, Phillip Haldane, 13
Gowans, Alan Wilbert, 74
Hanson, John Arthur, 111
Hazelhurst, Franklin Hamilton, 112
Jacobs, Stephen William, 200
Kalman, Harold David, 310

Kleinbauer, Walter Eugene, 223
McCormick, Thomas Julian, 313
McDonough, James Vernon, 77
Miller, Stephen Gaylord, 284
Murray, Steuben Butler, 2
Norton, Paul Foote, 92
Schneider, Donald David, 321
Schnorrenberg, John Martin, 183
Schwiebert, Ernest George, Jr., 209
Shear, Theodore Leslie, Jr., 210
Sheon, Aaron, 211
Smith, Jack Graham, 324
Soper, Alexander Coburn III, 52
Sprague, Paul Edward, 270
Tatum, George Bishop, 79
Ward, Clarence, 6
Wilber, Donald Newton, 70

Radcliffe College
Hall, Louise, 101
Hayes, Marian, 54
Lane, Barbara Miller, 157
Myer, Prudence Royce, 117
Sunderland, Alice L., 58
Sunderland, Elizabeth R., 27

Saint Louis University
Anderson, Philip James, 256

Southwestern Baptist Theological Seminary
Nichols J. B., 102

Stanford University
Taylor, Robert Ratcliffe, 288

Syracuse University
Gemmett, Robert James, 219
Katz, Martin Barry, 222
Mittenbuehler, Robert Logan, 266
Zielinski, Ann S., 327

Toronto (Canada), University of
Winter, Frederick Elliott, 127

Washington University
Serenyi, Peter, 244

Western Reserve University
Garnsey, Clarke Henderson, 156

Wisconsin, University of
Dennis, James Munn, 164
Jochem, Frederick L., 19
Lewis, Dudley Arnold, 158
Patton, Helen Frances, 193
Twombly, Robert Charles, 249

Yale University
Bohan, Peter John, 149
Boyle, Bernard Michael, 231
Branner, Robert J., 94
Brown, Frank E., 23a
Carrott, Richard G., 150
Chisolm, Lawrence Washington, 119
Collier, Margaret , 155
Cutler, John Baker, 260
Donnelly, Marian Card, 110
Evenson, Norma Doris, 165
Garvan, Anthony N. B., 61
Graybill, Samuel Huiet, Jr., 122

ARCHITECTURAL HISTORY

AUTHORS

PLANNING HISTORY

1936

1. WALLACE, WILLIAM
   The History of Eretria to 198 B.C.
   Johns Hopkins University

2. WOODBRIDGE, GEORGE
   La Roche-Sur-Yon, 1804–1814: An Experiment in Town Planning Under Napoleon
   University of Wisconsin

1945

3. HALL, EDWARD T., JR.
   Early Stockaded Settlements in the Governador, New Mexico, A Marginal Anasazi Development from Basket Maker III to Pueblo I Times
   Columbia University

1958

4. CROSS, KEVIN JAMES
   Urban Development in Canada
   Cornell University
   DAI 19, pt. 10, 2573. UM 59-00119.

5. DE LA CROIX, HORST MAX ALBERT
   Problems in Sixteenth-Century Italian Urbanism: The Radial Plan From "Sforzinda" to Palmanova
   University of California at Berkeley

1962

6. BISHOP, JOHN JOSEPH
   The Role of the Circus and Crescent in Eighteenth- and Nineteenth-Century British Town Planning
   Boston University
   DAI 23, pt. 4, 1317. UM 62-04546.

1963

7. MURTAGH, WILLIAM JOHN
   Moravian Architecture and City Planning: A Study of Eighteenth-Century Moravian Settlements in the American Colonies with Particular Emphasis on Bethlehem, Pennsylvania
   University of Pennsylvania

1964

8. JOHNSTON, NORMAN JOHN
   Harland Bartholomew: His Comprehensive Plans and Science of Planning
   University of Pennsylvania
   DAI 25, pt. 7, 4074. UM 64-10386.

1966

9. HARDOY, JORGE ENRIQUE
   Ciudades Precolumbinas
   Harvard University

10. THOMPSON, SAMUEL
    An Analysis of the Origins and Development of Citizen Participation in City Planning
    Harvard University

1967

11. BOLSTERLI, MARGARET JONES
    Bedford Park: A Practical Experiment in Aesthetics
    University of Minnesota
    DAI 28, pt. 12-A, 5007. UM 68-07426.

12. HUGGINS, KOLEEN A. H.
    The Evolution of City and Regional Planning in North Carolina, 1900–1950
    Duke University

13. MILGRAM, GRACE SMELO
    The City Expands: A Study of the Conversion of Land from Rural to Urban Use, Philadelphia, 1945–1962
    University of Pennsylvania
    DAI 28, pt. 6-A, 2362. UM 67-12781.

14. PETERSON, JON A.
    The Origins of the Comprehensive City Planning Ideal in the United States, 1840–1911
    Harvard University

15. VIGIER, FRANÇOIS CLAUDE DENIS
    The Response of Local Government to Rapid Urbanization: A Case Study of Liverpool and Manchester During the Industrial Revolution
    Harvard University

1968

16. WOLF, PETER MICHAEL
    Eugene Hénard and City Planning of Paris, 1900–1914
    New York University
    DAI 30, pt. 11-A, 4894. UM 70-07398.

1969

17. ANDERSON, PHILIP JAMES
    The Simple Builders: The Shakers, Their Villages and Architecture
    Saint Louis University
    DAI 30, pt. 8-A, 3385. UM 70-01840.

18. CRAWFORD, JOHN STEPHENS
    Roman Commercial Buildings of Asia Minor and Their Relation to Urban Complexes
    Harvard University

19. CROUCH, DORA POLK
    Palmyra
    University of California at Los Angeles
    DAI 31, pt. 2-A, 698. UM 70-14268.

20. FEIN, ALBERT
    Frederick Law Olmsted: His Development as a Theorist and Designer of the American City
    Columbia University

21. PUNDT, HERMANN GUSTAV JOHANNES
    The Environmental Planning of Karl Friedrich Schinkel and His Transformation of Central Berlin
    Harvard University

22. ROTHBLATT, DONALD NOAH
Appalachia: An Experiment in Regional Planning
Harvard University

23. WEISMANTEL, WILLIAM LOUIS
Collision of Urban Renewal with Zoning: The Boston Experience, 1950–1967
Harvard University

1970

24. LOPEZ GUINAZU, ANTONIO A.
Modernization in Venezuela (1950–1961)
Colorado State University
DAI 31, pt. 7-A, 3676. UM 71-02434.

1971

25. BURCHELL, ROBERT W.
Planned Unit Development: Its Antecedents, Its Realities, Its Future
Rutgers University
DAI 32, pt. 9-A, 5377. UM 72-09611.

26. GARR, DANIEL J.
Hispanic Colonial Settlement in California: Planning and Urban Development on the Frontier, 1769–1850
Cornell University
DAI 32, pt. 11-A, 6577. UM 72-13155.

27. HEIFETZ, ROBERT JOSEF
Origins, Development, Case Studies, and Critique of Advocacy Planning: Implications for Planning Education
Columbia University
DAI 32, pt. 11-A, 6577. UM 72-15575.

28. KANTOR, HARVEY A.
Modern Urban Planning in New York City: Origins and Evolution, 1890–1933
New York University

29. KIES, EMILY BARDACK
The City and the Machine: Urban and Industrial Illustration in America, 1880–1900
Columbia University
DAI 33, pt. 4-A, 1615. UM 72-19132.

30. SIMUTIS, LEONARD JOSEPH
Frederick Law Olmsted's Later Years: Landscape Architecture and the Spirit of Place
University of Minnesota
DAI 33, pt. 3-A, 1130. UM 72-05620.

31. VOSS, JERROLD RICHARD
Town Planning of the Illinois Central Railroad
Harvard University

1972

32. BOYER-DARALIS, MARY CHRISTINE
The Language of City Planning: An Essay in Historical and Philosophical Understanding
Massachusetts Institute of Technology

33. HOBERMAN, LOUISA S.
City Planning in Spanish Colonial Government: The Response in Mexico City to the Problem of Floods, 1607–1637
Columbia University
UM 75-09338.

34. KARTAL, SATILMIS KEMAL
New Towns for Turkey
New York University
DAI 33, pt. 6-A, 3067. UM 72-31093.

35. LOGAN, THOMAS HARVEY
The Invention of Zoning in the Emerging Planning Profession of Late Nineteenth-Century Germany
University of North Carolina at Chapel Hill
DAI 33, pt. 4-A, 1882. UM 72-24813.

36. SERAGELDIN, MONA ANIS
Urbanization and Social Change in a Foreign Dominated Economy: Cairo, 1805–1930
Harvard University

37. TOBRINER, STEPHEN OSCAR
The Architecture and Urbanism of Noto, An Eighteenth-Century Sicilian City
Harvard University

Notes on Contributors

Lauren Weiss Bricker is architectural historian at the Foundation for San Francisco's Architectural Heritage. While completing her graduate studies in art history at the University of California, Santa Barbara, she was assistant curator of the Architectural Drawings Collections, University Art Museum.

Michael W. Brooks, professor of English at West Chester University, is the author of *John Ruskin and Victorian Architecture.* He is now at work on a study of the cultural significance of the New York City subway system.

Richard Cheek, an architectural photographer, has published seven all-color books on American buildings and landscapes. An avid collector of volumes on American architecture, he also serves as a bibliographic consultant and with Keith Morgan is compiling a bibliography of American architectural literature published between 1895 and 1941.

J. A. Chewning is assistant professor in the College of Design, Architecture, Art, and Planning at the University of Cincinnati. He holds a master's degree in regional planning from Cornell University and a doctorate in the history of architecture from the Massachusetts Institute of Technology. Formerly he taught at the University of Massachusetts and Ball

State University and was senior editor of the *Art and Architecture Thesaurus.*

Peter Fergusson specializes in the architecture of the reform orders in late twelfth-century England. His *Architecture of Solitude: Cistercian Abbeys in Twelfth-Century England* was published by Princeton University Press in 1984. He teaches in the art department at Wellesley College.

Lisa Koenigsberg holds a Ph.D. in American studies from Yale University and an M.A. in history from The Johns Hopkins University. She has served on the staff of the Landmarks Preservation Commission, New York City. She curated the exhibition *Renderings from Worcester's Past* for the Worcester Art Museum (1987) and organized an exhibition on *Selected Images of American Victorian Womanhood* for the Yale University Art Gallery (1982). From 1982 to 1986 she was a Smithsonian Fellow at the National Museum of American Art and the National Portrait Gallery.

George Kubler studied at Yale University with Henri Focillon and at the Institute of Fine Arts in New York City with Herbert Spinden. His interests include medieval architecture, the architecture of colonial Latin America, and, most recently, the aesthetic recognition of ancient American art and architecture since Discovery.

Elisabeth Blair MacDougall took an M.A. in art history at the Institute of Fine Arts, New York University, and a Ph.D. at Harvard University. Her special interests are in Italian Renaissance and baroque history of architecture and gardens. She taught at Boston and Harvard universities and founded the program of Studies in Landscape Architecture at Dumbarton Oaks. Retired as director of studies there since 1988, she is professor of the history of landscape architecture (emerita), Harvard University.

Tod Marder, an associate professor and former chair of the Department of Art History at Rutgers University, currently edits the *Journal of the Society of Architectural Historians.* He has published numerous articles on Italian Renaissance and baroque architecture.

Keith N. Morgan's publications include *Charles A. Platt, The Artist as Architect* and, with D. Arnold Lewis, *American Victorian Architecture.* He is an associate professor and chair of the art history department at Boston University. He and Richard Cheek are compiling a bibliography of American architectural literature published between 1895 and 1941.

William B. Rhoads is professor of art history at the State University College at New Paltz, New York. He completed his dissertation, "The Colonial Revival," in 1974 at Princeton University, where he studied under Donald Drew Egbert and David R. Coffin. Published studies include several on Franklin D. Roosevelt's architectural and artistic interests and one on artists' studio houses in the Hudson Valley.

Helen Searing, a graduate of Vassar College (1954), holds a Ph.D. in art history from Yale University (1971). She has taught since 1967 at Smith College where she is Alice Pratt Brown Professor of Art. She has been visiting professor at the graduate schools of architecture of Columbia University and the University of California, Berkeley.

Linda Seidel, associate professor at the University of Chicago since 1977, is the author of *Songs of Glory: The Romanesque Façades of Aquitaine.* Introduced to A. Kingsley Porter's photographic archives as a graduate student at Harvard, she has consulted it extensively in her work on the decoration and design of twelfth-century cloisters in southern France and on the programs and patrons of medieval doorways in western France. Recent studies concern the interaction of audiences and art in both medieval and modern times.

Eduard F. Sekler is the Osgood Hooker Professor of Visual Art and professor of architecture at Harvard University. A UNESCO consultant for historic conservation on many occasions, he has published several books, including *Wren and His Place in European Architecture* and *Josef Hoffmann, the Architectural Work.* He studied architecture at the Technical University in his native Vienna and architectural history under Rudolf Wittkower at the Warburg Institute.

Nancy Shatzman Steinhardt is the author of *Chinese Traditional Architecture* (New York, 1984) and *Chinese Imperial City Planning* (Honolulu, 1990) as well as numerous articles on Chinese architecture, city planning, and wall painting. She is an assistant professor of East Asian art at the University of Pennsylvania.

Suzanne Stephens is an architectural writer, editor, and critic. An adjunct professor at Barnard College, she teaches a seminar on architectural criticism. She edited *Building the New Museum* (Princeton Architectural Press, 1986) and is working on an annotated anthology of architecture criticism in American magazines and newspapers over the past 120 years.

Dell Upton teaches architectural history at the University of California, Berkeley. He is the author of *Holy Things and Profane: Anglican Parish Churches in Colonial Virginia* and the editor of *America's Architectural Roots: Ethnic Groups That Built America.* He also edited, with John Michael Vlach, *Common Places: Readings in American Vernacular Architecture.*

David Van Zanten earned his doctorate at Harvard University. He teaches art history at Northwestern University and earlier taught at McGill University and the University of Pennsylvania. His books include *Walter Burley Griffin: Selected Designs*, *The Architectural Polychromy of the 1830s*, and *Designing Paris*, as well as various articles and essays. He edited Donald Drew Egbert's book, *The Beaux-Arts Tradition in French Architecture*.

Robert Wojtowicz is a Ph.D. candidate at the University of Pennsylvania. His dissertation concerns the architectural criticism of Lewis Mumford. He holds a master's degree in art history and archaeology from Columbia University.

Mary N. Woods teaches architectural history at Cornell University. She received her doctorate in art history from Columbia University, where she worked with George R. Collins. In 1988–1989, she received the first junior fellowship awarded by the Temple Buell Center for the Study of American Architecture, Columbia University. Her work on architectural periodicals is related to a larger interest in the professionalization of American architecture.